D1711614

WILLIAM B. HAZEN

Captain 8th Infantry, U.S.A., Colonel 41st O.V.I.; Brig. Gen. U.S. Vols.;
Maj. Gen. U.S. Vols.; Colonel 37th Infantry, U.S.A.
Brigadier General U.S.A.

THE FORTY-FIRST

OHIO

Veteran Volunteer Infantry

IN

The War of the Rebellion.

1861-1865.

BY

Robert L. Kimberly and Ephraim S. Holloway,

With the Co-operation of the Committee of the Regimental Association. . .

CLEVELAND, OHIO:

W. R. SMELLIE, PRINTER AND PUBLISHER.

1897

Reprinted by

BLUE ACORN PRESS
P.O. Box 2684
Huntington, WV 25726

New Material Copyright 1999 by Blue Acorn Press

ISBN 1-885033-23-0

Manufactured in the United States

PREFACE.

It is the aim of this book to show, first, of what material the regiment it commemorates was composed; and second, the life of the regiment apart from its marches and battles. These latter are matters of official record, but the real life of the regiment, its personnel and characteristics, are nowhere given in connected form.

As to material, the regiment came from the Western Reserve of Ohio, and from counties south and west of the Reserve. The Reserve, largely settled by New Englanders, was a hotbed of anti-slavery sentiment always. It was the home of Giddings and Wade, of national repute in the abolition agitation days. Its only city, Cleveland, was the scene of several notable contests under the fugitive slave-law; and at one time, a popular frenzy which made the soberer ones tremble was quieted only by the majestic presence and admirable tract of Salmon P. Chase, then governor of the state. A slave girl, Lucy, claimed in Wheeling, W. Va., was confined in the county jail, awaiting the process of the United States court for the Northern District of Ohio. A mass meeting was assembled, companies coming from the Giddings district, forty miles to the eastward, and from Oberlin, to the westward. The Giddings district men carried hickory sticks, the bark removed, in imitation of the Connecticut colonists who met and turned back the king's stamp act commissioner, near Hartford. This demonstration was so threatening that Gov. Chase was summoned, and, coming by special train from the State capital, arrived when the crowd had been wrought to madness over the use of the county jails to serve the purpose of the hated fugitive slave-law. The governor mounted the platform in the midst of the multitude on Monument Square, and stood, uncovered and unannounced, before the frenzied peo-

ple. At the moment, a committee was on its way to take the slave
girl from the jail. With a word, Chase, the born ruler, turned the
furious mob into an orderly assemblage of sober citizens. "Fellow
citizens," he said, and paused. "Lawabiding fellow-citizens of the
Western Reserve!" What more he said mattered not; he had called them to their senses, and the Giddings district "Peeled Stick
Brigade" went quietly homeward with the rest.

I give this prominence to the incident because it is luminous in
illustration of the character of the people. A people slow to anger;
but, once aroused, equal to martyrdom. A people who would suf-
fer long before unsheathing the sword; but the naked steel, in hand
at last, never to be returned to the scabbard except in victory.

Through that section of the country, in the years before the
war, one might travel day after day without the sight of a pauper
or a family not comfortably and decently provided for. And one
might travel twice as far without seeing a soldier or any hint of
war. In the regiment, as it was organized, there was but one man
who had seen so much as a battalion in the field, and I am not able
to say whether that one had ever witnessed a battle. A solitary
militia company was maintained at Cleveland, but it was seldom
seen. The gathering of a thousand men out of such a population,
putting them into a rigid army organization, and taking them
through the great campaigns in Kentucky, Tennessee, Alabama and
Georgia, would necessarily bring a multitude of diverse experiences, all new to the men of the regiment, and many of them worth
preserving for succeeding generations. Some of these experiences
show thrilling heroism; others are impressive by the patient endurance they disclose; still others are touchingly pathetic; and in
some there is a savor of piquant drollery. All these went to make
up the life of the regiment during its term of service. It is this life
which is sought to be recorded in this book. The bare military
record of marches and fights has been written many a time, and is
a part of the records of State and national governments. The real
life of the regiment, as outlined above, is nowhere preserved in
records.

If the purpose of this book be achieved, the survivors of the
regiment will find here many a well remembered scene and incident;

a later generation will see in its pages a story of patriotic service well performed; and some will recognize the tales heard from the lips of fathers long since gone to the eternal camping ground.

It is proper that acknowledgment be made here of the patient effort of the late Gen. E. S. Holloway, from whom some of the statistical matter has come. For the narrative, the writer is wholly responsible; but very valuable help has been received from many comrades. For all this aid, the writer gratefully returns thanks.

R. L. K.

Cincinnati, September, 1897.

Regimental Association Committee on History,

DR. ALBERT G. HART,
WILLIAM J. MORGAN,
WILLIAM R. SMELLIE.

The Forty-first Ohio Infantry.

CHAPTER I.

MAKING THE REGIMENT.

The news of the disaster at Bull Run, the first general engagement of the Civil War, came upon the Northern Ohio communities as a stunning shock. Incredulity and consternation were the contending emotions among those who heard the earlier news by wire from Washington. The night was a long one to such as waited hour after hour for some contradiction of the story of defeat and rout. But the people quickly roused themselves to face the situation and retrieve what had been lost. The abiding effect of the disaster was to open the eyes of all to the fact that the armed defiance of the national authority was not to be put down by anything in the nature of a brief excursion to the South by fifty or seventy-five thousand men. The immense gravity of the contest that was now fairly opened was thoroughly appreciated, and among all classes the belief spread that the loyal States would be called upon for all their military strength.

Under these circumstances, the President's call for three hundred thousand volunteers came as a relief rather than as an unwelcome demand. Few were disposed to count the cost. The one solemn fact in every mind was that a victorious enemy of the government was bent upon its overthrow. The old-fashioned Fourth of July was still familiar to the people, with its patriotic panegyrics upon the glorious Revolution; and all schoolboys had heard Patrick

Henry's speech.   The common patriotism, indeed, was almost an abstraction.   Except for the friction arising under the fugitive slave-law, these people would hardly have been conscious of a national government at any time, so lightly had its functions touched them.   Not many had ever seen a United States soldier, or any insignia of national authority.   The actual government, its personnel and operation, was to them little more than a myth.   But very real, and very close to their hearts, were the deeds of 1776 and 1812; and when it seemed that a domestic foe was about to obscure the lustre of the old heroism and throw away its fruitage, these people rose in defence with none silent or dissenting.

Militia companies from Cleveland had responded to the first call for volunteers.   That was when the contest appeared likely to be short and trifling.   When half a million men were ordered for three years service, Ohio came promptly to the front.   Several gentlemen of prominence and influence with the Governor became actively interested in the military organization going rapidly forward,—among them, George B. Senter, Bushnell White, George A. Benedict, and some others.   An order was secured from the War Department, giving leave of absence to Lieut. William B. Hazen, of the Eighth U. S. Infantry, to take command of a volunteer regiment to be raised in Cleveland.   Many enlistments had been made, and several companies were in camp, when Col. Hazen arrived to take command.   Among those who were most active in the regimental organization before Col. Hazen's arrival were Col. John J. Wiseman, who had been a member of a New York militia regiment, and who was made Lieutenant Colonel of the Forty-first; George S. Mygatt, who had been on the Governor's staff, and who became Major of the regiment; and Junius R. Sanford, a Cleveland militiaman, who was commissioned Adjutant.   In various counties around, the work of enlistment was pushed by energetic men, and the first full companies at the rendezvous came from Geauga county, many miles away.   In other counties, and as far away as Wayne and Columbiana to the southward, and Lorain and Ottawa to the west, recruiting was urged forward by Wiley, Leslie, Steele, Toland, Bushnell, Mitchell and a score of others.   Many of these names do not appear in the records of the regiment's active service; the rigorous requirements of the West Point colonel causing them to be set aside for other men, not more patriotic, but better adapted to the service. Not the less are these active and willing organizers to have their meed of praise, because the work they did was in preparation, and not the deadly work of war. Some further references to this earlier work will be found in the sketches of companies in this volume.

The arrival of Col. Hazen to take command at the rendezvous, Camp Wood, in the Cleveland suburbs, brought an immediate transformation. In his first order, announcing himself as commander, he laid out the full process of turning recruits into soldiers. Drills, study, recitations, camp police duty, the cut of the hair and cleanliness of person, roll calls, meals, reveille and tattoo and taps, absence from camp or from any duty, sick calls—calls of all kinds and recalls almost as numerous—every minute detail of the daily routine and life, from sunrise to the putting out of lights at night, was specified and prescribed with the precision of a disciplinarian, until the men began to wonder if two days' work was not crowded into the twelve-hour program. Bugle calls for the various duties were incessantly sounded, and exercises trod on each other's heels in the ceaseless labor of each day. The commander seemed as insensible to fatigue as a threshing machine, and to think his men were like thirty-day clocks, wound up to run a month without stopping, and then wind up again. But, if the colonel sometimes seemed to err in his driving, it is to be said that he knew, better than any other in the command, the tests to which the regiment would be put, and also that the time for preparation would be far too short, crowd it how he would. It is to be said further that he put most work where there was most responsibility. Besides drilling the men, the officers had their special studies and drills. It was a tremendous pace the colonel set in this business so entirely new to the recruits— too fast for some to endure, and they, good men, but unable to keep up, were left behind, dropping out one after another. For lack of willing disposition, Hazen had no mercy; but to simple lack of adaptability he was widely charitable and considerate.

The work of instruction never ceased in any command of Col. Hazen's. Before a year was over, the officers of his regiment were provided, in addition to army regulations and tactics, with Jomini's work, Napier's Peninsular War, special books on field fortifications, instructions in topographical drawing and some other subjects; and had received teaching and practice in minor engineer work, the fixing of distances, the method of marching troops, and a score of things outside the regulation tactics. For the men, there was a return, whenever brief occasion offered, to rudimentary instruction, the school of the soldier.

Summing up, it may be said that the inflexible army discipline, coming suddenly upon men unused to associated effort, at first benumbed the minds of many, as if they went through prescribed motions like automatons. But this wore away, leaving the men practiced, alert and obedient, with no loss of spirit. So, too, the strict regulations as to care of the person were sometimes galling; now and then a man felt a degradation in inspection with shirt unbuttoned and bared feet; but this feeling also vanished as the wisdom of the regulation forced itself into recognition.

But what a change from all anticipations! Where was "the pomp and circumstance of glorious war?" Not in the unending drudgery of drill; or in sweeping dirt paths with brush brooms day after day; or in the sentinel's lonely pacing through the dead of night; or in the detail for fatigue duty; or in keeping rust off a Springfield rifle barrel and rubbing up buttons and brass plates; or in eating the little-varied army rations month after month, until the soldier would give a farm for one of his mother's pickles, and a year of life for a bite of home-made pie. Pomp and pageantry were scarce. There were no waving plumes for officers or men— not so much as a feather. There was a dearth of prancing steeds, pawing the earth and scenting the battle afar off. Let alone prancing, the field officers' horses evidently thought the whole business a bore, and had no heart in it. Even the fifes and drums palled on the musical ear while the drum corps rattled off four hours a day just beyond the parade ground.

Ideas of organization in those early days of the war were somewhat crude, even among regular army officers. Thus, the Forty-first was to have a battery of artillery and a full brass band.

Both were organized. Every old member of the regiment will remember little Wetmore, captain of the battery, a thoroughly instructed West Point man; slight in frame and smooth-faced, and with a permanent physical disability; courteously reserved in manner; full of kindness of heart, but full also of official dignity when on duty—one of the picturesque figures of those weeks at Camp Wood.. But only of those weeks. Wetmore's battery went into the field, but not attached to the Forty-first. Army organization was growing rapidly, not only as to numbers, but also as to methods; batteries were not to be attached to infantry regiments.

The band lasted longer as an attachment to the regiment, though its life was shorter. Jack Leland's band had a name in Cleveland long before the war. The leader joined and enlisted his men, and all entered with good heart upon the service. But the army band practice was not the same as that which the men were accustomed to, and when, some months after the regiment had gone to the field, the colonel called for a detail to blow the bugle, the leader explained that such service would "spoil the lip" of the man detailed. The colonel failed to appreciate the nicety of this objection, and a discouragement came upon the band. Another breaker of musical hopes was the regulation for hospital service, the requirement of instruction in bearing stretchers and caring for the wounded. All this made band life in the army very different from band life at home. Then again, the first winter out was passed in Camp Wickliffe, Kentucky, where nothing but mud and sickness abounded. No place could be found better calculated to take the spirit out of the men whose idea of duty comprehended a march over smooth streets, wearing clean uniforms and heading a showy procession of some kind. Nevertheless, Leland and his men held bravely on; but the War Department soon learned as part of its first practical lesson that one of the things to be dispensed with, in such service as its armies were in, was the full regimental band. The less pretentious drum corps succeeded Cleveland's crack band in furnishing music for the Forty-first.

Yet another disenchantment came—this to the chaplain. A pious and worthy gentleman had been appointed to the place; but, the regiment once in the field, he failed to find the expected opportunities for his holy office.   But this was not perhaps the worst. The opportunities provided him were wholly unexpected in their demands; and when it came to inspecting the soup kettles of the company messes, the chaplain broke down.   Perhaps he was not fond of soup made in big black kettles over open fires, and from cakes of desiccated vegetables.   The good man gave it up, mildly protesting in the interest of his palate and his stomach.

Among other delusions common throughout the regiment at the time of assembling, was the notion that it was a good thing to have a little private arsenal in addition to the arms furnished by the government.   Some of the men brought with them Colt's revolvers, often the gift of friends left behind.   The regimental order which required the men to divest themselves of such extra armament and rely wholly on the regulation supply, was a great surprise.   Afterward, plodding along roads ankle deep in either mud or dust, and participation in a battle or two, was abundant vindication of the colonel's wisdom in stripping his men of useless loads.   Many articles besides pistols went the same way—with no little heartache, when the prohibited things were the loving gifts of fathers, mothers or sisters.

Colonel Hazen took command at Camp Wood on the 16th of September, 1861.   He found two full companies, and the others still recruiting.   On the 29th of October the regiment was mustered into the service with a total of 931 officers and men.   A week afterward the regiment left its rendezvous on the way to the front. It had not yet received its arms, but had been drilled with two hundred old muskets belonging to the State.

From Cleveland the regiment was taken direct to Camp Dennison, near Cincinnati, received its arms and spent some uncomfortable days there.   Everything was strange about the quarters, if not entirely new.   It was far enough to be away from home, and yet too near to afford the relief of novelty.   Nobody was sorry when the transport steamer Telegraph No. 3, took the command aboard at Cincinnati to go up the Ohio river to Gallipolis.   In this river town the people and surroundings were not so familiar, and some of the men began to feel that they were really off to the war at last. None of them knew that for a few days the destination of the regiment was in some doubt. The colonel knew it and was concerned for the outcome. He had no desire to come under the command of Gen. Rosecrans, then in West Virginia. A more inviting field of operations opened up to his imagination on the line south from Louisville, where the operations promised to be on a grander scale than was possible in the West Virginia wildernesses. The home of a rebel, Colonel Jenkins, was on the southern side of the river a few miles below Gallipolis, and there were reports of some Confederate activity in that region. The regiment was taken there by boat one day, and a short march was made to the Jenkins place, without result. The colonel hurried his regiment back to Gallipolis that night, to escape possible complications with Rosecrans. The matter did not pass unnoticed by the latter, but Col. Hazen was soon gratified by an order to Louisville to report to Gen. Buell, then organizing the Army of the Ohio at that place.

The camp just out of Louisville was a great improvement. The grounds were pleasant, and near enough to the city to be visited by the people there. The Forty-first began to get some satisfaction out of drills and dress parades before audiences from the city, which included some ladies of the loyal families. The men were becoming better accustomed to the close association of army organization; and, though the work of instruction was not intermitted for a day, it had become less onerous and tiring. The soldiers were coming to handle their guns with confidence, for it was not until they were pitted against the Confederate Enfield rifles that the uselessness of the Greenwood rifled muskets became apparent. This latter was the arm which had been furnished by the government, sorely pushed to outfit its gathering armies. The camp at Louisville was one of the bright spots in the record.

At Louisville the Forty-first was assigned to the Fifteenth brigade, Nelson's division, and, when this was done, it was fairly in the field for three years' service. Already it had a character peculiarly its own, and this distinction was helped by several outward signs. The men never wore the regulation army cap, but were supplied with the neater cadet cap. The manual of arms in which they were drilled was that of the old Scott tactics, sometimes called the "heavy infantry manual." The most noticeable feature of this manual, in comparison with the later "light infantry drill," was the position of the piece at shoulder arms. It was carried in the left hand, the barrel to the front—a much better show of arms than is given by the light infantry position at shoulder arms. This manual was adhered to throughout the service, and always marked the regiment for notice at reviews, parades and when marching with shouldered arms. There may have been other regiments using the old Scott manual, but the Forty-first fell in with none such.

CHAPTER II.

DOWN TO THE FRONT.

The march from Louisville southward to the vicinity of New Haven, Kentucky, was made under the careful and precise detailed orders of Gen. Don Carlos Buell, a master of the art of moving troops, as he was of the army system of organization. The Forty-first felt his directing hand while in Louisville very slightly, for the reason that the preliminary instruction of the regiment had been as thorough and painstaking as the time would allow. When it came to a march of some length, however, the case was different. It was a new experience. Each day's march was carefully marked out; times of halts for rest were prescribed; cautions as to speed of marching were given; directions for filling canteens were laid down; inspections were ordered to make sure that the raw soldiers did not over-load themselves, beyond the regulation outfit; and very little detail seemed to be prescribed. As a result, the first continued marching of these troops was done with comparative ease and precision, and there was very little straggling.

The camp in which the Forty-first spent the winter of 1861-2 was named Camp Wickliffe. Whatever the ground may have been in the summer season, during that winter it was almost continually a slough of mud. The regiment went to this camp as a part of Haskell's Fifteenth Brigade, Nelson's Division, Army of the Ohio. Not long after its arrival a new brigade, the Nineteenth, was organized, and Col. Hazen was assigned to the command of it. The brigade was made up of the Forty-first, the Sixth Kentucky, and the Forty-sixth and Forty-seventh Indiana. This organization was short-lived. The Indiana regiments were commanded by Colonels Fitch and Slack, prominent politicians of Indiana before the war; and these gentlemen, for some reason not discoverable by others, were the reverse of favorites with imperious Gen. Nelson. He made them uncomfortable, and even put some petty slights upon them. They soon secured the transfer of their commands to more congenial associations.

The fighting, that winter in Camp Wickliffe, was continuous, but it was fighting a more potent foe than the Southern army. Disease of various kinds played havoc with the men, and no precautions served to avoid it. Measles was perhaps the most calamitous visitation; many men who recovered from the direct attack were left to fall into some other ailment more or less serious. Battles of great note have been fought with less loss than was sustained by the troops at Camp Wickliffe. The medical staff of the Forty-first was well qualified professionally and well instructed as to army duties. The colonel's watch was upon this and the other regiments of the brigade; everything was done that was possible in caring for the men's health; but the season and the ground were not to be withstood. All in all, no more uncomfortable and dismal camp was ever occupied by the Forty-first.

The work of instruction was not given up, but the interference with drill, through storm and mud, was very great. This was the dreary season that sent the Chaplain home in disappointment, and sickened the regimental band. Many changes occurred among commissioned and non-commissioned officers. The losses in half a dozen fights would hardly make so great a change, in this regard, as had come over the regiment since it left Cleveland. Everything at Camp Wickliffe seemed untoward, if not calamitous—a very rough initiation into army life in inclement winter weather. Even the jokers and wits among the companies felt the depression, and their efforts were but half-hearted. No one was sorry when, with the approach of spring, orders came to march.

The destination was Nashville. Nelson's division marched to West Point and took steamers down the Ohio and up the Cumberland river. The country along the lower Cumberland was flooded. In many places the channel of the river was only to be guessed at, and the boats were tied up to the tops of submerged trees at night, to avoid running over the sunken forests.

Of course, it was known before arrival at Nashville that the enemy had passed on. The steamers came up to the levee and the troops debarked and marched up into the town. A solitary Texas cavalryman was found in the St. Cloud Hotel, where he had lingered under the influence of deep potations. This was the first armed foe the regiment had seen. Passing along High street, Gen. Buell himself riding at the head of the column, a woman came out from one of the better residences, and advanced to the sidewalk shouting for Jeff Davis. That house was taken for a Union Hospital.

The Forty-first was marched out of the city and took position on a height along the Franklin pike. During the day, a commotion was seen on a distant road running along the river; and later it was learned that a detachment of Southern cavalry had ridden down that road to the levee and burned a steamer. Camp report had it that this exploit was done by the Texas Black Horse Cavalry. It may be difficult to understand how the color of cavalry horses can give military renown; but it did so at that time. The Texas Black Horse Cavalry was much talked about, but the Forty-first never knew that it got nearer to that force than it was on the day the squad burned the steamer—too far away to see and admire the awful prowess of the black steeds.

The regiment finally went into camp on the grounds in front of the Ewing house, on the Murfreesboro road. Some notable incidents occurred during the stay at this camp. The first of these was a night alarm, very soon after the arrival. Nelson had had attached to his division a squadron of very new cavalry, and a battery of artillery almost as fresh. A detail of this cavalry was sent out a mile or so on the pike, toward Murfreesboro, as a picket, with a vidette a little distance further on. A section of the artillery was posted, guns unlimbered, on the pike in front of the Forty-first, whose camp was laid out parallel with the pike. Between the regiment and the pike was a high stone wall,—the artillery being outside the enclosure, on the pike, the regiment inside, facing the pike. The troops of the division were not camped in line. The first or second night after this marvellous disposition of force was made, while everybody but the sentinels was soundly sleeping, a single carbine shot rang out on the midnight air from the direction of the cavalry picket. An instant later there was a little fusillade in the same direction, and then a tremendous clatter of hoofs on the pike and coming toward the camps. The regiment was on its feet in a moment, the men hurriedly clutching their arms. The common thought was, "The Black Horse Cavalry!" The clatter on the pike was as if a thousand horsemen were thundering down upon them, and the companies got into line before commands could be given. The next thought was to form square against cavalry, and instantly it was done. Meantime the lieutenant-colonel and the major were hastening to mount their horses, which they accomplished just as the square was complete. Some thoughtful friend had given the major a pair of holster pistols, and no sooner was he in the saddle than he drew one of these from its holster. The lieutenant-colonel's horse was standing with his head close beside the major, when the major's pistol, by some accident, was fired. It was the first gun of the war for lieutenant-colonel's horse, and he promptly dumped his rider on the ground, while the major made his way inside the square. The clattering cavalry on the pike were close at hand. On they came, pell-mell, till they encountered the artillerymen's guns on the pike, which they failed to see until they had tumbled over them, horses and riders together. But when the cavalry outpost was in, the pike to the front was once more silent; no enemy followed. It turned out that the vidette in front of the outpost was sitting on his horse polishing his carbine, when he carelessly discharged it, pointed backward toward the outpost. The men there took the shot for an attack, sprang to their saddles, fired their carbines down the road and started back at a run. They had been stuffed with the imminent deadly hazard of outpost duty until they could see enemies anywhere in the darkness, in full tilt at them. There was no enemy near, nor was it likely there would be one. We can laugh at such incidents now, knowing that the men who figured in them abundantly proved themselves afterward on a score of fields. And the incident shows that rawness was not confined to the rank and file, but sometimes got into high official places. Gen. Nelson, it should be said in fairness, was an accomplished naval officer, but quite out of familiar lines in the army.

A second incident was of a very different character. An enlisted man had been into Nashville one day and found too much to drink. On his return he was halted by the camp guard, and some words ensued with the corporal on duty there.   At last the tipsy man struck the corporal.   Of course he was instantly overpowered and placed in confinement.   The division general thought this was a fit time to give a lesson in army discipline.   He had the tipsy man court-martialed for offering violence to "a superior officer"—over-looking or not knowing the fact that the word "officer" in the army regulations means a commissioned officer, and does not therefore include corporals.   The court-martial sentenced the man to be shot, and Gen. Nelson, approving the finding, and not sending it up to army headquarters as he should have done, proceeded to carry out the death sentence.   He posted his division on sloping ground that all might see, and placed the firing squad with the condemned man in front.   The official murder then took place.   The guns of the firing squad were loaded for them, the men being told that one piece was charged with only a blank cartridge, and none knowing whose piece it was that was thus charged.   Each man can in this way aim at a vital part, as he sights the gun at his comrade, and thereafter may console himself, if he can, with the belief that his piece contained the one blank cartridge, and so it was not his bullet that did the kill-ing.   In this instance, any one of four or five bullets that pierced the unfortunate would have killed him, had no other struck him. The effect of this exhibition killing was not good.   Rather, it was remembered with horror, not with a heightened sense of duty and respect for authority.

Still another incident of the stay at Nashville was a marching pilgrimage to the Hermitage, Jackson's old home.   It was one of Gen. Nelson's freaks one day to take his command out to this place. The march was not arranged with Gen. Buell's skill.   Nelson put a favorite regiment in the lead, and exercised no control over its pace. The leaders of a marching column can always quickly wear out those who follow, if their movement is not controlled.   It happened so in this instance, and the day was a most fatiguing and uncomfortable one.   So far as military exercise was concerned no benefit came from the expedition; on the contrary, it was hurtful to the marching habit of the men.   The General was a Kentuckian and a great admirer of Jackson; but the people where the Forty-first came from had not canonized Old Hickory.   The political significance of this toilsome and hurtful pilgrimage—it had no military phase—was distasteful to the greater number.

At Nashville, as at Camp Wickliffe, there were many changes among officers and non-commissioned officers; but, this over, such changes were less frequent.

The Forty-first marched from Camp Wickliffe February 14th, and reached Nashville on the 27th of the same month. About the middle of March the army began the march to Savannah, on the Tennessee river, to join Grant's forces near that point. The first part of the march was through a beautiful and well cultivated country. Coming to Duck river, it was thought necessary to bridge it, and that work was given to the division in advance of Nelson on the road. After several days of waiting for the bridge, impatient Nelson offered to ford the river with his division, and did so, the men stripped up to the waist and holding their arms aloft as they waded. This movement put Nelson in the lead on the march to Savannah. Getting farther down into the country, it became rougher, until the roads were so bad that heavy details were necessary to bring the trains along. Apparently bottomless mud made hard marching, and it was very exhausting to the details with the trains. These early experiences seem now never to have been outdone by later ones. Certainly the regiment was very much worn with marching when, on the 5th of April, it bivouacked two miles from Savannah, with the trains still miles in the rear struggling through the mud. This was on a Saturday. Next morning began Beauregard's assault on Grant's army in position on the other side of the river some miles above.

CHAPTER III.

SHILOH.

Saturday night, the 5th of April, 1862, came to the Forty-first in as weary a condition as it had ever known. The road passed over during the day was deep with mud, and the latter part of the long march from Nashville had been pressed a little harder than before. The wagon train was away back on the road when the regiment bivouacked near Savannah, and the men went quickly to their rest. Sunday morning broke fair, and officers and men thought of a day spent in putting things in order after the late hard work. But the morning had scarcely come when there was a sound of firing some distance up the river. Hazen with his staff rode on to Savannah, to the little tavern where Grant was sitting on the porch. Hazen was convinced, by the increasing din of firing in the distance, that a general engagement was on between Grant's forces and the Confederates. All others were soon convinced to the same effect.

A guide was furnished, and the whole division started soon after noon to march to a point opposite Pittsburg Landing, which was the landing for Grant's position on the other side of the river. Through the low and marshy bottom lands near the river the troops made their way, sometimes slowly, and did not finish the march till late in the afternoon. Coming out from the forest path they had been following, and approaching the river bank, the troops heard over their heads, from the high bank opposite, some whistling bullets and a shell or two. During the march the sounds of battle had swelled and lulled at intervals, and every one knew that a severe and protracted battle was in progress. There was a steamer in waiting to cross the troops. Hazen's brigade was the second one taken over. The night was near at hand, but the scene on the farther shore was distinct enough as the boat slowly made her way across. The bank down to the water's edge was covered with fugitives from the battlefield, and as the Forty-first moved off the boat and up the bank, the men picked their way among the crowds of runaways. All of them belonged to regiments which had been "cut to pieces" in the

battle—so they said.   Pretty large pieces some of them had been cut
into, it seemed.   At the top of the bank, the Forty-first was deployed
and moved forward a few yards; but the battle was just ending for
the day, and the regiment was not engaged.   In front, and sweeping
around toward the river above and below was the line of artillery
which enclosed the foothold left to the Union forces on that side of
the river.   It looked small to hold an army.   It is not attempted,
with reference to this matter, to give measurements and accurate
data—only to set down appearances as they showed to the newly-
arrived troops.   Neither is there in this narrative an indulgence in
denunciation of the fugitives on the river bank, since those men,
under more experienced leadership, afterward became thoroughly
reliable soldiers and made an honorable record on many a field.

Darkness had fallen, and all was still on the ground where the
battle ended, when the Forty-first was moved forward to take its
place in the line of battle formed for the next day's operations.   All
common landmarks on that field were obliterated; it was only a
stretch of ground covered everywhere with wagon and artillery
tracks coming from all directions and going everywhere.   The night
was dark, and locating the troops was slow and very wearisome
work.   At last, after many a wait and some turnings, the Forty-
first was halted and faced to the front.   It was in a thin wood, the
ground trodden and cut up, though this could be only felt, for the
intense darkness permitted no man to see his next fellow's face.
The men lay down where they stood when halted, and made themselves as comfortable as they could.   Now and then some one
stumbled over the dead body of a soldier, and moved a yard away
to lie down for the night.

In the first sleep of weariness, the men were aroused by the roar
of a heavy shell flying high overhead and crashing down through
the forest in the distance.   For hours during the night this was repeated at intervals sufficiently short to break up the night's sleep
into fitful spells, and in the morning leave a feeling as if no sleep at
all had been had.   No one knew at the time what this firing meant,
but afterward it was known that the shells came from a gun-boat
anchored in the river—our own of course—and were intended to
fly toward the ground the Confederates were supposed to occupy,

and so keep them uncomfortable and unresting throughout the night. That was the effect on the Union soldiers, however it was with the Confederates. This firing was one of the early stupidities of the war—a most annoying blunder.

The regiment stood to arms before daylight, in readiness to receive attack. None came, and finally the command, bedraggled and unsatisfied of rest, was started forward in line of battle, skirmishers out. Everywhere about was the wreckage from yesterday's battle. On a bare spot just outside a clump of bushes lay the lieutenant colonel of an Illinois regiment, flat on his back, sword as it dropped from his hand, a bullet hole in the forehead above the staring eyes and ghastly cheeks. A little beyond this, the skirmishers drew the enemy's fire, and then a solid shot from a field piece came bowling along the ground straight toward the advancing line. The men in the front rank saw it and stepped aside, but it struck a soldier behind them. The battery which fired it was located in a heavy wood on the left front, and kept up its fire for some time, with solid round shot. The skirmishers advanced to the fence of an open lot beyond which was the battery in the wood. Later in the war, those skirmishers would have made short work of that artillery. Mendenhall's battery came up and sent some quieting shells into the wood on the left front, and there were sounds that indicated the coming up of troops on the right.

Finally, the regiment, with the others of the brigade, was called to attention and started to charge the Confederate line in its front. Gen. Buell, anxious for the conduct of the men in their first encounter, rode with his staff close behind the line of battle as it started forward. The start was from an open wood; then came some underbrush and then open ground. The brigade crossed this at a dash, and the Confederates' first and second lines gave way before the onslaught. But the command was inexperienced, and the movement quickly went beyond control in a headlong pursuit; all formation was lost, and the enemy, with fresh troops, seized his ground again, driving back the scattered assailants. The Forty-first was speedily reformed on ground in the rear, and, although it had suffered severely, was in hand for any duty. But its first battle was ended.

Three hundred and seventy-three officers and men (one company, G, was back with the wagon train) were present for duty on the morning of that day.   In the fight, which lasted hardly more than half an hour, one hundred and forty-two were killed or wounded, and none were missing—total loss, thirty-nine per cent. of the number engaged.   This was a greater per cent. of loss than was sustained by any other regiment in either Buell's or Grant's army in that battle, except the Ninth Illinois infantry, which lost fifty per cent.   Three officers and three enlisted men, who at different times bore the colors of the Forty-first, were killed or wounded.   The killed and the mortally wounded (dying soon after the battle) together numbered forty-four, an unusually large per cent., due to the square standup fighting at short range when the enemy was first encountered in the charge.   The prolongation of this fighting was due in large measure to the ineffective guns of the Forty-first, which, inflicting on the enemy less execution than he was doing, enabled him to stay longer in the fight.

The distinctive feature of this engagement was that neither force was in position, but advancing, when the firing began.   The Confederate troops were coming to attack, or were getting into position, when the charge of Hazen's brigade was ordered; and the charge was ordered on the theory that raw troops would have a better chance when moving to attack than when standing to receive an attack on an unprotected line.   Whatever the merits of that theory, the Forty-first was never again so handled in action.

The regiment went into position on the night of the battle on the Tan Bark road, this being on the left of the Union line.   During the night before, rain fell almost constantly on the already sodden ground where the men lay without cover; and the like experience came the night after.   Many of the soldiers, lying down in their blankets, awoke in little puddles of water.   The whole field seemed a wilderness of mud.   Camp and garrison equipage was all behind at Savannah, and did not come up until the fifth day after the battle.   Meanwhile the regiment was sadly uncomfortable with the continued exposure, and much sickness resulted.   The battle field was strewn with unburied bodies of men and horses.   Heavy details were sent to put these under ground; and in some instances the rain of the following night undid the work of burial and laid bare the decaying corpses. The burial details found dead men in strange attitudes. They came across a Confederate kneeling beside a big log, his head and shoulders bent forward over it, and his gun in his hands as he had held it in the position of aiming when he met instant death from a Union bullet. Some of the dead faces bore signs of agony, but not many; a very few were torn by shot or shell. The deadly work at Shiloh was done by musketry, not artillery. On some of the Confederate dead were found large knives, designed for fighting—evidences that crude notions of war found lodgement among the fiery Southerners. None of the butcher knives were stained with blood; but some of them showed painstaking finish and polish, only to be rusted in the rain.

The battle occurred on Monday, April 7th; the camp equipage arrived on Friday, the 11th; and on Sunday, the 13th—that is, after an interval of a week for burying the dead and cleaning up the survivors—the Forty-first was astonished with an order to resume drills and study the following day. Officers and men thought themselves hardly yet recovered from the tremendous strain of the battle; the necessary period of rest after the exhaustion of march and fight seemed to have hardly begun. The difference between the theory and the practice of war had been made sharply prominent by the late experience in practice, while the connection and value of the theory had been rendered correspondingly dim and indefinite. The days of squad drill and the school of the soldier were far back in the past, with a whole campaign of actual war between them and the present. But there was the order, and the soldier's first duty is obedience. Obedience was rendered in this instance, but it was hardly of the cheerful kind—the men had been too roughly used, and too recently.

What, in other ways, of those days immediately following the first battle? Well, for one thing, the regiment slowly realized that it had received, between sunrise and sunset of one day, more and infinitely better teaching than all that could come from books—the invaluable lesson of experience. There was much of disenchantment in it—the most notable thing in this way, perhaps, being the

absence in practice of the element of show.   No music, for the drum
corps are stretcher-bearers for the wounded.   No bright uniforms,
even on the mounted officers.   Save for a two-inch bit of gold
embroidery on the shoulder, a major-general on the battlefield may
be scarcely distinguishable from his orderly, if the latter has had a
good pick of horses.   There is not often the inspiration that comes
of seeing great masses of troops in motion or in action.   In a country like the South at the time of the war, it is sometimes possible
to see a brigade in line of battle; but many a considerable engagement has been fought through without either side catching full sight
of so much as a regiment of the enemy.   The battles about Chattanooga were, perhaps, the only ones in the central South where
divisions entire could be seen in action.   To sum up, then, the real
business of war, the fighting, is relieved by none of the supposed
embellishments; it is a business sombre and heavy, lightened only
when the unspeakable exaltation of victory is vouchsafed to the
soldier.   Finally, the notion which possesses most new soldiers,
and others, that the battle is the only test, and that armies go in to
fight at their best of strength and heart, is an illusion.   In nine cases
out of ten, the marching to be done before the troops are set for
the fight is enough to tire out bodies and break down hearts in
sheer weariness of toil and deprivation of even the soldier's scanty
fare.   The labor of the campaign is not in the battle, but in the
preparation for it.

It hardly needs to be said that the greatest of all depressions in
the soldier's life is felt after the battle, when he has leisure to think
of the comrades lost or gone to the hospital for weary weeks or
months, if not forever.   He counts them over, one by one, with the
grief of comradeship, and feels almost as sore for the badly wounded
as for the dead, knowing the lack of opportunity for good treatment
which the best of surgeons cannot make good.   After its share in
the action at Shiloh was done, the Forty-first passed near a field
hospital where the wounded were being brought in and laid on the
ground to await the care of the overworked surgeons.   In a corner
of a rail fence near by was a pile of severed arms and legs, the pile
growing as the faithful doctors hastened their grim work.   This is
one of the spectacles which do not fade out of mind.

CHAPTER IV.

EVENTS, BUT NO BATTLES.

May 2d, 1862, the advance of the Union armies on Corinth, Mississippi, was begun. Everybody knew that there had been a new army organization, or disposition, and that Halleck was chief in command, with Grant second; that the Army of the Mississippi, Gen. Pope, was to be the left; the Army of the Ohio, Gen. Buell, the center; and the Army of the Tennessee, Gen. Thomas, the right. The Forty-first was still in Hazen's brigade of Nelson's division, with its long-time companions, the Ninth Indiana and the Sixth Kentucky.

There was really no period of rest after the Shiloh fight and before the advance on Corinth. Fatigue duty was heavy, while drill and study seemed more than ever burdensome. The order to march was therefore not unwelcome; it would at least intermit drill and camp duty. The first march was ten miles, to the vicinity of Monterey and about ten miles from Corinth, where the Confederates were posted. A great deal of road repairing had already been done, and more was done after the movement was begun. Hazen's brigade at one time advanced to within five miles of Corinth, acting as guard to the heavy details at work on the roads. Now and then, scouting Confederate cavalry was encountered, but in those days horsemen counted for little; they were very considerate of infantry, and did not bother. The country was wild and only thinly settled, seeming to produce not much besides thickly timbered land and mud. It was an excellent place for corduroy roads. A week or more was occupied with short marches of two to four miles, as the roads permitted, for sometimes the repairs of a day were washed out by the rain of the following night. On the 9th of May, heavy artillery firing was heard in the direction of Pope's army, and indicated that the Union forces were being closed in upon the enemy. But the next day a regular camp was established on fairly comfortable ground, and the day was spent in cleaning up.

On the 17th, the division line was advanced to within two miles of Corinth, and again halted on good ground. Though there was much picket and guard duty in these days before Corinth, the time was really the most restful the regiment had seen since leaving Spring Hill in March. There was sunshine overhead and dry ground under foot, instead of clouds and rain and depths of mud. Men were coming up from the hospital, and some recruits joined. It was a time of recovery, in spirit and in numbers, from the loss and fatigue of the Shiloh campaign. Communications had been re-established, and there was news from home. The sutler put in his first appearance, and did a lively business, acquiring some valuable experience. The story went that Private Hoover, of H company, rode to the sutler's tent in an officer's coat, obtained no one knew how, and by his ponderous, brusque manner convinced the new sutler that he was Gen. Nelson, and carried away some bottles, pay to be collected that night at the general's quarters. If the bottles had been barrels they could not have held more merriment than came from the anticipated reception of the sutler when he should present his bill to Nelson. Sunday morning inspections had been resumed, and began to find the soldiers in their accustomed good condition. There was even a flag presentation one Sunday, from the Sixth Ohio to the Twenty-fourth Ohio; and one of these regiments being Gen. Nelson's favorite, he ordered out the whole division to do honor to the occasion, himself figuring as the presentation orator.

The siege of Corinth was fairly on for the Forty-first by the 19th of May, when it went on picket duty at half past 3 o'clock in the morning and stood through the day to protect the men who were digging the first parallel. There was skirmishing at intervals through the day; but one man slightly wounded was the only loss sustained by the regiment. Next morning it was moved into the trenches for twenty-four hours, and there was much firing, but there were no losses. Sometimes the enemy's artillery opened at intervals, without effect. This was the first and the last regular siege work done by the regiment. Field tactics had moved from one extreme to the other. Thus, at Shiloh little attention was given to even such advantage as the ground offered; at Corinth the advance was by parallels. Each morning at half past 3, the troops not in the trenches stood at arms until daylight. It was a very formal and precise style of warfare, not excessively tiresome, and not particularly lively and rapid. On the 28th a new line was established within a half mile of the enemy's lines; and on the 30th the whole affair of the siege came to an end. The Confederates had been evacuating Corinth at their leisure, and on the morning of the 30th nothing remained there but a small rear guard, all ready to go, which it did at once, without offering or receiving molestation. This Corinth campaign lived in the memory of the regiment as a military demonstration, not as a visible result, and therefore the memory was faint rather than vivid—a colorless campaign.

Corinth was finally left behind on the 4th of June, the march being on the Rienzi road, and one of the objects the support of Pope, who reported having overtaken the enemy at Boonville. Nothing came of it, and after short marches for several days, the regiment finally started toward the Tennessee river, reaching Iuka on the 16th. A stop of some length was made at this place, broken by two or three expeditions along the line of the Memphis and Charleston railway. A bridge was being rebuilt at Bear river, and the regiment did some guard duty there, besides helping the engineer regiment on the bridge.

In the camp near Iuka drill was resumed, as usual when there was a halt. There was a review of the brigade one Sunday, by Gen. Nelson, which brought a little ruffle of the peace between the General and Col. Whitaker, of the Sixth Kentucky. The General's order to form column by companies was not heard by Whitaker, whose regiment remained in line when the movement was executed by the other regiments. Ponderous Nelson on his ponderous horse rode toward Whitaker, demanding with an oath why he did not put his command into column. The hot little Kentuckian spurred his horse toward Nelson, and demanded with an oath why the order was not properly given. It was an even balance between the two.

One of the delights of this camp was the abundance of blackberries afforded by the country around. Up to this time, the regiment had profited very little by additions to the regular rations out of the country. The blackberries were large and finely flavored, and made a luxury in the messes.

On the 22d of June, the march was resumed in the direction of Tuscumbia, Alabama, which place was passed two days later, and further on the Tennessee river was reached. On the 27th the regiment was ferried across the river, and next day moved toward Athens. Elk river was forded on the 29th, and on the 1st of July the command went into camp near Athens, afterward known as Camp Houghton. Since leaving Shiloh on the 2d of May, nine men had died of disease—no other deaths, and but one wounded.

The movement along the Memphis and Charleston railway, in which Buell's army was engaged at this time, was meant to threaten Chattanooga, which was the Confederate stronghold in that direction. Gen. Buell protested against a plan of campaign which stretched his army out along two hundred miles of railroad, but the commander-in-chief held to his plan.

The stay at Camp Houghton continued until July 17th. All drills were, of course, resumed. Col. Hazen, absent on sick leave since about the middle of May, rejoined his brigade. Berries were plentiful in the country; camp and drill grounds were good; water supply excellent; and the health of the regiment was improved. The Fourth of July was celebrated by a division review and a march through the town of Athens, all the natives round about turning out to see it.

July 17th orders came for Hazen's brigade to rebuild the Nashville & Decatur railroad to Reynolds' Station. As the order called for four regiments, the Twenty-seventh Kentucky was added to the brigade. Three days of marching brought the regiment to the scene of the work ordered, and it camped at Richland creek, on the plantation of Lieut.-Col. Brown, of the Twenty-seventh Tennessee Confederate regiment. The twelve days spent in this camp were a continuing feast for the regiment. A hundred negroes were on the place, and, of course, were friendly. There was fresh pork and a variety of garden vegetables, and the slaves regularly drove a herd of milch cows to the camp at milking time. No hotel ever spread such fare before the Forty-first as Col. Brown's plantation afforded. The fatigue duty was not overhard, and the time went on wings.

On the 1st of August, the regiment marched to Reynolds' Station, and was transported by rail to Nashville, and then to Murfreesboro, the brigade having been assigned to garrison that town after the capture of its garrison (July 13) by Forrest's cavalry. Guard and picket duty at this place was severe, but the country was pleasant and the nearness of Nashville was an advantage. The troops were called up without reveille at 3 o'clock each morning, and stood to arms until after daylight—this to guard against surprise by Forrest's enterprising cavalrymen. Major Wiley (promoted from Captain June 12), who had been absent on account of a wound received at Shiloh, rejoined the regiment and was in command, Lieut.-Col. Mygatt being absent on leave. Capt. W. R. Tolles had declined his promotion to Major.

CHAPTER V.

THE KENTUCKY CAMPAIGN.

Gen. Buell, grand master that he was of the art of moving armies, concentrated his widely separated forces at Nashville with marvellous exactness. Scattered over hundreds of miles of country, with numberless and various obstacles of bad roads and unbridged streams between them and the point of rendezvous, the remotest detachments came to Nashville with scarcely a half-day's delay beyond the calculated time. Minute orders for the march were given to each command, suiting the conditions of its line of movement. The movement was a masterpiece of quick concentration of scattered forces. Gen. Buell had been assigned the task of following Bragg in his march for the Ohio river country. The Confederate design was to gain recruits in Kentucky through the inspiration of the presence of a Southern army, with the possible further incentive that would come from some successful encounters. Bragg had moved out of Chattanooga while the railroad and bridge building was going on along the line of Halleck's menace of Chattanooga. Moving far to the eastward of the country occupied by the Union forces in Tennessee, Bragg could go as he pleased. It pleased him to get so good a start that he could not be intercepted, but entered Kentucky when and where he would. In the race for the Ohio river which began when Buell's army left Nashville, the two forces were moving on parallel lines, with the advantage on the Confederate side.

A very hard march it was from Nashville to Louisville, including night movements for position, and bivouacs on ground chosen for its military advantage rather than for the comfort and convenience of the worn-out soldiers. There was, perhaps, never much chance of bringing Bragg to a fight—he could always make his choice, having too good a start to be headed off. It was with some surprise that the men who had, several times during that race, gone into position in the night, that Buell might be able to take advantage of

WILLIAM B. HAZEN

Colonel 41st Ohio Volunteer Infantry

AQUILA WILEY

Colonel 41st O.V.I.; Brevet Brig. Gen. U.S. Vols.
Gen. Hazen called Wiley "the most efficient
regimental commander, regular or volunteer, I ever knew."

any opening to bring the Confederates to battle, afterward learned that the Northern newspapers were abusing Buell because he had not made Bragg fight. Often a bivouac was on ground where the only water to be had was in sink-holes frequented by cattle and hogs; and on one occasion the water supply was in caves beneath the ground on which the troops bivouacked. At no other time was the regiment for so long a time without the comforts that abundant water brings. Ordinary care of the person was out of the question, and when the regiment marched into Louisville it was scarcely recognizable, so ragged and worn and dirty were officers and men. But there was the Ohio river, never before so beautiful in the eyes of that begrimed soldiery. And, lying on the island, they looked across the river to the Indiana shore—"God's country," they called it—and thought of homes and friends in the free land.

The brief stay here was improved to remove the marks of the toilsome march just ended. Being in Louisville was next thing to being in Ohio. Communication with home was short and speedy, and there were some visiting relatives and friends. Some of the officers had acquaintances among the loyal families of the city, who made the time a pleasant one for them.

One of the notable happenings during the stay at Louisville was the killing of Gen. Nelson, the old commander of the division to which the Forty-first belonged. The general was shot by Gen. Jeff. C. Davis in resentment of such grossly abusive language as no army officer could submit to and keep his standing among men. Nelson had been absent from his division, on duty in Kentucky, for some time, and very few of the old division rejoiced at the prospect of his return to its command. No one doubted Nelson's loyalty; no one questioned his bravery; but, whatever his qualities as a naval officer, which was his profession, he had developed no capacity that warranted his rank in the army, and he was by nature and habit wholly unfit for a commander of men, especially the volunteer soldiery of the Rebellion. With a fresh recollection of many petty slights and some downright abuse given under cover of his rank, the Forty-first could not repress a feeling of relief while it joined in sorrow at the manner of his invited death. The regiment had been under his command for nearly a year.

On the 1st of October the advance on Bragg's army was begun. The brigade had been reinforced, and in this movement included the Twenty-seventh Kentucky, the One Hundred and Tenth Illinois, Cockerill's Ohio battery, and part of the time Wolford's Kentucky cavalry. The brigade was in Gilbert's corps, which formed the right of the army when it was gathered in front of Perryville. Skirmishing began on the second day out from Louisville, and the movement was retarded by repeated deployments when it was thought the enemy might be in force in the vicinity. So the days went on until the night of October 7th. The command had come again into a country where water was scarce. This night, after dark, the regiment marched several miles in search of a water supply, part of the distance in the dry bed where sometimes a creek flowed. Next morning the troops went into line of battle at 10 o'clock. Two or three hours afterward, some dismounted Confederate cavalrymen took possession of a farm house in front, and began firing. The skirmishers of the Forty-first, with a detachment from Wolford's cavalry, soon dislodged them, and Cockerill's battery threw some shells at the retreating horsemen. The regiment took no further part in the battle of Perryville, which was fought by the corps on the left, under McCook. From about 8 o'clock in the morning the sounds of the fighting away to the left were plainly heard. Much has been said and written—some of it immediately after the battle, and with the purpose of securing Buell's removal from command— about the eagerness of Gilbert's corps to advance and succor McCook that fateful 8th of October. Such talk is nonsense. Not even the brigade and division generals knew anything of the situation on the left, except that there was fighting; even the general in command of the army had some difficulty in getting at the facts. As for the men of the Forty-first, they simply wanted to do their duty, then as at all times, and they were not so foolish as to be impatient to assume, without knowledge, the direction of the battle. The much-talked-of eagerness to help McCook was developed after the battle, when it was known, as it was not known during the battle, that McCook sadly needed help. The Forty-first was little given to nonsense of that sort.

The morning after the battle, the line of battle in which was the Forty-first moved forward to Perryville, which the enemy had left during the night. One of the scenes on this advance was a Confederate field hospital in and about a small farm house. The long porch was crowded with wounded men, and, just as the regiment passed, the surgeons were taking off, near the shoulder, the arm of a poor fellow. Two attendants held the writhing man while the surgeon carved him—for they had no anæsthetics to put him into kind insensibility.

Two days after the battle, the Forty-first was in a reconnaissance toward Danville, finding no enemy; but the next day, advancing upon Danville, the Confederate rear guard was found in the town, and driven out by the brigade, the Ninth Indiana leading. The enemy, with cavalry and artillery, was in line at the fair grounds, and the skirmish was a lively one, artillery being used on both sides. Four men of the brigade were slightly wounded. Danville seemed to be a very inviting place, and perhaps this impression was heightened by the fact that the people were overjoyed to greet the Union troops as they entered. Nearly 400 sick Confederates were found in the hospitals, and 30 able-bodied men were captured. On the 12th of October the brigade was pushed forward near Camp Dick Robinson, encountering the Confederate cavalry in a sharp skirmish. On the 14th began a long chase of the enemy's rear guard by way of Stanford and Crab Orchard. Beyond the latter place the country becomes rougher as the mountains are approached. Wheeler's cavalry was the Confederate rear guard, and they made trouble in plenty. At every favorable point, they lay in wait, concealed until the advance was close upon them; then would come shells from two small field pieces, and a show of making a stand, to compel the deployment of a regiment or two. When the deployed force advanced, the nimble cavalrymen would be gone, artillery and all, to lie in wait again at the next favorable place.

In this way the march was kept up until the mountains were reached and crossed—a lonely country, with marches of half a day without seeing so much as a hut by the wayside. The enemy took to obstructing the narrow road by felling timber across it, and on one day the brigade made only three miles progress, most of the time being occupied with clearing the road. On the 19th the top of Wild Cat Mountain was reached, and about dark the advance arrived at Pittman's Cross Roads, where the enemy was in position, having had an infantry regiment sent to aid in holding back the pursuit. The Forty-first had the lead, and was within a hundred and fifty yards of the enemy's line before it was discovered. Then came a discharge from the artillery. The Forty-first replied with a volley, but the dusk of evening was deepening and the Confederates moved off. The commands of their officers could be heard distinctly, but nothing could be seen. And this was the last encounter with the Confederate rear guard. A prisoner taken at this point proved to be a man from the famous Washington Artillery of New Orleans, and a member of a well known loyal family of Louisville. Col. Hazen took his informal pledge and sent him to his friends in Louisville, in charge of an officer of the Forty-first, who was going to Ohio on duty. The two rode back unattended, by way of Nicholasville and Lexington, and were received everywhere with open arms by the Confederate sympathizers, who entertained them with true Southern hospitality. Wherever they stopped a feast was spread in honor of the Washington Artillery. In return, the Union officer with no little difficulty passed his prisoner safely through the lines at Lexington and delivered him to his family in Louisville. He kept his pledge and did not return to the Confederate service.

This pursuit of the Confederate rear guard involved some hard service, but no fighting, except the slight encounters when Wheeler made his stops to delay the pursuit. Several attempts were made to get flanking parties to his rear, but the wary and active cavalryman was not to be caught with infantry. The pursuit ended within a few miles of Loudonville, the Sixth Kentucky making the farthest advance in a reconnaissance toward that place. Several beef cattle were captured here, and they were welcome, for rations were short and the country destitute of forage. After two days' rest, the return march was begun, October 22d, and Mt. Vernon was passed on the 25th, the direction from thence being toward Somerset. The next night six inches of snow fell, and this made the march of the following day one of the most trying the regiment ever encountered. Rations were exhausted, and the private attempts at foraging brought little beside a barrel of applejack found in a distillery. The finders filled their canteens and on their return to the regiment passed the fiery stuff around among their comrades. It had the less effect, because the men were so nearly exhausted by exposure and hunger. By night, Somerset was reached, and rations were waiting there, never more welcome. A day's rest was given to recovery, and then the march was resumed, going toward Columbia. This place was reached on the 31st, and the regimental camp and garrison equipage was waiting. It had been left at Nashville on the 8th of September. At Columbia also were about a hundred recruits for the Forty-first, which were distributed among the companies, F and G getting the larger number. A number of commissions were received here, and the regiment was mustered for pay; clothing was issued, and the officers got needed supplies from the sutler—a general rejuvenation, indeed. On the 6th of November the regiment was paid at Glasgow, where the command made a halt from the 3d to the 12th of the month. The usual drills were resumed on the 5th and continued during the stay.

The regiment broke camp on the 12th and moved toward Gallatin in a moderate rain. The army was returning to Tennessee to operate southward with Nashville as a base. On the 15th the Cumberland river was crossed on a trestle foot-bridge, and the halt at night was near Silver Springs, Tennessee. At this place was witnessed the only scene of its kind in the history of the regiment. A lieutenant and private had been sentenced by court martial, the former to dismissal in disgrace, and the latter to the ceremony known as "drumming out of camp." The division was formed in columns closed in mass, on three sides of a square, and the culprits were marched under guard to the open side, where the division adjutant read the charges and the finding of the court. He then tore the shoulder-straps from the officer's coat, while the private was marched around the square, a placard on his back marked "Thief," and the drum corps playing the rogue's march. The two were then taken under guard through the lines and turned loose.

At this camp, Lieut.-Col. Geo. S. Mygatt, having resigned, bade farewell to the regiment, leaving Major Wiley in command. Several changes of camp were made—first to Stone river, then to Mill creek—and there was a great deal of picket and forage train duty, with some long marches. A reconnaissance or two helped to fill out the period, and on these occasions the Confederate cavalry was encountered without serious result. There were the usual drills, camp and police duty, brigade and division inspections, and a review by the department commander.

The Christmas present that year was an order to put three days' rations in haversacks and march at 6 o'clock next morning. The army was under its new commander, Rosecrans, and events were hastening toward the battle of Stone River. Since September 6th the regiment had marched 726 miles, over 600 miles without camp equipage. No battle had been fought by this command, but it had encountered the enemy scores of times in skirmish. It had become a well-seasoned and well-drilled body of soldiers; disciplined, confident and effective; and it had acquired that invaluable shoulder-to-shoulder quality, the unconscious recognition of the value of order and organization, which marks the true soldier.

CHAPTER VI.

STONE RIVER.

The advance from Nashville to Murfreesboro began on the 26th of December, and on the night of the 30th the army was in position about two miles and a half from Murfreesboro. On some parts of the line there was fighting to get into position, but less of this on the left, where the Forty-first was posted. On the way there had been skirmishing at intervals, and at Lavergne artillery had been used against the enemy. Hazen's brigade had been detached on the 27th, to move to the left of the line of advance, and save a bridge over Stewart's Creek, on the old Jefferson road. The movement was a rapid one, the latter part at double-quick step when the bridge was in sight. In this running skirmish the enemy was driven over the bridge without time to destroy it. There was a house to the left of the road near the bridge, and when the foremost of the brigade came in sight of it, two or three Confederate cavalry officers were delaying their mount and retreat to say good-bye to a young lady on the porch. The farewell may have been tender, but it was hurried by the rapid advance of Hazen's men. The young lady was not cast down by the departure of her Confederate friends, but sang "The Bonnie Blue Flag" that evening to entertain her new guests.

On the 29th the brigade returned to its division on the Nashville pike, and at midnight of the 30th went to its place in the line of battle, to the left of the pike and near the Cowan house. The new division general was John M. Palmer, of Illinois, one of the few volunteer officers (that is, those having no regular military education) who maintained themselves with credit from first to last, in the higher ranks and commands. The corps was the left of Rosecrans' line, but Palmer's division was not the left of the corps on the night before the battle. The bivouac of the Forty-first was on the edge of the thickly wooded ground afterward known as "The Cedars." Between the wooded ground and the pike was a cotton field, and just beyond the pike was the railroad, which crossed the pike at a sharp angle about 500 yards to the front. Stone River made a bend around the left toward the rear of this position, the southern bank being the higher one, with lower ground or flats on the northern side.

At daylight on the 31st two companies of the Forty-first, D and I, relieved A and F, which had been on the skirmish line during the night. Firing was heard far to the right early in the morning, increasing in volume rapidly, and coming nearer. Nevertheless, at about 8 o'clock the order to advance to the attack was given, and the line started forward in the direction of the Cowan house. Before the movement had made a hundred yards, it was stopped, and the line withdrawn to the point from which it started. The sound of battle on the right was moving toward the Union rear, and it was plain that misfortune had come upon the right of the army. Directly in front, also, the enemy appeared, advancing in line across the open country beyond and about the Cowan house. The Forty-first was in no position, in the cotton field, to receive an attack—the field was commanded on all sides by ground affording cover. The regiment was quickly moved by the left flank, crossing the pike and taking position on a slight crest of open woodland, the left near the railroad. The enemy came on in fine style to the attack of this position. The Forty-first was in the front line, and Cockerill's battery on its left. The fire of the regiment was held until the enemy was within easy range, and then let go with tremendous effect. The enemy was staggered, struggled forward a few yards further, but could make no more headway. When the Forty-first had exhausted its ammunition, the Ninth Indiana was ordered up to relieve it. Here occurred a marvellous thing. The Indianians had come to the war with a feeling that some taint was on them because an Indiana regiment in the Mexican war met with harsh censure on its conduct. The Ninth Indiana, from the day it took the field, was set to prove that the men from its state would fight. At Stone River the Ninth was commanded by Lieut.-Col. W. H. Blake, every inch a fighter. He brought his regiment up, marching by the flank, a few paces in rear of the Forty-first, which was then engaged and under a severe artillery fire. Here Blake gave the command: "On the right by file into line. March!" and proceeded, amid the whistling bullets and exploding shells, to set out his guides as the line grew toward the left. In the middle of this magnificent but useless bravado, a shell flying waist high exploded at the point where the fours were wheeling to take place in the line. Strange to say, the missile took but four men, two before it and two behind, and it caused not an instant's pause in the movement. With the precision of the drill ground, the Indianians finished their formation and advanced to relieve the Forty-first. They had proved that they could be as steady in fight as men cut out of stone.

Having replenished cartridge boxes, the Forty-first was placed on the right of the brigade, extending obliquely across the pike. Here it again engaged the enemy, until a Confederate battery opened on its right flank. Rosecrans' whole line to the right of Hazen's position had been driven back, and the cedars to the right and rear of that position were full of the victorious Confederates. The brigade took position behind and parallel with the railroad, the Forty-first on the left. The regiment suffered much from artillery in this place, one shell killing or wounding eight men. Afterwards, Lieut. Col. Wiley took the command to the support of a section of artillery which was resisting a cavalry attempt to cross the river to the left rear. Again, Gen. Rosecrans in person posted the regiment to meet an expected attempt to cross the river. Here also the regiment suffered much from the Confederate artillery, while it was in a position where it could do no service. Some moments before, and only a few yards from the Forty-first, Garesche, Rosecrans' chief of staff, riding with the general, had been literally beheaded by a Confederate shell. The Forty-first was not again engaged on that day. It had had the honor of playing a prominent part in holding the only point in Rosecrans' line of battle which was maintained throughout the day. A stone monument, erected by a detail from the brigade, and suitably inscribed, stands by the side of the railroad at this famous point.

The two days following were passed in bivouac as the troops stood. In the afternoon of the second day came Breckinridge's assault on Van Cleave's division, which had been posted across the river—a sort of detached left of the army. Hazen's brigade was moved hastily over to the support of Van Cleave when the sudden attack came. Breckinridge's onset was so fast and furious that it swept everything before it, and then his troops themselves went to pieces in their hot pursuit, and all formation and control were gone. When the Forty-first had got over, the ground in front was covered with crowds of men from both sides, but no organized bodies of troops were in sight. Breckinridge's scattered men, of course, made little show of resistance, but took themselves off. The regiment advanced in line for some distance, finding no occasion to fire, until it was halted at the skirt of a wood and ordered to deliver a volley in the direction of a Confederate battery two or three hundred yards away, which was throwing its shells far to the rear. The volley was delivered, and the battery fired no more. It was found afterward that it lost a man or two by the volley, besides several horses, leaving on the field one caisson, for lack of horses. This ended the fighting at Stone River.

The Forty-first went into the battle with a total of 413 officers and men. It lost 14 killed and 106 wounded, and four were reported missing. Five of the wounded are to be credited to the affair in support of Van Cleave, two days after the battle; all other losses fell in the main action. Except Van Cleave, who suffered mainly in the fight across the river, the loss of Palmer's division (25.40 per cent. of the men engaged) was heavier than that of any other division in the army. The three divisions of Crittenden's corps (Wood's, Palmer's and Van Cleave's) lost more heavily than any other divisions in the army. The loss, killed and wounded, of the whole army was 8,778, or 20.22 per cent. of the number engaged, which was 43,400. The Confederate force was 37,712, and the total loss was 10,266, or a fraction over 27 per cent.

Stone River was the first sustained action in which the Forty-first took part. At Shiloh the whole fighting was in a single headlong charge—severe in its losses, it is true, but very quickly over. At Corinth there was nothing more than skirmish or picket firing, and the same at Perryville. At Stone River it was a stand-up fight almost from daylight on, and a fight wholly on the defensive, with the fortune of the day steadily unfavorable—a very severe test, although the regiment was no longer considered a raw soldiery.

The formal and precise official records will, in the main, determine the history of this and other battles. But such records may or may not contain all that influences the soldier as he acts his part in the event. Mistaken ideas and erroneous reports, impossible of correction at the time, go to influence the spirit and make up the life of the soldiers, quite as certainly as do correct ideas and truthful reports. What is here set down, then, has no purpose of overturning established history. It is written because, right or wrong, it entered into the life of the regiment at the time, and so is to be taken into account.

First, as to the new general of the army. Rosecrans had come to that army heralded by the northern newspapers as what would be called, in the phrase of this later time, an "up-to-date" commander. Buell was sent to the rear as out of date. Many of the promises and pretenses put forth, not by the new commander, but in his behalf, everybody in the army knew to be simply foolish, and some of them were known to be false. The Forty-first came into immediate contact with Rosecrans, for the first time, at a review and inspection just before the army moved from Nashville toward Stone River. A single reported incident of this occasion will suffice. A private soldier in the line under inspection attracted the general's notice—his shoes were not new, or his pants were fringed at the bottom, or something of that sort. Rosecrans asked the soldier why he did not get a new article (whatever it was—pants, probably), and the man replied that he had asked for it, but had not received it. The general, with a certain peculiar gusto, told the soldier to make a requisition on his first sergeant; if that didn't do, make a requisition on his captain; if that didn't do, make a requisition on the regimental quartermaster, on the brigade and division quartermasters, etc.; and finally, if he did not get what he wanted, to come to him, the general. This is a good specimen of ad captandum style; but think what must be the effect of such talk on men who had been made pretty well acquainted with the army regulations! The story went the round of the camps, and was written up by an army correspondent. It had its effect—the better disciplined the soldier who heard it, the worse the effect. I do not vouch for the story; the essential fact is that it was taken up and circulated by the general's admirers.

At Stone River, during the battle, as has been mentioned before in this narrative, Rosecrans in person put the Forty-first in position at one time. This was while the hazard of the day was still undecided, and when the ablest commander might well have been overburdened with weightier affairs than posting a single regiment, and that for a duty not the most important conceivable. But it was the general's manner, rather than his command, which had the greater effect. He failed to produce an impression as one who grasped the whole momentous situation with the hand of a master. After this came the usual supply of stories about the battle, and, true or false, they had their effect on the army's estimate of its commander. It was doleful enough, the story of the camp fires built away beyond the right of the line to deceive the enemy; but it was the very irony of fate which brought the Confederate attack not upon that ghostly line, but upon the attenuated real line, finding it unready, artillery with guns not in battery, and a priest saying mass in the general's quarters. No after explanations could blot out the memory of the broken regiments of the right as they swarmed from the cedars into the open ground to the right and rear. Somewhere there had been lack of the vigilance to which the Forty-first was accustomed.

The weather following the battle was cold and wet, and it was a relief when, on the 7th of January, the regiment left the field and marched through Murfreesboro, turning eastward toward McMinnville and going into camp after a short march. The regiment had buried its dead on the ground where they fell—the place now marked by a monument. Except for these comrades, left forever behind, the Forty-first had no sorrow connected with that field; but the spirit of the army was not buoyant, and new scenes were welcome.

CHAPTER VII.

A WINTER REST.

The first days of January, 1863, had gone before the Forty-first left the vicinity of Murfreesboro. For the remainder of the winter, it was to be stationed at Readyville, twelve miles out on the Mc-Minnville road. Readyville was a name, not a town. The place afforded a good camping ground, and although the command was always on the alert, and the habit of standing to arms before daybreak became chronic, the duty on the whole was not hard. It was a season of rest, and of resumption of drills and studies. Many supplies beyond the army ration were obtained, not so much from the country, which was not over-rich, as from the markets northward. The Forty-first had its council of administration, with funds to procure certain desirable things not to be had from the commissary or the quartermaster. So it sometimes happened that the messes of officers and men were supplied with eatables from the northern markets. Quarters had been made as comfortable as possible, and the time was really an enjoyable one.

The Confederate cavalry was on the McMinnville road a few miles further on, and its patrols made frequent calls upon the brigade outpost about a mile from camp. On one occasion, these horsemen dashed down the pike to the bridge which spanned a creek running in front of the camp, and were turned back by the picket reserve at the bridge. At another time two horsemen thought to run down a solitary Forty-first vidette in advance on the pike; but he defended himself with his bayonet while he backed into a fence corner so that they could not flank him, and then easily held them at bay until succored by neighboring pickets. There was good fishing in the creek, and one day a party of officers who were just outside the lines catching bass, narrowly escaped capture. Some of Cluke's cavalry galloped down the pike until they drew the fire of the picket reserve, and then dashed off the road to escape the bullets. They rode within a rod of the fishermen, who were lying flat on their faces on the sloping bank of the creek; but the cavalrymen were in a hurry and did not see the unarmed fishers.

There was a diversity of entertainment in the army life at Readyville. In the hills back of the camp there was a mill which was put to work. Some of the officers were set to making topographical maps of the surrounding country. This required explorations outside the lines, and then there was added to the zest of map-making the duty of keeping a sharp lookout for the Morgan cavalry. At one time Hazen carefully planned an expedition to take in Cluke's force at the little town of Woodbury, a few miles on the road to McMinnville. Flanking parties were arranged and sent out in advance, the whole expedition marching so as to reach Woodbury at daylight. It was a failure so far as a capture was concerned. The main force, moving on the pike, got to the Confederate position in time for a brisk skirmish with Cluke's horsemen, but they declined to stay and be caught by the flanking parties.

The drill and parade ground was on a level field below the camps. There was some regulation target practice here, for at last the regiment had discarded the miserable Greenwood rifled muskets, and was supplied with Springfield rifles. The target practice was a great help in making the men familiar with their new weapons.

Among the satisfactions of the camp at Readyville, not the least was the mail communication with home. The regiment never did much in the way of furloughs; even leaves of absence for officers were scarce at all times. Next thing to a furlough is regular mail communication, and this the command enjoyed at this camp. It was a great time of rest, recuperation, enjoyment and instruction. The stay at Readyville was from January 10th to June 24th.

Leaving Readyville, the start was for Tullahoma, but the enemy had left that place before the Forty-first came near. A camp was made at Manchester, where the regiment remained for some days. Nothing of moment occurred here; the weather was very warm, and on the whole the stay was not remembered for its comfort. Tents were struck August 15th, and the regiment moved toward Chattanooga by the way of Dunlap and the Sequatchie Valley. The start was made in the middle of the day, the sun being intensely hot.

Somebody ordered the issue of a ration of whisky before starting. It was dealt out, and the march was begun immediately afterward. The way lay through a blackjack barren, and the road was a narrow cart track, the blackjacks closing in thick on both sides and shutting off all movement of air, while the trees were too low to afford shade. It was a trying march; those who drank their ration of whisky fell out by the score, and the regiment bivouacked a mere skeleton. All night long the stragglers were coming in. Never before or afterward was the regiment so completely done up.

The march through the Sequatchie Valley to the foot of Waldron's Ridge was made comfortably and expeditiously. Here the brigade was to watch the Tennessee river in the vicinity of Harrison's Landing, above Chattanooga. The nearest neighbors up the valley were twenty miles away—Minty's cavalry force. During the stay here, the building of a large barge was begun in a creek near the Tennessee. It was to be used in crossing the river when the time came; but before it was finished, Bragg had moved out of Chattanooga and the crossing could be made at leisure and whereever there was a ford. The weather here was delightful, and the duty light. There was leisure for short excursions to see the natural curiosities of Waldron's Ridge, and more than the usual liberty was allowed the command.

The order to move from this camp came suddenly, on the 8th of September. The regiment moved in the night to the mouth of West Chickamauga Creek, and forded the Tennessee early next morning. The same day it joined its division at Graysville, and was in movement toward Gordon's Mills and the country where the battle of Chickamauga was fought soon afterward.

CHAPTER VIII.

CHICKAMAUGA.

From the moment of crossing the Tennessee, above Chattanooga, on the morning of the 10th of September, all the movements of the troops indicated that the army was being manœuvered in presence of the enemy. The irregular marches, and bivouacs in places chosen not because they were good camping ground, were proof enough that our forces were feeling their way, held in readiness for emergencies. The general direction of the movement was toward Lafayette, by way of Gordon's Mills. The Forty-first encountered the Confederate cavalry near Ringgold, and again beyond Gordon's Mills—merely detachments for observation, giving little trouble. The weather was warm and dry, and the movement, especially after Gordon's Mills had been passed, was tiresome. In one place was a shed by the roadside, the ground within covered with bark and chips. Every man who came into this shed, though the halt lasted but a few moments, went away loaded with vermin. This was no light infliction, since nothing short of boiling the clothing, blankets, etc., would get rid of the pests, and for that there were few opportunities on this campaign.

Afterward it was known that the movement on the Lafayette road was for the purpose of bringing the army together, McCook having moved in parallel roads on the other side of Lookout Mountain. These marches and halts consumed the time until the 18th of September, and then, near the middle of the day, the bivouac was suddenly broken up, and a rapid march backward toward Gordon's Mills was begun. The reason for this was evident enough when the regiment came upon some high ground from which a sweep of country to the right was in view. Three or four miles away, on the other side of the Chickamauga, a long line of dust was rising above the tree tops. It stretched away in the distance toward Gordon's Mills and our road to the rear. Bragg's army was there, moving to get in rear of the Union forces and cut them off from Chattanooga. No one was disappointed when no halt was called at dark, but the march went on into the night. The regiment passed Gen. Rosecrans' headquarters at the side of the road, and some officers from Palmer's division stopped to greet acquaintances. The general of the army was in bad humor, and could hardly be civil.

It was after midnight when the regiment, having passed Gordon's Mills, went into bivouac in a thicket near the road. The men felt that they were on a battlefield, and were glad enough of the scanty rest that was to be had before daylight should call them to action again. Nothing could be seen of the position, but it was certain that the troops were massed rather than strung out in line, and the road was jammed with artillery and trains. In the morning the regiment with the rest was moved further along toward Rossville on the Chattanooga road, until it was near the Widow Glenn house, where Rosecrans' headquarters had been established. Further down the road and apparently to the right of it, there broke out, about the middle of the forenoon, the sound of a severe engagement. This was renewed again and again, and the report went about that a force sent to dispute the enemy's passage of the Chickamauga needed more than one reinforcement. Finally, soon after noon, Palmer's division was deployed in echelon and moved straight across the Rossville road to the attack. No enemy was in sight when the movement began. The formation in echelon was with the object of striking and crushing the enemy's left flank. The movement started in an open wood; beyond this was a large open field, and about half way across it a strip of woodland. The Forty-first was in the first echelon, and advanced to the woodland. But beyond this the fighting was terrific. From the edge of the woods in front there came a storm of rifle balls, and back of this were batteries in rapid action. Away to the right the battle swept, and it was plain that the enemy's flank was not found. The Forty-first fired its last cartridges and was recalled to replenish the boxes. This was done hurriedly, back in the open wood, and it was hardly finished when the enemy fell furiously on Van Cleave's division, which was on the right of Palmer's. Col. Hazen was near the Forty-first when this happened. Some idle batteries were at hand, and Hazen quickly

posted these to check the onslaught, for Van Cleave's men were beginning to come back. Then the brigade was moved into the path
of the storm which was bearing back the division of Van Cleave.
Col. Wiley broke his line to the rear by companies, to let the retreating crowds pass through, and then wheeled back into line. The
Forty-first was still in the open wood, and in front was a large cornfield. Through this the Confederates were swarming, but their first
line had spent its force and lost its formation. Close behind came a
second line in perfect order. Van Cleave's retreating regiments had
broken up Hazen's line as they swept through, but the Forty-first
had kept in form by breaking to the rear to let the fugitives pass,
as has been told. Wiley opened on the Confederate second line
with volleys by front and rear ranks, and the advance was instantly
checked. But it was soon apparent that the regiment was outflanked. Shots began to come from the right rear. Then Wiley
made a change of front to face to the right, and sent a volley into the
gathering enemy there. Then a change back, to face the front and
check the main advance. Never had the marvellous effect of volley
firing been more clearly demonstrated; the fiery Confederates could
not stand against it. The closed ranks of the Forty-first were in
sharp contrast with the loose line in front and the wandering foes on
the right. A hundred yards at a time the regiment fell back while
loading, and easily held the enemy at bay. Then a commanding
crest was reached, where a battery had taken post. Here it was proposed to stand, but the enemy did not come on. He was reforming
his lines, as could be plainly seen from the crest. But night drew
near, and the battle was over for the day.

Much of the night time was taken up with getting into a new
position—slow and tiresome marching in the darkness. Next morning, before the enemy moved, the Forty-first was lying behind a
barricade of rails and logs, an open field behind it. There were
troops to right and left, showing that a general line of battle was
posted. Rations were not abundant, and of water there was none at
all. A detail was sent to fill canteens; the men did not return, but
fell into the hands of the enemy, who held the water supply that was
ours the day before. The intense suffering occasioned by this lack
of water can hardly be imagined; pangs of hunger seemed mild in

comparison. Before night, men's tongues were swollen and their lips blackened and cracked until the power of speech was gone. It was far on into the next night when that time of awful thirst was ended.

The morning was well along when it became apparent that the enemy was advancing upon the Union lines. Nothing was to be seen in the woods to the front, but soon the well-known Confederate yell was heard, and the skirmishers became engaged, falling back before the enemy's line of battle. Then the line itself was in view, coming on with true Southern impetuosity. From behind its barricade of rails, the Forty-first opened fire, and to right and left the fight was on. The Confederates returned the fire with spirit, but their advance was checked, and they did little or no damage to the men behind the barricades. The attacking line rapidly thinned out under the steady fire; then it became unsteady, and finally it turned and fled. This was the regiment's first experience behind a defended line. Slight as was that defense of rails, it changed the whole character of the fighting. The enemy was severely punished, as was plainly to be seen, and had been able to make no return in kind. The men began to wonder if an attacking force could cover three hundred yards or so, before a well directed fire should destroy it.

But the battle was not over with this one successful defense. The Confederate line overlapped the Union left and had forced it back until it was stretched across the open field in rear, and at a right angle with the general line. Then there was a brave fight on both sides in the open ground. It was plainly seen from the position held by the Forty-first, and it was most eagerly watched. If those men on the flank failed to maintain their ground, the whole line would be taken in rear while it was assaulted in front. There were some moments of intense anxiety, and then it was seen that the Confederate assault had spent its force. It was as stubborn a fight as one could wish to see, but the staying quality of the Union troops won. Baird's and Johnson's divisions were on the left of Palmer's.

This doubling up of a flank occurred again that day—the second time, the right flank. This came from a break in the Union line, made not by the enemy, but by order from the commanding general. A division (Wood's) was withdrawn from its place in line, and at once the enemy entered the gap. The army was cut in two, and most of the right was driven from the field. The general of the army went as far as Chattanooga. The Confederates pushed their advantage toward the Union left, until the division next on the right of Palmer's (Reynolds') was bent back to the rear. This, like the flank attack on the left, was in view from the position of the Forty-first, and was watched as anxiously. Also like the other flanking operation, this one failed, thanks to nothing but the steadiness of the Union troops.

In rear of Reynold's original position on the right of Palmer was a log house which had been taken for a field hospital the night before. It contained men too badly wounded for transportation from the field, and bore on its gable the usual hospital flag. When Reynold's line was forced back, the log house was between the contending lines. It was riddled by the Confederate artillery, and somehow—probably by a bursting shell—it was set afire. This sickening horror was in full view from the position of the Forty-first, three hundred yards away. Men shuddered and turned pale as they saw the torn house and thought of the poor fellows in it.

But, while these things were taking place in front and on both flanks another peril began to grow in the consciousness of the men who could not be driven from front or flank. The cartridge boxes were being rapidly emptied, and no ammunition train was near. Everything seemed to have been swept away with the right wing. Then from the woods across the open field in rear, bullets began to whistle toward the backs of the men in the line. These shots were supposed to come from sharpshooters in the trees. A company of the Forty-first was faced about and delivered a volley into the treetops across the open. This had a good effect, there was one danger the less. But the question of ammunition pressed. Nobody knew where to find it. The four divisions of the left wing were holding their ground, but they were out of communication with the rest of the army, wherever that might be, and they had no supplies of any kind. The division generals came together, and the question of a commander came up. The three corps of the army were represented in those four divisions, but there was no corps commander present. None of the division generals coveted the responsibility of command, but it was plain that something must be done. There was heavy firing off to the right, and it was guessed that somewhere in that direction Thomas was holding out against the enemy that had swept away the right wing. Finally, Hazen volunteered to take his brigade across the interval, and make communication with whatever Union force might be still in the field. The brigade was withdrawn from the line, marched somewhat to the rear, and then started off through the unexplored woods toward the sound of battle. The movement was made cautiously but rapidly, the brigade constantly in readiness for any fortune that might befall. There were some scattered Confederates in the woods, and a Confederate skirmish line was struck obliquely, but no other force was encountered. The way seemed miles longer than it was, and the relief was great when the leading regiment came upon the left of the position where Thomas had stopped the victorious enemy and held him steadfastly. Thomas himself, beloved of all the army, rode up to take Hazen by the hand. The arrival was just in time. A desperate assault was about to come on the left of Thomas' line. Hazen's men marched through a cornfield to the crest of a low hill, and were there massed in column of regiments. Scarcely was this done when the Confederate storm burst. The slope in front of the brigade was open ground, and in a moment this was covered with heavy masses of the enemy making for the top. Hazen's regiments were lying flat. The foremost sprang to its feet, delivered its volley and went down again to load, and the next regiment just behind rose to fire and fall flat while the third put in its work; and so on. The slope was strewn with Confederate dead and wounded, but not a man could reach the crest. Along the rest of the line also the defense was successful. Night was falling fast, and the battle of Chickamauga was over.

But not quite so. When all had quieted on Thomas' front, there rose, a mile away to the left, loud and continued cheering. There was little doubt in the minds of those who knew the shrill Confederate cheer. It meant disaster, more or less, to the divisions that had stood all day as the left of the army.

When the fighting ended with the repulse of the enemy's final assault, a skirmish line was pushed forward through the cornfield on the left of Hazen's position, and halted at the edge of the field. This was the only outlying force as darkness fell; beyond the skirmish line was anybody's ground. Soon after dusk, the order came to withdraw, leaving the skirmishers in place until the troops were well on to the Rossville road. The remnant of the army yet on the field of Chickamauga was to fall back, if it could, to Mission Ridge and Chattanooga. The men moved off silently and were lost in the darkness. A field officer of the Forty-first was left to withdraw the skirmish line when the last of the troops had got well off toward the road. This officer dismounted and went down through the cornfield to the skirmishers. No order could be spoken aloud, lest the enemy in front be apprised of the movement. The word was passed along from man to man, and thus the line withdrew in silence. The officer charged with the withdrawal had returned to the upper edge of the field and sat there on his horse to see that all the skirmishers came in. When the last of them were passing, the officer heard a rustling in the cornfield—in front and to right and left; it came nearer, and then footsteps could be heard in slow and cautious movement. The officer turned his horse's head and followed his departing skirmishers; but a hundred yards away he looked to the rear, and there on the open crest, their figures standing out against the lighter sky, were the Confederate skirmishers who had followed up through the cornfield. On both sides it was a good-bye without words.

The way down to the Rossville road was made sad enough by the appeals of wounded men here and there, who had crawled out of the battle, but were unable to go farther. With piteous supplication, and sometimes with reproachful words wrung from them by their misery and pain, they begged their fellows not to leave them behind. Some asked for water—water, which the passing soldiers had not seen for twenty-four hot and toilsome hours. Listening to these poor fellows by the wayside was harder than facing another Confederate charge. But the march was a hurried one; the saddening appeals quickly died out in the black night behind, and the suffering comrades were left to the mercies of Confederate surgeons and prisons. Many a heart was filled with bitterness as the troops, under cover of darkness, were hastened away from a field where they had faced the enemy all day and won in every encounter—a field won by the soldiers and lost by the general.

Some time after getting on the Rossville road, water was found close at hand—the greatest relief the Forty-first had ever experienced in any strait. Lack of rations was forgotten—there was the blessed water! They drank their fill, and hurried on to Rossville. At daylight next morning, the division lay on Mission Ridge to the left of the Rossville pass, in position to meet any pursuit that Bragg might undertake. But no molestation came, and when the trains had been safely gathered at Chattanooga, the Forty-first, with its division, went to that place and took its assigned place in the defensive lines.

Looking back over the campaign, from the crossing of the Tennessee river on the 10th of September to the arrival at Chattanooga on the night of the 21st, the Forty-first had reason for congratulation. It had suffered no disaster. Though in the first day of the battle, the ill starred attack in echelon failed, yet the regiment performed its part with credit; and afterward rendered conspicuous service in staying the pursuit of Van Cleave. Next day it shared in the steady success of the brigade in every position it occupied. Not a foot of any ground was yielded to the enemy until the retreat was ordered after the battle was over. A good record from first to last. As to individual records, it may be said that the missing were the men detailed to go for water on the morning of the second day of battle; these men fell into the enemy's hands unawares. No exceptions are to be made when it is said that all duty was faithfully done by the whole command.

Some months after this battle, it is said, the opinion was held by some of Grant's officers that the spirit of the Army of the Cumberland had been broken at Chickamauga. The operations about Chattanooga, in the October and November following, were a sufficient contradiction of such notions. So far as concerns the Forty-first, it is certain that it came away from Chickamauga with firmer confidence in itself than it ever had before. It had been handled in action as few regiments ever were, and had not failed to respond effectively to every command.

CHAPTER IX.

BESIEGED AT CHATTANOOGA.

When the Army of the Cumberland reached Chattanooga from the field of Chickamauga, it was put into lines closely enveloping the town and resting the flanks on the Tennessee river above and below. These lines were quickly fortified, and some earthworks more pretentious were thrown up here and there for artillery. The position of the Forty-first was well toward the left of the line, and along a slight railroad cutting which made an excellent defense and saved much digging. There was great haste in getting this line in order, the army commander seeming to expect that Bragg would advance to attack with as little delay as possible. There were two houses in front of the regiment's line, and they were ordered to be destroyed, that the ground might be cleared of all that could afford cover for an attacking force. One of the houses was a large dwelling some distance to the front; the other, a smaller domicile, near the railroad cut. Of course, both places were deserted by their owners or occupants, but they had left behind everything in the way of furniture and furnishings. A piano was rescued from the larger house, and taken to headquarters. In the small house, some most excellent hams were not allowed to go to waste, and a feather bed was taken out. There was some fancy fishing tackle and a shot gun or two, to show the tastes of the former occupant. Evidently he had had short warning, for his bedroom was left as one would leave in case of fire, springing from bed and running with clothing in hand. The destruction of these houses was a new experience for the Forty-first. Things lying about the places were snatched up by the men merely for the novelty of it. Except the hams, nothing was found that was really useful—not even the feather bed could go under that description.

By the close of the day of arrival, the Forty-first was well off as to its fortified line, and the ground in front was cleared of obstructions for some hundreds of yards.   For a day or two afterward the enemy was closing in his enveloping lines, occupying the slight eminences in Chattanooga Valley, and the heights of Mission Ridge and Lookout Mountain to the left and the right.   Lookout Mountain, and with it railroad communication with the Nashville base of supplies and the North, had been abandoned by Rosecrans, as if the army could not have too short a line for its ability in defense. Close and tight were the Chattanooga lines.   The enemy might almost send an Enfield rifle ball across the whole ground from flank to flank, or from the front across the river in the rear.   When Bragg's dispositions were complete, he could and did drop shells on nearly all parts of the Union ground.

Across the Tennessee river a pontoon bridge was laid, and this at once became the only line for supplies.   These must come by wagon, running the gauntlet of the unguarded Sequatchie Valley, and laboriously crossing Waldron's Ridge.   Many wagons were lost with their greatly needed loads.   Occupying Raccoon Mountain, to the right and rear of Chattanooga, the Confederates cut off the wagon road which ran close to the river level on the opposite side. The effect of all this was quickly apparent.   In less than a month the commissary was issuing three day's half rations to last five days— less than one-third of a ration a day—and this of only the principal articles in the regular ration.   When it came to forage for the animals, there was little or none to be had.   Officers' horses had to be sent across the Tennessee on the pontoon bridge, to eat weeds and keep alive.   Artillery horses and the animals of the wagon trains died or became too weak for service.   Sometimes a few ears of corn came for the starving creatures, and then hungry men would pick up the scattered kernels about the feeding places and roast them to eke out their scanty food.   Quartermasters' stores, of course, were not more plentiful than commissary's; none had been issued for several months, and the men were badly off for shoes and clothing.

On the 19th of October, Gen. Rosecrans was relieved of the command, Gen. Thomas succeeding him.   A complete reorganization of the army followed.   Hazen's brigade was now made up of the First, Forty-first and Ninety-third Ohio, the Fifth Kentucky and the Sixth Indiana; and the division, commanded by Gen. Thomas J. Wood, was assigned to Gordon Granger's Fourth Army Corps.

The routine of camp life was relieved by watching the dress-parades of the Confederates on Mission Ridge, and the occasional practice of the artillery on Lookout Mountain. Except for the lack of supplies, the time would have gone well enough. The quarters had been made fairly comfortable, and the duty was not hard.

On the 23d of October, Grant arrived at Chattanooga—slipping in at the back door as it were, and fortunately escaping the Confederate riders across the river, for he brought with him no forces. There had been rumors of a corps from the Potomac under Hooker, and of the coming of Sherman's men from Vicksburg. Grant's arrival confirmed the belief that the Army of the Cumberland would not much longer remain in the box where Rosecrans had packed it. The men were anxious to go anywhere and do anything to get out.

One of the stories that went the rounds in the Forty-first at this time was that private Hoover, of H company, being intensely home-sick, thinking besides that there was little to do in Chattanooga, and knowing there was not enough to eat, asked for a furlough. The petition was discouraged by captain and colonel, and then Hoover asked leave to go to Gen. Thomas in person. He succeeded in getting to the general, and made his plea, ending with the statement, "Why, General, it's nigh on to two year since I've seen my wife." "Well, my man," said Thomas, "I haven't seen my wife for more than three years." Hoover was staggered, but recovered. He straightened himself into the position of "Attention" and made his salute as he answered, "Well, General, me and my wife ain't that kind of folks."

CHAPTER X.

BROWN'S FERRY.

Arriving in Chattanooga on the 23d of October, Gen. Grant soon acquainted himself with the situation, the strength and condition of Thomas' army, and the plans of that commander. There was no question as to the first step; it must be the recovery of the line of communication abandoned by Rosecrans, the railroad running close under Lookout Mountain. An attack on Lookout from Chattanooga would involve the whole army, and at great disadvantage. A foothold on the left bank of the Tennessee below Lookout would serve, with two pontoon bridges, allowing the use of the railroad to within a few miles of Chattanooga. A detachment could make the attempt to secure such a foothold, and the army would remain in its fortified lines.

Three days after Grant's arrival, an order came to Hazen for the detail of a field officer to report to Gen. W. F. Smith (Baldy Smith) at headquarters. Lieut. Col. Kimberly, of the Forty-first, was sent on this detail. Smith mounted his horse and led the way over the pontoon bridge in rear of Chattanooga, and then struck off to the left towards Raccoon Mountain. The two officers crossed the neck of land made by the sharp bend at Lookout Mountain, and came to the river again at a point known as Brown's Ferry. On the opposite shore was a high ridge, its river side almost precipitous. At the point known as the Ferry this ridge was cut almost to the level of the valley beyond it. All along the crest of the ridge the Confederate pickets were to be seen, and in the cut at the Ferry there was a company of infantry. Gen. Smith explained to Kimberly the plan of operation. The latter was to act as guide for an expedition that was to attempt a landing on the Confederate side, driving the enemy first from the ridge and the cut, and afterward clearing the valley beyond, up to Lookout Mountain. The detail for the expedition was Hazen's brigade, from which were to be taken as many picked officers and men as could be carried in fifty-two pontoons, twenty-five men to each pontoon. They were to embark at Chattanooga and pass down the river to the point of attack. Of course it must be a night expedition, so calculated as to reach Brown's Ferry just at daylight. The river bank was closely picketed on the Confederate side, from Lookout Mountain down, and the pontoons would pass within pistol shot of these pickets— this for several miles. It was not an inviting prospect, especially the pontoon part of it. These rough boats were heavy and as clumsy in the water as a square box.

The details for the pontoons were very carefully made, both officers and men. The force which was to attack at the Ferry was to be led by Lieut.-Col. Foy, of the Twenty-third Kentucky, and Col. Wiley was to lead the men in the rear pontoons, who were to scale the ridge. These officers were taken quietly to the spot where Baldy Smith had given the plan to Kimberly, and shown the scene of the coming attack.

At 3 o'clock on the morning of October 27th, the expedition embarked at Chattanooga, the pontoons being strung along the shore so that all might be pushed off together. It was found that the pontoons were so crowded that the men must stand, steadying themselves with their guns. A detail from Stanley's Michigan engineer regiment had been provided to man the oars, but they could do little in the crowded pontoons; the movement must rely mainly on the current of the river, which chanced to be running high. The night was not dark, but a fog hung over the river and filled the lower grounds. As the pontoons drifted past the right of the Union lines at Chattanooga, the buglers were sounding reveille. Half an hour later the expedition was floating past the point of Lookout Mountain. The talk of the Confederate pickets on the point, three hundred feet above the river, could be heard, with now and then a snatch of song.

The men had been carefully instructed in the need of keeping silence, and not a word passed above the breath. Opposite Lookout, however, a sharp cry rose from one of the leading pontoons; an officer of the Twenty-third Kentucky had been swept overboard by a snag projecting above the water. The commander of the pontoon growled an angry reprimand, but the poor fellow overboard was under water. No one expected to see or hear of him again, with the swift current and the darkness; but he came to the surface and was picked up by one of the rear pontoons.

There were two miles of drifting, close to the enemy's shore, between Lookout Mountain and the point of attack. The fog hung thick over the river, however, and there was no noise from the pontoons; the oars were useless for anything but helping to keep the course, and there was little rowing. The two miles were passed, and there had been no discovery. The leading pontoon, in which was the officer who was to command the attack at the cut, reached that point and was floating by in mistake, when Hazen, who followed close, called out: "Pull in, Col. Foy; pull in! pull in!" That command gave the alarm; the nearest sentinel in the cut fired, his bullet singing over the heads of the men in a pontoon. The alarm was taken up instantly. In a moment the company on duty in the cut was tumbling into line, and through the camps in the valley beyond the drums and bugles were carrying it on. There was no further need of silence, and the officers in the pontoons shouted their commands to the oarsmen to pull for the landing place. Foy's pontoon was quickly at the shore, and he led his men straight up the bank. On the opposite shore Turchin's brigade and the remainder of Hazen's were waiting to cross when the pontoons had discharged their loads. A dozen of Turchin's men, without orders, fired straight across the river, knowing nothing of what was there. The balls flew close to Foy's men as they ran up the bank, but no one was hurt. The surprised Confederate guard had hardly got into line when Col. Foy charged it at a run. The guard opened a wild fire, which was returned with effect, and the assailants dashed at them. The guard turned and fled, leaving some men wounded. The other pontoons came in close order, and the men sprang from them and joined the rest in the cut. Companies were sent to right and left to climb the ridge and dislodge the Confederate pickets. Four hundred yards above the landing, Wiley led his detachment straight up the steep face of the ridge, the men clinging to root and sapling as they mounted. The dawn was just breaking, and progress was easier. The crest was gained without a moment's halt.   The companies that started from the cut went rapidly along, dislodging the Confederates without stopping.   In a few moments the men from the pontoons held the ferry landing and the ridge on both sides, prepared to defend the position.   Meanwhile the unloaded pontoons were rapidly bringing over the remainder of the brigade.   Soon twelve hundred men were on the captured ridge. The alarm had traveled to Lookout Mountain, and its heavy batteries belched in aimless thunder, for the gunners could see nothing of what was going on two miles down the river.

It was not expected that the troops in the valley beyond the crest would submit without an effort.   A prisoner taken at the landing said it was McLaw's brigade of Longstreet's corps that held the valley.   A line of skirmishers was pushed forward from the main body at the landing.   The fog still hung on, but the quick words of command could be heard as the officers got McLaw's men together and put them into position.   The Union skirmishers quickly came upon an opposing line, the two almost running together in the fog.   A rod apart they stood and fired, and Hazen's men pushed on, bearing the enemy before them in hasty retreat.   Soon afterward, a line came forward to attack the ridge, and there was sharp fighting, but brief; the Confederates had no chance of dislodging the captors.   A second attack followed, but this was faint-hearted and called for little effort in the repulse.   There were occasional shots from the skirmishers after this, but the fighting was over.   A Confederate battery, however, came down the road from the direction of Lookout, and went into position in front of the ridge.   Its commander's orders could be heard, but the fog prevented seeing. The guns were unlimbered and several shells were fired over the ridge, doing no harm.   This was understood as a cover to the retreat of whatever forces might be in the valley.   Hazen pushed his skirmish line forward as rapidly as possible, in hope of getting the battery before it could withdraw.   The fog hindered, and although the skirmishers were very near the battery, they could not reach it in time. A solitary horseman was posted two hundred yards in front of the battery, and as soon as he saw the advancing skirmish line, he wheeled about and gave the warning.   The battery went off at a run.   When the fog finally dissolved, not a Confederate was to be seen in all the valley. Meantime the laying of the pontoon bridge at the ferry had gone forward rapidly. Turchin's brigade was moved across and posted on the left of the line, and both brigades made themselves secure in their positions.

Once more the line of supplies was open to the Army of the Cumberland. The way for the junction of Sherman's and Hooker's coming reinforcements was also open. The enemy still held Lookout Mountain, but the valley in which was the railroad from Bridgeport was in possession of the Union forces. Before the sun went down, the advance of Hooker's corps came marching down the valley with full haversacks, which the men of Thomas' army had not seen since Chickamauga. The newcomers were generous. Hooker's troops went into position on the left of Hazen. That night they had some desperate and bloody fighting with a strong force which had been sent down from Lookout to make a final effort at recovery of what had been so quickly lost. The enemy had miscalculated both the number and the temper of the Union force in the valley. Though he made a brave attempt and inflicted some loss, he could make no headway, and soon withdrew.

The operation at Brown's Ferry was of a kind not often occurring. It was extra hazardous because of the employment of the pontoons in the swift current of the river. There was good luck as well as good generalship in the affair. The surprise of the enemy was complete. Finally, the notion that the Army of the Cumberland had its spirit broken at Chickamauga was forever dispelled. Not a brigade in any army could have responded more promptly and effectively than did Hazen's brigade in this enterprise. The importance of the movement was immediately recognized by the Confederate authorities. A Richmond paper said mournfully that by one brilliant effort the Union forces had broken Bragg's grasp on the position at Chattanooga, and that the maintenance of that position was no longer problematical.

What of the relief to the men of the Union army? It was beyond description. The depression which had lasted from the days at Chickamauga was gone. The troops felt as if they had been in prison, and were now free. There was relief of actual hunger, too, and a prospect of much-needed supplies of all sorts.

One of the incidents of the morning of the fight may be told. In front of the Forty-first as it lay on the ridge after the enemy had gone, was a farmhouse a few yards from the base of the ridge. There was a corncrib near the house, and its contents were quickly distributed. Then, as the men sat about their little fires, a savory odor was observed, coming from a kettle in one of the men's messes. A little crowd was attracted by the grateful smell, and it was ex‑ plained that two of the men had caught a couple of rabbits down by the farmhouse. There were many hungry sniffs of the odors from that little kettle. An hour afterward, two elderly maiden ladies, occupants of the farmhouse, came up to complain that "you uns have carried off our cats." Well, they smelled as good as rab‑ bits while they were cooking. Not many hours afterward, there was an issue of fresh beef—an earnest of the good things coming in the wake of Hooker's men. By all odds, it was the finest and best-flavored beef ever issued to hungry soldiers.

The Forty-first remained on the ridge long enough to make some exploration of the valley, and even of the sides of Raccoon Mountain opposite. A queer little mill was found in one of the ravines here, and it ground some corn for the Yankees. But the stay was short. The valley was full of Hooker's men, and there was no need of longer delay. The regiment returned to its old place in the lines about Chattanooga. It had acquitted itself well in one of the most important and difficult operations of the war.

One of the incidents of this expedition was the meeting for the first time with troops from the East—Hooker's men. What was particularly noticeable about these men was the completeness of their outfit; beside the scantier outfit of the western troops, they looked something like walking museums of buttons and brass plates and ornaments. Some of their furnishings had never been dreamed of by the western soldiers. Everything, too, was fresh and in good condition—a contrast not relished by the men whose campaigns had been over long distances, taking them far from the base of supplies and compelling the wearing of wornout articles for months at a time. The advantages of campaigning on short lines and near the seat of government was apparent enough in this case.

CHAPTER XI.

MISSION RIDGE.

The re-establishment of freer communications with the base of supplies and the North brought much comfort. After the Brown's Ferry affair there was no fear of starvation. All the supplies needed were not forthcoming, but there was little disposition to find fault on that score. Although the Confederates still showed on Mission Ridge and Lookout Mountain, and from their positions in the valley between, they were no longer in the rear, blocking "the cracker line." Never were army rations more enjoyed than in those days after the taking of Brown's Ferry.

Regular camp duty was resumed, and there were some days of rest. Sherman's army arrived in time, and it was felt that active operations were not to be long delayed. But the beginning came without a word of warning. A court martial was in session in the brigade, and other of the ordinary affairs of camp life were going on as usual, when at noon of the 23d of November the assembly was sounded from brigade headquarters. When the men had got into ranks, the regiments of the brigade were moved out and deployed on the plain in front of the lines. Then a skirmish line was thrown forward, and the advance begun toward Mission Ridge. The word went around that it was to be a reconnaissance, or a demonstration to help some movement unknown, at another point. The location of the Confederate pickets was known to be just in front of a low wooded ridge half way between the Union lines and Mission Ridge.

These pickets were soon approached. Apparently they had no thought that a fight was coming. They remained quiet until the opposing skirmish line was far within the range of their rifles. On Mission Ridge, too, the enemy was seen idly gathering in little knots to look at the Union troops as they came nearer the wooded ridge, which was known as Orchard Knob. But at last the Confederate pickets understood. They opened fire, and were at once driven back by the advancing skirmishers. The little ridge at this point was covered with a thick undergrowth of forest, in which the Confederate pickets disappeared. The skirmishers followed and encountered a heavy fire from the ridge to the right of Orchard Knob. The Forty-first was in the first line, immediately behind the skirmishers. There were no orders to halt, and the regiment went on until it came up with the skirmishers and was receiving the enemy's fire from his position, which was concealed by the underbrush. For a moment Col. Wiley was in doubt; to go farther was to bring on an engagement, for it was plain that a strong force, not a slight picket reserve, was in front. Wiley sent an officer to Hazen for orders, but before these could be returned he had decided for himself and ordered the regiment forward. It opened fire and pressed through the underbrush. Approaching the crest of the little ridge, it was found that the slope for forty or fifty yards in front of the Confederate position had been cleared of the underbrush, and that the enemy was strongly posted behind a low breastwork. To the right of the attacking force the Confederate line bent forward and outflanked the assailants. A galling fire across the front came from this outflanking line. The Forty-first lost heavily each moment, with the rapid and steady fire in front and from the right. But the enemy was in sight when the underbrush had been passed, and the regiment's fire began to tell on the men behind the breastwork. At the edge of the cleared ground the Confederate fire forced a check in the advance. The line of the Forty-first was fast thinning out, and gaps in the ranks were many and widening. The color guard attempted to go forward, but the enemy's fire was withering. Lieut. Col. Kimberly seized the colors and was instantly dismounted, his horse shot dead. A rod away, the same fortune befell Wiley as he spurred into the open ground, calling his men to make a dash for the breastwork. But the fight was telling on the Confederates as well. Many of them lay on their backs and thrust their guns over the breastwork above their heads, firing thus at random. Then the Forty-first responded to the call and rushed upon the breastwork. As they mounted it, most of the enemy were lying flat; a few were standing, some of these having thrown down their guns, and fewer still were running through the brush toward

Mission Ridge. One or two of the fellows who had been lying on their backs and firing over their heads, did this after the Union troops were on the breastwork and over it, and a man of the Forty-first was killed by a wild shot of this kind. The man who fired that shot was crazed with the fight, not seeing what was going on, for at the moment the men of the Forty-first were over the breast-work and the rest of its defenders had surrendered. It was said that the brother of the Forty-first man who was thus killed after the surrender was maddened at the sight, and with his bayonet pinned the fear-crazed Southener to the ground as he lay.

The defenders of the breastwork were the Twenty-eighth Ala-bama, whose colors, presented by the ladies of Selma, fell into the hands of the Forty-first, with many of its men prisoners. An hour or two after the fight, Grant and Thomas rode along the line, and Thomas called for the officers of the regiment. Then he told Col. Wiley to present to officers and men his thanks for the fight they made—"a gallant thing, Colonel, a very gallant thing," added the grim old warrior. It is to be said here, as something not to be for-gotten, that the Ninety-third Ohio was with the Forty-first in this fight, and shared fully the honor of the victory. Its commander, Major William Birch, a true soldier, died two days after, of wounds received while leading his men in this desperate struggle.

The regiment lay that night on the ground taken from the enemy. There were a few shells, by way of practice, from the Con-federate artillery on top of Mission Ridge, but no damage was done. Still in the same position next day, the men had a full view of Hooker's action on Lookout Mountain. The Confederate uniform was not of a color to be easily seen at a great distance, but the Union troops could be seen very plainly. The fight was eagerly watched as Hooker's line swept around the end of the mountain on the broad slope below the summit. The enemy made his last stand on some fenced ground near a farm house, well around on the Chattanooga side. While the fight was going on here, the side of the mountain below the fighting ground was covered with haze or fog, and from this circumstance the action was called "a battle above the clouds."

Next day, the 25th of November, Sherman began his attack on the enemy's right flank, which was on Mission Ridge, far to the left of the line at Orchard Knob. Grant's headquarters were established at the latter point, and all of Thomas' army was on the line. Hooker's troops were in the valley in front of Chattanooga, to operate in the direction of Rossville. The line of the Army of the Cumberland squarely faced Mission Ridge, and nearly opposite the centre of that line was Bragg's headquarters on the Ridge. At the foot of the Ridge, directly in front of the Forty-first, was a line of log breastworks in front of a winter camp which the enemy had built. The shanties had stick-and-mud chimneys, all arranged for occupancy in cold weather. Above this camp, on top of the Ridge, artillery was in position, and this was added to during the earlier part of the day.

Almost from the beginning of Sherman's attack away to the left, the Confederates could be seen moving along the top of the Ridge in that direction. Relying on the natural strength of the position in front of Thomas' army, and not alarmed at Hooker's movement toward Rossville, Bragg was hurrying his troops to his threatened right flank. The weary hours dragged on with watching of this movement on the Ridge, but at last the order came. Six guns were to be fired from Grant's headquarters at Orchard Knob, as a signal for a general advance on the Ridge.

The men were called to attention and the stacks of arms broken. The color-bearers unfurled the flags and shook them out. Field and staff officers took their places. In the rear the surgeons mustered their stretcher-bearers. Everything was in readiness when the six guns were fired from Orchard Knob, and instantly the army moved briskly forward in well-ordered lines. Passing the strip of bushy woodland on the little ridge from which the start was made, the lines came out into the open plain which stretched to the foot of Mission Ridge. It must have been the sight of a lifetime to the Confederates on the Ridge—those double lines of blue, marked at intervals with the crimson flags and fringed with the glittering arms carried at a right shoulder; stretching away to right and left, division after division, along the plain above and below. But their artillerymen took little time to admire the splendid pageant. Fifty

guns massed to the left of Bragg's headquarters burst forth in rapid
fire, and the air above the Union lines was filled with bursting shells.
But these were all too high; the fragments fell far behind the advancing lines.   The first effect of that tremendous discharge of artillery was stunning; but in a moment it was plain that no harm was
being done.   The much-talked-of moral effect of big guns was
missing; there was no wavering in the lines.   Rather, a feeling of
new confidence came upon the men as they moved on, always too
fast for the Confederates' depressing of their pieces.   In the Forty-
first, one man was struck on the shoulder by a fragment of shell,
but this was the extent of the casualties from several tons of shells.

At the moment of starting, the Confederate infantry could be
seen still hurrying on toward Sherman.   But this was quickly
stopped when Thomas' magnificent menace came into view.   Better
risk Sherman on the right with too few men, than this host steadily
moving on the centre.   The Ridge was high and steep, and the
ascent was obstructed with gullies and felled timber.   But this on-
coming army—would it storm the Ridge, disdaining the obstructions?   Brown's Ferry, Orchard Knob, Lookout Mountain—these
were samples of the enterprise which Bragg must face.   He could
not recall the men gone against Sherman, but he could stop that
movement, and he did.

As the Forty-first, in its place in line, approached the log breastworks at the foot of the Ridge, the Confederates posted there sprang
up and ran up the Ridge, taking paths that led obliquely to the top.
The battery on Orchard Knob fired at these flying men on their
way up the Ridge, but this was mere boy's play, and likely to do
more mischief to friend than to foe.   The order given out when the
start was made was to take the line at the foot of the Ridge.   This
line was abandoned by the enemy before the assailants could reach
it, as has been told.   Coming up to the line of logs, the Forty-first
threw itself down against the logs for shelter, and the second line
of troops followed and did the same.   The infantry on the Ridge
had opened a severe fire, and the artillery, by firing obliquely down
the face of the steep slope, was able to be effective.   Both arms
together made the firing hot, and damage was done.   The shelter
of the logs was insufficient for refuge for a single line, and two were

here. Then the logs were laid at angles like a rail fence, and some
of the faces thus formed were enfiladed from the top of the Ridge.
The mounted officers, of course, had dismounted—whatever was
to be done, it was plain that horses could go no farther in that fight.
The animals were set loose, and most of them galloped off to the
rear. But Col. Wiley's horse, bewildered by the din of battle, hung
about the feet of the prostrate men, and was likely enough to tread
on them. The Colonel rose from the ground to turn the horse's
head to the rear and drive him away. Wiley's hand was on the
bridle as he turned the horse about, when he himself sank to the
ground, his leg shattered at the knee by a rifle ball. The command
of the battalion thus fell to Lieut. Col. Kimberly.

The Confederate fire was increasing, and they were getting
the range more accurately with both small arms and artillery. No
fight could be made from that insufficient and overcrowded shelter,
but there were no orders for any further movement—all orders
given had been fulfilled. It was destruction to remain, it was impossible to withdraw without confusion and great loss. The roar
of battle from the Ridge was deafening; no command could be
heard at the distance of a company front. Hazen lay on the ground
a rod away from Kimberly, and signalled to go forward. Kimberly
and a dozen officers and men nearest him sprang to their feet shouting to the others, then jumped the logs and ran forward to the
shanties of the winter camp. This movement instantly spread right
and left, and the whole battalion dashed forward to the ascent of the
Ridge. It was the intention to gather the men behind the shanties
for a better beginning of the ascent, but this could not be done. The
oblique fire of the Confederate artillery knocked the shanties about
the heads of the men, while the infantry riddled them with bullets.
So the start was made as it could be. Once the ascent was begun,
however, the men came together, for the gullied and broken face
of the Ridge afforded shelter not to be found on the level ground
below. All the Confederate fire was also less effective, though it
was not lessened. On went the assailants, closing together as they
made their way over or around obstructions. As they neared the
top, a battery to the right, which from first to last had done more
damage than all the rest, came into full view at little more than

pistol range. Kimberly called to his nearest men to pick off the gunners. When the first of these men dropped on one knee and fired, an artilleryman plunged headlong to the ground in the act of passing a cartridge. A dozen other shots followed instantly, and that battery fired no more. The artillery immediately in front could not sufficiently depress its guns, so steep was the ascent, and when the battery to the right was still, there was an end of the trouble from artillery.

The Forty-first was near the top, the enemy's line of works in full view, not a stone's throw away. Just to the left of the Forty-first, Bassett Langdon was leading his First Ohio straight at the works, himself the foremost figure, his men following as they could keep up with his long legs. For an instant he was seen to stagger as a rifle ball went through his cheeks from side to side; then recovered, ran to the works, and fired every cartridge in his revolver at the enemy. But they were leaving their works. The Forty-first came up and over, the enemy a confused mass of fugitives a hundred yards or so down the slope to the rear. Not that their spirit was all gone; two or three of their officers began to rally them, and in a moment had half a regiment in line. The victors were flushed, jubilant, and for the moment careless. Then the flag of the Forty-first was advanced toward the gathering Confederate force, and the men leaped forward into line. That was enough for the enemy; brave as they were, they had just then no heart to stand another charge. Meantime, Fetterly, Kramer and others of the Forty-first had seized the destructive battery to the right. One of the pieces was wheeled to the right, pointing toward Bragg's headquarters, where the enemy was still holding out. The piece was loaded, but the men had no primer. They emptied a cartridge into the vent, and then one of them discharged his Springfield rifle over it. The shell skimmed the ground and burst in front of the Confederate headquarters. In another moment, Newton's division had them all in flight. In the coming dusk a horseman was seen to ride down the rear slope from Bragg's quarters. He was said to be Braxton Bragg himself—I do not know.

About Hazen's headquarters that night were gathered eighteen pieces of captured artillery. Six of these fell to the Forty-first and its comrades in the fight, the Ninety-third, and the Forty-first had a Confederate battle flag.

While the men were still exulting over the victory, the new division commander, Gen. Thomas J. Wood, rode in among them. He, too, was jubilant. "Men," he cried, "I'll have you all court-martialed. You were ordered to take the rifle-pits at the foot of the Ridge, and here you've got the Ridge itself and all of Bragg's artillery!"

In the two days of battle here, the Forty-first lost 115 men, nearly all of them the first day, at Orchard Knob. That brief but desperate struggle was, with one exception, the most costly one encountered by the regiment. Compared with Orchard Knob, the general action which carried the apparently impregnable position on Mission Ridge was but a trifle, so far as losses in the Forty-first are concerned. In the second fight there was a loss not to be esti-mated in numbers. Col. Wiley lost his leg as the result of the wound which has been mentioned above. Perhaps the loss of this commander may be best understood by reading the characterization of him in Hazen's book of recollections of army service. "Wiley," says Hazen, "was the most efficient regimental commander, regu-lar or volunteer, I ever knew."

One of the minor incidents which deserves to be recorded as of the kind that can not be forgotten, occurred when the regiment was half way up Mission Ridge in the assault. A boy who was enlisted in A company as a drummer, but who went into this battle carrying a gun, came tremblingly to the regimental commander when the fight was hottest. He stood at attention, but he could not salute, for with his right hand he held across his breast his shattered left arm. He was faint with the shock and the loss of blood; and his face, as smooth and fresh as a girl's, was pallid under the pain he bore. But he would report himself. "Colonel," he said, "I must go and have my arm fixed." And tottered off down the Ridge through the storm of battle.

There has been much dispute about the details of the Mission Ridge fight, especially as to orders or absence of orders to assault the Ridge after the line at the foot had been gained, and as to the troops first in the works at the summit. In regard to orders to assault the Ridge, there can be no question so far as Hazen's brigade is concerned. No command could have been communicated to the brigade as it lay close to the ground behind the line of logs. In the din of the tremendous fusillade from the summit, it was impossible to make a command heard by so much as a regiment. Orders could go only from man to man, in the way described above, as the beginning of the movement of the Forty-first. Gen. Wood's words of greeting to the victors on the Ridge, heretofore quoted in this narrative, seem to be conclusive proof that no orders for the assault were given by or through the division commander. It is certain, then, that Wood's division had no orders; Hazen always said he had none; what orders the Forty-first had, and how they came, is told above. The assault, by this part of Thomas' army at least, was the voluntary movement of an intelligent soldiery, without direction from the higher officers of the army. It was the judgment of the soldiers, not the orders of the commanders, which brought about the assault.

As to the first arrivals at the summit, no attempt will be made here to settle that question. The essential fact is that the enemy in front of the Forty-first were driven from their works by that regiment; if any other command had cleared its front before the Forty-first entered the Confederate works, that fact did not affect the fight of this regiment, the enemy in its front holding out until the regiment was right upon them, ready to use the bayonet.

The victory was a new experience to the Forty-first. It carried its point of attack at Shiloh only to waste itself in wild and fruitless pursuit. In the defensive fighting at Stone River and Chickamauga, it kept its ground, gaining nothing beyond the repulse of the enemy. At Brown's Ferry it made the capture, barren of trophies and leaving the enemy still in the field, aggressive as opportunity offered. But in the two days of Mission Ridge, there were substantial fruits of victory. The first day's fight left the defenders of the line at Orchard Knob prisoners in our hands, with their captured flag testifying the completeness of the conquest. When Mission Ridge was crowned, there remained no organized enemy in front—nothing but crowds of flying soldiers hunting the security of the woods beyond the Ridge, anxious only to get away from the field on which they left their dead and wounded and prisoners, with their artillery. There was an indescribable exhilaration among the victors; they trod on air as they went about amid their trophies. Was not Chickamauga avenged? Under its new leadership, what should balk this army? And yet, they did not fully know the importance of that day's work—that the taking of Mission Ridge was one of the marvellous feats of arms of all ages.

CHAPTER XII.

EAST TENNESSEE AND A VETERAN FURLOUGH.

There was little time for rest after the Mission Ridge battle. The whole vicinity of Chattanooga was now clear of the enemy. The pontoons on the Tennessee river were no longer essential, since the railroad undei the point of Lookout could be restored through to Chattanooga. All supplies could come in abundance. Many stores were needed, but there was no time to wait for them. Knox ville was threatened, and a corps from the Army of the Cumberland must hasten to its relief. The lot fell to the Fourth Corps, and the march was begun under orders to press forward with all possible speed.

There followed some marching experience that was new to this regiment. The nights were cool at the outset, and grew colder as the march progressed. It soon fell out that there was a frozen crust on the roads in the mornings, and this was very hard on the men's shoes, already too much worn. In two or three days there were many with shoes which had ceased to be a protection to the feet, if they were not entirely gone. The command was ordered to forage the country, and regular details were made for this duty. Sheep and some beef cattle were brought in. The pelts and hides were given to the shoeless men, and out of them they made clumsy coverings for the feet, rudely after the style of an Indian's moccasin. It was something in the way of warmth, though the soft green skins afforded small protection from the sharp points in the frozen roads. With it all, there was real suffering on this march. There was some compensation in the food supply from the forage parties. Many a smoke-house, well stocked with the delicious unsalted hams peculiar to that region, yielded its store for the mess tables. The supply of fresh beef and mutton was fair, and occasionally there were fowls. The foragers had many tales to tell of adventures and escapes far off the line of march. Often they encountered natives who had little desire to contribute, and some were openly hostile. In one or two instances the foragers escaped cunningly-laid traps only by nights of sleepless watching.

Before Knoxville was reached, it was known that the enemy had given over his attempt to take the place, warned of the approaching reinforcements. The Forty-first, with the rest, marched through the town. Passing the headquarters of the commanding general, the troops were closed up and marched to the step as in review. The general recognized the Forty-first by its guns at the left shoulder, and said some complimentary things about the regiment.

The march was continued twenty miles or more beyond Knoxville, toward Clinch Mountain, and finally the regiment went into camp at Blaine's Cross Roads. Winter weather had come in earnest, and the camp was an uncomfortable one, not properly made for winter quarters. While here, the regimental commander received a communication from the Governor of Ohio, stating that the Forty-first, like many other Ohio regiments, was so much reduced in numbers that it was in danger of consolidation with some other regiment. Its vacant colonelcy could not be filled, and thus promotions were stopped, while in case of consolidation there would, of course, be surplus officers to be disposed of by discharge. The Governor urged that the regimental commander at once set about re-enlisting the regiment under the War Department orders. In that case, the whole command would have a thirty-day furlough with transportation to Cleveland. This would afford an opportunity to recruit the regiment so that its organization and name might be preserved and not lost in a consolidation. The Governor was confident that if the regiment re-enlisted and came home, plans that had been matured would fill its wasted ranks and preserve its organization and identity. One chilly morning late in December, the ground being partly covered with snow and slush, Lieut. Col. Kimberly had the regiment paraded without arms, and read to the men the War Department order providing for the re-enlistment of regiments whose term of service was about to expire. The purport of the letter of the Governor was also told, and the matter was left with the men. There were 188 present at that camp, and 180 of these at once re-enlisted under the War Department order.

On the 5th of January, 1864, the Forty-first left the camp above Knoxville, on its way to Ohio on veteran furlough. It marched to a point on the Tennessee river, where a steamboat was waiting to transport it to Chattanooga. There was a scarcity of rations on the trip down the Tennessee, and on one day at least the men were hungry until a supply was purchased from a farmer, near whose place the boat stopped for fuel. At Chattanooga, Col. Wiley was found in his old quarters, his amputation still tender of course, but his spirit the same as ever. He greeted the commander of the re-enlisted Forty first with these words. "Kimberly, you've won the greatest victory the regiment ever had"—referring, of course, to the re-enlistment.

The Forty-first reached Cleveland on the 2d of February, and before the men dispersed to their homes, a public reception and dinner was tendered the regiment by the city government. Marching to the big tent of the Northern Ohio Sanitary Commission, on Monument Square, the veterans were greeted by Charles W. Palmer on behalf of the Mayor and Council. Lieut. Col. Kimberly replied for the Forty-first, saying the regiment was re-enlisted for the war, and inviting the people of Northern Ohio to fill up its depleted ranks. No returning soldiers were ever more warmly welcomed or accorded greater honor. The dinner was the choicest that land of plenty could afford, and the service was by the willing hands of ladies whose husbands, fathers and friends were battling for the Union. A noble welcome, truly.

This ceremony being over, officers and men were soon dismissed to seek home and friends. A day or two afterward, Kimberly was summoned to Columbus to meet the Governor and the Adjutant-General of the State. The Governor repeated the substance of the letter heretofore mentioned, regarding the recruiting of the regiment; and ended by exhorting Kimberly to set every officer and man at work to secure recruits and save the regimental organization. The lieutenant colonel explained that the members of the regiment had already gone to their homes, and that one of the inducements to re-enlistment was the promise of a month among their families and friends after more than two years' absence. A detail on recruiting service had certainly not been thought of; but for himself, Kimberly promised to give earnest attention to the recruiting business. The Adjutant-General then gave the names and location of a number of men to whom had been issued "recruiting commissions"—that is, commissions conditioned on the enlistment of a certain number of men. Kimberly was offered the choice of two of these conditionally commissioned men, who should then recruit for the Forty-first, thus bringing to the regiment the men for two companies. The choice was made—two men located in the section where the regiment was raised—and they were assigned to the Forty-first. The two men went to the work of winning their commissions by getting recruits. Some of the men they enlisted went with them for the avowed purpose of joining the Forty-first. The two companies were enlisted and mustered in, but they never came to the Forty-first. They were assigned to make up a battalion of six companies in order to give a lieutenant colonel's commission to a man who held it four months and then resigned.

So much space is given to this matter because it is fairly typical of certain methods grossly unjust to the soldiers in the field, while they were not at all understood by the devoted and self-sacrificing friends of those soldiers. Had the two companies been sent to the Forty-first as promised, there would still have been a great injustice in commissioning their officers as payment for recruiting service, over the heads of men who had won promotion by two years of faithful service on hard-fought fields. Not to send the companies as promised was to leave the regiment short of the number required to allow promotions, making officers perform the duty of a rank to which they could not be commissioned. As to enlisting men expressly for a preferred regiment, and then, after muster in, assigning them to another command, nothing whatever need be said.

This affair was the one cloud that hung over the veteran furlough days. What days they were! Never were skies so blue, and early spring sunshine so warm, and homes so bright and cheerful, and friends so kind and loving, and all familiar sights and sounds so grateful to eye and ear. Those days went swiftly, and the time for return was quickly at hand. The veterans reported promptly at Cleveland. There were nearly a hundred recruits where there should have been three hundred.

Making no display, and without a public leave-taking, the Forty-first marched quietly to the railway station one morning, and was soon on the way to the front. It rejoined its division in East Tennessee on the 26th of March.

CHAPTER XIII.

A HUNDRED DAYS UNDER FIRE.

When the Forty-first rejoined its division from veteran furlough, the Atlanta campaign was about to begin. The regiment
was put into a battalion with the First Ohio, the command falling
to Lieut. Col. Kimberly. Hazen still commanded the brigade,
Wood the division, and Thomas the Army of the Cumberland—
the whole a part of Sherman's grand army.

The start for Atlanta was along the line of the railroad. The
enemy was encountered at Rocky Face Ridge, where Thomas'
troops amused him while a flanking force worked around to the
right. The Forty-first was not engaged, but in the field tactics it
was sent, in column doubled on the center, into an open field at
long rifle range from the Ridge. At once it was a target for the
Confederates on the Ridge. Two or three changes of position
were made before getting out of the galling fire, and the regiment
was complimented for its steadiness in these movements. A few
days afterward, at Resaca, the Forty-first made a dash and gained
a position less than a hundred yards from the enemy's main line,
and from this place kept his artillery idle during the day. At night,
both sides pushed skirmishers a few yards to the front, and they
almost met. This was such close quarters that the regiment was
kept on the alert the greater part of the night. Soon after dark,
the enemy opened a fusillade along that part of the line, and it
was replied to by the troops on right and left; but the fire of the
Forty-first was reserved until there should be some sign of attack
by the enemy. On both sides, a great deal of ammunition was
wasted in the darkness. The enemy's purpose was not attack, but
to cover a retreat.

When Resaca was passed, the army was fairly on the long and
tedious Atlanta campaign, during which there was hardly a day
out of a hundred when the regiment was not under fire. Wagon

ROBERT L. KIMBERLY

Lieut. Col. 41st O.V.V.I.; Col. 191st O.V.I.; Brevet Col. U.S. Vols.;
Brevet Brig. Gen. U.S. Vols.; Major U.S.A. (not accepted);
Brig. Gen. U.S. Vols. (appointed, not confirmed, war having ended).

EPHRAIM S. HOLLOWAY

Lieut. Col. 41st O.V.V.I.;
Col. 41st O.V.V.I. (appointed, not mustered, war having ended).

trains, with camp equipage, were, of course, left behind. One wagon to a regiment was the allowance, and even this was not often seen. The commands were supposed to be so equipped that they could go on indefinitely, without dependence on any transportation beyond that of rations and ammunition. The Forty-first had a special provision for such campaigns. Its one wagon carried a large chest, in which each regiment had a thin box sufficient for the carrying of such papers as were necessary for keeping musters and accounts. Company commanders were thus enabled to keep up accounts and records during the campaign. The regular company desk was a convenience, but not an absolute necessity.

After passing Resaca, the regiment drove the enemy from Calhoun to Adairsville in a day's march. It was necessary to keep out a skirmish line the entire distance, but nevertheless the road was cleared so that the march of the column was not delayed. Those were days of hard marching, with not much in the way of variety to relieve the tediousness. Near Cassville, the regiment one day came upon a store of tobacco, which was a prize, for the sutler was conspicuously absent on that march. Just beyond, and within sight of Cassville, the command was deployed on the crest of a high ridge. In the valley below, a considerable force of Confederates were manoeuvering in plain sight, but they quickly withdrew to the cover of woods. The troops marched down to the plain, and the division was deployed and moved forward a short distance toward the wood where the enemy disappeared. Then came a halt, and a concentration of most of the artillery of the corps on the front line. The town of Cassville was to be shelled, but the order was countermanded, and then the infantry was again sent forward in line of battle. It came to the edge of the wood, and the skirmishers were beginning to exchange shots with the enemy, when an order came to halt and bivouac on the spot. A Confederate soldier came in and gave himself up. He said that Johnston's army (Johnston had succeeded Bragg after the Mission Ridge battle) was in a strong position just in front. It was here that Johnston's famous battle order was read to his troops. But it was by this time too near dark to bring on a general engagement. Everything looked favorable for a battle in the morning. Firing had been heard from

Schofield's corps far to the right, and the corps which was advancing on a parallel road to the left was also heard from in firing that indicated the presence of the main body of the enemy. While the alternate advances and halts above noted were in progress, Sherman himself was immediately in rear of the Forty-first, and the orders came direct from him. Part of the time he was half reclining in a corner of rail fence, and once or twice gave his orders without so much as looking up. Of course, his calculations included factors miles away and far beyond sight. Either of the advances ordered would have brought on a battle if it had been allowed to go on for fifteen minutes, and the history of the war would have been changed —to whose advantage no one can say. But Sherman was apparently undecided for a time. Next morning the enemy had gone.

Much was heard at this time about Allatoona Pass. Nobody but the generals knew where or what it was, but the talk was of a wonderfully strong position there, which Johnston would not surrender without hard fighting. The Forty-first was with that part of the army which moved off to the right of this marvellous pass. The country here was wilder than before, and when a place called Burnt Hickory was reached, there was nothing to be seen except a heavily timbered wilderness, and the timber was not hickory, but pine. The march wandered through such country for several days. The most enterprising foragers for the officers' messes failed to find anything worth bringing in, and it was a time of fasting as to supplies from the country. A better region was entered as the army approached Dallas, where the enemy was in position. At Pumpkinvine Creek, the Forty-first passed through some of Hooker's troops and went on to the front. Hooker had had a severe fight while out of supporting distance. The camp talk was that he had been ambitious to fight a battle of his own, and that Johnston had been more than willing. The Forty-first, with some sharp skirmishing, gained a position on some rough ground, full of stumps and not especially inviting for its military advantages. But it was close to the enemy's line—no doubt of that. It had become the custom for the first line to make cover as soon as it went into position. Sometimes this was done with rails, and sometimes by throwing up a low embankment and standing in the ditch thereby made.

Work of this description was at once begun in this position, but the enemy was close enough in front to interfere and make the duty uncomfortable. Nevertheless, the cover progressed. It was fairly well along next day, when the brigade was relieved from the front line and marched off to the left for a considerable distance—beyond the left flank of the army, indeed. Here were corps and division generals in a group. The Forty-first was leading, and as it came up to the point where the generals sat on their horses, a halt was made, while Hazen and his regimental commanders were called up to receive orders. Kimberly, whose command was leading, was given a pocket compass, receiving at the same time the orders of the division general, Wood. The battalion was to march in line of battle, skirmishers out, a mile and a half due southeast by the compass; then wheel to the right and march due southwest until the enemy was found. The expectation was that the Confederate right flank would be taken in rear, or, if that flank were refused, that the attack would fall on or near its extreme right. The rest of the brigade was to follow in column by battalion front, and behind were to come four other brigades. The order was explicit and emphatic to attack the instant the enemy was found, waiting for no further orders under any circumstances, whether the enemy were found in position or not, behind fortifications or otherwise. The parting word of the general to Kimberly was to remember that five brigades were behind him.

The ground on which the regiment stood when this order was given, was high and open. But there was only a short view in any direction. The country was generally wooded, though cleared land was frequently found; a hilly country, with little or no level ground even in the valleys; it was down one hill and up another with scarcely breathing space. The regiment was put into line facing the southeast, and moved off down an open slope into a wooded valley, and so on, keeping the line of battle, whatever obstacles were encountered. Three-quarters of a mile from the starting point, some Confederate cavalrymen were seen on a hill in front, but they quickly disappeared and were seen no more. When a mile and a half had been covered in this direction, a wheel to the right was made, and the march went on, over the same kind of country, due southwest. The second line should have been two or three hundred yards in rear of the first, following its change of direction; but the country was so broken and so full of obstacles that this must have been a difficult thing to do. When the movement had gone about a mile in the new direction, the regiment came upon a large open ground, sloping upward to a wooded crest. There, in full view, five hundred yards away, was a large force in position, the men busily intrenching their line. The column of attack had come upon the rear of that line, which faced the wrong way for the enemy. Topographical calculations had been at fault. The attacking force was in rear of the left flank of the Union army, instead of being in rear of the right flank of the Confederates. Orders came to move by the left flank. Up and down hill, through ravines, across brooks and over fences, the march continued until the better part of the day seemed to be spent. At last the regiment was skirting an open ground, a slope at the upper edge of which fresh earthworks were visible. But these faced toward the attacking force; apparently it was the refused right of the Confederate army. The regiment moved on past the open ground to a thin wood. Here it was faced to the front and started forward. According to what could be seen, a movement straight to the front would pass a little to the left of the enemy's fortified line, which was something more than half a mile away.

The open wood through which the regiment was now moving sloped gradually for three hundred yards, and then there was a slight ravine, the opposite bank the more abrupt, and covered with a dense undergrowth, beyond which nothing could be seen. Off to the right front, across the big open field, were the enemy's fresh earthworks, on which a man or two could now and then be seen, but there was nothing to indicate that the presence of the attacking force was known. In front was the silent forest, no sign or sound of life. The regiment passed on down the slope into the little ravine, and began the ascent of the other side through the thick undergrowth. Suddenly then, like a lightning stroke from a cloudless sky, the storm burst. The bullets came like hail in sheets, with a sustained rapidity that showed the presence of more than one close line of infantry. Instantly the ranks of the Forty-first were torn as they had never been before. The men fell by dozens. A view was opened through the underbrush as the Confederate fire mowed it down. Fifty yards or so in front was a barricade packed with line after line of blazing rifles. Those of the Forty-first who were not shot down dropped to the ground and began to answer the furious Confederate fire. Their defense was not waist high, and they were fair marks as they stood in ranks. Then their fire slackened and stopped, and they went down behind their defense. A sergeant of the Forty-first saw something white thrust up above their cover, and called out that it was a white flag. The regiment sprang to its feet to advance, but instantly the Confederate rifles were again in action. The line was too thin with losses to breast that storm. On the right of the battalion was the First Ohio. While the fire in front was hottest, there came from the enemy's works across the open field to the right an enfilading fire of artillery and musketry. This smote the First Ohio heavily, but its major, Stafford, held it bravely to its post.

Where were the five brigades which were to follow? The minutes wore away, each bringing death to brave men, and no line came up in rear. Kimberly sent his adjutant to find the second line, and he did not return. A second messenger was sent, and no return. Then the adjutant of the First Ohio, and he was shot down before he had made a hundred yards to the rear. That explained the failure of the messengers sent before. No word reached the brigade commander. But that did not matter; Hazen had no second line to send. The battalion following the Forty-first had been deflected from its course, and was in action on the left. So with the others. Forty-five minutes passed, and no succor came. It was plain that the plan of attack had miscarried. The battalion was wasting away in a fruitless endeavor. Still, the men were not conquered. All knew that their line was too thin to make a successful assault; but they had found some shelter—it was easier to find, now there were fewer of them—and they were keeping the enemy close to his cover; there was no more standing up to fire, as at first. If only the second line were up! With that help, they could make a dash and drive the enemy. Sergeant Butler, of D company, came by the battalion commander, creeping to the rear half doubled up with the pain of a shot in the body, pressing both hands on the wound to stop the waste of blood. He had his message: "Colonel, don't fall back! Keep 'em at it. They'll take the position when the second line comes." Poor Butler! He dropped to the ground almost as he spoke, unable to hobble further back, and soon after fell into the enemy's hands. For it was plain enough that the second line was not coming. Just to the left, the One Hundred and Twenty-fourth Ohio, which should have been the second line, could be seen fighting as desperately as any. Along the whole line of the battalion, there was a constant drift to the ravine of men wounded but able to crawl to shelter, and these, of course, were but part of the casualties. Kimberly saw all this as minute after minute passed, until three-quarters of an hour had gone. Then he withdrew the remnant that was left. The men came back by command to the shelter of the little ravine, where the shrunken companies closed up in perfect order. Not a man who was unhurt was left behind by either the First or the Forty-first. Then the command was marched by the flank along the ravine, and so, keeping the shelter, to the point from which its forward movement started. Here were Hazen and a number of other general officers with their staffs—among them Gen. O. O. Howard, the corps commander. To Hazen, Kimberly reported his withdrawal without orders, expecting no censure and receiving none. The two torn and wasted regiments at that moment filing by, spoke louder than words.

The Forty-first went into this engagement with 262 men, and lost 108 killed and wounded. In one company, out of 22 men engaged, 20 were shot; and in a very small company, which took into the fight only 11 men, the loss was 9. The greater part of this heavy loss was sustained in the opening of the battle, which came like a volley from an ambush, and in the second attempt to storm the enemy's position, when the men, who had found some shelter, were called to their feet only to receive a fire as severe as that at the beginning of the fight. Finally, the wounds were made at short range; not a hundred yards separated the combatants. The exception to this was the enfilading fire from the right, where the enemy was a half mile away.

No part of the line on which the battle took place was held by the Union troops, but all fell back. It was a repulse from right to left. What would have happened had the original plan been carried out, is, of course, only matter of conjecture, the result depending largely on the dispositon and movement of the opposing army. One thing, however, may be taken as certain: Had a second and a third line, or even one line, come up while the Forty-first was still engaged, that one point in the enemy's position would have been carried. The failure of the movement as laid out, the deflecting of the line of march of the second line and those following, entirely changed the attack. It was to have been an attack in column of battalions with wide intervals; as it was made, so far as Hazen's brigade was concerned, it was an attack in echelon, without reserves.

The wounded who were unable to help themselves off the line of the fighting, fell into the enemy's hands; the dead were buried by him on the ground. Trenches were dug, and the bodies were thrown in with little care. Sometime afterward, when the army had passed on toward Atlanta, several of these trenches were opened, that certain bodies might be rescued, for friends in the North. Union and Confederate were found piled together, and none could be identified.

This action was called the battle of Pickett's Mill. In his book, "A Narrative of Military Service," Gen. Hazen says that "it was the most fierce, bloody and persistent assault of the Atlanta campaign." In his official report, Gen. Wood says of the right of the attacked position, where was the Forty-first, that "no troops could stay there and live." The Confederate force in front of the Forty-first was Cleburne's division, and it was reinforced during the fight. Confederate official reports mention the enfilading fire delivered from the right, and say that but two pieces of artillery were engaged. It is a fact worth notice, that while the Confederate reports of the Atlanta campaign minutely record the Pickett's Mill battle as one of the most prominent and important events of the campaign, Gen. Sherman's memoirs wholly ignore the action. As to the choice of commands to make the attempt on the enemy's right, Gen. Wood vigorously protested against taking his division out of the line which it had just fortified at no little hazard and with some losses. Gen. Howard's reply was that he had taken the commands which he thought most likely to succeed in the hazardous attempt. It was the fortune of the Forty-first to open the fighting at Mission Ridge, and again at Pickett's Mill. Hazen speaks of the change from the original plan of attack, but gives no explanation except by saying that the battalions following the Forty-first had drifted away to the left. He thought that the long delay of the flank movement to get away from the Union left, as hereinbefore described, was fatal to the enterprise, and says the attack could have been delivered two hours and a half sooner (it was near 5 in the afternoon when it was made), this interval having been employed by the Confederates in bringing up forces and strengthening their position. Confederate reports show that they were on the alert, and had expected a further movement against their right, that having been the trend of the Union tactics for a day or two before. The position of Cleburne, as it was seen during the battle, had the look of one chosen for the occasion—that is, to meet this attack—as his line was not a prolongation of the line of earthworks which could be seen to the right.

The withdrawal from the field of battle was not to a great distance. The Forty-first was moved to the right and rear, and took position on a wooded ridge. The enemy's line, on high ground across an open field, was in sight. The new position was at once fortified, and was occupied for several days. At one time, the enemy came down across the open ground to reconnoiter. His skirmish line was plainly seen from the start. They came up the wooded slope in front of the Forty-first with little resistance offered, the Union skirmishers falling back by order. The regiment stood behind its earthwork, and when the enemy was well up toward it, two volleys, by front and rear rank, set them off flying. Then the Union skirmish line, returning to its position, picked up a prisoner or two.

Very little in the way of recuperation and restoration was possible while occupying this position. It seemed to be peculiarly an out-of-the-way place; communications were not direct and easy; the roads were byways, not highways; there was nothing in the country within reach; it seemed as if the regiment had been put into a side pocket and forgotten.

A notable incident about this time was a severe thunder storm one afternoon. The lightning played around uncomfortably. Four men who were lying under their shelter tent were shocked, but not killed; and the brigade bugler, who had taken refuge in a hollow tree on a hillside, was upset by a bolt which shattered the tree and sent him rolling down the hill.

Pickett's Mills left the Forty-first much saddened, for many a comrade was missed from the ranks. The regiment was far below the two-hundred mark in strength, with no prospect of recovery in this regard. It had not half the men who started on the campaign, for although the greater loss was in the late battle, it was constantly suffering from sickness. No men were coming up from the rear, from hospital or as recruits. Far down in the heart of the enemy's country, with the base of supplies so distant as to be practically cut off as to anything but ammunition and crackers and coffee and bacon; with only the dog-tent for a shelter, and for cooking utensils tin cups and frying pans—the whole outfit for shelter and living carried on the soldier's back and in his haversack—why, two months or so of this, with little or no word from home, made life seem like banishment to a wilderness. A campaign in Africa would hardly be farther from home; and Crusoe on his island would not be in greater need of the common comforts of civilized life.

CHAPTER XIV.

CLOSING UPON ATLANTA.

The battle of Pickett's Mills was fought on the 27th of May, and on the 4th of June the Confederates left their position there. On the 6th, the Forty-first marched seven miles in the direction of Acworth. The enemy was in close proximity from day to day, and always there were more or less severe encounters along the lines. On the 10th of June, the regiment moved at 4 in the morning, and all day long was kept on the alert with movement, skirmish and wait; going into bivouac at dark only four hundred yards from the place of starting. This was the character of the work from day to day. On the 15th, a deserter came in and reported the death of the Confederate Gen. Polk, who had been killed by a shell while reconnoitering on a hill in plain view from the ground then occupied by the Forty-first. On the 17th, a movement in line of battle was begun, Kimberly's and Foy's battalions in the first line. The front seemed to be clear, but on each flank the enemy's skirmishers were active. Finally, Capt. Kile, of the Forty-first, was sent with four companies to clear the left front. The enemy was well posted in a farmhouse and its surroundings, but Kile charged the position and dislodged the Confederates. The advance was then possible, and was made, but brought on nothing more than desultory skirmishing.

Reveille at half past 3 in the morning, an advance at 4, and an all day skirmish—this was the order for day after day. It happened so on the 18th and again on the 21st, the enemy being driven about 400 yards on the latter day. On the 22d, Hooker's line was attacked, and the Forty-first was sent to fill a gap. Skirmishing as usual, but no serious fighting, for the hour was late. On the 23d, the regiment got within 75 yards of the Confederate main line, and a hastily made cover sufficed to hold the position until dark, which was near at hand, and during the night the line was fortified. On the 27th the regiment was at the base of Kenesaw Mountain.

The assault which was made at this point did not involve the Forty-first, except in skirmishing. The heavy fighting was to the right of the regiment's position in the line; but a skirmish line was sent up the steep and obstructed hill in front, until the enemy's fortified line stopped further progress. That night the regiment was sent on special service. An attack was expected some distance to the right. The opposing lines were close together and the night was very dark. Instead of relying on a skirmish line, it was somebody's notion to put a regiment between the lines as an outlying force, and the detail for this duty fell to the Forty-first. A staff officer was the guide. With great caution, to avoid discovery by the enemy, the regiment was led into the edge of a dense thicket, and halted. No commands were given above the breath. Now and then a word or two could be heard from the front—that was the enemy. Again, some slight sound would come from the rear—that was our own people. As regards any conception of the direction of lines, or of the configuration of the ground beyond the spot where the men stood, the regiment might as well have been in the bottom of a well. There was not even the pretense of a bivouac in line at this place. The men sat or lay down, guns in hand, and waited for the night to pass. Nothing came of it, except intolerable weariness, and just before daybreak the regiment was ordered back, stealing away as cautiously as it came.

In this way the campaign wore on. Some progress was made, on one part of the line or another, with every day. Sherman was hugging Johnston close, and pressing nearer and nearer to Atlanta. On the morning of July 2d, there came a departure from the regular order. The pickets were to fire briskly for ten minutes. By mutual understanding, there had been no useless picket firing, and so Col. Kimberly, the men of the Forty-first being at the front, gave due notice before the firing began. The purpose of this picket firing was never made known; its visible effect was nothing at all. On the 3d the enemy's position was found to be evacuated. A reconnoitering force was sent forward, developing nothing but the elaborateness of the enemy's defenses. There were traverses, abattis, chevaux-de-frise, advanced works, lunettes, and so on. It looked as though the Confederates had relieved time that hung heavily, by constructing all forms of field fortifications to be found in the military textbooks.

On the 5th of July, the Forty-first was detached to march by a parallel road to the Chattahoochie river, striking it at a point where was a pontoon bridge. A railroad station agent had given information that a portion of the enemy's trains were crossing the river on this bridge. The regiment was put on tne road and the march hastened. Approaching the river, the enemy's cavalry was found, but no trains. The skirmish line, commanded by Major Williston, went forward at a run across the flat ground, and so pushed the cavalry that the last man had barely time to cut the bridge loose and let it swing over to the Confederate side. The enemy opened up a lively fire across the river, and hurt some men, Major Williston receiving a shot in the shoulder. But, with the Chattahoochie between the armies, and later on Peach Tree Creek, the contending forces were not so close together as they had been.

From the crossing of the Chattahoochie to the arrival at Peach Tree Creek, the Forty-first was not brought into immediate contact with the enemy. At the latter stream, the enemy was disposed to resist the passage, and sharp fighting occurred just beyond the right of Hazen's brigade, and some also in front, the troops being within the enemy's range and suffering a few casualties, though not engaged. Just at dusk the brigade was crossed quickly and moved to the top of the steep bank. Here a line was formed to protect the crossing, and during the night it was strongly intrenched. The enemy was known to be in position not a thousand yards from the creek, and it was thought that when morning came he might attempt to crush any force that had crossed in the night. The Forty-first was in front, and built a good earthwork. The men had become expert in this work; intrenching tools were as much a part of the equipment as the rifle. After a regiment was halted in line, a few moments sufficed to produce a defense of no little value in case of attack, and a few hours would find it effectual against field artillery. At this point, most of the night was spent on the earthwork. The regiment stood to arms before daybreak, but no attack came. An occasional picket shot from a line of bushes along a fence in front, was the only indication of the enemy's presence. Peach Tree

Creek was crossed on the 20th of July. It was the last natural obstacle on the way to Atlanta, and on the 22d the regiment was fairly established in line before that city. This was the day saddened by the death of McPherson.

Before Atlanta, the position of the Forty-first was on a low ridge, slightly covered with a bushy growth, open ground in front and rear, and to the right. No troops joined the line on the right, for the ridge ran out there, and the ground was low for three or four hundred yards to a heavily wooded tract. Running obliquely across the front was the bed of a little stream, and beyond this an open slope, at the top of which were the Confederate works. On this open slope the enemy had well-constructed rifle pits, each one large enough to hold from four to six men. Off in the woods on the right front the enemy had a heavy siege gun, which sent some shells into the front of the little ridge where the Forty-first lay, and some others far overhead toward the left. These big missiles swept down from the Confederate lines with a tremendous roar, and when they burst the air was full of fragments. But that was all; they did not succeed in hurting anybody. The men soon came to hear them with indifference. Some one said that the big shells came as if they were firing a blacksmith shop at the Union line—this with reference to the quantity of iron let loose when the shell burst.

On the 25th of July, the brigade lost two good regiments, relieved from service because of expiration of term of enlistment. These were the First Ohio and the Fifth Kentucky. On the 27th, Gen. Stanley was assigned to the command of the Fourth Corps, Gen. Howard going to the Army of the Tennessee. On the 28th, the Forty-first was ordered to take the Confederate rifle pits on the open slope in its front. The regiment was deployed as skirmishers, made a quick and determined dash, and easily drove the enemy out, taking the reverse side of the pits for its shelter as it pelted the running Confederates. A battery in the rear (Bridge's), attempting to help an attack that needed no helping, exploded a shell directly over one of the rifle pits after it was taken—fortunately hurting no one. One or two more shells flew almost as close to the captors, and then somebody mercifully stopped the artillerymen. The

Forty-first had come to dread this battery more than it did those of the enemy, for on one or two former occasions, something like the experience just related had been encountered.

When the movement was made to the rear of Atlanta, to cut the enemy's line of communication, the Forty-first was a part of it. There was a great deal of marching, some of it in the night time; several positions taken up without encounter; and much tearing up of railroad track. The movement ended near Lovejoy Station, the Forty-first having some trifling skirmishing to end up the campaign. In this winding up of the long struggle, one singular thing occurred near the Forty-first. The Seventy-first Ohio, which had been at the battle of Shiloh with some ill fortune, and had afterward been kept in the rear on various kinds of guard duty with more ill fortune, was sent to the front at Atlanta. It looked like a brigade or a little division beside one of the regiments that had been through the campaign. Officers and men were anxious to wipe out the old stains, and a single opportunity occurred while the troops were near Lovejoy. A Confederate skirmish line was posted along a fence on the farther side of an open field, and some companies of the Seventy-first were deployed as skirmishers and sent against it. The line of Seventy-first men advanced into the field and began firing. The Confederate skirmishers were covered by the fence, those of the Seventy-first stood upright in the open ground. Not a man of them would take cover; they were set to prove that the regiment would stand and fight. They lost a dozen or more men in less than as many minutes, without accomplishing what a practiced regiment would have done with little or no loss. At that cost they made their point, and at least won the sympathy of those who saw the needless sacrifice.

After the evacuation, the Forty-first was encamped east of Atlanta for rest and recuperation. It began the campaign with 331 men, and had dwindled to 99. One hundred and fifty had fallen in battle, and more than 80 had succumbed to disease. No other campaign in the middle West equalled that one in duration, in marching service, and in frequent and close contact with the enemy. Many a day when there was no battle, it was a picket fight for breakfast, a skirmish for dinner, and another little fight to finish the day. For week after week, the din of musketry was ringing in the ears without cessation, save in the night; and the night itself was often broken by marching, or intrenching, or standing to arms. Those were a hundred days of unintermitted strain, with none but the commonest indispensable supplies, and those not always regular and in full quantity. The marvel was that anything at all was got over so long a line of supply. Nothing but the railroad, reconstructed as the army went forward, made it possible.

One of the happenings at the close of the campaign, important to the Forty-first and its old brigade, was the transfer of Gen. Hazen to the Army of the Tennessee, where he was given a division. His departure left Col. O. H. Payne, of the One Hundred and Twenty-fourth Ohio, in command as the senior colonel. This officer was well qualified to take the command, and he was certainly entitled to it by virtue of long and uniformly good and creditable service. Nevertheless, an Illinois colonel, whose regiment had never served a day with this command, was sent to take Hazen's vacant place. Col. P. S. Post, the officer referred to, was a good and worthy soldier—not a word to be said against his faithfulness or efficiency; but his assignment to this command over the heads of men as competent, and entitled to the preferment by long service with the command, was a grievous wrong. Hazen had some active and bitter enemies, and one of these, Gen. D. S. Stanley, was now commander of the corps. This officer's hostility extended to all who were connected with Hazen, or supposed to be friendly to him, and it did not stop when Hazen had left those connections and friends behind him. Indeed, Stanley's aggressive enmity did not cease with the ending of the war. He had the ear of Sherman as one of a coterie of regular officers who would be called a "ring" in politics. He seems to have taken umbrage at every good stroke Hazen made, and to have counted him always a rival for a coming brigadier generalship in the regular army. After the war, this hostile influence was able to banish Hazen to a post in the wilds of the far West and keep him there, while better posts were reserved for others. This was at all times a serious adverse influence for Hazen to contend with, and it affected very directly the fortune of his command. No proof can be made, but Hazen's friends had no doubt that the assignment of

Col. Post to command the old brigade, passing over competent men of the brigade, was due to the influence which Stanley conspicuously represented. The strength of Hazen's enemies was shown at the time of the Hazen-Stanley court martial long after the war, when the finding of the court was against Stanley, and the general of the army (Sherman) approved the finding, but reversed the penalty. Col. Payne's resignation quickly followed the ungracious and wrongful act which took from him what he had fairly won. It was a stigma which the old brigade did not deserve.

Some leaves of absence followed the ended campaign, and there was a prospect of freer communication with the North; but this was soon changed when Hood, leaving Sherman to do as he pleased, started the Confederate columns for Nashville.

CHAPTER XV.

AFTER HOOD.

When the Confederate army was set in motion for the attempt on Nashville, the Fourth and Twenty-third corps were detached from Sherman's army and given the task of taking care of Hood while Sherman made his jaunt to the sea. The Forty-first made so hasty a march to Chattanooga that there was little time for observations on the way. One of the sights, however, was Rome, Georgia —remembered as an oddly located little town. The latter part of the march to Chattanooga was greatly hastened, and on one day the regiment scored a march of thirty miles. From Chattanooga the regiment went by rail to Athens, Alabama, the transportation being in freight cars and most uncomfortable. At Athens, one hundred and sixty-four drafted men and substitutes were received. Compared with the worn clothing of the Forty-first, these new men were magnificently fitted out. Some of the outfit they got rid of on the first day's march toward Pulaski; the day was warm, the march hard on the recent arrivals, and they dropped many a brand new overcoat by the roadside.

At Pulaski there was a partial return to Atlanta campaign experiences. Elaborate earthworks were planned and thrown up. The supposition was that Hood's men were once more to be encountered, but this did not happen then. The next move was to Columbia, and it was a hurried one. There was no longer a doubt of the close proximity of the Confederate army, and that in numbers the two Union corps were overmatched. The Forty-first was sent across the river to look out for the flank and rear, while the troops went into position. There were crowds of negro refugees, eager to follow the army when they thought it was being driven out of the country never to return. There was rain here, though the weather was cold.

The principal duty in which the regiment was here engaged was a reconnaissance toward a ford several miles above Columbia. There was a report of Confederates crossing at this place early one morning, and the reconnaissance was ordered to determine the fact. The matter was important, for the road from the ford to Spring Hill, on the road to Nashville and in rear of Columbia, was shorter than the road from the army's position to Spring Hill. Marching several miles toward the road from the ford, the command at last came in sight of it across a wide stretch of open fields, and saw that it was full of passing baggage trains, hurrying toward Spring Hill. A staff officer from army headquarters was with the reconnaissance, and for some time he was convinced that these trains were a foraging expedition sent across the river, and not, as it proved, the trains of part of Hood's army which had already passed on toward the Union rear. The Forty-first was deployed and advanced to a farmhouse half a mile from the road. From this point it was plain to be seen that while the trains occupied the road, beside the wagons the way was crowded with infantry. Still the staff officer was not satisfied. A skirmish line was sent forward, and had not advanced far when a line of infantry rose to its feet behind a fence midway between the skirmishers and the road. That was enough; nobody doubted longer that a heavy force, a large part of the Confederate army, was rapidly putting itself between the Union forces and Nashville. The reconnaissance was quickly returned to Columbia, where the whole army was found in motion, or getting in motion, withdrawing from its position on the southern side of the river, to get back as fast as might be to Spring Hill. There were reports that a division which had been sent there late in the day had encountered the enemy actually on the Nashville road.

Night had now come, but the start was made at once. The Forty-first had the lead of its brigade, which was the first on the road. Till past midnight the hurried march was kept up, until the regiment was near to Spring Hill. This was familiar ground. Three hundred yards to the right of the pike was a wood where the regiment had camped on the way from Nashville to Shiloh. When the head of the column, the Forty-first, came in sight of this old camping-ground, it was recognized even in the night by the configuration of the ground. But it was now covered with fires of a bivouac—the long lines extending away on to the front until they seemed to bend to the left, as if crossing the pike near Spring Hill. The sight was like a reviving draught to a worn-out man. In the reconnaissance, the regiment had done a good day's duty before beginning another march with hardly a breathing spell. The night march was therefore the more wearisome and it was long. The men were going along half asleep, keeping their places by sheer force of habit. All talking had been given up hours ago, so tired were these soldiers; their weary footsteps on the ground made the only sounds to be heard. But here, on the old camp-ground, was a bivouac. That meant the end of the march near at hand; it meant coffee and supper and rest. At once the sleepy column was awake. The men began to show their revived spirit in talk, the usual jest and badinage, and thanks to good luck. The head of the column came up abreast of the nearest bivouac fires, when a horseman rode hurriedly out of a little lane which led from the pike to the bivouac, and spurred forward to the group of officers riding just in advance of the column. The officers halted when the horseman reached them, and the marching column closed up on them and halted too. The horseman from the lane was an orderly of division headquarters. He had dropped out and ridden up the lane toward the bivouac, to get an advance cup of coffee from some comrade there. A third of the way to the bivouac he was halted by a sentinel's challenge. Instead of replying to the challenge, the orderly, having his wits about him instantly, and more than a suspicion from the voice that came from the shadowy sentinel, demanded hastily, "What corps is this?" The sentinel was put off his guard and answered, "Cheatham's."

So, here was Wood's division marching by the flank past Cheatham's corps, hardly more than a pistol shot away. The orderly wheeled his horse and came back with his news. It was this that had halted the officers riding just in front of the troops. Wood and Stanley were there, with some others. There was some hurried consultation. Everybody had taken the bivouac to be that of our troops sent down in the afternoon. Wood came to the commander of the Forty-first, confirming the whisper that had already gone round. "Let your men keep well closed, and move in silence, Colonel," said he; "let the word be passed back quietly." This calm direction was from Wood, the division general. Wood, the old soldier and comrade, was revealed in the low words spoken just as he turned his horse's head to lead the way: "Kimberly, I hope the old division will come out of this all right; but I don't know what it is running into."

There was no need to pass the caution back along the road. The news had already gone; the talk was hushed and the men had closed together as if on drill, alert and ready. While this was passing, the enemy in the bivouac was seen to be alarmed; the sleeping men around the fires were being roused without drum or bugle. They rose up between the fires and the troops on the pike as if they sprang out of the ground. Hastily they got into line, and then were faced to their left and moved off into the darkness toward the rear of the Union troops on the pike.

The Forty-first led the way close behind Gen. Wood. On they went, quickly and silently. The long line of bivouac fires was found to be no nearer the pike as Spring Hill was approached, and finally that line, wherever it stretched, was out of sight. At Spring Hill, the Forty-first was halted on the pike, faced to the front and moved a rod or two off the road, pushing a skirmish line cautiously a few yards into the wood in front. Here the men were to lie down until daylight; no fires, and of course no coffee. The skirmishers were thirty or forty yards in advance, and two of them, coming to a house in the wood, saw a shadowy figure at the other end of the little building. This was a Confederate picket, and he wanted coffee— not fight, for these men on both sides, who had learned how to fight, had learned also the folly of useless picket quarrels.

The regiment lay on its arms the remainder of the night, the men sleeping as they could, all worn out and some hungry. There was no alarm. but the pike just behind was full of hurrying troops, with trains and artillery. In the gray of the morning, the regiment was called up and moved on toward Franklin, keeping off the pike a few yards, to give the way to the artillery and trains. At one point, while the regiment passed over an open field, some scattering shots came from the wood beyond, but a light fog was on the ground, and nothing could be seen but the flashes of the Confederate rifles. Of course, the enemy could see no better, and was firing at the noise of the trains on the pike. A little farther on, the road passed over a low wooded ridge, and as the Forty-first was coming to the summit, a squadron of Confederate cavalry galloped up from the right and reached the pike, which was filled with a double line of artillery and wagons. The cartridge boxes of the Forty-first were empty from the service of the day before, and bayonets were fixed for a charge on the cavalrymen. But the captain of a passing battery on the pike unlimbered a section on the other side of the wagon trains, and sent two or three shots among the cavalry, the teamsters of the wagon train clinging low down on the sides of their mules as they hurried by under the artilleryman's shells. The cavalry did not wait for the Forty-first, which had deployed and was coming on at a quick step.

Arrived at Franklin, the defensive lines were found to be well manned, and preparations still going on. The division was ordered across the Harpeth river as a reserve for the right and rear of the position in front of Franklin. Thus the Forty-first had no part in the severe battle which followed. During the day there were some indications of a Confederate attempt to work around the right and to the rear, but nothing came of it. The enemy was too severely punished in his attacks on the front to be very enterprising elsewhere. Wood's division held the crossing of the Harpeth river until the army had withdrawn after the battle, and the same day reached Nashville.

Since leaving Atlanta, the Forty-first had done some hard marching, the most rapid of which was below Chattanooga, and the most wearisome that between Athens and Nashville, which included night movements. The weather grew cold before the end of the marching, and at Columbia there was both cold and rain. The bivouac there, among the trains and the refugees, was one of the unpleasant ones to be remembered. The most notable event of the whole period was the night march along the Confederate front, which has been described. This was one of the extra-hazardous operations of the war, a very critical time for the army under Schofield. The failure to take advantage of the opportunity at Spring Hill decided the fate of Hood's campaign and his army.

Nashville was the base of supplies, and these were greatly needed. Here also was Thomas, energetically gathering forces to bring his command up to the strength required to beat back impetuous Hood. While this was in progress, the Forty-first had a brief season of rest. It was posted near the Granny White pike.

CHAPTER XVI.

A DECISIVE BATTLE.

The nucleus of the army with which Gen. Thomas fought and destroyed Hood's army was the Fourth and the Twenty-third Corps. The former was made up almost wholly of the veteran regiments of the Army of the Cumberland, which had served under Buell and Rosecrans. The Twenty-third was a newer organization, and was famous for the excellent flanking service it performed in the Atlanta campaign; but it was not strong in numbers. The two corps together were far too small for the task of encountering the Confederate army which had made Sherman's combined forces win almost every mile of the way from Chattanooga to Atlanta, meeting them in several general engagements, and putting their well-tried regiments to service as hard as had been found anywhere. No other army, no corps, was sent to Thomas; but he was set to create an army with the two corps as a nucleus. Troops from many places, unattached commands, regiments which had been on guard duty and the like, were gathered together to add to the effective force of the little army. These were the materials furnished to Thomas in preparation for the great work before him. And, with it all, the government at Washington was impatient and the newspaper generals at the North did not withhold their carping criticisms. An officer was on his way with orders to relieve Thomas, it was said, when that supreme folly was ended by the triumphant victory of Nashville.

The morning of the 15th of December, 1864, broke fair, but the weather had been damp and cold, and the ground was covered with a film of ice in many localities. By the preparations of the night before, it was expected to be the day of battle. The Forty-first was deployed as skirmishers and sent against the enemy's line about a brick house to the right of the Granny White pike. This line was well intrenched, with artillery, and behind it was a second line, also intrenched. The Forty-first was deployed behind a stone wall, beyond which, up to the enemy's line, the ground was open. The regiment went over the icy ground at a run, encountering a brisk fire, but unchecked. The line of works was carried with a rush, and two pieces of artillery and some prisoners fell into our hands. Beyond the brick house, the Confederates attempted to make a stand, but they were quickly put to flight again. The fighting was not all on one side; the enemy at first made a good defense and inflicted some loss. There was no further engagement that day.

On the 16th came the main battle. The Forty-first, with its brigade, moved up toward the Confederate position at Overton Knob, and passed some weary hours in waiting. The regiment was on high ground, a valley separating this from the higher Knob. The valley and Knob were thinly covered with wood. Finally, an assault was determined on. Artillery opened on the fortified line on the Knob, with a little effect. Some of the logs that crowned the earthworks were knocked out of place or splintered. There was no show of return fire from the enemy. After some minutes of this artillery practice, the brigade was ordered to the assault of the works, the Forty-first being again on the skirmish line. Its orders were to go as far as possible without the aid of the main line. The regiment moved briskly down the slope into the valley, and began the ascent of the long declivity stretching to the earthworks at the top. The enemy offered no resistance until the skirmishers were within about one hundred yards of the works; then he opened fire, but it was not severe in effect, and the skirmishers started on a run. It was seen that a line of abattis covered the works at about thirty yards distance; but no serious difficulty was expected in removing this before the main line should come up. When the skirmishers reached the abattis, it was found to be regularly constructed, and staked down— the only complete defence of this kind ever encountered by the regiment. There was no moving the abattis; it held the assailants under the fire from the works, unable to advance. They tugged ineffectually at the abattis a moment or two, and then threw themselves on the ground and opened fire on the works. These were well-made, and the logs along the top gave the defenders a good protection. While this was going on, two lines of infantry were seen to enter the works. Instantly they opened a tremendous fire on the assailants.

The line of battle behind could not advance to the skirmishers at the abattis. Some colored troops which had been sent in on the left were broken and thrown into confusion, and drifted over on to the ground behind the Forty-first, mingling with the troops there. That their officers did their best to hold these colored soldiers to the fight, is shown by the fact that nearly every one of the officers was killed or wounded. Col. Post, the brigade commander, was wounded and disabled, and the losses throughout the brigade were becoming heavy. Meantime several of the Forty-first skirmishers had penetrated the abattis by crawling through; private Kleinhaus, of I company, having thus forced a passage, ran up and leaped the works— a prisoner, of course. Col. Kimberly saw that the main line was making no headway, and could not; the attack on the left had failed entirely, and the colored men were no longer in the fight on their ground. The Forty-first was therefore withdrawn, but several men had passed the abattis, and these were left. The whole attacking force was in retreat. The regiment went back in skirmish line, as it had advanced, and rallied on the ground from which the assault started. The Confederate fire had slackened when this withdrawal was made, but it did not wholly cease as long as any men were in the valley.

While this severe and protracted fight was going on at Overton Knob, an advance and attack was ordered on the extreme right of the army. It was supposed that this would be favored by the concentration of the enemy on the Knob. However that may have been, the attack on the right succeeded, and instantly the backward movement was taken up along the whole Confederate line. The troops in the works at the Knob were seen to be moving, and a second advance was ordered, with the same brigade formation. Two of the Forty-first men who had penetrated the abattis in the first advance and been left there when the regiment fell back, were Sergeant Garrett of G company, and private Holcomb of A. These men, lying within twenty yards of the works, were first to know of the Confederate retreat; not waiting for the coming up of the new advance, they mounted the works. Some prisoners, four pieces of artillery and two battle flags fell into their hands. This artillery was afterward marked with the name of the Forty-first, by order of the chief of artillery of the army, and Gen. Thomas sent Garrett and Holcomb to Washington with their captured flags.

Of course, when the regiment came up to the works, the enemy was well started on his hasty retreat. The southern slope of the Knob, and the country beyond, were full of his retreating troops, going too rapidly to be overtaken, except by cavalry. The regiment moved some distance in the direction of the retreat, and then bivouacked, having been unable to come up with Hood's swiftly moving men. The pursuit was continued next day, but Thomas' cavalry were now in the lead on the road, and pushed the Confederates along far ahead of the reach of infantry. There were many complimentary reports of the cavalry, which permitted no stand of a Confederate force to cover the retreat. No sooner was a body of the enemy found in position to check the pursuit, than the cavalry charged and drove the harassed Confederates pell mell on their way. The Forty-first passed some fields by the roadside which were thickly strewn with the rifles of Hood's infantry, thrown down to lighten the load of the flying men. At Pulaski, a great quantity of ammunition and a piece or two of artillery were thrown into a pond, and at several points wagons from the trains were pulled off the road and abandoned.

When the Confederates turned their backs on Overton Knob, a decisive battle was over, for one of the combatants was never again to appear in the field. Hood's army was destroyed as a factor in the war of the rebellion. This was the army which had once shown itself before Louisville, and might have watered its horses in the Ohio river. Afterward it dealt a savage blow at Perryville, and swept Rosecrans' front from right to left at Stone River. Then it made Chickamauga a disastrous field for the same commander, and cooped him up in Chattanooga. It fought stubbornly at Mission Ridge against Grant's combined armies, and disputed with Sherman the road from Chattanooga to Atlanta, delivering several severe battles. Next it started for Nashville, and all the way was active, bold and enterprising. At Spring Hill it had Schofield's army in its grip, and lost it by only a narrow chance. At Franklin it made one of the fiercest battles of the war, and followed on to Nashville still bold and confident. But at Franklin its final opportunity passed. Nashville was strongly fortified, and abler generals than Hood, with stronger armies, might have beaten against it in vain. But Hood was yet bold and defiant. It remained for the matchless soldier Thomas to give the veteran Confederate army its quietus. He did this in an offensive battle which was without fault of generalship from beginning to end, exemplifying the best in the art of war from the opening skirmish to the vigorous pursuit of the beaten enemy, driven from the field never to reappear. How different this from the ineffective assault at Kenesaw, and the misdirected bloody battle at Pickett's Mills! The hand of a master was on the Union army at Nashville—yet at the very moment another man carried in his pocket an order to supersede that master in his command.

This was the last battle of the Forty-first, as it was the last in all the region it had traversed back and forth since 1862. But its service was not over.

CHAPTER XVII.

AFTER THE CAMPAIGNS.

Following the battle of Nashville came hard marching and rough weather. The pursuit was carried far beyond Pulaski, and there was rain and sleet, while the country was wild and the roads heavy. Some miles beyond Pulaski, during a day's halt, the Forty-first was sent on an expedition against a marauding cavalry force which was reported to have a rendezvous in the vicinity. It was near night when the designated point had been found and the country examined, and the return march was in the dark, over roads which were mere bridle paths in a wilderness, and often obstructed with fallen timber. Half the night was spent in wandering about in the woods, trying to follow the route. A storm of rain and sleet set in during this time; the march was thus made a trying one in several ways. When the regiment finally reached its bivouac, it was long past midnight, and the men were not only worn out with marching, but wet and cold. Toward morning the weather became much colder. The regiment was in no condition to move next day with the rest of the command, and was left behind to thaw out and dry itself, and recuperate.

The pursuit of Hood had ended. There was no longer a hope of encountering any of his army, which was largely scattered through the country to the southward, and nowhere in the field as an organization. The Fourth Corps was now destined for Huntsville, Alabama, and the march to that point was made without notable incident. The Forty-first was put in camp some miles below Huntsville, on a fine wooded ridge—an excellent camping-ground. Permanent winter quarters were constructed, and much care was taken in the work. A cotton gin house near by afforded some lumber for floors and the like, but the main reliance was on puncheons split from the abundant timber in the vicinity.

The Forty-first was not to pass the remaining winter months at rest, however. There was an order, afterward countermanded, for the corps to go northward, Nashville being its first destination. Artillery and trains were to be sent across country to the Tennessee somewhere near Tuscumbia; and the troops were to go by rail. The Forty-first, which, under General Stanley, was not likely to miss its share of undesirable service, was detailed to take the artillery and trains in charge for the march. The regiment was small for the duty, and the Forty-ninth Ohio, a strong regiment, was added to Col. Kimberly's command. The march was by way of Athens, and so on across to the Tennessee. Trains and artillery together stretched out for several miles on the road when well closed up, and an obstruction, even a rod or two of bad road, might double that length. The infantry must be disposed mainly in front and rear. All together it was a hard service. When Duck river was reached, it was to be forded; but the stream was swollen and rising. It seemed best to get over at once, lest fording should be impossible after a few hours. The crossing was made, and the march continued after dark, to get a favorable place for bivouac. Just after the halt was made, a courier from Stanley appeared with a dispatch ordering the immediate return of the whole body, and warning Col. Kimberly that Roddy's Confederate cavalry was in the vicinity of Duck river or beyond, with the purpose of attacking the train. Strict injunctions to be vigilant and to lose no time in returning, were added; and finally there was a specific order not to cross the river under any circumstances. This last order came too late; the whole command, trains and all, was several miles beyond the river when the courier arrived. What information about Roddy the general had, was never known. The fact was that neither then nor afterward were there indications of the presence of any force of the enemy in the neighborhood of the command. But no time was lost in recrossing the river next morning, which, fortunately, it was possible to do. The return march was made with due diligence, and with but one incident worth mention. Several mornings, before the day's march was taken up, Col. Kimberly was besieged by citizens from the country near by, with complaints of the taking of animals by men from the trains. Men would start out ahead of the column in the morning to prowl about the country during the day, and return at night. The complaining citizens were ready to claim protection as loyal men, and some of them brought vouchers for forage furnished a year or more before to a Union cavalry force which went through that region. Kimberly resolved to stop the plundering, and made a detail from the Forty-first, under a trusty lieutenant, to march before day, and take post at a bridge a few miles in advance. Most of the stragglers through the country would come to this bridge for a crossing, and the lieutenant was to arrest all who came up ahead of the column. The first man to come up was a commissary belonging to corps headquarters. He was promptly stopped and detained, in spite of vigorous protest. When Kimberly came along with the column, he placed the commissary in arrest and ordered him to the rear of his train. After arrival at the camp near Huntsville, he was released from arrest, and at once complained to Gen. Stanley, with a charge that an overissue of two day's rations had been made to the infantry on the march. Stanley sent for Kimberly, telling him of the charge. The latter produced a handful of the old forage vouchers brought in by the citizens along the road, which were given by Stanley's own command. Nothing more was heard about over-feeding the Forty-first.

About the first of March, Lieut. Col. Kimberly was promoted to Colonel of a regiment just raised for Hancock's corps, then in the Shenandoah Valley, and turned over the command of the Forty-first to Major Holloway, who continued its commander until the final muster out.

When a part of the forces about Huntsville were to be sent to Texas in the summer of 1865 it fell to the lot of the Forty-first to be selected for that unwelcome service. The government had many new and strong regiments which would have been glad of the Texas trip instead of a muster out. It seemed, therefore, a mistake to send regiments which had faithfully served for more than three years, and, having enlisted "for three years or during the war," were anxious to go home when the war was over.

CHAPTER XVIII.

DOWN IN TEXAS.

The Third Division of the Fourth Army Corps was ordered to Texas in June, 1865. It was transported to Johnsonville, Tenn., embarked on steamers, and on the morning of June 18, started down the Tennessee river en route to New Orleans. About 2 o'clock on the morning of the 19th, the fleet reached Cairo. The Forty-first was on the steamer Echo No. 2, and while the boat was rounding to, she collided with the monitor Oneida, which was anchored in the stream. Eight feet of the Echo's hull just forward of her boilers was crushed in, and she filled in a few moments. In less than ten minutes from the time of collision the boat went down. Fortunately she was lying close to the Monitor, and the men quickly escaped. There were 320 soldiers on board, and but one man was lost. But nothing was saved of the regimental effects, and the men came off with clothing barely sufficient to cover them—not always that. They were taken off the Monitor and landed in Cairo, and there the division quartermaster soon had the command outfitted anew. At 10 o'clock of the same morning the regiment went aboard the steamer Atlantic, then loading for New Orleans. The loss of regimental and company papers by the sinking of the Echo was irreparable, and caused great and serious trouble ever afterward.

The voyage down the Mississippi went on at once. The Atlantic was detached from the fleet at Memphis, as she carried freight and passengers for various points below. On the afternoon of the 24th, the boat reached New Orleans, and the Forty-first was marched to Camp Chalmet, seven miles south of the city, remaining there about two weeks. Here the lost arms and accoutrements of the men were replaced. July 7th, the regiment embarked on a steamer for Indianola, Texas, and that place was reached on the 11th. On the 13th, the regiment marched for Green Lake, moving in the night time to escape the scorching sun of the daylight hours.

This place in Southern Texas is in the cattle raising country, and there were few inhabitants besides the herdsmen. There was little to do, with opportunity to indulge in hunting and fishing, with now and then the shooting of a twenty-two-foot alligator. But the regiment suffered much from the intermittent fever known as "bone break fever."

On the 11th of September, the regiment marched for San Antonio. The first day of this march was, perhaps, the severest the regiment ever encountered. The sun was intensely hot, and the men fainted and fell out by the score. A flood of rain fell about 10 o'clock, and the dry prairie was turned into sheets of water. On the 23d, the regiment went into camp seven miles from San Antonio, where it remained until the 25th of October, when it was ordered to Galveston. A march was made to Alleton, where railroad transportation was obtained to Galveston, which city was reached on the night of November 2d. On the 5th, the regiment embarked for New Orleans. The Texas affair was over, and the troops were being withdrawn for discharge.

About the middle of November the Forty-first reached Columbus, and on the 26th of the month was mustered out of service. It had been in service four years and one month, and had borne on its rolls about 1,500 men from first to last.

A brief recapitulation: The Forty-first took part in the battle of Shiloh; in the campaign and slight fighting about Corinth; in the Kentucky campaign after Bragg, but was not engaged at Perryville; in the pursuit over the Wildcat Mountains; in the battle of Stone River; in the Tullahoma campaign; in the Chickamauga campaign and battle; in the Brown's Ferry, Orchard Knob and Mission Ridge engagements about Chattanooga; in the East Tennessee expedition to relieve Knoxville; in the Atlanta campaign, leading in the severest battle of that campaign; in the campaign after Hood, to Nashville, and in the victorious battle at that place, and in the toilsome pursuit of Hood afterward; and passed the last months of its service in Texas. In all this time and service, says Hazen in his "Narrative of Military Service," the regiment "never failed to respond to every call, and never failed to punish an enemy who attacked it."

CHAPTER XIX.

THE CAMP FIRE.

One of the notable personal incidents in the life of the Forty-first was the capture of W. A. Fetterly, of I company, and his escape from Andersonville. Fetterly was a very successful forager, and had many adventures while engaged in hunting up supplies from the country for the headquarters mess. When he returned empty-handed, there was nothing in the region roundabout. But he went out once too often, and was caught and taken to Andersonville. The story of that prison pen has been often told, and when Fetterly returned from it he was a living example of its terrors of hunger. He was thin and hollow-eyed, weak and worn—almost a wreck. But he had had strength enough to make his escape. He eluded pursuit by keeping to the bed of a stream for a long distance, thus destroying the scent for the dogs. He came to the regiment while it was lying at Atlanta. A native brought Fetterly into camp in a wagon; the native sitting in front and driving, while Fetterly sat behind, with a cavalryman's carbine across his knees. It was the persuasiveness of the carbine that made the native willing.

Perhaps the unluckiest man in the regiment was private Theodore Hawley, of G company. He made his way alone to the front and joined the regiment at Savannah the day before the Shiloh battle. In his first two battles, he was wounded before firing a shot, and each time was condemned to a long spell in hospitals and convalescent camps. He joined the regiment from the second of these enforced absences, on the day of the crossing of Peach Tree Creek, near Atlanta. The regiment crossed at dusk, and during the night threw up a strong earthwork. It was Hawley's first experience in this work, and he was very proud of the work in front of his company. When the gray dawn came, he was on the parapet, smoothing the surface and tamping it down. A sergeant called to him to come down, as the enemy's pickets would soon be firing. The warning was a moment too late, for as the sergeant spoke, a rifle ball came whizzing by, and took off the fingers of one of Hawley's hands. He jumped down behind the works, and tears rolled down his cheeks as he exclaimed that he was ruined for the army at last, and had not fired a shot for the flag. He had fought his way to the regiment when he joined it first; twice he had fought his way back to it through convalescent camps and provost guards; and this was the end of it all.

The command against leaving ranks in the march was so constantly repeated that it became like a worn out song. "No falling out for water" was the common form. When the men for the Brown's Ferry expedition were getting into the toppling pontoons, one of the wags of the regiment called out, "No falling out for water." This is one from Col. Wiley's store of humorous incidents.

Among the first to come into prominence as wags was Lieut. Harry Jones, of E company. If he ever had a serious moment, it was not discovered. In the quarters at Camp Dennison, one evening when Col. Hazen was absent, Jones organized an entertainment that was as full of fun as he could pack it. But it was also productive of noise that could be heard far beyond the limits of the regiment's quarters. When the officer of the day appeared, all was still and decorous as a Quaker meeting, and Jones was trying to torture his face into a serious expression. He looked incredulous when the officer of the day spoke of the tumult that was raging in those quarters a moment before; and finally, with much gravity, Jones called the officer whose quarters were next in line, and asked, "Captain, did you hear any noise about here a few minutes ago?"

At Rocky Face Ridge one night, the regiment lay in a wood directly under the precipitous face of the ridge. In the morning, the men were cautioned to put out fires at daylight, that the enemy's fire might not be drawn by smoke rising above the tree tops. One of the messes had a little colored boy who was its boast because he never failed to come up with his coffee. He was on hand that morning, and after he had served his mess, he started to make a pot of coffee for himself. He was squatting down blowing the fire to boil his coffee, when a Confederate bullet struck the tin pot, scattered the fire in all directions, and passed between the little darkey's legs. He sprang up, and with a single word, "Zip!" started straight to the rear on a run. He could be seen for three quarters of a mile, still at full speed, and he may be going yet, for he never returned to the regiment.

Brevet honors were slow in reaching the Western armies; it was said that all the hospital stewards in the East had been brevetted before any came as far west as Tennessee. A batch came at last, and the army being within reach of Nashville, the favored officers were soon seen in new uniforms. Possibly they seemed more numerous because none had been seen before; and some thought the business a little overdone. This was no doubt the opinion of a teamster who was heard one day swearing at his mules as "Brevet horses."

After the fall of Atlanta, there was an order to forage the country, and the Forty-first one day sent out a regular detail. One of the men was a private of K company whose rations were always short. Three or four miles out, this man was missed, but when the detail was returning toward evening, he was found in a fence corner, with the remains of a half-grown pig beside a fire. He had been there the better part of the day, and he was so full of fresh pork, roasted on his bayonet, that he could scarcely get up off the ground. His sergeant watched him struggling to his feet, and asked what ailed him. He pointed to the half-eaten pig and said faintly, "Makes me svell up like a leetle bup." For once his rations had held out.

While the Forty-first held the front line at Stone River, a caisson of Cotterell's battery, just to the left of the regiment, was blown up by a shell from the enemy. It was a tremendous affair in noise and appearance, but the injury to the men was surprisingly small. Cotterell's battery always had a warm place with the Forty-first.

Perhaps nothing in the history of the regiment spoke more or better for the general faithfulness of the men, than their prompt return from veteran furlough. They simply shut their eyes to all the enjoyments of home, and went cheerfully back to the Southern wildernesses. It proved that they went to even harder service than they had known before.

The large men of the regiment were mostly in A, B and F companies, though H had some, and also I. Perhaps E had most men of medium and small stature, but it was a very hardy company. It came, more largely than the other companies, from the city.

Only one detail for guard service in the rear ever fell to the Forty-first. That was at Columbia on the Hood campaign, when it was sent across the river to look after the trains of the army and the roads on the left, while the main body was in position on the front. This one experience of the rear of an army was enough. At this time the ground occupied by trains and guard was overrun by the black refugees who were trying to get back with the army, believing that the Yankees were being driven off by Mas' Hood, never to return. These people had no lofty ideas of freedom, but they were drawn to the Union side as the needle to the pole. Born and raised in that country, they hesitated not a moment to cast in their fortunes with the strangers who had come down there to fight their former masters. No lures were held out by the national forces, as none were possible; the refugees were kindly treated, but they were much in the way, and the army had no desire to encourage their congregating about its rear. A very large part of the refugees was made up of women, many of the men having been taken off into the Southern service with their masters.

A number of negro servants were with the regiment from first to last. With regimental headquarters was Thomason, a barber in Cleveland before the war. When the army moved from Louisville to Camp Wickliff, Thomason somehow fell in rear and was arrested and jailed in Louisville as a fugitive slave. It cost some trouble, but he was rescued and went on with the regiment. Another headquarter servant, a fairly intelligent fellow, was taken North from

Louisville by an officer going home, in the days before emancipation, and when negroes were closely watched. This man was told of the hazard, and provided with food that he might keep in hiding on the steamer from Louisville to Cincinnati. However he may have regarded freedom in the North, he could not keep himself out of sight on the steamer, but boldly presented himself at the servants' table for meals. He had a narrow escape from being put ashore in Kentucky for return to Louisville as a fugitive. Still another headquarters servant was captured at the Chattahoochie river. He was with his master in the Southern army; but he transferred his allegiance without demonstration of any kind, and made a most useful servant for many a day. Some of the company messes at different times had negro cooks. Often they were faithful and venturesome in coming up to the front when the regiment was facing the enemy; and almost without exception they were useful and convenient.

The only association the regiment ever had with colored troops was at the battle of Nashville. What happened there has been told elsewhere. Several officers of the Forty-first were given colored commands, and served with them with credit; but so far as this regiment had opportunity to observe, the previous condition of the negro was too great an obstacle to his armed service. At Nashville, for instance, there was little doubt that the Confederate fight had extra vigor when it was directed against Steadman's colored regiments. Their presence introduced an element of bitterness that would have been otherwise lacking.

Of all food supplies found in the country, the most valuable and most palatable was the hog. Chickens were too few to go around, but on several occasions stores of hams were captured and made a welcome relief from the army ration of bacon. A half-grown pig will go farther than a flock of hens, and as a rule will be better enjoyed. Of vegetables, the principal was the small red sweet-potato, very small and not very sweet. The men got tired of these long before the war ended.

The association of the Forty-first with other troops was not greatly varied, though there were several changes of brigade organization. This regiment remained to the last the representative and nucleus of the original organization at Camp Wickliff in the winter of 1861-62—the Nineteenth brigade, Army of the Ohio. Other regiments came and went, but the Forty-first remained; and, save for the short interval between Atlanta and the Nashville fight, the brigade was always commanded by an officer from the Forty-first. This would not have happened so, had the regular succession to command been left undisturbed when Gen. Hazen was transferred to the Army of the Tennessee. The command of the brigade should at that time have fallen to Col. O. H. Payne, of the One Hundred and Twenty-fourth Ohio. His resignation while Col. Post was in command, left the brigade to fall to Lieut. Col. Kimberly when Post was wounded in the Nashville battle; and this command continued until the end of the fighting period.

The regiments longest associated with the Forty-first in brigade organization were the Ninth Indiana and the Sixth Kentucky. Neither Col. Suman, of the Ninth, nor Col. Whitaker, of the Sixth, was able to get along with Hazen except with some friction. No trouble of this kind was found with the lieutenant-colonel of either of these regiments. Col. Payne, of the One Hundred and Twenty-fourth, of course had no difficulty in keeping on pleasant terms with the brigade commander. No more had Col. Berry, of the Fifth Kentucky; Col. Langdon, of the First Ohio; Col. Foy, of the Twenty-third Kentucky; Col. Bowman, of the Ninety-third Ohio, and some others who at different times were in Hazen's brigade. Perhaps the Ninety-third Ohio, next to the One Hundred and Twenty-fourth, was the regiment with which the Forty-first was in closest association. These two regiments formed one of the battalions of the brigade, with the First Ohio, during the Atlanta campaign. Their fortunes were therefore the same during that long and tedious struggle; and certainly the Forty-first never found occasion to complain of its companion regiments in any duty. Berry's Fifth Kentucky is remembered as an active and efficient command, and Col. Foy, of the Twenty-third Kentucky, had the respect of all in his command of his brave regiment. Payne's One Hundred and Twenty-fourth Ohio, coming from the section in which the Forty-first was raised, was like its own people to that regiment. These regiments were closest in sympathy of all that served in the brigade at any time. The Seventy-first Ohio and the Twenty-seventh Kentucky were hardly long enough in the command to become well acquainted.

As to association with commanders above the brigade, the regiment's first experience was not pleasant. Something of Nelson, the division commander, has already been said. A fairly illustrative incident may be given here. Col. Hazen was absent from Camp Wickliff when the order came to move, and the brigade rightfully belonged to one of the two Indiana colonels, Fitch and Slack. But Nelson had a quarrel—all his own—with both of these officers, and would recognize neither as in command in Hazen's absence. So the division general sent for the brigade adjutant, who found him sitting in his big Sibley tent, coatless and stretched in a chair before the fire. None of the customary civilities were offered to the adjutant, who stood patiently while Nelson framed this verbal command: "I want you to put three days' cooked rations in haversacks, and have Hazen's brigade on the road at 6 o'clock in the morning, to wait my august arrival, sir!" The adjutant asked if Col. Slack was in command, and was met with a storm of denial wild enough to blow a man out of the tent. After Nelson, the division fell to Wm. Sooy Smith for a brief spell, and then to Gen. Palmer. Smith's command was too short to leave any lasting impression. Palmer led the division at Stone River and Chickamauga. He was always popular with his command. The men not only had confidence in his soldierly ability, but they were attracted by his unpretentious, kindly manner, and his evident consideration for the welfare and comfort of the whole command. He had no favorites and showed no partialities—a man from the people and still of the people, a fine type of the American soldier. As to his military qualities, it has already been said in this book that he was one of the very few men without a West Point education who maintained themselves creditably in the higher commands of the army. All the men of that division hold John M. Palmer in affectionate remembrance.

Gen. Thomas J. Wood commanded the division on the Atlanta campaign and thereafter to the end of the fighting service. He was a regular army officer, but thoroughly appreciative of the volunteer soldiery—a careful, considerate man, knowing well his duty and looking constantly to proper discipline, yet always kind. He held the unquestioning confidence of his men, in all regards, and he had a soldierly pride in his division which prompted him to untiring care for it. When, on the Atlanta campaign, he thought his division was too often called on for service that others might share, he did not hesitate to protest in its behalf. His men thought no division of the army had a better commander, and few as good a one. It was easy for him to get the best service his men were capable of.

Above the grade of division general, the regiment was under Crittenden, the typical, courtly, but unfortunate Kentuckian—remembered yet with kindly feeling. Then came, for a brief season, Gordon Granger—too short a stay to become well acquainted. Next Gen. O. O. Howard, well known by reputation before he came to the West. But association with a corps commander is remote at best, and leaves no such vivid recollections as are called up by the name of the division general. There was nothing but good feeling toward Gen. Howard—a conscientious soldier, a kind and courteous gentleman. The last of the corps commanders, Gen. D. S. Stanley, has already been spoken of in the narrative of the Atlanta and Nashville campaigns. Nobody in the Forty-first questioned his ability as a general, but all felt that his unfortunate quarrel with Hazen was also unfortunate for the regiment and the brigade. Except at Nashville, the Forty-first had no fighting under his command.

Coming finally to the army commanders, it is to be said that the men believed in Buell, were uncertain and a little fearful of Rosecrans, and idolized Thomas. Grant and Sherman were farther away, and were known almost wholly by reputation. It was generally believed in the regiment that Grant's army was surprised at Shiloh, and would have fared badly the second day, but for Buell; but nobody believed the absurd newspaper stories about Grant after the battle. Between Sherman and Thomas, in any position, the

JOHN M. PALMER

THOMAS J. WOOD

choice would always be the latter with the men who served under both. It was known that Thomas did not favor the assault at Kennesaw mountain, and it went to his credit with the soldiers. The story went about that the Kennesaw fight was to show the enemy that the Union troops would assault fortified lines. Thomas thought such a demonstration unnecessary; yet when the time came, he did not hesitate to assault the strongly intrenched lines at Nashville. In both instances, the event sustained his judgment; he made a grand success of his assault, while that at Kennesaw was a costly failure. No proof was needed that the troops who had swept the enemy off Mission Ridge would attack fortifications on occasion.

One of the persistent faults of army commanders, following the traditions of the military art, was in the maintenance of secrecy about movements—this at all times, not alone when some critical enterprise was afoot, demanding great care that it be kept from any possibility of disclosure to the enemy. This habit of secrecy is a survival from the ancient system, and, whatever may have been in its favor some centuries ago and with an unintelligent soldiery, it was distinctly hurtful on several occasions during the war. A good illustration was afforded by the actions at and before Mission Ridge. The Orchard Knob fight might have been over much sooner than it was, and at less loss, if the purpose of the movement had been made known, at least to regimental commanders, before it was started. But there were no orders, and the Forty-first and Ninety-third were held for some minutes under fire, to no purpose. Had Col. Wiley been directed to drive in the Confederate pickets and their reserves, he would have made shorter work of it. But when the skirmishers had developed a heavy force in front, whose position and strength could not be determined except by attack, no regimental commander could know whether it was the general's intention to bring on an engagement. The same thing occurred when the troops were ordered to take the rifle pits at the foot of Mission Ridge, with no orders further, and found that they could neither remain at that point nor retreat from it without great loss. It would probably be found throughout all the armies, as it was in the experience of the Forty-first, that the most effective service was obtained when the orders were specific and the purpose of the movement was made known. With such troops as were in the Union armies, the better they are informed as to what is expected of them, and the resistance likely to be encountered, the better they will perform. Examples proving this are afforded by the Brown's Ferry affair and the battle of Pickett's Mills.

From first to last, the regiment traveled a great deal by steamboat. First, was the voyage up the Ohio river to Gallipolis, and the trip from that place to Louisville. Next the voyage down the Ohio and up the Cumberland to Nashville. Then came the voyage down from East Tennessee on veteran furlough; and last, the long voyage down the Mississippi to New Orleans and from there to Texas. None of these were pleasure trips, or productive of enjoyment in any way. The most uncomfortable railroad travel, perhaps, was the short ride from Chattanooga to Athens, on the Hood campaign to Nashville.

There were several bright spots in the commissary line, by unusual supplies from the country. The most notable of these was the camp near Reynolds Station while rebuilding the railroad just before Bragg's Kentucky campaign. The Confederate colonel's plantation afforded more luxuries than were found in any other place. The East Tennessee march, though a hard one in many ways, brought some good feeding from the country. The long Atlanta campaign yielded little in this way. Of actual and prolonged hunger, the only experience was at Chattanooga after the Chickamauga battle. The thirst on the second day of that battle was worse than any hunger. There was some of this, not so severe, in the Kentucky campaign.

The dead of the Forty-first lie in graves that stretch from Ohio to Texas. The places where the greater numbers are buried are: Shiloh, 40; Murfreesboro, 36; Chattanooga, 87; Nashville, 36. Four are buried in the Andersonville prison grounds. Those given above are mainly men killed in action or died of wounds. Many were buried at Louisville and other points, from hospitals. Thirty-seven who were killed in action at Pickett's Mills, or died of wounds received there, have been removed to cemeteries in other places; and some killed in the minor actions of the Atlanta campaign are scattered along the route. A total of 178 men were killed in action or died of wounds. The killed and wounded at Shiloh were 38 per cent. of the men engaged; at Stone River, 27 per cent.; and at Pickett's Mills, over 40 per cent. At the latter battle, one company (H) lost over 90 per cent. of its men, and another company (K) over 81 per cent.

Beyond comparison, the Atlanta campaign was the severest the regiment was engaged in. This was not alone because of long continuance, but also because of the unintermitted close contact with the enemy from Dallas nearly to Atlanta. The effect of this service was to reduce the number present for duty from 331 at the opening of the campaign, to 99 when it ended—about four months. Perhaps the most severe shorter marches were that of one day on the return to Chattanooga after the Atlanta campaign, when thirty miles were covered; the expedition after cavalry below Pulaski in the winter of the Nashville campaign; and one hot day's march in Texas. In the Kentucky campaign after Bragg, there were several night movements, always a severe strain on the men.

Most of the men who came home for muster out were left with more or less disability, often latent and to be developed in after years. There is a notion that army service toughens men and does not wear them out. Whatever foundation there may be for this notion, nothing of the kind was evident in the experience of the Forty-first. The severe demands of the service left almost all of the men permanently weakened, as perhaps all long-continued excesses must do.

In its quartermaster and commissary service, the Forty-first was always fortunate. There were at all times competent and energetic officers in those departments, and more than once it happened that the regiment was supplied when others were in more or less want. Of course, such lack as that at Chattanooga during the siege by Bragg, was not in any way connected with the efficiency of the quartermaster and commissary staff; but there were times when such officers as the Forty-first had were able to do much for the comfort of the regiment.

The regimental association of survivors was organized in 1868 and holds annual reunions. These have been held at various places, but in the last year or two, opinion seems to have settled on Cleveland as a central and accessible point. That city was therefore chosen for the reunions of 1896 and 1897. The survivors are widely scattered, some too far away to join the reunions. Nevertheless, these are always times of great enjoyment—reunions, often, of comrades separated for thirty years or more.

Largely through the efforts and attention of Gen. Wiley, a regimental monument has been erected to mark the position of the Forty-first at Chickamauga. It is one of many put up by different regiments on that field. The deeds of the regiment are thus recorded in stone on two fields—Stone River, in the brigade monument, and Chickamauga.

CHAPTER XX.

IN EIGHTEEN HUNDRED AND SIXTY-ONE.

Today, a scattered band of old men sit before their fires and stretch their stiffening joints, and, laying their heads back on the cushioned chair, fall into youth and vigor as the world fades out and the past lives again.

There is a tumult in the land. Rumors of gathering armies and insults to the fathers' flag are flying thick and fast. On farms and on the roads, in shop and school and at the fireside, the darkening clouds bear down. Then, here and there, little knots of men talk of the threatening storm, until earnestness grows into impatient desire, and desire into resolve, and resolve into action. From Wayne and Columbiana, from Trumbull and Geauga, from Lorain and Huron and Ottawa, and from divers others, they come to join the Cuyahoga men in marching to the rescue. They enter on the new life cheerfully and with good heart, making no murmur at its hardships, and accepting its surprises and disappointments without faltering. The machine of army discipline galls here and there, but this they make light of—they are out to end the war, not for pleasure.

They are at the front. The baptism of fire comes suddenly at Shiloh, and the ranks are stripped almost before they realize that they are in battle. The colors go down once, twice, half a dozen times, but always there is a new hand to raise the flag undismayed. There's many a gap that never will be filled—there's many a comrade gone forever.

Then, if any duty can be ignoble, they come upon such now in long days of fatigue detail, in march, in sickness, in unsheltered nights of storm. So they drift on to Corinth, and down through Mississippi, and back into Tennessee, and up to Louisville in a long race for the lead. Then down to the mountains, and back through cold and snow and rain, and finally to Nashville again. Out to Stone River, to stand on the only part of the line not overwhelmed, and leave six score comrades there.

A period of rest, and then on through the hot country toward Chattanooga, and down to Chickamauga. An ineffective, costly battle the first day, a successful defense the second day, with the tortures of thirst and the enemy on every side. Back to Chattanooga, to hunger a month, and then to steal down the river in the night and smite Longstreet's men closing the northern door. Over to Orchard Knob, opening the battles that were to free Chattanooga, and on to the glorious triumph of Mission Ridge. Up into inhospitable East Tennessee in winter weather, with feet half shod, to stand in snow and slush for reconsecration; and then a blessed respite at home.

Again at the front, veterans! Southward, past spiteful Rocky Face and tangled Resaca, and on along the footsore route to Atlanta. At Pickett's Mills, a bloody burial of brave endeavor—an offering without an altar, a hopeless sacrifice. Locked in close grip with the foe at morning, noon and night, some weeks of struggle till Atlanta is reached and won, with men enough left in ranks to make a company, no more.

A breathing-spell, and then away once more after Hood; up to Chattanooga, twenty, thirty miles a day; over to Athens, then the race for Nashville, holding off outnumbering enemies, running the narrow chance at Spring Hill, guarding flank and rear at Franklin, at last sheltered under Nashville's forts. Two weeks of waiting and then the crowning battle of the middle West—Overton Knob a capture, with cannon and prisoners, and in front only flying crowds of men who had been the opposing army. Next some toilsome service in the wilderness, a little rest at Huntsville, and a journey bent southward which should have been toward home when the war was over.

Again and again the visions pass, not always of the grand events, the march, the battle, the campaign. Here, at Pickett's Mills, a soldier lies prone on his back, scarce out of the sweep of balls that fly above him. Prone on his back and with closed eyes;

yet not dead. On his left breast a darker stain spreads and spreads over his army shirt, as his life pours out in the crimson spring. Above the earthworks on the hill to the right the sun's last rays are shining, but in the valley where the soldier lies, twilight is coming on. * * * In a fair Ohio home a mother lifts her baby boy and holds him close to a soldier's picture on the mantel. In the tree tops about the house the sun's last rays are lingering, and twilight comes. "Kiss papa good night till he comes home again," she says. * * * It is the self-same hour, on the battlefield and in the home; and the soldier-father's long good night is said.

Still the visions pass. Here is a lofty ridge, smoke-crowned but a moment ago, where thousands of blue blouses are gathering about their trophies of flags and cannon—treading on air, those exulting captors. Here is another height, reached by a difficult and obstructed way, but rich in spoils of the enemy who had turned his face forever from the fight. One by one the visions come and go— of battle smokes, of victorious attacks and triumphant defenses, of sudden dash and stubborn long resistance, of flags waving in sulphurous air, of comrades dead and dying, of hungry days and shelterless times of rain and cold, of captured arms, of brave endeavor not always with reward, of patient vigils in the wakeful night, of tardy news from home——.

But all this belongs to the times of eighteen hundred and sixty-one.

CHAPTER XXI.

"TO THE COLORS!"

Some facts concerning the flags of the Forty-first are not easy to determine at this late period. It seems to be fairly well settled that the first flag (the national colors) came from the Chardon Light Guards, and the second one from the ladies of Geauga county. In the early headquarter records is a letter from L. C. Ludlow, secretary of the Chardon Light Guards, asking what time would be convenient for presentation of a flag from that corps. This letter is dated "Recorder's Office, Geauga County, Oct. 24, 1861," and calls the flag proposed to be presented a "regimental banner." Under date of October 26, Col. Hazen replies, suggesting that the presentation be made on Monday, Oct. 28, as the regiment expected to move on the 29th. A file of the Geauga county paper, the Jeffersonian Democrat, is kept in the county auditor's office, and Comrade Silo P. Warriner has found in this file an extended account of the presentation. A jointed silver ferule on the staff of the flag bore this inscription:

"Presented to the 41st Regt., O. V. I., by the Chardon Light Guards of Geauga County, O., 1861." Then follows the account: "The regiment being drawn up in line, the flag was borne by the Chardon Light Guards in procession to the front, where it was handed to Col. Hazen. Company C, Captain Cole, being the color company, was called to the front and the flag handed to the color sergeant, when Company C marched back to the line. The regiment then formed on three sides of a square, and Judge M. C. Canfield, of Chardon, addressed them." Judge Canfield's address was eloquent and stirring, and the paper reports it at some length. The reply of Col. Hazen was as follows:

Gentlemen of the Chardon Light Guards and Citizens of Geauga County:—I am glad to meet you here today, to thank you for what your county has done for this regiment. She has furnished many men of whom we are all proud, of whom you and the country should be proud. You have come here today to present us the emblem of our country's greatness. We thank you for it, and will never tarnish the splendor of its purity. We are soon to leave you, perhaps some of us not to return; it is probably better that we all should not; but go where we will, we know your hearts go with us, and such as do return are sure of a hospitable welcome. We will do our duty, and may no one disinherit the greeting so dear to the soldier when the battle is over.

In behalf of the regiment, I thank you heartily for the happy compliment just paid them, and must bid you now adieu."

The flag thus presented is now in possession of Mr. Hunt, at his house in Geauga county. How long it was carried by the regiment, or why it was laid aside and found its way to its present location, is not known. An apparent error in the newspaper account quoted may be explained. Captain Cole's company is spoken of as receiving the flag as the color company. Wiley's company served as color company, but this may not have been the original arrangement. In the regimental records, under date of Nov. 2, 1861, appears a letter from Col. Hazen to the Adjutant-General of the State, proposing the following arrangement of companies: "1. Capt. Tolles'; 2. Capt. Bushnell's; 3. Capt. Cole's; 4. Capt. Stone's; 5. Capt. Wiley's; 6. Capt. Leslie's; 7. Capt. Hamblin's; 8. Capt. Pease's; 9. Capt. Williston's; 10. Capt. Goodsell's." It will be seen that this does not correspond with the final arrangement of the companies in line.

A flag came from the ladies of Geauga county, and this is now in the flag room at Columbus. On the staff is inscribed: "Presented to the 41st Regiment, O. V. I., by the Ladies of Geauga County." There can be no question about the service done by this flag; it was carried until it had almost ceased to be a flag, torn by shell and bullet, even the staff chipped and marred. It was probably presented for the ladies in a letter from Mr. J. O. Converse; but the date and circumstances are lost. The first color sergeant of the regiment was H. M. Billings, who says that the Chardon Light

Guard flag was presented before he was detailed as color-bearer, and that the two stands of colors were in the color box on the way to Shiloh.   There was also a large bunting flag, the regulation garrison flag, which was presented to the regiment by Gen. M. D. Leggitt and wife, one Sunday afternoon at Camp Wood.   This flag was loaned to some committee at the Northern Ohio Sanitary Fair at Cleveland, during the regiment's veteran furlough, and was not afterward in possession of the regiment.   These three flags may be taken as the original flags of the Forty-first.

At Chattanooga, during the siege by Bragg, Col. Wiley received a flag which he had ordered in Cincinnati, and he presented it to the regiment one evening at dress parade near the railroad cut which was the regiment's line.   Col. Hazen and some other officers happened to be passing as Wiley was handing over the colors. This was the regulation colors, and on it was embroidered the names of the principal battles of the regiment.

Gen. Hazen presented the regiment with a large and handsome banner, which at the time of presentation bore the names of Shiloh, Stone River and Chickamauga.   At the first regimental reunion after the war, an order was read from the general of the army, giving permission to put the names of other battles on this banner.   A committee was appointed, and Mrs. Capt. James McMahon was chosen to add the names.   She did the work beautifully by hand, in silk embroidery.   The added names were those of the battles after Chickamauga—Brown's Ferry, Mission Ridge, Resaca, Pickett's Mills, Nashville, etc.   This banner is now in possession of the regimental association.

On more than one occasion, the Forty-first responded to the call, "To the colors!"   Conspicuously at Orchard Knob and Mission Ridge the colors were advanced and the regiment rallied about them in the face of the enemy.   With the relics in the flag-room at Columbus are the captured flag of the Twenty-eighth Alabama Confederate regiment, presented by the ladies of Selma, and several battle-flags or guidons.

CHAPTER XXII.

A STATEMENT BY SURGEON ALBERT G. HART.

While the Regiment was at Chattanooga, Tennessee, in January, 1864, after two years and four months of service, and was completing the re-enlistment papers, the company commanders furnished the data from which was compiled the following table. It illustrates the rapid and fearful waste of human life following in the wake of war.

	COMPANIES.										
	A	B	C	D	E	F	G	H	I	K	Total
Original Recruits, 1861	84	98	89	86	86	87	89	82	85	86	872
New Recruits, 1862, 1863	19	36	12	2	11	18	23	1	7	1	130
Drafted Men		2	26			2	1	5			36
Total	103	136	127	88	97	107	113	88	92	87	1038
Killed in battle	8	7	7	1	7	7	4	8	9	2	60
Died of wounds	7	3	9	5	4	10	12	3	1	2	56
Died of disease	9	18	16	8	2	9	13	12	13	11	111
Discharged of wounds		4	2	3	6	6	1	4		2	28
Discharged of disease	23	25	13	22	22	17	25	20	13	27	207
Drafted men discharged		2	24			2	1	4			33
Absent		9	2	5	10	5	4	5	4	13	57
Invalid corps	1								2		3
Promoted and transferred	6	4	2	1		3	2	5	2	1	26
Prisoners of war	2		1	1	4	1		3	3		15
Absent sick and wounded	4	35	19	17	14	4	22	10	8	11	144
Absent on duty	12	8	4	2	6	1	4	4	5	4	50
Present with Regiment	31	21	28	23	22	42	25	10	32	14	248

This table shows that in two years and four months nearly one-fourth of those who enlisted had died, and almost as many more had been discharged as unfit for further service. There were also 145 others absent, sick or wounded, many of whom afterwards died or were discharged.

The following table is compiled from the Ohio State Roster, and shows the whole number enlisted, and our losses during our entire service as a regiment:

Whole number enlisted		1472
Killed in battle, ...	109	
Died of wounds, ...	69	
Died of disease, ...	141	
Died of accident, ...	3	
Total deaths, ...		322
Discharged from wounds, . . .	134	
Discharged from disease, . . .	291	
Total discharged, ...		425
Died and discharged, ...		747
		725

Let us trace briefly the conditions which contributed to our loss, as the table given shows, of 141 by death from disease, and 291 by discharge from disease—432 men, during our term of service.

The regiment was recruited chiefly from a farming community, and the men accustomed to moderate labor and regular meals and sleep. Our commander was a captain in the regular army, from whom much was expected, thoroughly loyal to the service, and with the advantage of considerable experience in Indian wars upon the frontier. He was naturally ambitious that his regiment should be capable of giving the best possible service to the country, and meet the high expectations of its friends. Acting upon the maxims received in his military education and experience, and urged forward by the evident military necessity that the regiment be ready to go into active service at the earliest possible day, he initiated long

hours of drill and camp duties—no time could be afforded for accli-
mation or to accustom the men to the great change from civil to
military life.

It was early seen by the medical officers that the severe and
unaccustomed strain upon the men was rapidly lowering their vital
tone, and rendering them less able to resist the camp and epidemic
influences they were sure to encounter. The repeated efforts made
even as early as Camp Wood, to urge this view upon the commanding officer, were always courteously received, but were met by the
assurance that his early experience contradicted the fears expressed
by the surgeons.

Nothing can be more certain to the writer than the fact that
nothing was gained by this continued working of the men at high
pressure; and that longer hours of rest and fewer of drill would have
accomplished more than the long hours of work by men rarely fully
rested from their duties. Our experience in our first camp was
only that of many other regiments. The results in our case were
soon to appear, and to leave a lasting impression on the history of
the regiment.

The movements of the command have already been given in
this history. We reached Camp Wickliff, Kentucky, sixty miles
below Louisville, December 15th, 1861, and marched out February
16th, 1862, just sixty days. The conditions surrounding us while
there have already been described. From letters I wrote from that
camp, I take the following facts: We had one case of measles, at
Louisville. A few days after our arrival at Camp Wickliff a number of cases occurred. Soon men were down in nearly all of our
fifty Sibley tents, unavoidably exposing every one. The disease
became epidemic, and the whole camp a focus of contagion. In
all there were 125 cases. It was impossible to find room in our
regimental hospital for so many. Most of the cases were mild and
the larger part remained in their tents, which were heated by sheet
iron stoves, and were visited daily by the surgeon and nursed by
their comrades. These cases did at least as well, if not better, than
those crowded together in our hospital. At the same time typhoid
fever prevailed to an alarming extent, and our cases of measles were

no sooner on their feet than a large proportion of them came down with that disease. Malaria, camp diarrhea and jaundice abounded. Including the convalescents there were at one time 300 men off duty.

About January 20th, our hospital cases were ordered sent to Louisville. My letters mentioned sending off 90 cases in three weeks, and before we left in all 125 had been sent under these orders. When we broke up camp, 125 convalescents were sent to Nelson Barracks. We had marched into the camp 930 strong; we left in sixty days with only 680 men.

The Ohio State Roster reports 9 deaths, from all causes, at Camp Wickliff. The same authority reports 33 of those we sent to Louisville as dying in hospital there within a few weeks—a larger number than we had killed on any battle field of the war.

Many of those sent back died at a later period or were discharged for disability. And a large number who applied after the war for surgeon's certificate, referred the origin of their disability to sickness at Camp Wickliff.

Few of those who went into the army knew anything of the duties to be required of them. With the most earnest purpose to do all for the best, and acting on all the light of that day, many mistakes on the part of officers and men were inevitable. All honor to those who did the best they knew or could know. With all its imperfections our army hospital service was far superior to that which had ever been furnished to the soldiers of any previous war.

The epidemic described was the only instance of the massing of our sick. All through the service we had the usual diseases incident to our army life, and the continued drain upon our numbers from death and discharge. Of the survivors whom I meet at our army reunions, many complain of disability, yet are living on—"the survival of the fittest." From the number still reported on our regimental roster as living, it is probable that of those enlisted from 40 to 45 per cent. still survive—32 years after the war. And the report of the Commissioner of Pensions for the year 1895 gives the death rate for that year of pensioners of the late war as being less than four per cent.

The soldiers of the Mexican War were granted a service pension 39 years after the close of that war. The bill required some degree of disability, or dependency, or that the claimant under its provisions should be 62 years of age, and that he should have served 60 days, or been actually engaged in a battle. Taking this as a precedent, it is safe to expect that if not before, then that 39 years after the close of our war, which will be in 1904, a service pension will be granted to the soldiers of the War of the Rebellion. The pension of the soldiers of the Mexican War is twelve dollars a month. Judging from the liberal provision of the Pension Act of 1890, such a pension bill will embrace all who served 60 days.

SURGEONS' ROSTER.

Surgeon Thos. B. Cleveland, appointed August 29th, 1861. Resigned May 17th, 1862. Resided at Cleveland, O., and resigned on account of ill health. Deceased.

Surgeon John C. Hubbard, appointed May 12th, 1862. Discharged for disability August 30th, 1862. Did duty as surgeon 18 days. Deceased.

Surgeon Albert G. Hart, appointed assistant surgeon September 5, 1861. Promoted surgeon August 30th, 1862. Resigned November 5th, 1864. Lives 102 Jennings avenue, Cleveland, O.

Surgeon John Hill, appointed December 16th, 1864. Mustered out with the regiment November 27th, 1865. Resides at Vincennes, Ind.

Assistant Surgeon Benjamin F. Cheney, appointed September 12th, 1862. Resigned August 22d, 1864. Resides at New Haven, Conn.

Assistant Surgeon John W. Bugh, appointed March 11th, 1863. Resigned January 5th, 1864. Lives at Bluffton, Ind.

Chas. E. Tupper, appointed September 8th, 1864. Deceased.

LIST OF BATTLES.

The following is a list of battles in which this Regiment bore an honorable part:

(Official Army Register, Part V, Page 116).

Shiloh, Tenn..April 6-7, 1862.
Stone River, Tenn...........................Dec. 31, 1862, Jany. 2, 1863.
Woodbury, Tenn...Jany 24, 1863.
Chickamauga, Ga..Sept. 19-20, 1863.
Brown's Ferry, Tenn....................................October 27, 1863.
Chattanooga, Tenn..................................November 23-25, 1863.
Orchard Knob, Tenn..................................November 23, 1863.
Mission Ridge, Tenn..................................November 25, 1863.
Rocky Face Ridge, Ga...................................May 5-9, 1864.
Resaca, Ga...May 13-16, 1864.
Adairsville, Ga..May 17-18, 1864.
Cassville, Ga..May 19-22, 1864.
Dallas, Ga..May 25 to June 4, 1864.
Picketts Mills, Ga..May 27, 1864.
Kennesaw Mountain, Ga..................................June 9-30, 1864.
Chattahoochee River, Ga................................July 6-10, 1864.
Atlanta, Ga. (Siege of)......................July 28 to September 2, 1864.
Lovejoy Station, Ga..................................September 2-6, 1864.
Franklin, Tenn......................................November 30, 1864.
Nashville, Tenn....................................December 15-16, 1864.

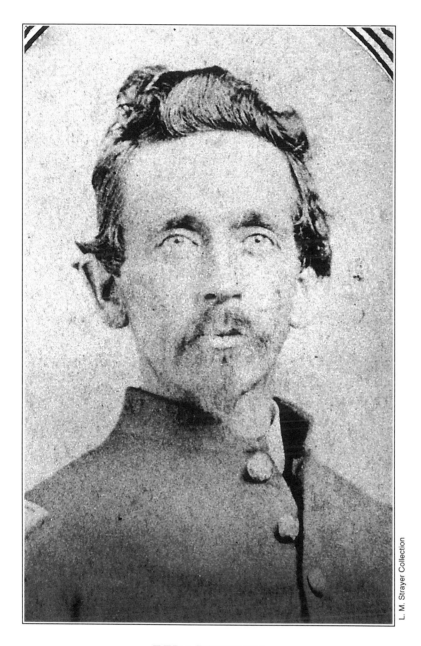

EZRA DUNHAM

Corporal, Sergeant, First Sergeant, Company C;
First Lieutenant, Co. C; Captain, Co. H
Major, 41st O.V.V.I.

WILLIAM C. CATLIN

Assistant Surgeon 41st O.V.I.
Assistant Surgeon 86th O.V.I.

Lotz House Museum, Franklin, Tenn.

EMERSON OPDYCKE

First Lieutenant and Captain, Co. A, 41st O.V.I.
Colonel 125th O.V.I.

JAMES McCLEERY

Second Lieutenant, First Lieutenant and Captain, Co. A;
Captain, Co. H; Brevet Major 41st O.V.V.I.; Acting Asst. Insp. Gen.
Hazen's staff; Brevet Brig. Gen. U.S. Vols.
Lost right arm at Shiloh; wounded at Stones River.

CHARLES W. HILLS

Corporal and Second Lieutenant, Co. A
Wounded at Shiloh and Brown's Ferry, Tenn.

JOHN L. BOWER

Private, Corporal and Sergeant, Co. B

Theme Prints Ltd., Bayside, N.Y.

HUBERT H. HARRINGTON

Private, Co. B

CHRISTOPHER C. WEBBER

Private, Co. B

Photographed by J. MARKILLIE, Hudson, O.

WILLIAM M. BEEBE

Second Lieutenant, Co. I; First Lieutenant, Cos. I and K
Captain, Cos. C and H
Lieut. Col. 128th U.S. Colored Troops

CUNNINGHAM HUSTON

Corporal and Sergeant, Co. C
Quartermaster Sergeant, 41st O.V.V.I.
First Lieutenant, Co. C

FERDINAND D. COBB

First Sergeant, Second Lieutenant, Co. F
First Lieutenant, Co. E
Wounded at Nashville, Dec. 16, 1864

EDWARD J. JOHNSON

Private, Co. E
Wounded and captured at Chickamauga

JAMES N. CLARK

Corporal, Co. C; Sergt. Major, 41st O.V.I.
Second Lieutenant, Co. C
First Lieutenant, Co. F

ROBERT A. GAULT

Corporal and Sergeant, Co. F
Sergeant Major, 41st O.V.V.I.
First Lieutenant and Captain, Co. G

PETER HERRIFF

Private, Corporal and Sergeant, Co. D
Commissary Sergeant, 41st O.V.V.I.
Second Lieutenant, Co. I; First Lieutenant, Co. G

LLOYD FISHER

First Sergeant, Co. D; Second Lieutenant, Co. G
Wounded at Chickamauga

OTIS A. SHATTOCK

Private and Corporal, Co. G

ALLISON P. VARNEY

Private, Co. G

HORATIO P. KILE

Second and First Lieutenant, Co. G
Captain, Co. H

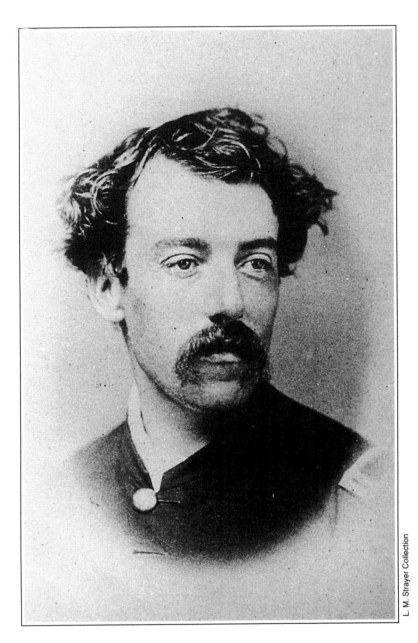

HARRY W. JONES

Second Lieutenant, Co. E; First Lieutenant, Cos. K and E

UNKNOWN

Note "41" numerals affixed to collar.

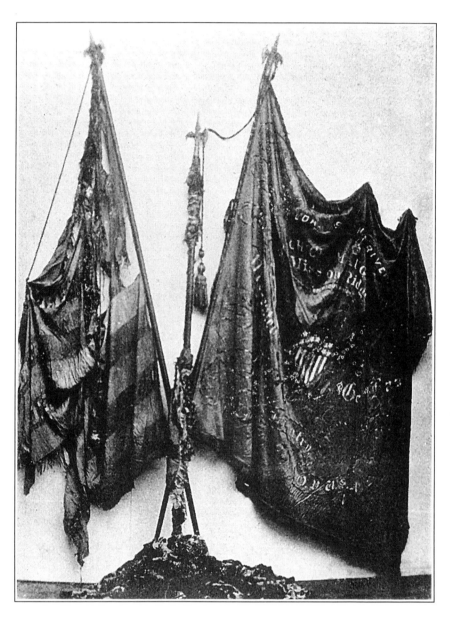

FLAGS OF THE REGIMENT

The colors in center the one presented by the Ladies of Geauga County, nothing left but the staff. The one at left was presented to the Regiment by Col. Wiley, and the banner at right the one presented by Gen. Hazen.

ROSTER

OF

THE FORTY-FIRST OHIO INFANTRY.

Mustered in Oct. 29, 1861, at Cleveland, O., by Jas. P. W. Neill, 1st Lieut., 18th Infantry, U. S. A. Re-enlisted for three years more as a Regiment, January 1, 1864, at Blain's X-Roads, Tenn. Mustered out Nov. 27th, 1805 at Columbus, O., by Chas. Sprawl, Capt. and A. A. D. C.

FIELD AND STAFF.

COLONELS.

WILLIAM B. HAZEN. Age 35. Entered the service Aug. 7, 1861, 3 years. Promoted from Captain 8th U. S. Infantry, Aug. 7, 1861; to Brig. Gen. of Volunteers April 15, 1863. Afterward to Major General.

AQUILA WILEY. Age 26. Entered the service September 19, 1861, 3 years. Captain Company C. Promoted to Major March 1, 1862; to Lieut. Colonel Nov. 20, 1862; to Colonel Nov. 29, 1862; to Brevet Brig. General. See Co. C.

LIEUTENANT COLONELS.

JOHN J. WISEMAN. Age 34. Entered the service Aug. 7, 1861, 3 years. Resigned March 1, 1862.

GEORGE S. MYGATT. Age 36. Entered the service August 7, 1861, 3 years. Promoted from Major March 1, 1862. Resigned November 20, 1862.

ROBERT L. KIMBERLY. Age 25. Entered the service September 27, 1861, 3 years. Promoted from 2nd Lieut., Co. D. to 1st Lieut. and Adjutant January 21, 1862; to Captain March 17, 1862; Major November 20, 1862; Lieut. Colonel January 1, 1863; Colonel 191st Ohio Regiment February 28, 1865; Brevet Colonel March 13, 1865; Brevet Brig. General——.

EPHRAIM S. HOLLOWAY. Age 30. Entered the service Oct. 10, 1861, 3 years. Promoted from 1st Lieut. Co. F to Captain September 8th, 1862; to Major Nov. 26, 1864; Lieut Colonel March 18, 1865; Colonel May 31, 1865, but not mustered. Brevet Brig. General at expiration of service. Mustered out with regiment Nov. 27th, 1865.

MAJORS.

JOHN H. WILLISTON. Age 28. Entered the service Sept. 16, 1861, 3 years. Promoted from Captain Co. I to Major, Jan. 1, 1863. Wounded July 6, 1864, in action at Chattahoochee River, Ga. Discharged on surgeon's certificate of disability Oct. 22, 1864, on account of wound.

EZRA DUNHAM. Age 23. Entered the service Sept. 19, 1861, 3 years, as Private Co. C. Promoted to Major March 18, 1865; mustered out with regiment Nov. 27, 1865. See Co. C.

SURGEONS.

THOMAS G. CLEVELAND. Age 37. Entered the service August 29, 1861, 3 years. Resigned May 17th, 1862.

ALBERT G. HART. Age 39. Entered the service Sept. 5, 1861, 3 years. Promoted from Assistant Surgeon August 30th, 1862. Resigned Nov. 9th, 1864.

JOHN C. HUBBARD. Age 41. Entered the service May 12, 1862, 3 years. Discharged Aug. 30, 1862.

JOHN HILL. Age 30. Entered the service Dec. 16, 1864, 3 years. Mustered out with regiment Nov. 27, 1865.

ASSISTANT SURGEONS.

BENJAMIN H. CHENEY. Age 26. Entered the service Sept. 12, 1862, 3 years. Resigned Aug. 22, 1864.

JOHN W. BUGH. Age 37. Entered the service March 11, 1863, 3 years. Resigned January 5, 1864.

CHARLES E. TUPPER. Age 36. Entered the service Sept. 8, 1864, 3 years. Mustered out with regiment Nov. 27, 1865.

ADJUTANTS.

JUNIUS R. SANFORD. Age 26. Entered the service Aug. 23, 1861, 3 years. Resigned Jan 5, 1862.

RUFUS B. HARDY. Age 22. Entered the service Sept. 19, 1861, 3 years. Promoted from 2d Lieut. Co. C to 1st Lieut. Jan. 21, 1862; appointed Adjutant June 21, 1862. Resigned April 4, 1864. See Co. C.

SAMUEL B. ASDELL. Age 18. Entered the service Sept. 19, 1861, 3 years, as Sergt. Co. C. Promoted to 1st Lieut. and Adjt. Nov. 20, 1862. Died Nov. 17, 1863. See Co. C.

SEWARD S. PALMER. Age 19. Entered the service Aug. 2, 1861, 3 years, as Corporal Co. A. Promoted to 1st Lieut. and Adjt. Nov. 26, 1864; Captain March 18, 1865. Mustered out with regiment as Captain Co. A Nov. 27, 1865. See Co. A.

GEORGE J. A. THOMPSON. Age 27. Entered the service Sept. 18, 1861, 3 years, as Private Co. D. Promoted to 1st Lieut. Nov. 26, 1864; appointed Adjutant May 1, 1865. Mustered out with regiment as Adjutant Nov. 27, 1865. See Co. D.

REGIMENTAL QUARTER MASTERS.

WILLIAM S. CHAMBERLAIN. Age 31. Entered the service Aug. 24, 1861, 3 years. Resigned Dec. 10th, 1861.

HENRY W. JOHNSON. Age 26. Entered the service Aug. 20, 1861, 3 years, as 2nd Lieut. Co. B. Promoted to 1st Lieut Jan. 9, 1862; appointed Quarter Master Jan. 13, 1862; promoted to Captain Nov. 20, 1862; Captain and Assistant Quarter Master June 14, 1865. See Co. B.

WALTER BLYTHE. Age 39. Entered the service Aug. 25, 1861, 3 years. Promoted to 2nd Lieut. Co. E from Quarter Master Sergt. April 19, 1862; 1st Lieut. and Reg. Quarter Master Oct. 1, 1862. Mustered out on expiration of term of service Jan. 17, 1865.

JAMES M. KIRKPATRICK. Age 21. Entered the service Oct. 10, 1861, 3 years, as Private Co. F. Promoted to 1st Lieut. Co. B, Nov. 26, 1864; appointed Reg. Quarter Master March 1, 1865. Mustered out with regiment Nov. 27, 1865. See Co. F.

CHAPLAIN.

ORMAN A. LYMAN. Age 44. Entered the service Dec. 16, 1861, 3 years. Resigned May 31, 1862.

SERGEANT MAJORS.

EDWIN B. ATWOOD. Age 23. Entered the service Sept. 19, 1861, 3 years. Promoted to 2nd Lieut. Co. G Jan. 21, 1862; to 1st Lieut. Co. A, Sept. 8, 1862; tranferred to Co. D, Dec. 9, 1862; promoted to Captain April 13, 1864; transferred from Co. D Oct. 20, 1864; Brevet Major March 13, 1865; transferred to Co. K March 28, 1865. Mustered out with company Nov. 27, 1865.

LESTER T. PATCHIN. Age 26. Entered the service Aug. 20, 1861, 3 years. Promoted to Sergt. Major Jan. 21, 1862; to 2nd Lieut. Co. I March 17, 1862; to 1st Lieut. Sept. 1, 1862. Died Jan. 18, 1863, of wounds received Dec. 31, 1862 in Battle of Stone River, Tenn.

JAMES N. CLARK. Age 19. Entered the service Sept. 19, 1861, 3 years. Promoted from Corporal to Sergt. Major July 21, 1862; to 2nd Lieut. Sept. 17, 1862; to 1st Lieut. Co. F March 24, 1863. Mustered out Jany. 17, 1865 on expiration of term of service.

EUGENE R. EGGLESTON. Age 23. Entered the service Sept. 10, 1861, 3 years. Promoted to Sergt. Major from 1st Sergt. Co. G Nov. 1, 1862; to 2nd Lieut. Co. C March 24, 1863. Resigned Sept. 30, 1864.

ROBERT A. GAULT. Age 22. Entered the service Oct. 10, 1861, 3 years, as Corporal Co. F. Appointed Sergt. Mar. 17, 1862; promoted to Sergt. Major May 1, 1863; to 1st Lieut. Co. G Nov. 26, 1864; to Captain March 18, 1865. Mustered out with Co. G Nov. 27, 1865. See Co. F.

JOHN CRONKHITE. Age 19. Entered the service Oct. 5, 1861, 3 years, as Private Co. I. Appointed Corporal Feb. 4, 1862; Sergeant, Nov. 23, 1863; 1st Sergt. Dec. 6, 1864; promoted to Sergt. Major Feb. 1, 1865; 1st Lieut. April 20, 1865. Mustered out with regiment Nov. 27, 1865. See Co. I.

HENRY J. ENGLEBECK. Age 21. Entered the service Sept. 16, 1861, 3 years, as Private Co. I. Appointed Corporal April 18, 1863; promoted to Sergt. Major May 1, 1865. Mustered out with regiment Nov. 27, 1865. See Co. I.

QUARTER MASTER SERGEANTS.

THOMAS H. SOMERS. Age 26. Entered the service Sept. 16, 1861, 3 years, as Corporal Co. H. Appointed Sergt. Dec. 27, 1861; promoted to Sergt. Major June 20, 1862; to 2nd Lieut. Co. F May 29, 1863. See Co. H.

LYMAN ALLEN. Age 23. Entered the service Aug. 2, 1861, for 3 years, as Private Co. A. Appointed Corporal ———; promoted to Q. M. Sergeant June 17, 1863. Discharged at Chattanooga, Tenn., Oct. 7, 1863.

CUNNINGHAM HUSTON. Age 21. Entered the service Sept. 19, 1861, 3 years, as Corporal Co. C. Appointed Sergt. May 1, 1862; promoted to Q. M. Sergeant March 28, 1864; to 1st Lieut. March 18, 1865. See Co. C.

LESTER F. MILLER. Age 22. Entered the service Sept. 26, 1862, 3 years, as Private Co. F. Appointed Sergt. July 8, 1864; promoted Q. M. Sergt. May 1, 1865; to 2nd Lieut. May 11, 1865. See Co. F.

LEROY E. BOSLEY. Age 19. Entered the service Aug. 20, 1861, 3 years, as Private Co. B. Appointed Corporal April 8, 1862; Sergt. Jany. 20, 1864; promoted to Q. M. Sergt. June 1, 1865. Mustered out with regiment Nov. 27, 1865. See Co. B.

COMMISSARY SERGEANTS

WILLIAM E. BOOTH. Age 26. Entered the service Sept. 21, 1861, 3 years. Promoted to 2nd Lieut. Co. F Sept. 19, 1862; to 1st Lieut. Co. B May 29, 1863. Resigned Sept. 22, 1864.

PETER HERRIFF. Age 19. Entered the service Sept. 2, 1861, 3 years, as Private Co. D. Appointed Corporal April 28, 1863; Sergt., March 27, 1864; promoted Com. Sergt. Dec. 9, 1864; to 2nd Lieut. Co. I April 28, 1865; to 1st Lieut. Co. G May 11, 1865. See Co. D.

JAMES J. MATTOCKS. Age 31. Entered the service Aug. 2, 1861, 3 years, as Corporal Co. A. Appointed Sergt. Nov. 21, 1861; 1st Sergt. Dec. 25, 1862; promoted to Com. Sergt. May 1, 1865. See Co. A.

HOSPITAL STEWARDS.

CHARLES COLVIN. Age 24. Entered the service Sept. 23, 1861, 3 years. Mustered out at the expiration of term of service, Sept. 23, 1864.

CHARLES W. SWANK. Age 34. Entered the service Oct. 10, 1861, 3 years, as Private Co. F. Promoted to Hospital Steward May 1, 1865. Mustered out with the regiment Nov. 27, 1865. See Co. F.

REGIMENTAL BAND.

Mustered in Oct. 22, 1861, for 3 years. Mustered out at Corinth, Miss., June 6th, 1862 by General Order No. 90.

Jackson M. Leland, Leader of Band.....................1st E Flat Cornet.
William Carl ....2nd E Flat Cornet.
John Messer...2nd E Flat Cornet
Julius Seidel...1st B Flat Cornet
Charles Dickinson ....2nd B Flat Cornet
George Little...2nd B Flat Cornet.
Jacob Kehris..Solo Alto E Flat.
Daniel L. Moore ....2nd Alto E Flat
Mendon L. Prentiss ....2nd Alto E Flat.
Thomas Phillips.......................2d Alto and Band Sergeant.
Henry Dormeyer..B Flat Tenor.
James W. Dickinson ....B Flat Tenor.
Albert Dickinson ....B Flat Bass.
Hamilton Stickney ....E Flat Bass.
George Breymeier. ....E Flat Bass.
Wm. S. Lovejoy..Bass Drum.
Andrew L. Leland......................................Drum.

COMPANY A.

Company "A" was gathered largely by Seth A. Bushnell, a well-to-do farmer living in the town of Hartford, and made up of men from Hartford, Vernon, Kinsman, Bazetta and other towns adjoining. They were many of them young men, and the very pick of a wealthy farm section on the Western Reserve. A large portion of them enlisted at a mass meeting held at Hartford, August 2d, 1861, where the war topics were discussed, and the hearts of young men were fired with the spirit of Wade, Hutchins and Giddings, and their faces set like a flint toward the nation's honor and safety.

About the middle of August the company gathered at Warren, the county seat of Trumbull county and there, after the sad parting from wives and sweethearts, took the train for Cleveland. Eighty-four men were taken to Cleveland, and there Charles W. Hills, the Cutlers and others from Mayfield, Cuyahoga Co., 16 in all were secured to complete the quota. Organization was effected by the election of S. A. Bushnell of Hartford, Captain; Emerson Opdycke, of Warren, as 1st Lieutenant and James McCleery, of Bazetta, as 2d Lieutenant. C. C. Hart of Hartford was made 1st Sergeant; Augustus D. Druery, of Hartford, 2d Sergeant; Elmer Moses, of Hartford, 3d Sergeant; Seward S. Palmer, 4th Sergeant; Charles Gallup, 5th Sergeant.

The company took part in all the battles with the regiment from Shiloh, April 6th and 7th, 1862, to Nashville, Tenn., Dec. 15th and 16th, 1864, and in skirmishes without number. It had enrolled during the war 165 men. There were killed in action three corporals, Ames, Braden and Smith, and seven privates. Twenty-one died of wounds and disease; two were taken prisoners and never heard of. The officers when mustered out Nov. 27, 1865, at Columbus, were Captain, Seward S. Palmer; 1st Lieut., P. A. Bower. The non-commissioned officers were: 1st Sergt., Andrew C. Parker; 2d Sergt., Joseph Jackson; 3d Sergt., Geo. F. Haynes; 4th Sergt., Charles Settle; 5th Sergt., Sheldon Crooks. Corporals: Daniel I. Holcomb, Sullivan D. Ralph, Alfred J. Henry, Isaac A. Gamber, Adolphus Flint. The former officers were: Captains S. A. Bushnell, Emerson Opdycke, James McCleery; 1st Lieuts., Opdycke, McCleery, Hart, Fuller, McMahon, Palmer; 2d Lieuts., McCleery, Hart, Fuller and Charles W. Hills. Of the 165 men only five came home without a wound of some sort to stand as evidence of their prowess at the front during the whole war. They were never a day on any detached service, or left in the rear at some stockade, but always at the front. The company holds its record second to none.

CAPTAINS.

SETH A. BUSHNELL. Age 43. Entered the service Aug. 2, 1861, 3 years. Resigned Nov. 27, 1861.

EMERSON OPDYCKE. Age 31. Entered the service July 26, 1861, 3 years. Promoted from 1st Lieut. Jany. 9, 1862 to Colonel 125th Regiment, O. V. I., Sept. 17, 1862. Wounded April 7th, 1862, in battle of Shiloh, Tenn.

JAMES McCLEERY. Age 22. Entered the service Aug. 20, 1861, 3 years. Promoted to 1st Lieut. from 2d Lieut. Jany. 9, 1862; lost right arm April 7, 1862, in battle of Shiloh, Tenn. Promoted Captain Sept. 17, 1862, wounded Dec. 31, 1862 in battle of Stone River. Tenn.; transferred to Co. H April 28, 1865. Mustered out Nov. 27, 1865.

SEWARD S. PALMER. Age 19. Entered the service Aug. 2, 1861, 3 years. Appointed Sergeant from Corporal Feb. 9, 1802; 1st Sergt. July 17, 1864. Promoted to 1st Lieut. and Adjutant Nov. 26, 1864; Captain March 18th, 1865. Mustered out with the company Nov. 27, 1865. VETERAN. In battles of Shiloh, Corinth, Iuka, Rockyface Ridge, Resaca, and all the Atlanta campaign and Nashville to end of war with regiment.

1st LIEUTENANTS.

EDWIN B. ATWOOD. See Field and Staff.

CALVIN C. HART. Age 31. Entered the service Aug. 20, 1861, 3 years. Appointed 1st Sergt. from Sergt. ——; promoted to 2d Lieut. Jan. 9, 1862; 1st Lieut. Sept. 9, 1862. Killed Dec. 31, 1862 in battle of Stone River, Tenn.

DAVIS C. FULLER. Age 20. Entered the service Aug. 20, 1861, 3 years. Promoted to 2d Lieut. from Sergeant May 21, 1862; 1st Lieut. Jany. 1st, 1863; discharged on Surgeon's certificate of disability June 27, 1863.

JAMES McMAHON. See Company H.

PHILIP A. BOWER. Age 26. Entered the service Aug. 15, 1861, 3 years. Appointed Corporal Dec. 20, 1862; Sergeant May 1, 1863; 1st Sergeant Dec. 6, 1864. Promoted to 1st Lieut. March 18, 1865. Mustered out with the company Nov. 27, 1865. VETERAN.

2d LIEUTENANT.

CHARLES W. HILLS. Age 21. Entered the service Aug. 24, 1861, 3 years. Appointed Corporal, Sergeant, and promoted to 2d Lieutenant. Wounded in the battle of Shiloh, Tenn. April 7, 1862, and wounded in right hand at Brown's Ferry, Tenn. Battles engaged in were Shiloh, Stone River, Chickamauga, Brown's Ferry. Resigned on account of wounds Oct. 28, 1864.

1st SERGEANTS.

TRUMAN C. CUTLER. Age 24. Entered the service Aug. 24, 1861, 3 years. Appointed Sergt. ——; promoted to 2d Lieut. Feb. 8, 1862, and assigned to Co. D, 1st Lieut. May 21, 1862 and assigned to Co. E.

ANDREW C. PARKER. Age 23. Entered the service Aug. 18, 1861, 3 years. Appointed Corporal Dec. 1, 1863; Sergeant Jany. 26, 1864; 1st Sergeant March 27, 1865. Mustered out with company Nov. 27, 1865. Wounded April 7, 1862, at the battle of Shiloh, Tenn. VETERAN.

SERGEANTS.

JOSEPH JACKSON. Age 18. Entered the service Aug. 22, 1861, 3 years. Appointed Corporal Nov. 1, 1862; Sergeant Dec. 6, 1864. Mustered out with company Nov. 27, 1865. VETERAN.

GEORGE F. HAYNES. Age 25. Entered the service Aug. 8, 1861, 3 years. Appointed Corporal Jany. 26, 1864; Sergeant Feb. 20, 1865. Mustered out with company Nov. 27, 1865. VETERAN.

CHARLES SETTLE. Age 19. Entered the service Aug. 10, 1861, 3 years. Appointed Corporal May 2, 1864; Sergeant, March 28, 1865. Mustered out with company Nov. 27, 1865. VETERAN.

SHELDON CROOKS. Age 23. Entered the service Aug. 2, 1861, 3 years. Appointed Corporal Oct. 17, 1865; Sergeant ——. Mustered out with company Nov. 27, 1865. VETERAN.

CHARLES H. BENNETT. Age 19. Entered the service Aug. 2, 1861, 3 years. Mustered as Private. Appointed Sergeant ——. Died Dec. 9th, 1863, in hospital at Nashville, Tenn., of wounds received Oct. 27, 1863 in battle of Brown's Ferry, Tenn.

ELMER MOSES. Age 30. Entered the service Aug. 2, 1861, 3 years. Appointed from Corporal ——; discharged October —, 1862 to accept commission in the 125th Regiment, O. V. I.

AUGUSTUS D. DRUERY. Age 33. Entered the service Aug. 20, 1861, 3 years. Discharged January 6, 1863, at Camp Dennison, Ohio, on surgeon's certificate of disability.

JAMES N. DILLEY. Age 21. Entered the service Aug. 8, 1861, 3 years. Mustered as Private; appointed Sergeant ——; discharged January 21, 1865, at Cincinnati, Ohio, on surgeon's certificate of disability. VETERAN. Wounded while on picket, July 9, 1864, at Chattahoochee River, Ga. Was in battles of Shiloh, Stone River, Chickamauga, Mission Ridge, Resaca.

LESTER W. PERHAM. Age 25. Entered the service Aug. 12, 1862, 3 years. Appointed Corporal July 7, 1864; Sergeant, May 1, 1865. Mustered out at San Antonio, Texas, on expiration of term of service, Oct. 16, 1865.

JAMES J. MATTOCKS. Age 31. Entered the service Aug. 2, 1861, 3 years. Appointed from Corporal Nov. 1, 1861; First Sergeant, Dec. 25, 1862. Promoted to Com. Sergeant May 1, 1865. VETERAN. Mustered out with company, Nov. 27, 1865.

CORPORALS.

DANIEL I. HOLCOMB. Age 18. Entered the service Aug. 20, 1861, 3 years. Appointed Corporal Feb. 20, 1865. Mustered out with company Nov. 27, 1865. VETERAN. Fought in all battles of the Regiment, except Shiloh. Was wounded at Chickamauga.

SULLIVAN D. RALPH. Age 26. Entered the service Aug. 22, 1861, 3 years. Appointed Corporal Feb. 20, 1865. Mustered out with company Nov. 27, 1865. VETERAN.

ALFRED J. HENRY. Age 18. Entered the service Aug. 10, 1861, 3 years. Appointed Corporal Aug. 17, 1865. Mustered out with company Nov. 27, 1865. VETERAN. Wounded in battle of Woodbury and in battle of Pickett's Mills. Was in all battles of the Regiment.

ISAAC A. GAMBER. Age 17. Entered the service Aug. 24, 1861, 3 years. Appointed Corporal Aug. 17, 1865. Mustered out with company Nov. 27, 1865. VETERAN.

ADOLPHUS FLINT. Age 21. Entered the service Aug. 10, 1861, 3 years. Appointed Corporal Dec. 6, 1864. Mustered out at Cincinnati, Ohio, by order of the War Department May 25, 1865. VETERAN.

HORACE B. AMES. Age 21. Entered the service Aug. 15, 1861, 3 years. Killed April 7, 1862, in battle of Shiloh, Tenn. Supposed to be the first man in the Regiment killed in battle.

WALLACE B. BRADEN. Age 19. Entered the service Aug. 22, 1861, 3 years. Killed Sept. 19, 1863, in battle of Chickamauga, Georgia. Wounded twice at battle of Shiloh, Tenn., April 7, 1862.

CHARLES R. SMITH. Age 19. Entered the service Aug. 15, 1861, 3 years. Appointed Corporal ——. Killed May 27, 1864, in battle of Pickett's Mills, Ga.

HENRY H. BROWN. Age 25. Entered the service Aug. 24, 1861, 3 years. Appointed Corporal ——. Died Sept. 13, 1864, in Rebel prison at Andersonville, Ga. Captured at battle of Chickamauga, Ga., Sept. 19, 1863.

WILLIAM McCARNAHAN. Age 37. Entered the service Aug. 2, 1861, 3 years. Discharged at Columbus, Ohio, on surgeon's certificate of disability Aug. 8, 1862.

HARRISON DAILY. Age 19. Entered the service Aug. 15, 1861, 3 years. Appointed Corporal ——. Mustered out on expiration of term of service Aug. 26, 1864.

JULIAS A. CUTLER. Age 30. Entered the service Aug. 24, 1861, 3 years. Appointed Corporal ——. Discharged at New Market, Tenn., on surgeon's certificate of disability March 24, 1865. VETERAN.

CHARLES A. GALLUP. Age 24. Entered the service Aug. 2, 1861, 3 years. Appointed Corporal ——. Discharged at Louisville, Ky., on surgeon's certificate of disability June 12, 1862.

THOMAS C. SNYDER. Age 18. Entered the service Aug. 18, 1861, 3 years. Appointed Corporal ——. Discharged at Columbus, Ohio, on surgeon's certificate of disability Aug. 19, 1862.

ORLANDO W. HAYNES. Age 23. Entered the service Aug. 8, 1861, 3 years. Discharged at Columbus, Ohio, on surgeon's certificate of disability Feb. 13, 1863. Wounded at the battle of Shiloh, Tenn., April 7, 1862.

ROBERT A. JOHNSON. Age 22. Entered the service Aug. 2, 1861, 3 years. Appointed Corporal ——. Discharged at Cleveland, Ohio, by order of War Department June 13, 1865. VETERAN.

LYMAN ALLEN. Age 23. Entered the service Aug. 2, 1861, 3 years. Appointed Corporal ——. Promoted Q. M. Sergeant June 17, 1863. Discharged at Chattanooga, Tenn., Sept. 7, 1863.

PRIVATES.

ADAMS, HENRY S. Age 33. Entered the service Sept. 27, 1864, 1 year. Drafted. Mustered out at Nashville, Tenn., by order of War Department June 13, 1865.

ALLEN, WILLIAM. Age 37. Entered the service Sept. 28, 1864, 1 year. Drafted. Mustered out at Nashville, Tenn., by order of the War Department June 13, 1865.

BENNETT, SAMUEL. Age 27. Entered the service Aug. 23, 1861, 3 years. Killed April 7, 1862, in battle of Shiloh, Tenn.

BENNETT, AVERY. Age 18. Entered the service Aug. 2, 1861, 3 years. Died January 17, 1863, at Murfreesboro, Tenn., of wounds received Dec. 31, 1862, in battle of Stone River, Tenn.

BROCKWAY, DANIEL W. Age 25. Entered the service Aug. 31, 1861, 3 years. Died March 27, 1864, at Cleveland, Ohio.

BACON, CLINTON. Age 20. Entered the service Aug. 22, 1861, 3 years. Died Sept. 26, 1863, at Nashville Tenn., of wounds received Sept. 19, 1863, in battle of Chickamauga, Ga.

BEECH, CARTLIN. Age 17. Entered the service Aug. 20, 1861, 3 years. Died Nov. 17, 1862, at Silver Springs, Tenn.

BARBER, HENRY. Age 18. Entered the service Aug. 23, 1861, 3 years. Mustered out Aug. 26, 1864, on expiration of term of service. Battles engaged in: Shiloh, Stone River, Chickamauga, Resaca. Wounded in right arm at the battle of Shiloh, Tenn., April 7, 1862.

BARNES, GEORGE D. Age 22. Entered the service Aug. 8, 1861, 3 years. Killed May 27, 1864, in battle of Pickett's Mills, Ga. VETERAN.

BARNHART, JAMES A. Age 19. Entered the service Aug 20, 1861, 3 years. Mustered out on expiration of term of service Aug. 26, 1864. Battles engaged in: Stone River, Chickamauga, Brown's Ferry, Mission Ridge. Wounded in the battle of Mission Ridge Nov. 25, 1863.

BENNETT, DANIEL. Age 28. Entered the service Aug. 23, 1861, 3 years. Discharged at Columbus, Ohio, on surgeon's certificate of disability July 1, 1862.

BENNETT, JOSEPH M. Age 31. Entered the service Aug. 24, 1861, 3 years. Discharged May 15, 1862, at Columbus, Ohio, on surgeon's certificate of disability. Battles engaged in: Shiloh, Tenn., April 6 and 7, 1862.

BIRD, JAMES T. Age 20. Entered the service Oct. 8, 1864, 1 year. Substitute. Mustered out at San Antonio, Texas, on expiration of term of service Oct. 16, 1865.

BURR, EDMUND. Age 37. Entered the service Aug. 20, 1861, 3 years. Discharged at Cincinnati, Ohio, on surgeon's certificate of disability March 20, 1863.

BRADEN, GEORGE. Age 18. Entered the service Aug. 22, 1861, 3 years. Mustered out on expiration of term of service Aug. 26, 1864. Battles engaged in: All that the Regiment was in to Atlanta. Wounded at battle of Stone River slightly.

BECKER, MARTIN. Age 30. Entered the service Aug. 25, 1864, 1 year. Mustered out at Nashville, Tenn., by order of War Department June 13, 1865.

BURNETT, MATHEW. Age 38. Entered the service Sept. 21, 1864, 1 Year. Drafted. Mustered out at Nashville, Tenn., by order of War Department June 13, 1865.

CURTIS, FRANK. Age 31. Entered the service Aug. 24, 1861, 3 years. Died January 22, 1862, at Louisville, Ky.

CLAUSE, MICHAEL. Age 25. Entered the service Sept. 21, 1864, 1 year. Drafted. Mustered out at Nashville, Tenn., by order of War Department June 13, 1865.

CRESTON, JOHN. Age 18. Entered the service Sept. 29, 1864, 1 year. Mustered out at Nashville, Tenn., by order of War Department June 13, 1865.

CLARK, GEORGE A. Age 18. Entered the service Aug. 15, 1861, 3 years. Discharged at Cleveland, Ohio, by order of War Department June 7, 1865. Battles engaged in: Shiloh, Stone River, Chickamauga, Pickett's Mills. VETERAN. Was taken prisoner at battle of Stone River, Tenn. Was imprisoned in Castle Thunder 27 days and paroled.

CHAMBERS, ROBERT. Age 18. Entered the service March 7, 1864, 3 years. Discharged at Nashville, Tenn., by order of War Department Oct. 26, 1865.

DREYER, AUGUSTUS T. Age 32. Entered the service Aug. 22, 1861, 3 years. Discharged at Columbus, Ohio, on surgeon's certificate of disability Feb. 9, 1863.

DUCHER, ALBERT V. G. Age 19. Entered the service Aug. 22, 1861, 3 years. Discharged at Columbus, Ohio, on surgeon's certificate of disability June 2, 1865. Battles engaged in: Stone River, Woodbury, Chickamauga, Orchard Knob, Mission Ridge, Resaca, Pickett's Mills. Wounded in left hip at battle of Pickett's Mills May 27, 1864.

DAVIS, JEREMIAH M. Age 19. Entered the service Oct. 8, 1864, 1 year. Substitute. Mustered out at San Antonio, Texas, on expiration of term of service Oct. 16, 1865.

DOTY, ALFRED. Age 37. Entered the service Sept. 12, 1864, 1 year. Drafted. Mustered out at Nashville, Tenn., by order of War Department June 13, 1865.

DRUM, JOHN. Age 30. Entered the service Sept. 24, 1864, 1 year. Drafted. Mustered out at Nashville, Tenn., by order of War Department June 13, 1865.

EAKIN, ROBERT. Age 18. Entered the service Aug. 23, 1861, 3 years. Mustered out on expiration of term of service Aug. 26, 1864.

ELY, LEROY. Age 18. Entered the service Aug. 15, 1862, 3 years. Discharged at Nashville, Tenn., on surgeon's certificate of disability Feb. 27, 1863.

FANCHER, JAMES. Age 18. Entered the service Oct. 8, 1864, 1 year. Substitute. Mustered out at Nashville, Tenn., by order of War Department June 12, 1865.

FROST, ALBERT G. Age 18. Entered the service Aug. 23, 1861, 3 years. Mustered out on expiration of term of service Aug. 26, 1864.

FLINT, BENJAMIN. Age 21. Entered the service Aug. 12, 1862, 3 years. Mustered out at San Antonio, Texas, on expiration of term of service Oct. 16, 1865.

GOODELL, JOHN. Age 20. Entered the service Feb. 22, 1864, 3 years. Mustered out with the company at Columbus, Ohio, Nov. 27, 1865.

GAMBER, JOHN. Age 19. Entered the service Feb. 23, 1864, 3 years. Mustered out at Camp Chase, Ohio, by order of War Department June 17, 1865.

GRIDLEY, HOMER. Age 18. Entered the service Aug. 23, 1861, 3 years. Discharged at Murfreesboro, Tenn., on surgeon's certificate of disability Aug. 18, 1862.

GEE, CHRISTOPHER W. Age 36. Entered the service Aug. 24, 1861, 3 years. Discharged at Cincinnati, Ohio, on surgeon's certificate of disability Aug. 15, 1865. VETERAN.

HOLCOMB, VIRGIL. Age 26. Entered the service Aug. 31, 1862, 3 years. Died June 25, 1863, at Reederville, Tenn.

HOLCOMB, JUDSON B. Age 20. Entered the service Aug. 15, 1862, 3 years. Died Feb. 13, 1864, at Nashville, Tenn., of wounds received Sept. 19, 1863, in battle of Chickamauga, Ga.

HOLCOMB, MARQUIS D. Age 35. Entered the service Feb. 29, 1864, 3 years. Died June 9, 1864, in Field Hospital of wounds received May 27, 1864, in battle of Pickett's Mills, Ga. Shot through the neck.

HALL, MORGAN. Age 28. Entered the service Aug. 24, 1861, 3 years. Discharged at Columbus, Ohio, on surgeon's certificate of disability Sept. 15, 1862.

HALL, GEORGE. Age 24. Entered the service Aug. 15, 1861, 3 years. Discharged at Camp Wickliffe, Ky., on surgeon's certificate of disability Feb. 15, 1862.

HARNESS, ELIJAH. Age 29. Entered the service Oct. 4, 1864, 1 year. Substitute. Mustered out at San Antonio, Texas, on expiration of term of service Oct. 16, 1865.

HAYES, ORLANDO. Age 20. Entered the service Aug. 22, 1862, 3 years. Mustered out at San Antonio, Texas, on expiration of term of service Oct. 16, 1865.

HERVEY, THOMAS. Age 40. Entered the service Aug. 5, 1861, 3 years. Discharged at Louisville, Ky., on surgeon's certificate of disability June 14, 1862.

HERVEY, GEORGE. Age 18. Entered the service Aug. 22, 1862, 3 years. Discharged ——, 1863, on surgeon's certificate of disability.

HERVEY, SAMUEL. Age 18. Entered the service Oct. 5, 1862, 3 years. Mustered out at San Antonio, Texas, on expiration of term of service Oct. 16, 1865.

HILLS, AUGUSTUS T. Age 25. Entered the service Aug. 24, 1861, 3 years. Discharged at Murfreesboro, Tenn., on surgeon's certificate of disability May 11, 1863.

HELPBURN, WILLIAM. Age 21. Entered the service Sept. 22, 1864, 1 year. Drafted. Mustered out at Nashville, Tenn., by order of War Department June 13, 1865.

HOOKS, REUBEN. Age 24. Entered the service Sept. 21, 1864, 1 year. Drafted. Mustered out at Nashville, Tenn., by order of War Department June 13, 1865.

HEWETT, ASBURY. Age 18. Entered the service Aug. 30, 1862, 3 years. Wounded and captured May 27, 1864, at battle of Pickett's Mills, Ga. No further record found. To put this soldier and his relatives in a proper light I wish to say that I was in command of Co. A at said battle, and retreated from our position at 9 p. m., and he must have been wounded or dead or he would have been with his company. It was very dark, and we could not see each other. The ground was captured by the enemy fifteen minutes after we left. James McMahon, Captain.

JONES, ALBERT. Age 25. Entered the service Aug. 10, 1861, 3 years. Discharged at Nashville, Tenn., on surgeon's certificate of disability Dec. 22, 1862.

KESLER, HIRAM. Age 19. Entered the service Aug. 24, 1861, 3 years. Transferred to Co. A, 15th Regt., Veteran Reserve Corps, Aug. 25, 1863. Wounded in right hip in battle of Stone River, Tenn.; also right elbow. Discharged at Chicago, Ill., Aug. 1864.

KIES, HENRY. Age 18. Entered the service Oct. 6, 1864, 1 year. Substitute. Mustered out at San Antonio, Tex., on expiration of term of service, Oct. 16, 1865.

KEPNER, ALLEN. Age 19. Entered the service Aug. 10, 1861, 3 years. Mustered out at Columbus, Ohio, on expiration of term of service Feb. 25, 1865.

LYNN, JACOB. Age 28. Entered the service Aug. 15, 1861, 3 years. Discharged at Nashville, Tenn., on surgeon's certificate of disability June 3, 1862.

LYNN, JACOB. Age 28. Entered the service Feb. 29, 1864, 3 years. Discharged by order of War Department July 1, 1865.

LANE, JOHN D. Age 21. Entered the service Feb. 28, 1865, 3 years.

LANE, ENOS. Age 18. Entered the service Aug. 22, 1861, 3 years. Mustered out on expiration of term of service Aug. 22, 1864.

LEHMAN, THADDEUS. Age 27. Entered the service Oct. 6, 1864, 1 year. Substitute. Mustered out at San Antonio, Texas, on expiration of term of service Oct. 16, 1864.

LINCOLN, ADDISON. Age 21. Entered the service Aug. 12, 1862, 3 years. Mustered out at San Antonio, Texas, on expiration of term of service Oct. 16, 1865. Was in all battles with Regiment, except the battle of Shiloh. Wounded in head at the battle of Chickamauga, Ga. Slightly wounded at Pickett's Mills. Taken prisoner at Stone River; thirty days in Castle Thunder.

MacDONALD, FINLEY A. Age 18. Entered the service Aug. 24, 1861, 3 years. Mustered out with the company Nov. 27, 1865. Was in all battles of the Regiment. Wounded in battle of Chickamauga. VETERAN.

McFARLAND, ALBERT. Age 18. Entered the service Aug. 30, 1862, 3 years. Killed Dec. 31, 1862, in battle of Stone River, Tenn.

MacDONALD, FRANK. Age 20. Entered the service Oct. 1, 1862, 3 years. Mustered out at Nashville, Tenn., by order of War Department May 13, 1865.

McCANN, ARCHIBALD C. Age 36. Entered the service Oct. 7, 1864, 1 year. Substitute. Discharged at St. Louis, Mo., on surgeon's certificate of disability June 16, 1865.

MINER, HENRY. Age 19. Entered the service Aug. 23, 1861, 3 years. Mustered out with company at Columbus, Ohio, Nov. 27, 1865. VETERAN. Was in all the battles of the Regiment.

MINER, GEORGE R. Age 23. Entered the service Aug. 23, 1861, 3 years. Mustered out at Nashville, Tenn., by order of War Department June 13, 1865.

MURRY, LAFTUS L. Age 18. Entered the service Aug. 21, 1862, 3 years. Died Jan. 26, 1863, in hospital at Nashville, Tenn.

MELVIN, BRUMMEL A. Age 30. Entered the service Sept. 28, 1864, 1 year. Drafted. Mustered out at Nashville, Tenn., by order of War Department June 13, 1865.

MILLER, SAMUEL. Age 24. Entered the service Aug. 3, 1861, 3 years. Mustered out on expiration of term of service at Chattanooga, Tenn., Aug. 26, 1864. Was in all battles of the Regiment up to the date of discharge.

NORTON, GEORGE. Age 23. Entered the service Aug. 8, 1861, 3 years. Died March 11, 1862, at Louisville, Ky.

NEPHEW, BENJAMIN. Age 33. Entered the service Aug. 8, 1861, 3 years. Discharged at Nashville, Tenn., on surgeon's certificate of disability March 2, 1863.

O'BRIEN, JAMES. Age 18. Entered the service Oct. 25, 1864, 1 year.

PELTON, JAMES. Age 27. Entered the service Aug. 16, 1861, 3 years. Died Feb. 16, 1862, at Louisville, Ky.

PHILLIPS, IRA N. Age 21. Entered the service Oct. 12, 1864, 1 year. Drafted. Died Dec. 11, 1864, at Nashville, Tenn., of wounds received Dec. 7, 1864, in action.

PARKER, ALBERT L. Age 34. Entered the service Feb. 29, 1864, 3 years. Died Sept. 17, 1865, at Victoria, Texas.

PATTERSON, JOHN R. Age 30. Entered the service Sept. 28, 1864, 1 year. Drafted. Mustered out at Nashville, Tenn., by order of War Department June 13, 1865.

PETTEGREW, WALTER C. Age 23. Entered the service Aug. 20, 1861, 3 years. Mustered out at Nashville, Tenn., by order of War Department June 13, 1865.

PIERCE, DAVID E. Age 20. Entered the service Aug. 22, 1861, 3 years. Discharged at Columbus, Ohio, June 4, 1862, on surgeon's certificate of disability.

PFOUTS, EDWARD. Age 20. Entered the service Aug. 10, 1861, 3 years. Discharged at Columbus, Ohio, on surgeon's certificate of disability June 17, 1864.

QUIGLEY, WILLIAM. Age 41. Entered the service Sept. 22, 1864, 1 year. Drafted. Mustered out at Louisville, Ky., by order of War Department May 15, 1865.

RITCHIE, MILO. Age 19. Entered the service Aug. 15, 1861, 3 years. Killed Nov. 25, 1863, in battle of Mission Ridge, Tenn.

RATLIFF, WILLIAM. Age 20. Entered the service Aug. 10, 1861, 3 years. Died Dec. 24, 1861, at Camp Wickliffe, Ky.

RALPH, RANSON. Age 23. Entered the service Aug. 15, 1862, 3 years. Died Sept. —, 1863, at Nashville, Tenn., of wounds received Sept. 19, 1863, in battle of Chickamauga, Ga.

RICHMOND, WELFORD J. Age 16. Entered the service Aug. 24, 1861, 3 years. Died April 13, 1862, at Mound City, Ill., of wounds received April 7, 1862, in battle of Shiloh, Tenn.

SADDLER, THOMAS. Age 18. Entered the service Aug. 18, 1861, 3 years. Killed Oct. 27, 1863, in battle of Brown's Ferry, Tenn.

SETTLE, JOHN. Age 19. Entered the service Aug. 12, 1862, 3 years. Died March 23, 1863, at Annapolis, Md., of disease contracted in Rebel prison.

SPENCER, OWEN. Age 21. Entered the service Aug. 8, 1861, 3 years. Died Aug. 17, 1863, at Hillsboro, Tenn.

SPENCER, JAMES. Age 20. Entered the service March 1, 1864, 3 years.

SHIRCY, WILLIAM. Age 18. Entered the service Aug. 12, 1862, 3 years. Died Sept. 25, 1863, at Chattanooga Tenn., of wounds received Sept. 19, 1863, in action.

SHEPHERD, DWIGHT. Age 27. Entered the service Aug. 8, 1861, 3 years. Discharged at Columbus, Ohio, on surgeon's certificate of disability July 23, 1863.

SHULL, ABRAHAM. Age 20. Entered the service Aug. 8, 1861, 3 years. Mustered out at Nashville, Tenn., by order of War Department June 13, 1865.

SKINNER, ARCHIBALD. Age 28. Entered the service Aug. 30, 1862, 3 years. Mustered out at Nashville, Tenn., by order of War Department May 9, 1865.

SMITH, WILLIAM. Age 34. Entered the service Sept. 23, 1864, 1 year. Drafted. Mustered out at Nashville, Tenn., by order of War Department June 13, 1865.

SMITH, JOHN M. Age 37. Entered the service Aug. 20, 1861, 3 years. Discharged at Cincinnati, Ohio, by order of War Department Aug. 15, 1865. VETERAN. Fought in all the battles of the Regiment, except Shiloh.

SHEALOR, WILLIAM W. Age 18. Entered the service Feb. 10, 1865, 1 year. Mustered out with the company Nov. 27, 1865.

SNIDER, COLUMBUS. Age 22. Entered the service Sept. 26, 1864, 1 year. Drafted. Mustered out at Nashville, Tenn., by order of War Department June 13, 1865.

SWACKHAMER, ISAAC. Age 23. Entered the service Sept. 24, 1864, 1 year. Drafted. Mustered out at Nashville, Tenn. by order of War Department June 13, 1865. See Roll of Honor.

TOLMAN, JOSEPH. Age 40. Entered the service Oct. 6, 1864, 1 year. Substitute. Mustered out at San Antonio, Tex., on expiration of term of service Oct. 16, 1865.

WAGONER, JOHN. Age 20. Entered the service Aug. 10, 1861, 3 years. Killed Dec. 31, 1862 in battle of Stone River, Tenn.

WARD, JOHN. Age 21. Entered the service Aug. 8, 1861, 3 years. Killed April 7, 1862 in battle of Shiloh, Tenn.

WADWORTH, JAMES. Age 23. Entered the service Aug. 8, 1861, 3 years. Died Nov. 17, 1862 at Nashville, Tenn.

WEBB, ALMON. Age 20. Entered the service Aug. 30, 1862, 3 years. Mustered out at San Antonio, Tex., on expiration of term of service Oct. 16, 1865.

WEBBER, JOHN A. Age 35. Entered the service Oct. 4, 1864, 1 year. Substitute. Mustered out at San Antonio, Tex., on expiration of term of service Oct. 16, 1865.

WEBBER, JOSHUA. Age 18. Entered the service Oct. 6, 1864, 1 year. Substitute. Mustered out at San Antonio, Tex., on expiration of term of service Oct. 16, 1865.

WEBBER, WILLIAM. Age 19. Entered the service Oct. 4, 1864, 1 year. Substitute. Mustered out at San Antonio, Tex., on expiration of term of service Oct. 16, 1865.

WILLIAMS, JOHN C. Age 18. Entered the service Aug. 8, 1861, 3 years. Discharged at Gallipolis, Ohio, on surgeon's certificate of disability May 13, 1863.

WITTEN, PETER. Age 38. Entered the service Sept. 21, 1864, 1 year. Drafted. Mustered out at Nashville, Tenn., by order of War Department June 13, 1865.

WILSON, ELI. Age 33. Entered the service Sept. 21, 1864, 1 year. Drafted. Mustered out at Nashville, Tenn., by order of War Department June 13, 1865.

WILSON, ALEXANDER. Age 18. Entered the service Oct. 4, 1864, 1 year. Absent, sick in hospital Dec. 15, 1864. Discharged by order of War Department June 29, 1865.

WORTS, RICHARD, Jr. Age 24. Entered the service Aug. 24, 1861, 3 years. Discharged at Columbus, Ohio, on surgeon's certificate of disability Aug. 29, 1865.

WORDELL, BENJAMIN. Age 26. Entered the service Sept. 27, 1864, 1 year. Drafted. Mustered out at Nashville, Tenn., by order of War Department June 13, 1865.

WRIGHT, WILLIAM. Age 26. Entered the service Sept. 21, 1864, 1 year. Substitute. Mustered out at Nashville, Tenn., by order of War Department June 13, 1865.

COMPANY B.

This company was originally recruited from Geauga county farmers, generally consisting of young men from sixteen to twenty-three years of age. It was originally organized at Burton, Geauga county, on the 20th day of August, 1861.

General Hazen, in his "Narrative of Military Service," published in 1885, has the following to say of the nucleus of the 41st Ohio, and the organization of Company B, which had started out under the name of "The Hitchcock Guards."

"The Forty-first Ohio, when I joined it, was recruiting rapidly. It had its inception in Geauga county, under the immediate care and patronage of the Hon. Peter Hitchcock, of Burton, a widely and most honorably known citizen. Three young men, Elias A. Ford (nephew of the late Governor Seabury Ford), Henry W. Johnson and Lester T. Patchin, were the nucleus. They went from village to village, and from neighborhood to neighborhood, with the old flag flying, to the step of fife and drum, and the first company was soon enrolled, as the result of their good work. Patchin was killed in one of the early battles. Ford was shot at Stone River, but recovered, and is a well-known railroad man in Pittsburg. Johnson was my efficient quartermaster in the war. He afterward declined a commission in the regular army, and is now a manufacturer at Michigan City."

General Hazen has stated the matter correctly, except that there were four others who stepped to the front with Ford, Johnson and Patchin, when the President first called for three-year volunteers, and their names were Chauncey H. Talcott, Henry Hotchkiss, James B. Cleveland and Martin Taylor. These seven were the organizers of Company B, in conjunction with the most valuable services of the Hon. Peter Hitchcock, and enrolled the first company around which the 41st Ohio Regiment was formed at Camp Wood.

Company B participated in all of the battles in which the 41st was engaged, and carried an honorable record through them all.

From first to last the company had 141 men on its rolls. It lost, in killed in battle and died of wounds, 16 men; died of disease, 19; drowned, 1. Fifteen were mustered out at expiration of term of service, before the close of the war, and 19 veterans were mustered out after the war ended.

CAPTAINS.

WILLIAM R. TOLLS. Age 37. Entered the service Aug. 20, 1861, 3 years. Promoted to Lieut. Colonel 105th Regiment, O. V. I., Aug. 20, 1862.

HENRY W. JOHNSON. Age 26. Entered the service Aug. 20, 1861, 3 years. Promoted to 1st Lieut. from 2d Lieut. Jan. 9, 1862; appointed Regt. Quartermaster Jan. 13, 1862; promoted to Captain Nov. 20, 1862; Captain and Asst. Quartermaster June 14, 1865; Brevet Major to date, March 13, 1865, for meritorious service. Was with the Division all through the service, and mustered out July 27, 1866.

ALONZO D. HOSMER. Age 26. Entered the service Aug. 27, 1861, 3 years. Appointed 1st Sergeant from Private Jan. 20 ,1864; promoted to 1st Lieut. March 13, 1865; Captain, March 18, 1865. Mustered out with company Nov. 27, 1865. VETERAN. Was in all the battles of the Regiment. Was wounded at Shiloh, Chickamauga, and twice at Pickett's Mills, Ga., May 27, 1864.

1st LIEUTENANTS.

WILLIAM W. MUNN. Age 32. Entered the service Aug. 20, 1861, 3 years. Promoted to Captain of Co. G, Jan. 8, 1862. Died Dec. 2, 1863, of wounds received Nov. 23, 1863, in battle of Orchard Knob, front of Chattanooga, Tenn.

JOHN D. KIRKENDALL. See Co. F.

ELIAS A. FORD. Age 21. Entered the service Aug. 20, 1861, 3 years. Promoted to 2d Lieut of Co. E from 1st Sergeant Feb. 3, 1862; transferred to Co. K April 17, 1862; promoted to 1st Lieut. Sept. 17, 1862. Resigned June 3, 1863. Was wounded at the battle of Stone River, Tenn., Dec. 31, 1862, severely, through right lung.

WILLIAM E. BOOTH. See Field and Staff.

JAMES M. KIRKPATRICK. See Co. F.

2d LIEUTENANTS.

KENETH MAHER. Entered the service Jan. 9, 1862, 3 years. Assigned to Co. B Jan. 26, 1862. Resigned Aug. 17, 1862.

WILLIAM H. PIERCE. See Co. H.

1st SERGEANTS.

GEORGE E. TURRELL. Age 21. Entered the service Aug. 20, 1861, 3 years. Appointed Sergeant from Corporal Jan. 10, 1862; 1st Sergeant, April —, 1862. Killed April 7, 1862, in battle of Shiloh, Tenn.

CHARLES H. WILLIAMS. Age 22. Entered the service Aug. 20, 1861, 3 years. Killed Nov. 25, 1863, in battle of Mission Ridge, Tenn.

EDWARD MORSE. Age 22. Entered the service Aug. 20, 1861, 3 years. Appointed Sergeant from Corporal Jan. 20, 1864; 1st Sergeant, March 31, 1865. Mustered out with the company Nov. 27, 1865. VETERAN.

SERGEANTS.

JOHN L. BOWER. Age 18. Entered the service Aug. 20, 1861, 3 years. Appointed Corporal Jan. 20, 1864; Sergeant, July 9, 1864. Was in all the battles of the Regiment. Mustered out with the company Nov. 27, 1865. VETERAN.

JOHN HANSARD. Age 21. Entered the service Aug. 20, 1861, 3 years. Appointed from Corporal April —, 1862. Killed April 7, 1862, in battle of Shiloh, Tenn.

JOHN V. MOORE. Age 24. Entered the service Aug. 20, 1861, 3 years. Appointed from Corporal April 8, 1862. Died Nov. 25, 1863, of wounds received in action.

JAMES B. CLEVELAND. Age 27. Entered the service Aug. 20, 1861, 3 years. Promoted to 2d Lieut., Co. H, March 1, 1862; 1st Lieut., May 24, 1862. Resigned March 24, 1863.

LESTER T. PATCHIN. Age 26. Entered the service Aug. 20, 1861, 3 years. Promoted to Sergeant Major Jan. 21, 1862; to 2d Lieut., Co. I, March 17, 1862; 1st Lieut., Sept. 1, 1862. Died Jan. 18, 1863, of wounds received Dec. 31, 1862, in battle of Stone River, Tenn.

CHAUNCEY H. TALCOTT. Age 28. Entered the service Aug. 20, 1861, 3 years. Promoted to 2d Lieut., Co. C, Jan. 21, 1862. Killed April 7, 1862, in battle of Shiloh, Tenn.

LEROY E. BOSLEY. Age 19. Entered the service Aug. 20, 1861, 3 years. Appointed Corporal April 8, 1862; Sergeant, Jan. 20, 1864; promoted to Q. M. Sergeant June 1, 1865. Mustered out with the regiment Nov. 27, 1865. VETERAN.

CORPORALS.

CLARKSON STRICKLAND. Age 20. Entered the service Aug. 20, 1861, 3 years. Appointed Corporal March 31, 1865. Mustered out with the company Nov. 27, 1865. VETERAN.

HARVEY BELDEN. Age 25. Entered the service Oct. 25, 1861, 3 years. Appointed Corporal April 8, 1862. Died Nov. 30, 1863, of wounds received in battle of Mission Ridge, Nov. 25, 1863.

EDWARD A. CARLETON. Age 18. Entered the service Aug. 20, 1861, 3 years. Appointed Corporal ———. Died Dec. 25, 1863, of wounds received in battle of Chickamauga, Sept. 19, 1863.

DANIEL CORLISS. Age 21. Entered the service Aug. 20, 1861, 3 years. Died Sept. 15, 1862, at Nashville, Tenn.

FRANKLIN SAVAGE. Age 25. Entered the service Aug. 20, 1861, 3 years. Appointed Corporal April 8, 1862.

FRANCIS FERRIS. Age 23. Entered the service Aug. 20, 1861, 3 years. Appointed Corporal ——. Discharged on surgeon's certificate of disability May 29, 1862.

THOMAS BUNDY. Age 24. Entered the service Aug. 20, 1861, 3 years. Discharged on surgeon's certificate of disability July 29, 1862.

LEVI PATCHIN, Jr. Age 27. Entered the service Aug. 20, 1861, 3 years. Promoted to 1st Lieut. in 15th Regiment, U. S. Colored Troops.

HENRY A. WEBBER. Age 21. Entered the service Aug. 27, 1861, 3 years. Appointed Corporal April 8, 1862. Mustered out on expiration of term of service Sept. 8, 1864.

CHARLES A. SNOW. Age 21. Entered the service Aug. 20, 1861, 3 years. Appointed Corporal April 8, 1862. Mustered out on expiration of term of service Sept. 8, 1864.

CHARLES P. BAIL. Age 35. Entered the service Aug. 30, 1862, 3 years. Appointed Corporal Nov. 6, 1862. Mustered out by order of War Department at Rock Island, Ill., June 13, 1865. Took part in the battles of Stone River, Chickamauga, Brown's Ferry, Orchard Knob, Mission Ridge. Wounded at Mission Ridge.

THEODORE F. HAWLEY. Age 23. Entered the service April 1, 1862, 3 years. Appointed Corporal April 27, 1864. Discharged on surgeon's certificate of disability Feb. 8, 1865. Was in all battles of Regiment, except Nashville, Dec., 1864. Wounded in battles of Shiloh, Stone River, Chickamauga, Orchard Knob, Mission Ridge and Peach Tree Creek.

LEVI DUNNING. Age 23. Entered the service July 30, 1862, 3 years. Appointed Corporal July 9, 1864. Mustered out by order of War Department June 13, 1865. Battles engaged in: Stone River, Chickamauga, Mission Ridge and Orchard Knob; all battles in the siege of Atlanta, and all after battles of the Regiment.

WILLIAM C. HODGES, Musician. Age 30. Entered the service Aug. 20, 1861, 3 years. Discharged on surgeon's certificate of disability April 1, 1863.

THOMAS R. CHRISTIE, Wagoner. Age 26. Entered the service Aug. 20, 1861, 3 years. Mustered out Sept. 5, 1864, at Columbus, Ohio, on expiration of term of service.

PRIVATES.

ANDREWS, FLETCHER. Age 19. Entered the service March 16, 1864, 3 years. Mustered out with the company Nov. 27, 1865.

ANDREWS, HOMER. Age 18. Entered the service Aug. 27, 1861, 3 years. Died Jan. 23, 1862.

ANDREWS, EDWARD. Age 22. Entered the service Aug. 27, 1861, 3 years. Discharged on surgeon's certificate of disability June 3, 1862.

BARTLETT, GEORGE S. Age 29. Entered the service Aug. 20, 1861, 3 years. Killed April 7, 1862, in battle of Shiloh, Tenn.

BARTLETT, DAVID R. Age 21. Entered the service Aug. 16, 1862, 3 years. Mustered out by order of War Department June 13, 1865. Battles engaged in: Stone River, Chickamauga, and all battles of the Atlanta campaign and Nashville, Tenn. Wounded in Stone River and Chickamauga battles.

BARTHOLOMEW, C. A. Age —. Entered the service Sept. 27, 1862, 3 years. Discharged on surgeon's certificate of disability Jan. 22, 1863.

BUCK, WILLIAM H. Age 18. Entered the service Aug. 20, 1861, 3 years. Killed Dec. 31, 1862, in battle of Stone River, Tenn.

BOSLEY, WILLIAM H. Age 20. Entered the service Aug. 27, 1861, 3 years. Died June 16, 1862, at Shiloh, Tenn.

BURNETT, ROBERT P., Jr. Age 26. Entered the service Aug. 20, 1861, 3 years. Died May 7, 1862, of disease at Shiloh, Tenn.

BENTON, ORLANDO. Age 19. Entered the service Aug. 20, 1861, 3 years. Died May 7, 1862, at 4th Division Hospital, Shiloh, Tenn.

BALLARD, LUTHER M. Age 27. Entered the service Aug. 30, 1862, 3 years. Died Nov. 30, 1863, at Chattanooga, Tenn., of disease. Battle engaged in: Chickamauga, Ga.

BURTON, DAVID O. Age 40. Entered the service Aug. 20, 1861, 3 years. Discharged on surgeon's certificate of disability July 7, 1862.

BURTON, RANSON D. Age 23. Entered the service Aug. 27, 1861, 3 years. Mustered out by order of War Department June 13, 1865.

BUNDY, LEARTUS. Age 28. Entered the service Aug. 20, 1861, 3 years. Discharged on surgeon's certificate of disability April 24, 1863. Battle engaged in: Shiloh, Tenn., April 6 and 7, 1862.

BENNET, ELMER J. Age 18. Entered the service Aug. 20, 1861, 3 years. Discharged on surgeon's certificate of disability July 11, 1862.

BLAKESELL, CHARLES W. Age 19. Entered the service Aug. 16, 1862, 3 years. Discharged at Camp Harker, Tenn., on surgeon's certificate of disability June 6, 1865.

BOOTH, CHARLES. Age 18. Entered the service Sept. 30, 1862, 3 years. Discharged on surgeon's certificate of disability Oct. 30, 1863.

BURKE, JOHN A. Age 44. Entered the service Sept. 15, 1862, 3 years. Discharged on surgeon's certificate of disability Sept. 20, 1863.

160   THE FORTY-FIRST OHIO INFANTRY.

BEARDSLEY, WILLIAM. Age 23. Entered the service Oct. 8, 1862, 9 months. Drafted. Mustered out on expiration of term of service July 7, 1863.

CHAMBERLAIN, LEWIS A. Age 20. Entered the service Aug. 16, 1862, 3 years. Discharged on surgeon's certificate of disability May 18, 1865.

CHELLIS, JOHN. Age —. Entered the service Aug. 30, 1862, 3 years. Discharged on surgeon's certificate of disability May 18, 1865.

COTTAM, MORTIMER L. Age 18. Entered the service Aug. 27, 1861, 3 years. Mustered out by order of War Department June 13, 1865.

CONRAD, JOHN D. Age 42. Entered the service Aug. 20, 1861, 3 years. Discharged on surgeon's certificate of disability July 18, 1862.

COUSINS, LEVI B. Age 18. Entered the service Aug. 20, 1861, 3 years. Discharged on surgeon's certificate of disability, March 9, 1862.

COVERT, JOHN. Age 29. Entered the service Aug. 27, 1861, 3 years. Discharged on surgeon's certificate of disability July 11, 1862.

DAVIDSON, HENRY T. Age 26. Entered the service Aug. 20, 1861, 3 years. Mustered out with the company Nov. 27, 1865. VETERAN.

DEWEY, WALLACE B. Age 18. Entered the service Aug. 20, 1861, 3 years. Mustered out with company Nov. 27, 1865. VETERAN.

DINES, JAMES A. Age 18. Entered the service Aug. 20, 1861, 3 years. Killed July 5, 1864 in action near Chattahoochee river, Ga. VETERAN.

DINES, WILLIAM, Jr. Age 23. Entered the service Aug. 20, 1861, 3 years. Mustered out on expiration of term of service Sept. 8, 1864. Wounded in battle of Mission Ridge, Tenn., Nov. 25, 1863.

DINES, PHILLIP. Age 19. Entered the service Aug. 20, 1861, 3 years. Mustered out on expiration of term of service Sept. 8, 1864. Battles engaged in: Stone River, Chickamauga, Orchard Knob, Mission Ridge. Wounded in battle of Mission Ridge, Nov. 25, 1863.

DOOLITTLE, SOBOSKI. Age 18. Entered the service Aug. 20, 1861, 3 years. Mustered out at expiration of service, Sept. 8, 1864.

DANFORTH, CHARLES. Age 37. Entered the service Aug. 21, 1862, 3 years. Transferred to Co. I, 5th Regiment, Veteran Reserve Corps. Dec. 15, 1863. Discharged July 5, 1865 by order of War Department.

DUNNING, CURTIS. Age 20. Entered the service Aug. 30, 1862, 3 years. Mustered out at Louisville, Ky. by order of War Department May 30, 1865. Battles engaged in: Stone River, Chickamauga, Resaca. Wounded at Chickamauga, Ga.

DEVOICE, HENRY. Age 28. Entered the service Sept. 8, 1862, 3 years. Discharged on surgeon's certificate of disability March 22, 1863.

ELDRIDGE, NATHAN. Age 18. Entered the service Sept. 26, 1862, 3 years. Mustered out by order of War Department June 13, 1865.

FARRELL, WILLIAM. Age 18. Entered the service Aug. 27, 1861, 3 years. Discharged on surgeon's certificate of disability June 30, 1862.

FISHER, HERBERT. Age 20. Entered the service Aug. 20, 1861, 3 years. Discharged on surgeon's certificate of disability Aug. 12, 1862.

FISHER, ORANGE. Age 44. Entered the service Aug. 30, 1862, 3 years. Discharged by order of War Department April 18, 1863.

FULLER, LEWIS. Age 23. Entered the service Aug. 30, 1861, 3 years. Mustered out on expiration of term of service Sept. 8, 1864.

FOSTER, JAMES M. Age 42. Entered the service Aug. 30, 1862, 3 years. Mustered out by order of War Department June 13, 1865.

GREEN, WARREN F. Age 18. Entered the service Aug. 20, 1861, 3 years. Mustered out with company Nov. 27, 1865. VETERAN.

GILBERT, HARRISON W. Age 23. Entered the service Aug. 27, 1861, 3 years. Killed Sept. 19, 1863 in battle of Chickamauga, Ga.

GRAY, ERASTUS. Age 47. Entered the service Sept. 30, 1862, 3 years. Died May 17, 1863 at Nashville, Tenn.

GOULD, LEVERINGS. Age 27. Entered the service Aug. 30, 1862, 3 years. Discharged at Cleveland O. on surgeon's certificate of disability April 27, 1864.

GOODE, JOHN T. Age 18. Entered the service Aug. 16, 1862, 3 years. Discharged on surgeon's certificate of disability Feb. 8, 1865. Battles engaged in: Stone River, and all engagements of the Atlantic campaign up to June 21, 1864. Wounded June 21, 1864, at Kennesaw Mountain, Ga. in right arm and hand.

GAGER, MARTIN. Age 18. Entered the service Aug. 20, 1861, 3 years. Discharged on surgeon's certificate of disability Oct. 20, 1862.

GOODRICH, WILLIAM. Age 22. Entered the service Aug. 20, 1861, 3 years. Mustered out by order of War Department June 13, 1865.

HICKOCK, GEORGE H. Age 18. Entered the service Aug. 20, 1861, 3 years. Mustered out with company Nov. 27, 1865. VETERAN.

HAYES, ANDREW J. Age 28. Entered the service Aug. 20, 1861, 3 years. Mustered out with company Nov. 27, 1865. VETERAN.

HARRINGTON, HUBERT. Age 21. Entered the service Aug. 27, 1861, 3 years. Mustered out with the company Nov. 27, 1865. VETERAN.

HARRINGTON, LEAMAN. Age 20. Entered the service Aug. 10, 1862, 3 years. Died Nov. 22, 1862 at Nashville, Tenn.

HARRINGTON, WILLIAM. Age 18. Entered the service Aug. 20, 1861, 3 years. Discharged on surgeon's certificate of disability June 19, 1863.

HAMILTON, JOHN M. Age 22. Entered the service Feb. 27, 1864, 3 years. Mustered with the company Nov. 27, 1865.

HINKSTON, HARMON. Age 35. Entered the service Aug. 20, 1861, 3 years. Discharged on surgeon's certificate of disability Sept. 26, 1862.

HOTCHKISS, HENRY. Age 30. Entered the service Aug. 27, 1861, 3 years. Mustered out on expiration of term of service Sept. 8, 1864.

HILL, ANDREW J. Age 26. Entered the service Aug. 20, 1861, 3 years. Mustered out on expiration of term of service Sept. 8, 1864.

HILL, JOSEPH. Age 42. Entered the service Sept. 30, 1862, 3 years. Discharged on surgeon's certificate of disability Oct. 8, 1863.

HAMMOND, LEONARD D. Age 19. Entered the service Aug. 16, 1862, 3 years. Mustered out by order of War Department July 13, 1865. Battles engaged in: Stone River, Chickamauga, Mission Ridge, Atlanta campaign, Franklin, Nov. 30, 1864, Nashville, Dec. 15 and 16, 1864.

JUDD, CHARLES F. Age 21. Entered the service Aug. 27, 1861, 3 years. Mustered out with company Nov. 27, 1865. VETERAN.

JOHNSON, JAMES B. Age 19. Entered the service Aug. 7, 1862, 3 years. Discharged on surgeon's certificate of disability April 4, 1863.

KINNEY, ALBERT R. Age 18. Entered the service Aug. 20, 1861, 3 years. Discharged at Columbus, O. on surgeon's certificate of disability Feb. 7, 1863.

KUBLER, CHRISTOPHER. Age 18. Entered the service Aug. 13, 1862, 3 years. Mustered out by order of War Department June 13, 1865.

LAWDOW, ALBERT. Age 19. Entered the service Aug. 27, 1861, 3 years. Mustered out with the company Nov. 27, 1865. VETERAN.

LANNING. ISAAC. Age 26. Entered the service Aug. 27, 1861, 3 years. Mustered out with company Nov. 27, 1865; was in all the battles of the Regiment. Wounded at the battle of Chickamauga, Ga. VETERAN.

LONG, SETH. Age 37. Entered the service Sept. 23, 1864, 1 year. Drafted. Mustered out at Louisville, Ky. by order of War Department May 16, 1865.

LATHAM, MARCUS L. Age 20. Entered the service Aug. 20, 1861, 3 years. Discharged on surgeon's certificate of disability July 17, 1864. Battles engaged in: Stone River, Chickamauga, Orchard Knob. Wounded in battles of Stone River and Orchard Knob, Tenn.

LATTIN, EUGENE. Age 22. Entered the service Aug. 20, 1861, 3 years. Discharged on surgeon's certificate of disability Jan. 17, 1863.

McNISH, AMOS A. Age 18. Entered the service Aug. 20, 1861, 3 years. Discharged at Columbus, O., Jan. 16, 1865.

MORTON, DAVID C. Age 21. Entered the service Aug. 20, 1861, 3 years. Died Dec. 30, 1861.

MORTON, DELOS. Age 19. Entered the service Aug. 20, 1861, 3 years. Mustered out on expiration of term of service Sept. 8, 1864.

MASON, MILTON A. Age 18. Entered the service Aug. 27, 1861, 3 years. Mustered out on expiration of term of service Sept. 24, 1864.

NEACE, SHUBAL. Age 18. Entered the service Aug. 30, 1862, 3 years. Mustered out by order of War Department June 13, 1865.

NETTLETON, DANIEL. Age 34. Entered the service Aug. 20, 1861, 3 years. Transferred to Co. I, 12th Regiment, V. R. C., Nov. 13, 1863.

PARKS, BURNETT. Age 24. Entered the service Aug. 20, 1861, 3 years. Mustered out with the company Nov. 27, 1865. VETERAN.

PEBLES, LYMAN W. Age 19. Entered the service Aug. 27, 1861, 3 years. Died March 24, 1862 at Louisville, Ky.

PELTON, HENRY C. Age 28. Entered the service Aug. 20, 1861, 3 years. Drowned March 26, 1862, in the Ohio river.

PELTON, HARLOW. Age 24. Entered the service Aug. 20, 1861, 3 years. Discharged on surgeon's certificate of disability Oct. 30, 1862.

PATCHIN, PALMER. Age 20. Entered the service Sept. 30, 1862, 3 years. Mustered out by order of War Department June 13, 1865.

PATCHIN, BERNARD. Age 30. Entered the service Sept. 20, 1862, 3 years. Died December 17, 1862 at Nashville, Tenn.

PRATT, HARVEY H. Age 21. Entered the service Aug. 27, 1861, 3 years. Mustered out on expiration of term of service Aug. 26, 1864. Battles engaged in: Orchard Knob and Mission Ridge, Tenn. Wounded slight in Mission Ridge battle.

PATTERSON, GEORGE B. Age 19. Entered the service Aug. 20, 1861, 3 years. Discharged on surgeon's certificate of disability July 5, 1864.

POTTER, JOHN. Age 21. Entered the service Aug. 20, 1861, 3 years. Discharged on surgeon's certificate of disability Jan. 4, 1865. Battles engaged in: Shiloh, Corinth, Miss., Stone River, Woodbury, Chickamauga, Mission Ridge, Rockyface Ridge, Resaca, Pickett's Mills. Wounded in last named battle.

ROSE, NELSON E. Age 22. Entered the service Aug. 20, 1861, 3 years. Killed Sept. 19, 1863, in battle of Chickamauga, Ga.

RICHARDSON, GEORGE. Age 20. Entered the service Aug. 27, 1861, 3 years. Discharged on surgeon's certificate of disability June 12, 1862.

ROOT, RILEY. Age 39. Entered the service Oct. 8, 1862, 9 months. Drafted. Died of disease July 17, 1863, at Murfreesboro, Tenn.

SPRINGER, CHARLES H. Age 20. Entered the service Aug. 20, 1861, 3 years. Killed May 27, 1864 in battle of Pickett's Mills, Ga.

SMITH, JAY C. Age 23. Entered the service Aug. 20, 1861, 3 years. Died January 29, 1862 at Louisville, Ky.

SMITH, GUY. Age 18. Entered the service Aug. 20, 1861, 3 years. Discharged on surgeon's certificate of disability July 3, 1862.

SMITH, ADDISON. Age 27. Entered the service Aug. 30, 1862, 3 years. Discharged June 13, 1865 by order of War Department.

SAVAGE, EDWARD. Age 22. Entered the service Aug. 20, 1861, 3 years. Died January 26, 1862 at Louisville, Ky.

SEELY, ANDREW J. Age 31. Entered the service Aug. 27, 1861, 3 years. Died June 12, 1864 near Atlanta, Ga.

SLITOR, ENOCH. Age 28. Entered the service Aug. 20, 1861, 3 years. Died March 20, 1862 at Louisville, Ky.

SLITOR, GEORGE. Age 20. Entered the service Aug. 20, 1861, 3 years. Discharged on surgeon's certificate of disability Feb. 10, 1862. Mustered into the service as James G. Slitor.

SHEPHERD, CHARLES R. Age 19. Entered the service Aug. 20, 1861, 3 years. Discharged on surgeon's certificate of disability July 11, 1862.

SCOTT, THOMAS A. Age 23. Entered the service Aug. 20, 1861, 3 years. Mustered out on expiration of term of service Sept. 8, 1864.

SANBORN, EDMUND M. Age 23. Entered the service Aug. 27, 1862, 3 years. Discharged by order of War Department April 15, 1865.

TAYLOR, MARTIN. Age 23. Entered the service Aug. 20, 1861, 3 years. Died May 2, 1863.

TISDALE, PHILO. Age 23. Entered the service Aug. 20, 1861, 3 years. Mustered out by order of War Department June 13, 1865.

TURRELL, WILLIAM C. Age 22. Entered the service Aug. 20, 1861, 3 years. Discharged on surgeon's certificate of disability Sept. 7, 1862.

WILSON, BUELL. Age 25. Entered the service Aug. 27, 1861, 3 years. Died April 9, 1862 at Louisville, Ky.

WHITE, JAMES. Age 42. Entered the service Sept. 30, 1862, 3 years. Died Feb. 14, 1865.

WHITE, WILLIAM. Age 43. Entered the service Sept. 27, 1862, 3 years. Died Dec. 20, 1862.

WILDER, GEORGE. Age 40. Entered the service Aug. 20, 1861, 3 years. Died Feb. 19, 1863, at Murfreesboro, Tenn.

WORDEN, MILTON. Age 22. Entered the service Aug. 20, 1861, 3 years.

WILBER, ALBERT G. Age 19. Entered the service Aug. 27, 1861, 3 years. Discharged on surgeon's certificate of disability Aug. 26, 1862.

WHITLAM, JOHN. Age 24. Entered the service Aug. 20, 1861, 3 years. Discharged on surgeon's certificate of disability June 3, 1865. VETER-AN.

WATTERS, LORRIN C. Age 23. Entered the service Aug. 27, 1861, 3 years. Discharged on surgeon's certificate of disability Aug. 26, 1862. Fought in battle of Shiloh, Tenn. April 6 and 7, 1864.

WESLEY, JOHN Age 23. Entered the service Sept. 0, 1862, 3 years. Mustered out at Hartford, Ct. by order of War Department June 10, 1865.

WINCHELL, LUTHER. Age 18. Entered the service Sept. 27, 1862, 3 years. Mustered out by order of War Department June 13, 1865.

WEBBER, CHRISTOPHER C. Age 19. Entered the service Aug. 20, 1861, 3 years. Mustered out with the company Nov. 27, 1865. VETERAN.

COMPANY C.

Company "C" was recruited in September, 1861, at Wooster, Wayne County, by Captain Aquila Wiley, who had served as Captain of Company "C" of the 16th Regiment, in the three months' service. At the time it was raised, commissions had been issued to citizens of the county to raise five other companies for the 16th Regiment, for three years service, and a camp of rendezvous was established at Wooster for that regiment. The men who had served in Company "C" of the 16th divided up, some of them receiving commissions in the new companies authorized to be raised for the 16th regiment. This made recruiting for Wiley's company slower than it would have been under other circumstances. On September 19th it proceeded to Camp Wood at Cleveland, with three officers and seventy-five enlisted men. The remainder of the company joined a week or two afterward. The following extract from a letter of Captain Wiley to the Wooster Republican will recall some of the incidents connected with the arrival at Camp Wood. The letter was dated September 23, 1861, and speaks of the kindness of the Wooster people while the company was forming, and of the enthusiastic greetings at railway stations on the way to Cleveland. Of the reception there, Capt. Wiley wrote:

"We reached Euclid street station about 6½ o'clock, P. M., and marched from there to camp. When we reached the camp, we found all the troops drawn up in open ranks at the entrance, to receive and welcome us. The Major conducted us to our quarters, tents having been pitched for our use. One of the companies prepared supper for us, carried down our blankets and camp equipage from the Quartermaster's building, and before 9 o'clock we had our supper and were in our tents, many of us comfortably enjoying our first night's sleep in camp.

We are all well pleased with the neatness, cleanliness, order and discipline of our camp. I may some other time try to give you an idea of what system and order can accomplish for the comfort and convenience of troops in camp.

Messrs. Schuckers, Lightner and Miller accompanied us with their martial music, contributing thereby greatly to the pleasure of the company, and of the crowds who met us at the station. We shall remember them kindly."

The following is a list of those who were killed, or died of wounds received in action:

1st Lieutenant, Franklin E. Pancoast; 2d Lieutenant, Chauncey H. Talcott; Color Sergeant, John Dunn; Sergeants, Louis Reed and Franklin W. Eckerman; Corporals, William S. Anderson, Edward Leininger, Solomon Miller, John Shelly, Samuel Graybill and Joseph Rossiter; and Privates, John Axe, Thomas Bonham, Anthony Camp, Joseph Carlin, David Cocklin, William F. Harley, Hiram Harmon, Jacob Jackson, Samuel Lautzenheiser, John Markwalder, Thomas McGonigal, Joseph Sweeny, Jacob Shanklin, Simon Wagoner and John Weaver.

CAPTAINS.

AQUILA WILEY. Age 26. Entered the service Sept. 19, 1861, 3 years. Promoted to Major Mar. 1, 1862; to Lieut. Colonel Nov. 20, 1862; to Colonel Nov. 29, 1862; to Brevet Brig. General. Wounded Apr. 7, 1862, in battle of Shiloh, Tenn.; wounded Nov. 25, 1863, in battle of Mission Ridge, Tenn., leg amputated. Resigned June 4, 1864.

WILLIAM RYMERS. Age 33. Entered the service Sept. 10, 1861, 3 years. Promoted from 1st Lieut. Co. I, March 1, 1862. Resigned Sept. 9, 1862.

JAMES H. COLE. Age 25. Entered the service Sept. 7, 1861, 3 years. Original Captain of Co. D, resigned March 17, 1862; recommissioned Captain Co. C, Aug. 26, 1862. Resigned to accept commission in Veteran Reserve Corps, March 29, 1864.

WILLIAM M. BEEBE. Age 21. See Co. I.

JOHN P. PATTERSON. Age 18. Entered the service Sept. 19, 1861, 3 years. Appointed Corporal from Private ——; Sergt., March 25, 1864. Promoted 1st Lieut. Nov. 26, 1864; Captain Co. H March 18, 1865; transferred from Co. H March 28, 1865. Mustered out with company Nov. 27, 1865. VETERAN. Was in all the battles of the regiment except Shiloh and Chickamauga. Slightly wounded.

1st LIEUTENANTS.

FRANKLIN E. PANCOAST. Age 24. Entered the service Sept. 19, 1861, 3 years. Died May 16, 1862, of wounds received April 7, 1862, in battle of Shiloh, Tenn.

RUFUS P. HARDY. Age 22. Entered the service Sept. 19, 1861, 3 years. Promoted from 2d Lieut. January 21, 1862. Appointed Adjutant, and transferred from Co. E June 21, 1862. Resigned April 4, 1864.

EZRA DUNHAM. Age 23. Entered the service Sept. 19, 1861, 3 years. Appointed Corporal Jan. 10, 1862; Sergt. March 10, 1862; 1st Sergt. May 1, 1862; promoted to 1st Lieut. Oct. 12, 1864; to Capt. Co. H Nov. 26, 1864; to Major March 18, 1865. Mustered out with the company Nov. 27, 1865. VETERAN.

CUNNINGHAM HUSTON. Age 21. Entered the service Sept. 19, 1861, 3 years. Appointed Sergt. from Corporal May 1, 1862; promoted to Q. M. Sergt. March 28, 1864; 1st Lieut. March 18, 1865. Mustered out with the company Nov. 27, 1865. VETERAN.

2d LIEUTENANTS.

CHAUNCEY H. TALCOTT. Age 28. See Co. B.

SAMUEL B. ASDELL. Age 18. Entered the service Sept. 19, 1861, 3 years. Appointed 1st Sergt. from Sergt. Dec. 16, 1861; promoted to 2d Lieut. April 7, 1862; 1st Lieut. and Adjutant Nov. 20, 1862. Died Nov. 17, 1863.

JAMES N. CLARK. Age 19. Entered the service Sept. 19, 1861, 3 years. Promoted from Corporal to Sergeant Major July 21, 1862; 2d Lieut. Sept. 17, 1862; 1st Lieut. Co. F March 24, 1863. Mustered out on expiration of term of service Jan. 17, 1865.

EUGENE R. EGGLESTON. Age 23. See Co. G.

1st SERGEANTS.

RUSH JAMESON. Age 19. Entered the service Aug. 30, 1862, 3 years. Appointed Sergt. from Private July 9, 1864; 1st Sergt. Dec. 9, 1864; promoted 2d Lieut. Co. I April 20, 1865; 1st Lieut. July 10, 1865; but not mustered. Mustered out with Co. I Nov. 27, 1865.

WILLIAM C. COOK. Age 18. Entered the service Sept. 19, 1861, 3 years. Appointed Sergeant from Musician July 9, 1864; 1st Sergeant, Jan. 9, 1865. Mustered out with the company Nov. 27, 1865. VETERAN.

SERGEANTS.

SIMON NORRIS. Age 18. Entered the service Sept. 19, 1861, 3 years. Appointed Corporal July 9, 1864; Sergeant Dec. 9, 1864. Mustered out with the company Nov 27, 1865. VETERAN.

JOHN BEELER. Age 19. Entered the service Sept. 19, 1861, 3 years. Appointed Corporal July 9, 1864; Sergeant Dec. 9, 1864. Mustered out with company Nov. 27, 1865. VETERAN.

WILLIAM FEASEL. Age 18. Entered the service Sept. 19, 1861, 3 years. Appointed Corporal July 9, 1864; Sergeant Dec. 9, 1864. Mustered out with the company Nov. 27, 1865. VETERAN.

JAMES M. HUSTON. Age. 22. Entered the service Sept. 19, 1861, 3 years. Appointed Corporal July 9, 1864; Sergeant July 1, 1865. Mustered out with the company Nov. 27, 1865. VETERAN.

SAMUEL BERRY. Age 21. Entered the service Sept. 19, 1861, 3 years. Appointed from Corporal Jan. 1, 1862. Died Feb. 22, 1862, at Wooster, Ohio.

JOHN DUNN. Age 24. Entered the service Sept. 19, 1861, 3 years. Died April 13, 1862, on the field, of wounds received in action April 7, 1862, in battle of Shiloh, Tenn.

LOUIS REED. Age 21. Entered the service Sept. 19, 1861, 3 years. Died May 11, 1862, at Massillon, Ohio, of wounds received April 7, 1862, in battle of Shiloh, Tenn.

FRANKLIN W. ECKERMAN. Age 24. Entered the service Sept. 19, 1861, 3 years. Appointed from Corporal March 25, 1864. Died July 4, 1864, of wounds received May 27, 1864, in battle of Pickett's Mills, Ga.

REUBEN B. COOK. Age 28. Entered the service Sept. 19, 1861, 3 years. Appointed Sergeant Aug. 9, 1862. Discharged March 31, 1864.

CORPORALS.

JOHN HOMAN. Age 19. Entered the service Sept. 19, 1861, 3 years. Appointed Corporal Dec. 0, 1804. Mustered out with the company Nov. 27, 1865. VETERAN.

MILTON FLETCHER. Age 18. Entered the service Sept. 19, 1861, 3 years. Appointed Corporal April 1, 1865. Mustered out with the company Nov. 27, 1865. VETERAN.

WILLIAM S. ANDERSON. Age 18. Entered the service Sept. 19, 1861, 3 years. Appointed Corporal ——. Killed Nov. 25, 1863, in battle of Mission Ridge, Tenn.

EDWARD LEININGER. Age 19. Entered the service Sept. 19, 1861, 3 years. Appointed Corporal ——. Killed May 27, 1864, in battle of Pickett's Mills, Ga.

SOLOMON MILLER. Age 21. Entered the service Sept. 19, 1861, 3 years. Killed May 31, 1864, in battle near Dallas, Ga. Appointed Corporal ——.

JOHN SHELLEY. Age 21. Entered the service Sept. 19, 1861, 3 years. Appointed Corporal ——. Killed Nov. 25, 1863, in battle of Mission Ridge, Tenn.

SAMUEL GRAYBILL. Age 18. Entered the service Sept. 19, 1861, 3 years. Appointed Corporal March 25, 1864. Died June 15, 1864, at Nashville, Tenn., of wounds received May 27, 1864, in battle of Pickett's Mills, Ga. VETERAN.

JOSEPH ROSSITER. Age 22. Entered the service Sept. 19, 1861, 3 years. Appointed Corporal March 10, 1862. Died April 10, 1862, on the field, of wounds received April 7, 1862, in battle of Shiloh, Tenn.

THOMAS WELLS. Age 19. Entered the service Sept. 19, 1861, 3 years. Died Dec. 29, 1862, at Louisville, Ky.

JAMES CARLIN. Age 19. Entered the service Sept. 19, 1861, 3 years. Appointed Corporal ——. Discharged at Nashville, Tenn., on surgeon's certificate of disability, April 20, 1863.

JAMES E. DORLAND. Age 18. Entered the service April 30, 1862, 3 years. Appointed Corporal ——. Discharged at Nashville, Tenn., by order of War Department, June 13, 1865. Was present during the Atlanta Campaign.

SILAS BROWN. Age 26. Entered the service Sept. 19, 1861, 3 years. Dicharged at Nashville, Tenn., on surgeon's certificate of disability, March 10, 1863.

JOHN GALLOWAY. Age 18. Entered the service Sept. 19, 1861, 3 years. Appointed Corporal ——. Discharged at Jeffersonville, Ind., on surgeon's certificate of disability, June 2, 1865.

JAMES SNYDER. Age 22. Entered the service Sept. 19, 1861, 3 years. Discharged at Columbus, O., on surgeon's certificate of disability, Oct. 20, 1862.

WILLIAM ERWIN. Age 18. Entered the service Feb. 18, 1864, 3 years. Appointed Corporal July 1, 1865. Mustered out with the company Nov. 27, 1865.

ALONZO RAYAL. Age 20. Entered the service Sept. 19, 1861, 3 years. Died March 3, 1862, at Louisville, Ky.

PRIVATES.

AXE, JOHN. Age 28. Entered the service Feb. 16, 1864, 3 years. Died July 20, 1864, at Jeffersonville, Ind., of wounds received May 27, 1864, in battle of Pickett's Mills, Ga.

ARNOLD, GEORGE. Age 23. Entered the service Sept. 19, 1861, 3 years. Discharged at St. Louis, Mo., on surgeon's certificate of disability, June 18, 1862.

ALBER, MATHIAS. Age 33. Entered the service Sept. 29, 1864, 1 year. Substitute. Mustered out at Nashville, Tenn., by order of War Department, June 13, 1865.

ANDERSON, ELBERT H. Age 38. Entered the service Sept. 29, 1864, 1 year. Drafted. Mustered out at Nashville, Tenn., by order of War Department, June 13, 1865.

BITZER, JAMES. Age 18. Entered the service March 6, 1865, 1 year. Mustered out with the company Nov. 27, 1865.

BOND, ISAAC. Age 18. Entered the service Oct. 8, 1864, 1 year. Substitute. Died Jan. 10, 1865, at Huntsville, Ala.

BONHAM, THOMAS. Age 19. Entered the service Sept. 19, 1861, 3 years. Killed Sept. 19, 1863, in battle of Chickamauga, Ga.

BUHLER, GEORGE. Age 23. Entered the service Sept. 19, 1861, 3 years.

BROWN, REASON. Age 25. Entered the service Oct. 8, 1862, 9 months. Drafted. Mustered out at Manchester, Tenn., on expiration of term of service, July 17, 1863.

BELLMAN, EMANUEL. Age 37. Entered the service Sept. 19, 1861, 3 years. Transferred to Co. B, 1st Regt. Veteran Pioneers. July 29, 1864. VETERAN.

CHACEY, SAMUEL H. Age 18. Entered the service Sept. 19, 1861, 3 years. Mustered out with company Nov. 27, 1865. VETERAN.

CHACEY, OBEDIAH. Age 18. Entered the service March 6, 1865, 1 year. Mustered out with the company Nov. 27, 1865.

CAMP, MATHIAS. Age 18. Entered the service Sept. 19, 1861, 3 years. Died Feb. 10, 1862, at Louisville, Ky.

CAMP, ANTHONY. Age 35. Entered the service Aug. 30, 1862, 3 years. Killed Nov. 25, 1863, in battle of Mission Ridge, Tenn.

CAMP, SILAS. Age 39. Entered the service Sept. 30, 1862, 3 years. Mustered out at Nashville Tenn., by order of the War Department, June 13, 1865.

CASWELL, H. S. Age 22. Entered the service Aug. 30, 1862, 3 years. Died Dec. 1, 1862, at Nashville, Tenn.

CARLIN, JOSEPH. Age 18. Entered the service Sept. 19, 1861, 3 years. Died Dec. 9, 1863, at Chattanooga, Tenn. of wounds received Nov. 23, 1863, in battle of Orchard Knob, Tenn.

COCKLIN, DAVID. Age 22. Entered the service Sept. 19, 1861, 3 years. Died May 10, 1862, at Cincinnati, O., of wounds received April 7, 1862, in battle of Shiloh, Tenn.

CLARK, SAMUEL V. Entered the service Sept. 19, 1861, 3 years.

CAPLISH, JOSEPH. Age 19. Entered the service Oct. 6, 1864, 1 year. Substitute.

CHAFFIN, NORMAN. Age 22. Entered the service Sept. 19, 1861, 3 years. Mustered out at Columbus, Ohio, on surgeon's certificate of disability, Oct. 4, 1864.

CULLEY, JAMES. Age 20. Entered the service Sept. 19, 1861, 3 years. Discharged at Columbus, Ohio, on surgeon's certificate of disability, July 8, 1862.

CULLEY, THOMAS. Age 20. 3 years. Transferred to Co. E, 6th Regt. Veteran Reserve Corps, March 13, 1865. VETERAN.

CLIPPINGER, ISRAEL. Age 44. Entered the service Oct. 8, 1862, 9 months. Drafted. Mustered out at Manchester, Tenn., on expiration of term of service, July 17, 1863.

COOK, DELORMA F. Age 19. Entered the service Oct. 8, 1862, 9 months. Drafted. Mustered out at Manchester, Tenn., on expiration of term of service, July 17, 1863.

COX, JACOB F. Age 31. Entered the service Oct. 8, 1862, 9 months. Drafted. Mustered out at Manchester, Tenn., on expiration of term of service, July 17, 1863.

CAMPBELL, DANIEL H. Age 18. Entered the service March 6, 1865, 1 year. Mustered in as David H. Campbell. Mustered out at Camp Dennison, Ohio, by order of War Department, July 27, 1865.

DUNHAM, JOSEPH. Age 21. Entered the service Sept. 19, 1861, 3 years. Discharged at Camp Dennison, Ohio on surgeon's certificate of disability, April 18, 1864.

DEVOIR, JOHN. Age 18. Entered the service Oct. 8, 1862, 9 months. Drafted. Mustered out at Manchester, Tenn., on expiration of term of service, July 17, 1863.

DEMOND, JOHN A. Age 36. Entered the service Oct. 7, 1864, 1 year. Substitute. Mustered out at San Antonio, Tex., on expiration of term of service, Oct. 16, 1865.

FLICKINGER, JOHN. Age 23. Entered the service Sept. 19, 1861, 3 years. Died April 11, 1862, at Nashville, Tenn.

FRANCE, JOHN T. Age 20. Entered the service Sept. 19, 1861, 3 years. Discharged at Camp Dennison, Ohio, on surgeon's certificate of disability, Feb. 29, 1864.

FIRESTONE, JOHN. Age 25. Entered the service Oct. 8, 1862, 9 months. Drafted. Mustered out at Manchester, Tenn., on expiration of term of service, July 17, 1863.

FOGLE, ELISHA. Age 18. Entered the service Oct. 8, 1864, 1 year. Substitute. Mustered out at San Antonio, Tex., on expiration of term of service, Oct. 16, 1864.

GALLOWAY, GEORGE. Age 18. Entered the service March 6, 1865, 1 year. Mustered out with the company Nov. 27, 1865.

GALLOWAY, DAVID W. Age 21. Entered the service Sept. 19, 1861, 3 years. Died Aug. 8, 1862, at Murfreesboro, Tenn.

GALLOWAY, DANIEL. Age 20. Entered the service Sept. 19, 1861, 3 years. Transferred to 25th Co., 2d Battalion, Veteran Reserve Corps, Sept. 16, 1863.

GRAFTON, THOMAS. Age 22. Entered the service Sept. 19, 1861, 3 years. Discharged at Columbus, Ohio, on surgeon's certificate of disability, June 20, 1862.

GARVER, AMOS L. Age 25. Entered the service Oct. 8, 1862, 9 months. Drafted. Mustered out at Manchester, Tenn., on expiration of term of service, July 17, 1863.

GEISSLER, FREDERICK. Age 21. Entered the service Sept. 21, 1864, 1 year. Drafted. Mustered out at Nashville, Tenn., by order of War Department, June 13, 1865.

GRATER, HENRY A. Age 21. Entered the service Sept. 19, 1861, 3 years. Transferred to Co. B, 1st Regt., Veteran Pioneers, July 29, 1864. VETERAN.

GEORGE, WILLIAM. Age 20. Entered the service Sept. 19, 1861, 3 years. Died Feb. 24, 1862, at Louisville, Ky.

HARLEY, WILLIAM F. Age 18. Entered the service Feb. 18, 1864, 3 years. Killed May 27, 1864, in battle of Pickett's Mills, Ga.

HENDERSON, THOMAS. Age 18. Entered the service Sept. 19, 1861, 3 years. Mustered out with the company Nov. 27, 1865. VETERAN.

HESS, JOHN. Age 33. Entered the service Feb. 9, 1864, 3 years. Mustered out with the company Nov. 27, 1865.

HARMON, HIRAM. Age 20. Entered the service Sept. 9, 1861, 3 years. Died Feb. 4, 1864, at Salisbury, N. C.

HUMMEL, ALBERT. Age 20. Entered the service Sept. 19, 1861, 3 years. Discharged Oct. 31, 1862, at Cincinnati, O., for wounds received April 7, 1862, in battle of Shiloh, Tenn.

HAVERSTOCK, FRANKLIN. Age 20. Entered the service Sept. 19, 1861, 3 years. Mustered out at Cincinnati, Ohio, on expiration of term of service, Nov. 25, 1864.

HINKLE, RICHARD C. Age 18. Entered the service Sept. 19, 1861, 3 years. Mustered out at Atlanta, Ga., on expiration of term of service, Sept. 23, 1864.

HAMMON, DAVID. Age 23. Entered the service Oct. 8, 1862, 9 months. Drafted. Mustered out at Manchester, Tenn., on expiration of term of service, June 17, 1863.

HOMAN, EBER. Age 26. Entered the service Oct. 8, 1862, 9 months. Drafted. Mustered out at Manchester, Tenn., on expiration of term of service, June 17, 1863.

HOPKINS, WILLIAM. Age 19. Entered the service Oct. 6, 1864, 1 year. Substitute. Mustered out at San Antonio, Tex., on expiration of term of service, Oct. 16, 1865.

HOUSER, DILLION. Age 18. Entered the service Oct. 6, 1864, 1 year. Substitute. Mustered out at San Antonio, Tex., on expiration of term of service, Oct. 16, 1865.

HELLER, JOSEPH. Age 26. Entered the service Sept. 26, 1864, 1 year. Drafted. Mustered out at Nashville, Tenn., by order War Department, June 13, 1865.

HIESTAND, JONAS. Age 29. Entered the service Sept. 23, 1864, 1 year. Drafted. Mustered out at Nashville, Tenn., by order of War Department, June 13, 1865.

HUBBERT, JASPER. Age 22. Entered the service Sept. 19, 1861, 3 years. Mustered in as Jasper Hubbard. Transferred to 155th Co., 2d Battalion, Veteran Reserve Corps, Feb. 2, 1864.

JACKSON, JACOB. Age 18. Entered the service Sept. 19, 1861, 3 years. Killed May 27, 1864, in battle of Pickett's Mills, Ga.

JACKSON, JAMES. Age 19. Entered the service Sep. 19, 1861, 3 years. Died June 24, 1862, at Iuka, Miss.

JONES, SAMUEL B. Age 38. Entered the service Sept. 20, 1864, 1 year. Drafted. Mustered out at Nashville, Tenn., by order War Department, June 13, 1865.

KESSLER, JAMES E. Age 26. Entered the service Sept. 19, 1861, 3 years. Absent in hospital at Jeffersonville, Ind. Mustered out Nov. 27, 1865, by order of War Department. VETERAN.

KESSLER, JOSEPH. Age 21. Entered the service Sept. 19, 1861, 3 years. Discharged at Nashville, Tenn., on surgeon's certificate of disability, Feb. 2, 1863.

KLINE JOSIAH. Age 20. Entered the service Sept. 19, 1861, 3 years. Died May 10, 1862, at Evansville, Ind.

KAICHNER, CONRAD. Age 42. Entered the service Oct. 5, 1864, 1 year. Substitute. Mustered out by order of War Department, May 22, 1865.

KRAINNER, JOHN. Age 43. Entered the service Sept. 29, 1864, 1 year. Drafted. Mustered out at Nashville, Tenn., by order of War Department, June 13, 1865.

LAUTZENHEISER, SAMUEL. Age 19. Entered the service Sept. 19, 1861, 3 years. Died June 20, 1864, at Chattanooga, Tenn., of wounds received May 27, 1864, in battle of Pickett's Mills, Ga. VETERAN.

LONGBERRY, JOHN. Age 18. Entered the service Oct. 6, 1864, 1 year. Substitute. Discharged by order of War Department May 7, 1865.

LILLEY, LEVI. Age 20. Entered the service Sept. 19, 1861, 3 years. Discharged at Nashville, Tenn., on surgeon's certificate of disability, July 12, 1863.

LILLEY, JAMES J. Age 23. Entered the service Aug. 13, 1862, 3 years. Mustered out at Nashville, Tenn., by order of War Department, June 13, 1865.

LANCASTER, NICHOLAS. Age 34. Entered the service Sept. 19, 1861, 3 years. Discharged at Louisville, Ky., on surgeon's certificate of disability, June 17, 1862.

LONG, SETH. Age 37. Entered the service Sept. 23, 1864, 1 year. Drafted. Mustered out at Nashville, Tenn., by order of War Department, June 13, 1865.

MYER, JOHN. Age 22. Entered the service Sept. 19, 1861, 3 years. Mustered out with company Nov. 27, 1865. VETERAN.

MEEK, SAMUEL. Age 30. Entered the service Oct. 6, 1864, 1 year. Substitute. Absent sick in division hospital since Nov. 29, 1864. Mustered out —— on expiration of term of service.

MAXWELL, ALEXANDER. Age 28. Entered the service Oct. 8, 1862, 3 years. Died March 21, 1863, at Readyville, Tenn.

MARKWALDER, JOHN. Age 19. Entered the service Sept. 19, 1861, 3 years. Died Dec. 25, 1863, of wounds received Nov. 25, 1863, in battle of Mission Ridge, Tenn.

McGONIGAL, THOMAS. Age 26. Entered the service Sept. 9, 1862, 3 years. Died Jan. 1, 1863, at Murfreesboro, Tenn., of wounds received Dec. 31, 1862, in battle of Stone River, Tenn.

McCLELLAN, ALFRED. Age 27. Entered the service Oct. 8, 1862, 9 months. Drafted. Mustered out at Manchester, Tenn., on expiration of term of service, July 17, 1863.

McCLELLAN, JESSE M. Age 19. Entered the service Feb. 9, 1864, 3 years. Transferred to 150th Co., 2d Battalion, Veteran Reserve Corps, Oct. 7, 1864.

McGONIGAL, JOSEPH. Age 19. Entered the service Sept. 19, 1861, 3 years. Mustered out at Columbus, Ohio, on expiration of term of service, Sept. 29, 1864.

MARTIN, CYRUS. Age 35. Entered the service Oct. 8, 1862, 9 months. Drafted.

MARTIN, JOHN H. Age 22. Entered the service Oct. 8, 1862, 9 months. Drafted. Mustered out at Manchester, Tenn., on expiration of term of service, July 17, 1863.

MARTIN, HENRY R. Age 44. Entered the service Oct. 8, 1862, 9 months. Drafted. Mustered out at Manchester, Tenn., on expiration of term of service, July 17, 1863.

MYERS, JACOB C. Age 21. Entered the service Oct. 8, 1862, 9 months. Drafted. Mustered out at Manchester, Tenn., on expiration of term of service, July 17, 1863.

MOFFITT, JAMES. Age 30. Entered the service Oct. 8, 1862, 9 months. Drafted. Mustered out at Manchester, Tenn., on expiration of term of service, July 17, 1863.

MOUSER, LEVI T. Age 40. Entered the service Sept. 27, 1864, 1 year. Drafted. Mustered out at Nashville, Tenn., by order of War Department, July 13, 1865.

MORRIS, HENRY. Age 25. Entered the service Sept. 19, 1861, 3 years. Transferred to 155th Co., 2d Battalion, Veteran Reserve Corps, Feb. 2, 1864.

MITCHELL, CHARLES. Age 18. Entered the service Oct. 5, 1864, 1 year. Discharged Sept. 29, 1865, at Camp Dennison, Ohio. Battles engaged in: Columbia; Springhill; Franklin, Tenn., and Nashville, Tenn. Poisoned at Bull's Gap and sent to field hospital.

NOAH, PAUL. Age 23. Entered the service Sept. 4, 1864, 1 year. Substitute. Mustered out at Nashville, Tenn., by order of War Department, July 13, 1865.

OCKER, HENRY. Age 27. Entered the service Sept. 19, 1861, 3 years. Mustered out at Atlanta, Ga., on expiration of term of service, Sept. 23, 1864.

OMWEG, SAMUEL. Age 28. Entered the service Sept. 19, 1861, 3 years. Transferred to 43d Co., 2d Battalion, Veteran Reserve Corps, Aug. 14, 1863.

PAINTER, JOHN. Age 32. Entered the service Oct. 8, 1862, 9 months. Drafted. Mustered out July 17, 1863, at Manchester, Tenn., on expiration of term of service. Not in "Roster of Ohio Troops."

PATTERSON, ROBERT C. Age 18. Entered the service March 6, 1865, 1 year. Mustered out with the company Nov. 27, 1865.

PERKINS, LEONIDAS. Age 24. Entered the service Sept. 24, 1864, 1 year. Drafted. Died March 8, 1865, at Nashville, Tenn.

PLUMMER, SAMUEL. Age 21. Entered the service Sept. 19, 1861, 3 years. Mustered out at Camp Dennison, Ohio, on expiration of term of service, Oct. 17, 1864.

PUDDY, SMITH H. Age 28. Entered the service Sept. 21, 1864, 1 year. Drafted. Mustered out at Nashville, Tenn., by order of War Department, June 13, 1865.

PFLUEGER, MICHAEL. Age 40. Entered the service Sept. 4, 1864, 1 year. Drafted. Mustered out at Nashville, Tenn., by order of War Department, June 13, 1865.

ROBENSON, JEFFERSON T. Age 18. Entered the service Sept. 19, 1861, 3 years. Discharged at Columbus, Ohio, Feb. 13, 1863, for wounds received in action.

RAYL, BOSTON. Age 18. Entered the service Aug. 30, 1862, 3 years. Mustered out at Nashville, Tenn., by order of War Department, June 13, 1865.

REIDER, CYRUS. Age 18. Entered the service Aug. 30, 1862, 3 years. Mustered out at Nashville, Tenn., by order of War Department, June 13, 1865.

REIDER, EMANUEL. Age 27. Entered the service Oct. 8, 1862, 9 months. Drafted. Mustered out at Manchester, Tenn., on expiration of term of service, July 17, 1863.

REED, THOMAS. Age 32. Entered the service Oct. 8, 1862, 9 months. Drafted. Mustered out at Manchester, Tenn., on expiration of term of service, July 17, 1863.

RICCARD, ZEANOCH. Age 31. Entered the service Sept. 29, 1864, 1 year. Drafted. Mustered out at Nashville, Tenn., by order of War Department, July 13, 1865.

RICARD, ANDREW. Age 38. Entered the service Sept. 29, 1864, 1 year. Drafted. Mustered out at Nashville, Tenn., by order of War Department, July 13, 1865.

RUNYAN, HENRY. Age 25. Entered the service Sept. 29, 1864, 1 year. Drafted. Mustered out at Nashville, Tenn., by order of War Department, July 13, 1865.

RHODES, ISAAC. Age 26. Entered the service Sept. 23, 1864, 1 year. Drafted. Mustered out at Cincinnati, Ohio, by order of War Department, May 17, 1865.

SWEENY, JOSEPH. Age 19. Entered the service Sept. 19, 1861, 3 years. Killed April 7, 1862, in battle of Shiloh, Tenn.

STOUFFER, JACOB. Age 21. Entered the service Sept. 19, 1861, 3 years. Mustered out with the company Nov. 27, 1865. VETERAN.

STOUFFER, ANTHONY. Age 19. Entered the service Sept. 19, 1861, 3 years. Mustered out at Atlanta, Ga., on expiration of term of service, Sept. 25, 1864.

STRINE, HARRISON. Age 18. Entered the service Sept. 19, 1861, 3 years. Died March 3, 1862, in Wayne County, Ohio.

STRINE, MARTIN V. Age 20. Entered the service Aug. 30, 1862, 3 years. Mustered out June 13, 1865, at Nashville, Tenn., by order of War Department. Battles engaged in: Stone River; Chickamauga, Ga.; Mission Ridge; The Atlanta Campaign; Franklin and Nashville, Tenn., 1864.

SNYDER, PETER. Age 22. Entered the service Oct. 8, 1862, 9 months. Drafted. Died March 23, 1863, at Readyville, Tenn.

SNYDER, CHRISTIAN. Age 36. Entered the service Oct. 8, 1862, 9 months. Drafted. Mustered out at Manchester, Tenn., on expiration of term of service, July 17, 1863.

SHANKLIN, JACOB. Age 20. Entered the service Sept. 19, 1861, 3 years. Died Nov. 27, 1863, at Chattanooga, Tenn. of wounds received Nov. 25, 1863, in battle of Mission Ridge, Tenn.

SHANKLIN, JAMES. Age 18. Entered the service Sept. 19, 1861, 3 years. Mustered out at Atlanta, Ga., on expiration of term of service, Sept. 23, 1864. Was in all battles of the regiment up to date of discharge. Wounded in hand at battle of Orchard Knob, Tenn., Nov. 23, 1863.

SHANER, WILLIAM. Age 18. Entered the service Sept. 19, 1861, 3 years. Discharged at Nashville, Tenn., on surgeon's certificate of disability, Oct. 6, 1862.

SERGEON, JOSEPH. Age 25. Entered the service Oct. 8, 1862, 9 months. Drafted. Mustered out at Manchester, Tenn., on expiration of term of service, Aug. 4, 1863.

SPAYD, ADAM. Age 23. Entered the service Oct. 8, 1862, 9 months. Drafted. Mustered out at Manchester, Tenn., on expiration of term of service, July 17, 1863.

SCOTT, LEVI T. Age 35. Entered the service Oct. 8, 1862, 9 months. Drafted. Discharged at Bowling Green, Ky., on surgeon's certificate of disability, Feb. 17, 1863.

SOUTH, ARNOLD. Age 40. Entered the service Sept. 21, 1864, 1 year. Drafted. Mustered out at Louisville, Ky., by order of War Department, June 8, 1865.

SELIX, PATTERSON. Age 24. Entered the service Oct. 6, 1864, 1 year. Drafted. Mustered out at San Antonio, Tex., on expiration of term of service, Oct. 16, 1865.

TEMPLE, JOHN. Age 24. Entered the service Sept. 21, 1864, 1 year. Drafted. Mustered out at Nashville, Tenn., by order of War Department, June 13, 1865.

TITUS, CORNELIUS F. Age 33. Entered the service Sept. 19, 1861, 3 years.

THOMAS, THOMAS. Age 36. Entered the service Sept. 21, 1864, 1 year. Drafted. Mustered out at Nashville, Tenn., by order of War Department, June 8, 1865.

TIVENAN, JOHN. Age 20. Entered the service Oct. 6, 1864, 1 year. Substitute. Mustered out at San Antonio, Tex., on expiration of term of service, Oct. 16, 1865.

ULGENER, PETER. Age 30. Entered the service Oct. 6, 1864, 1 year. Substitute. Mustered out at San Antonio, Tex., on expiration of term of service, Oct. 16, 1865.

VALLANDINGHAM, C. L. Age 19. Entered the service Sept. 19, 1861, 3 years. Transferred to 157th Co., 2d Battalion, Veteran Reserve Corps, Feb. 15, 1864.

WARNER, PETER. Age 29. Entered the service Sept. 19, 1861, 3 years. Discharged at Louisville, Ky., on surgeon's certificate of disability, Feb. 24, 1863.

WARNER, SAMUEL J. Age 21. Entered the service March 6, 1865, 1 year. Mustered out with company Nov. 27, 1865.

WILSON, JOHN M. Age 20. Entered the service Sept. 19, 1861, 3 years. Discharged at Cincinnati, Ohio, on surgeon's certificate of disability, April 3, 1863.

WRIGHT, JOHN. Age 20. Entered the service Sept. 19, 1861, 3 years. Mustered out at Atlanta, Ga., on expiration of term of service, Sept. 23, 1864.

WEIKER, WILLIAM. Age 30. Entered the service Aug. 30, 1862, 3 years. Discharged at Nashville, Tenn., by order of War Department, Jan. 17, 1863.

WALTON, THOMAS. Age 29. Entered the service Oct. 6, 1864, 1 year. Substitute. Mustered out at San Antonio, Tex., on expiration of term of service, Oct. 16, 1865.

WAGONER, SIMON. Age 21. Entered the service Sept. 19, 1861, 3 years. Killed April 7, 1862, in battle of Shiloh, Tenn.

WEAVER, JOHN. Age 18. Entered the service Sept. 19, 1861, 3 years. Killed April 7, 1862, in battle of Shiloh, Tenn.

WYNN, GEORGE. Age —. Entered the service Sept. 9, 1862, 3 years. Discharged Sept. 13, 1865, at Columbus, Ohio.

CLARK, PHENIES F. Age 31. Entered the service Oct. 8, 1862, 9 months. Substitute. Mustered out July 17, 1863, at Manchester, Tenn., on expiration of term of service.

COMPANY D.

This company was recruited in Cleveland, though many of the men came from the country southward, notably from Bedford and its vicinity. The company contained both town and country men. James H. Cole, Harvey E. Proctor and Robert L. Kimberly were among those concerned in raising the company, and were made its first officers. It had an unusual number of young men of medium stature, trim and solid, and bright in intellect. The company lost heavily in the earlier battles, and during the greater part of the term of service was not strong in numbers. Its dead count 25, three-fifths of them by wounds, the others by disease. One of its members, Edward W. Kelley, was left on the field of Chickamauga, wounded, and died of starvation in Andersonville prison pen. Four of the six killed in action were at Pickett's Mills, and two others died of wounds received there.

CAPTAINS.

JAMES H. COLE. Age 25. Entered the service Sept. 27, 1861, 3 years. Resigned March 17, 1862. See Co. C.

ROBERT L. KIMBERLY. Age 25. Entered the service Sept. 19, 1861, 3 years. Promoted 1st Lieut. and Adjutant from 2d Lieut. Jan. 21, 1862; Captain March 17, 1862; Major Nov. 20, 1862; Lieut. Colonel Jan. 1, 1863; Colonel 191st Regt. O. V. I. Feb. 28, 1865; Brevet Colonel March 13, 1865; Brevet Brigadier General ——.

HARVEY E. PROCTOR. Age 24. Entered the service Sept. 27, 1861, 3 years. Promoted from 1st Lieut. Sept. 19, 1862. Resigned some time in 1864.

1st LIEUTENANTS.

EDWIN B. ATWOOD. Age 23. See Field and Staff.

GEORGE J. A. THOMPSON. Age 27. Entered the service Sept. 18, 1861, 3 years. Appointed Corporal Jan. 8, 1862; Sergt. Jan. 12, 1863. Promoted to 1st Lieut. Nov. 26, 1864. Appointed Adjutant May 1, 1865. Mustered out with regiment Nov. 27, 1865. VETERAN.

CHARLES HAMMOND. Age 23. Entered the service Sept. 27, 1861, 3 years. Appointed Sergt. from Corporal July 1, 1862; 1st Sergt. March 27, 1864. Promoted to 1st Lieut. Co. G March 18, 1865. Transferred from Co. G June 1, 1865. Mustered out with company Nov. 27, 1865. VETERAN. Battles engaged in: Stone River, Chickamauga, Mission Ridge, Franklin, Nashville. Wounded at Chickamauga, Ga.

2d LIEUTENANTS.

TRUMAN C. CUTLER. Age 24. See Co. A.

WILLIAM HANSARD. Age 19. See Co. G.

GEORGE C. DODGE. Age 18. Entered the service Oct. 2, 1861, 3 years. Promoted from Sergt. January 1, 1863. Discharged Dec. 27, 1864.

1st SERGEANTS.

LLOYD FISHER. Age 20. Entered the service Sept. 27, 1861, 3 years. Promoted to 2d Lieut. Co. G Nov. 20, 1862; 1st Lieut. April 13, 1864; but not mustered. Discharged May 27, 1864, on surgeon's certificate of disability from wound received in battle of Chickamauga, Sept. 19, 1863. In all battles to date wounded.

JOHN H. WAKEFIELD. Age 22. Entered the service Sept 22, 1861, 3 years. Appointed Corporal Nov. 24, 1861; 1st Sergt. April 27, 1863. Reduced to the ranks for not re-enlisting with the regiment, March 27, 1864. Mustered out at Columbus, O., on expiration of term of service, Nov. 4, 1864. Wounded Sept. 19, 1863, in battle of Chickamauga, Ga., also May 27, 1864, in battle of Pickett's Mills, Ga. Arm amputated.

ARTHUR O. EMERSON. Age 19. Entered the service Oct. 8, 1861, 3 years. Appointed Corporal Dec. 13, 1862; Sergt. Dec. 9, 1864; 1st Sergt. April 1, 1865. Mustered out with company Nov. 27, 1865. VETERAN. In battles: Shiloh and all battles of the Regt. Wounded April 7, 1862, in battle of Shiloh, Tenn. Wounded Nov. 25, 1863, in battle of Mission Ridge, Tenn., and Pickett's Mills, Ga.

SERGEANTS.

EDWARD CLIFFORD. Age 18. Entered the service Sept. 2, 1861, 3 years. Discharged at Camp near Spring Hill, Tenn., by order of War Department, March 28, 1862.

HENRY M. BILLINGS. Age 25. Entered the service Sept. 2, 1861, 3 years. Discharged at Columbus, Ohio, by order of War Department, July 11, 1862.

SPENCER A. SAWYER. Age 18. Entered the service Oct. 5, 1861, 3 years. Appointed Corporal March 24, 1864; Sergt. Dec. 9, 1864. Was in all battles of the regiment with the exception of Atlanta Campaign after battle of Pickett's Mills. Wounded at battle of Stone River. Captured and 3 months in prison. Wounded at Pickett's Mills. Mustered out with the company Nov. 27, 1865. VETERAN.

JASON LOCKWOOD. Age 19. Entered the service Sept. 27, 1861, 3 years. Appointed Corporal March 24, 1864; Sergt. April 1, 1865. Mustered out with company Nov. 27, 1865. VETERAN. Wounded July 5, 1864, in action at Chattahoochee River, Ga.

SALATHIEL FANCHER. Age 21. Entered the service Sept. 2, 1861, 3 years. Appointed Corporal March 24, 1864; Sergt. July 1, 1865. Mustered out with company Nov. 27, 1865. VETERAN.

WILLIAM H. MARSHALL. Age 19. Entered the service Oct. 5, 1861, 3 years. Appointed Corporal Dec. 9, 1864; Sergt. July 1, 1865. Was in all battles of the regiment. Mustered out with company Nov. 27, 1865. VETERAN.

BURR FISHER. Age 27. Entered the service Sept. 27, 1861, 3 years. Appointed from Corporal Feb. 12, 1862. Discharged at Columbus, O., by order of War Department, Jan. 12, 1863.

ELON G. BOUGHTON. Age 22. Entered the service Sept. 10, 1861, 3 years. Appointed from Private May 18, 1862. Mustered out by order of War Department, June 13, 1865. Battles engaged in: Shiloh, Stone River, Chickamauga. Wounded Nov. 25, 1863 in battle of Mission Ridge, Tenn. After recovering from wounds served the remainder of service in Veteran Reserve Corps.

THOMAS BUTLER. Age 43. Entered the service Sept. 21, 1861, 3 years. Appointed Corporal Dec. 13, 1862; Sergt. March 27, 1864. Wounded Nov. 25, 1863, in battle of Mission Ridge. Wounded and captured May 27, 1864, at the battle of Pickett's Mills, Ga. Discharged June 17, 1865, at Camp Chase, O., by order of War Department. VETERAN.

PETER HERRIFF. Age 19. Entered the service Sept. 2, 1861, 3 years. Appointed Corporal April 28, 1863; Sergt. March 27, 1864. Promoted Com. Sergeant Dec. 9, 1864; to 2d Lieut. Co. I April 28, 1865; 1st Lieut. Co. G May 11, 1865. Mustered out with the regiment Nov. 27, 1865. VETERAN.

CORPORALS.

DANIEL TROWBRIDGE. Age 24. Entered the service Sept. 2, 1861, 3 years. Died May 9, 1862, of wounds received April 7, 1862, in battle of Shiloh, Tenn. One of the Color guards. Wounded while carrying the Colors in battle stated.

ORWIN OSBORN. Age 20. Entered the service Sept. 27, 1861, 3 years. Appointed Corporal Feb. 28, 1862. Discharged at Columbus, O., by order of War Department, Aug. 15, 1862.

WILLIAM H. H. FLICK. Age 20. Entered the service Sept. 2, 1861, 3 years. Wounded April 7, 1862, in battle of Shiloh, Tenn. Discharged at Columbus, O., by order of War Department, Dec. 11, 1862.

EMERY DAVIS. Age 22. Entered the service Sept. 2, 1861, 3 years. Discharged at Columbus, Ohio, by order of War Department, Oct. 22, 1862.

WILLIAM DUNKEE. Age 20. Entered the service Sept. 18, 1861, 3 years. Appointed Corporal July 11, 1862. Died Nov. 25, 1863, at Chattanooga, Tenn., of wounds received Nov. 25 1863, in battle of Mission Ridge, Tenn. In all battles of the regiment to time of death.

EMERSON W. SMELLIE. Age 16. Entered the service Sept. 2, 1861, 3 years. Died Nov. 26, 1863, at Chattanooga, Tenn., of wounds received Nov. 25, 1863, in battle of Mission Ridge, Tenn. Was in all battles of the regiment up to the date of his death. Appointed Corporal Feb. 11, 1863.

ANSON B. WARD. Age 18. Entered the service Sept. 2, 1861, 3 years. Wounded Oct. 27, 1863, in battle of Brown's Ferry, Tenn. Mustered out on expiration of term of service, Nov. 5, 1864.

MARTIN V. B. LOGAN. Age 22. Entered the service Sept. 14, 1861, 3 years.

T. VIRGIL RICHMOND Age 22. Entered the service Sept. 21, 1861, 3 years. Appointed Corporal Dec 9, 1864. Wounded Sept. 19, 1863, in battle of Chickamauga, Ga. Mustered out with company Nov. 27, 1865. VETERAN. Was in all battles of the regiment except Brown's Ferry, Tenn.

JULIUS JONES. Ag 21. Entered the service Sept. 10, 1861, 3 years. Appointed Corporal Dec. 9, 1864. Mustered out with company Nov. 27, 1865. VETERAN.

WILLIAM H. DEISMAN. Age 21. Entered the service Oct. 11, 1861, 3 years. Appointed Corporal April 1, 1865. Wounded Dec. 31, 1862, in battle of Stone River; Sept. 19, 1863, at Chickamauga, Ga., and May 27, 1864, at Pickett's Mills, Ga. Discharged at Nashville, Tenn., Aug. 12, 1865. VETERAN.

ALBERT HERRIMAN. Age 18. Entered the service Sept. 25, 1861, 3 years. Appointed Corporal July 1, 1865. Was in all battles of the regiment. Mustered out with company Nov. 27, 1865. VETERAN.

NEHEMIAH M. FLICK. Age 18. Entered the service March 1, 1864, 3 years. Appointed Corporal July 1, 1865. Mustered out with company Nov. 27, 1865.

ABLE P. ROSCOW. Musician. Age 42. Entered the service Oct. 22, 1861, 3 years. Discharged at Columbus, O., by order War Department, Aug. 4, 1865.

PRIVATES.

ATHERTON, ALLEN. Age 26. Entered the service Sept. 18, 1861, 3 years. Killed May 15, 1864, in battle of Resaca, Ga. VETERAN. Was in all battles of the regiment to time of death.

ASHBURN, JAMES W. Age 25. Entered the service Sept. 2, 1861, 3 years. Discharged ——, near Mt. Pleasant, Tenn., by order of War Department.

ALLEN, STEPHEN G. Age 36. Entered the service Oct. 4, 1864, 1 year. Substitute.

BUTTON, VERNEUEL. Age 18. Entered the service Feb. 9, 1864, 3 years. Mustered out with company Nov. 27, 1865.

BROWN, WILLIAM. Age 33. Entered the service Oct. 7, 1864, 1 year. Substitute, but never reported.

BROWN, BENJAMIN. Age 39. Entered the service Sept. 21, 1864, 1 year. Drafted. Mustered out at Nashville, Tenn., by order of War Department, June 13, 1865.

BROWN, JOHN W. Age 22. Entered the service Sept. 30, 1864, 1 year. Substitute. Mustered out at Nashville, Tenn., by order of War Department, June 13, 1865.

BAXTON, GEORGE. Age 21. Entered the service Oct. 12, 1864, 1 year. Substitute, but never reported.

BUSARD, GEORGE. Age 19. Entered the service Oct. 13, 1864, 1 year. Substitute, but never reported.

BERGER, EDWARD. Age 19. Entered the service Sept. 23, 1864, 1 year. Substitute. Mustered out at Nashville, Tenn., by order of War Department, June 13, 1865.

BATES, ALVIN. Age 18. Entered the service Oct. 1, 1864, 1 year. Substitute. Discharged at San Antonio, Tex., on expiration of term of service, Oct. 16, 1865.

BUTLER, JOHN D. Age 41. Entered the service Sept. 21, 1861, 3 years. Transferred to Co. B, 1st Regt., U. S. Veteran Engineers, July 29, 1864. VETERAN.

CORKAL, EDWARD. Age 18. Entered the service Sept. 17, 1861, 3 years. Died May 18, 1862, at Iuka, Miss.

CLEVELAND, JAMES. Age 27. Entered the service Sept. 10, 1861, 3 years.

CONNOR, MICHAEL. Age 22. Entered the service Oct. 2, 1864, 1 year. Substitute, but never reported.

COWAN, JOHN F. Age 18. Entered the service Sept. 10, 1861, 3 years. Discharged at Readyville, Tenn., by order of War Department, Feb. 14, 1863.

COWAN, WILLIAM. Age 29. Entered the service Oct. 8, 1862, 3 years. Discharged at Nashville, Tenn., by order of War Department, March 6, 1863.

CARR, ASA P. Age 22. Entered the service Sept. 14, 1861, 3 years. Mustered out on expiration of term of service, Nov. 5, 1864.

CORLISS, PATRICK. Age 30. Entered the service Oct. 5, 1864, 1 year. Substitute. Mustered out at Cincinnati, O., by order of War Department, May 13, 1865.

CLASKY, GEORGE H. Age 18. Entered the service Sept. 17, 1861, 3 years. Wounded Sept. 19, 1863, in battle of Chickamauga, Ga. Mustered out at Columbus, O., on expiration of term of service, Nov. 3, 1864. Correct name is Geo. H. Klasgye.

COOK, JOHN M. Age 33. Entered the service Sept. 23, 1864, 1 year. Drafted. Mustered out at Nashville, Tenn., by order of War Department, June 13, 1865.

CONWAY, FRANCIS, M. Age 22. Entered the service Sept. 24, 1864, 1 year Drafted. Mustered out at Nashville, Tenn., by order of War Department, June 13, 1865.

DUNHAM, ROYAL. Age 18. Entered the service Feb. 29, 1864, 3 years. Killed May 27, 1864, in battle of Pickett's Mills, Ga. Battles engaged in: all regiment battles from Chattanooga, May 1, 1864, to the battle he was killed in.

DAVIDSON, JESSE. Age 19. Entered the service Sept. 2, 1861, 3 years. Died April 22, 1862, at Louisville, Ky.

DAVIDSON, JOSEPH. Age 20. Entered the service Sept. 2, 1861, 3 years. Wounded Nov. 25, 1863, in battle of Mission Ridge, Tenn. Discharged at Camp Dennison, O., by order of War Department, Aug. 24, 1864.

DOANE, JAMES. Age 32. Entered the service Oct. 7, 1864, 1 year. Substitute, but never reported.

DETRICK, JOHN. Age 29. Entered the service Sept. 24, 1864, 1 year. Drafted. Mustered out at Nashville, Tenn., by order of War Department, June 13, 1865.

DANA, JOHN. Age 18. Entered the service Oct. 4, 1864, 1 year. Substitute. Mustered out at San Antonio, Tex., on expiration of term of service, Oct. 16, 1865.

ELLS, JAMES A. Age 18. Entered the service Sept. 20, 1861, 3 years. Discharged at Columbus, O., by order of War Department, Feb. 22, 1863.

FITZPATRICK, THOMAS. Age 29. Entered the service Sept. 2, 1861, 3 years. Died Dec. 8, 1863, at Chattanooga, of wounds received Nov. 23, 1863, in battle of Orchard Knob, Tenn.

FLICK, JOSIAH. Age 18. Entered the service Sept. 27, 1861, 3 years. Discharged at Columbus, O., by order of War Department, Dec. 6, 1862.

GREGORY, THEODORE. Age 25. Entered the service Sept. 2, 1861, 3 years. Wounded May 27, 1864, in battle of Pickett's Mills, Ga. Mustered out with company Nov. 27, 1865. VETERAN.

GARDNER, JOHN. Age 35. Entered the service Sept. 17, 1861, 3 years. Killed Nov. 25, 1863, in battle of Mission Ridge, Tenn.

GREY, SAMUEL H. Age 24. Entered the service Oct. 5, 1864, 1 year. Died Dec. 25, 1864, at Chattanooga, Tenn. Substitute.

GIBBS, CHARLES H. Age 19. Entered the service Oct. 7, 1864, 1 year. Substitute, but never reported.

GIBBONS, FRANCIS. Age 21. Entered the service Sept. 17, 1861, 3 years. Discharged at Columbus, O., by order of War Department, July 14, 1862.

GLASCOW, WILLIAM. Age 30. Entered the service Sept. 10, 1861, 3 years. Wounded April 7, 1862, in battle of Shiloh, Tenn. Discharged at Cincinnati, O., by order of War Department, Nov. 3, 1862.

GREER, ENOCH. Age 23. Entered the service Sept. 26, 1864, 1 year. Drafted. Mustered out at Nashville, Tenn., by order of War Department, June 13, 1865.

GADE, HENRY. Age 40. Entered the service Oct. 12, 1864, 1 year. Substitute. Mustered out at San Antonio, Tex., on expiration of term of service, Oct. 16, 1865.

HARRIS, FRANCIS. Age 18. Entered the service Sept. 2, 1861, 3 years. Died March 25, 1862, at Louisville, Ky.

HARRIS, MARTIN. Age 28. Entered the service Sept. 2, 1861, 3 years. Discharged at Murfreesboro, Tenn., by order of War Department, July 24, 1862.

HIST, JOSEPH. Age 19. Entered the service Oct. 3, 1861, 3 years. Died January 28, 1863, at Nashville, Tenn., of wounds received Dec. 31, 1862, in battle of Stone River, Tenn.

HECKELMEIER, THOMAS. Age 43. Entered the service Oct. 5, 1864, 1 year. Died Jan. 15, 1865, at Nashville, Tenn., of wounds received Dec. 16, 1864, in battle of Nashville, Tenn. Substitute.

HAMPTON, GEORGE. Age 29. Entered the service Sept. 25, 1861, 3 years.

HART, LUCIEN. Age 23. Entered the service Oct. 10, 1864, 1 year. Substitute, but never reported.

HART, HUGH. Age 35. Entered the service Sept. 17, 1861, 3 years. Wounded April 7, 1862, in battle of Shiloh, Tenn. Discharged by order of War Department, Oct. 11, 1862.

HORNIG, ALEXANDER. Age 20. Entered the service Sept. 27, 1861, 3 years. Mustered out at Pulaski, Tenn., on expiration of term of service, Nov. 5, 1864.

HEWETT, JOHNSON C. Age 18. Entered the service Sept. 14, 1861, 3 years. Wounded Sept. 19, 1863, in battle of Chickamauga, Ga. Mustered out by order of War Department, Nov. 27, 1865.

HIGHLEYMAN, RICHARD R. Age 25. Entered the service Sept. 22, 1864, 1 year. Drafted. Mustered out at Nashville, Tenn., by order of War Department, June 13, 1865.

HUNTER, LOUIS H. Age 24. Entered the service Sept. 23, 1864, 1 year. Drafted. Mustered out at Nashville, Tenn., by order of War Department, June 13, 1865.

HILLS, AMOS W. Age 19. Entered the service Oct. 5, 1864, 1 year. Drafted. Mustered out at Camp Dennison, Ohio, by order of War Department, July 27, 1865.

IVES, ERASTUS P. Age 18. Entered the service Sept. 21, 1861, 3 years. Died Feb. 20, 1862, at Louisville, Ky.

JONES, DAVID M. Age 16. Entered the service Sept. 27, 1861, 3 years. Died Feb. 6, 1863, at Bedford, Ohio.

JOHNSON, WILLIAM. Age 38. Entered the service Oct. 6, 1864, 1 year. Substitute, but never reported.

JOHNSON, WILLIAM M. Age 28. Entered the service Sept. 26, 1864, 1 year. Drafted. Mustered out at Nashville, Tenn., by order of War Department, June 13, 1865.

KELLOGG, BENOAH, Age 19. Entered the service March 2, 1864, 3 years. Wounded May 27, 1864, in battle of Pickett's Mills, Ga. Mustered out by order of War Department, Nov. 27, 1865.

KELLEY, EDWARD W. Age 18. Entered the service Sept. 2, 1861, 3 years. Wounded and captured Sept. 20, 1863, at battle of Chickamauga, Ga. Died Aug. 15, 1864, in Rebel prison, at Andersonville, Ga. Wounded at the battle of Shiloh, Tenn., April 7, 1862. Fought in all battles of the regiment up to his capture.

MINOR, JONATHAN. Age 18. Entered the service Oct. 4, 1864, 1 year. Substitute. Wounded Dec. 16, 1864, in battle of Nashville, Tenn. Mustered out by order of War Department, Nov. 27, 1865.

MEAD, LEVI. Age 21. Entered the service Sept. 2, 1861, 3 years. Died April 7, 1862, at Louisville, Ky.

MUDGE, BIRDACIE. Age 28. Entered the service Oct. 4, 1861, 3 years.

MATHEWS, ORLO C. Age 19. Entered the service Oct. 9, 1861, 3 years. Captured Oct. 23, 1864, at ——. Discharged at Columbus, Ohio, June 22, 1865. VETERAN.

MIER, JOHN. Age 40. Entered the service Sept. 22, 1864, 1 year. Drafted. Mustered out at Nashville, Tenn., by order of War Department, June 13, 1865.

MANLEY, ASHER B. Age 18. Entered the service Oct. 4, 1864, 1 year. Substitute. Mustered out at San Antonio, Tex., on expiration of term of service, Oct. 16, 1865.

MYERS, GEORGE W. Age 18. Entered the service Oct. 4, 1864, 1 year. Substitute. Mustered out at San Antonio, Tex., on expiration of term of service, Oct. 16, 1865.

NEWCOMB, JAMES F. Age 20. Entered the service Sept. 21, 1861, 3 years. Teamster. Mustered out with company Nov. 27, 1865. VETERAN.

NEEDHAM, BENJAMIN F. Age 23. Entered the service Sept. 18, 1861, 3 years. Discharged at Cleveland, Ohio, on surgeon's certificate of disability, July 6, 1864. Battles engaged in: Shiloh, Stone River, Woodbury, Chickamauga, Orchard Knob. Wounded April 7, 1862, in Battle of Shiloh, Tenn., also Nov. 23, 1863, in battle of Orchard Knob, Tenn.

O'BRIAN, MICHAEL. Age 42. Entered the service Sept. 25, 1861, 3 years. Discharged at Camp Wickliffe, Ky., by order of War Department, Jan. 30, 1862.

PRICE, FRANCIS M. Age 28. Entered the service Feb. 17, 1865, 1 year.

PRIEST, PETER. Age 43. Entered the service Oct. 7, 1864, 1 year. Substitute, but never reported.

PETTY, JOHN. Age 18. Entered the service Oct. 13, 1864, 1 year. Substitute, but never reported.

PERCEY, CHARLES. Age 19. Entered the service Feb. 20, 1864, 3 years. Assigned to the company, but never reported.

PIERCE, THOMAS. Age 29. Entered the service Sept. 30, 1861, 3 years. Discharged at Bowling Green, Ky., by order of War Department, Jan. 20, 1863.

PEASE, JAMES. Age 18. Entered the service Sept. 17, 1861, 3 years. Mustered out at Pulaski, Tenn., on expiration of term of service, Nov. 5, 1864. Wounded Nov. 23, 1863, in battle of Orchard Knob, Tenn.

PEASE, ENOS. Age 45. Entered the service Oct. 27, 1861, 3 years. Discharged at Nashville, Tenn., by order of War Department, April 30, 1863.

PRESSING, LEONARD. Age 26. Entered the service Sept. 23, 1864, 1 year. Drafted. Wounded April 1, 1865, at Bull's Gap, Tenn., by guerillas. Mustered out at Nashville, Tenn., by order of War Department, June 13, 1865.

POWERS, WILLIAM. Age 35. Entered the service Sept. 2, 1861, 3 years. Transferred to Co. E, 12th Regt., Veteran Reserve Corps, Aug. 6, 1863.

RAMSEY, CHARLES. Age 18. Entered the service April 14, 1864, 3 years. Mustered out with company Nov. 27, 1865.

RANO, JULIUS. Age 18. Entered the service Sept 14, 1861, 3 years. Discharged at Columbus, O., by order of War Department, July 12, 1862.

RATTLE, WILLIAM. Age 18. Entered the service Sept 14, 1861, 3 years. Killed May 27, 1864, in battle of Pickett's Mills, Ga. VETERAN.

RICHARDSON, LUTHER. Age 18. Entered the service Sept. 2, 1861, 3 years. VETERAN. Killed May 27, 1864, in battle of Pickett's Mills, Ga.

SAMPSON, SAMUEL. Age 19. Entered the service Sept. 14, 1861, 3 years. Died Dec. 5, 1865, at post hospital, Cairo, Ill. VETERAN.

STUDER, THOMAS. Age 19. Entered the service Oct. 5, 1861, 3 years. Died Feb. 16, 1862, at Louisville, Ky.

STUDER, JACOB. Age 18. Entered the service Sept. 30, 1864, 1 year. Substitute. Mustered out at Nashville, Tenn., by order of War Department, June 13, 1865.

SMITH, HENRY W. Age 30. Entered the service Sept. 25, 1861, 3 years. Discharged on surgeon's certificate of disability, Dec. 3, 1862. Re-enlisted Feb. 20, 1864. Died June 22, 1864, at Chattanooga, Tenn., of wounds received May 27, 1864, in battle of Pickett's Mills, Ga.

SMITH, J. STALE. Age 18. Entered the service Oct. 4, 1864, 1 year. Substitute, but did not report.

SMITH, WILLIAM E. Age 19. Entered the service Oct. 15, 1861, 3 years. Mustered out at Nashville, Tenn., by order of War Department, June 13, 1865. Battles engaged in: Shiloh and Stone River, Tenn. Wounded Dec. 31, 1862, in battle of Stone River, Tenn. Served his time out in Veteran Reserve Corps.

SMITH, PETER. Age 25. Entered the service Sept. 23, 1864, 1 year. Drafted. Mustered out at Nashville, Tenn., by order of War Department, June 13, 1865.

SANDMAN, JOHN. Age 40. Entered the service Sept. 16, 1861, 3 years.

STILLINGER, JACOB R. Age 23. Entered the service Oct. 4, 1864, 1 year. Substitute, but did not report.

SIMPSON, WILLIAM. Age 26. Entered the service Sept. 18, 1861, 3 years. Discharged at Pulaski, Tenn., by order of War Department, June 12, 1862. Battle engaged in: Shiloh, Tenn.

SLOCUM, OLIVER. Age 28. Entered the service Sept. 2, 1861, 3 years. Discharged at Nashville, Tenn., by order of War Department, Nov. 29, 1862.

SMELLIE, WILLIAM R. Age 15. Entered the service May 26, 1862, 3 years. Discharged at Cleveland, Ohio, Sept. 14, 1864, on surgeon's certificate of disability from wound received at Pickett's Mills. Battles engaged in: Corinth, Miss.; Stone River; Woodbury; Chickamauga; Brown's Ferry; Orchard Knob; Mission Ridge; Rocky Face Ridge; Resaca, and Pickett's Mills. Wounded twice at Woodbury and twice at Pickett's Mills, Ga., May 27, 1864.

SCHEER, FREDERICK. Age 18. Entered the service Oct. 5, 1864, 1 year. Substitute. Mustered out at San Antonio, Tex., on surgeon's certificate of disability, Oct. 16, 1865.

TRUMP, ANDREW. Age 18. Entered the service Sept. 14, 1861, 3 years. Killed May 27, 1864, in battle of Pickett's Mills, Ga.

TOMPKINS, MOSES. Age 32. Entered the service Feb. 12, 1864, 3 years. Died June 21, 1864, at Chattanooga, Tenn., of wounds received May 27, 1864, in battle of Pickett's Mills, Ga.

TENNIS, JOHN S. Age 18. Entered the service Sept. 14, 1861, 3 years. Discharged at Readyville, Tenn., by order of War Department, Feb. 14, 1863.

TUMBLESON, JAMES. Age 18. Entered the service Sept. 30. 1864. 1 year. Substitute. Mustered out at Nashville, Tenn., by order of War Department, June 13, 1865.

THURSTON, JAMES. Age 27. Entered the service Sept. 26, 1864, 1 year. Drafted. Mustered out at Nashville, Tenn., by order of War Department, June 13, 1865.

TULLIS, DAVID. Age 18. Entered the service Oct. 1, 1864, 1 year. Substitute. Mustered out at San Antonio, Tex., on expiration of term of service, Oct. 16, 1865.

UNDERHILL, DANIEL R. Age 19. Entered the service Sept. 10, 1861, 3 years. Died Jan. 15, 1862, at Camp Wickliffe, Ky.

VENOAH, CHARLES. Age 48. Entered the service Sept 18, 1861, 3 years. Mustered out at Columbus, Ohio, on expiration of term of service, Nov. 29, 1864. Wounded Nov. 25, 1863, in battle of Mission Ridge, Tenn., also Feb. 19, 1864, at Readyville, Tenn.

VARNHOLT, JOHN. Age 22. Entered the service Oct. 5, 1864, 1 year. Substitute. Mustered out at San Antonio, Tex., on expiration of term of service, Oct. 16, 1865.

WICK, WILLIAM, Age 18. Entered the service Sept. 27, 1861, 3 years. Mustered out with company Nov. 27, 1865. VETERAN.

WOOD, WILLIAM. Age 18. Entered the service Feb. 25, 1864, 3 years. Mustered out with company Nov. 27, 1865.

WOOD, ELISHA. Age 40. Entered the service Oct 28, 1861, 3 years. Discharged at Columbus, O., by order of War Department, Nov. 25, 1862.

WHEELER, ZENAS. Age 18. Entered the service Sept. 27, 1861, 3 years. Discharged at Cincinnati, Ohio, by order of War Department, Nov. 19, 1862.

COMPANY E.

During July, 1861, F. D. Stone and W. J. Morgan began recruiting a company in Cleveland. On the 17th of August Captain Stone received orders from the Adjutant General of the state of Ohio to march his company to an unbroken field, which afterward became "Camp Wood." The company proving to have only sixty men, it could go into camp with only a 1st Lieutenant. W. J. Morgan, being the prospective Lieutenant, got the men together and marched them out to the field, climbed over the fence, and went into camp, aligned the men in proper order, and solemnly swore them into the service of the United States; and by previous instruction or intimation, named the field "Camp Wood." They remained in camp that day, with James McMahon acting as 1st Sergeant. At sunset Morgan mustered the company and gave them permission to go to their homes for the night, with strict injunctions to report in the morning for roll-call, which was faithfully done. During this day, Acting Quartermaster Sergeant W. S. Blythe reported to Lieut. Morgan with carpenters, lumber, etc. Result, a building, and before night loads of bread, meat, coffee, sugar, etc., and Blythe dealt out rations in good military form. Recruits were constantly added to the company, and in a few days, other companies came into the camp. Lieut. Morgan's company being now about complete in numbers, at least to the minimum, F. D. Stone was made Captain and took charge of the company; W. J. Morgan, First Lieutenant; Harry Jones, Second "Principal Ornament," as he called it; Ab Virgil, First Sergeant. Sergeant McMahon was given to Capt. Pease' Oberlin company (H) as First Sergeant. Pease wanted a man of McMahon's experience, and McMahon deemed his chances better in H company.

During its service the company lost nine men killed in action, six died of wounds, and only three of disease. Three of the killed in action were at Shiloh, and three others died of wounds received there.

CAPTAINS.

FRANK D. STONE. Age 23. Entered the service Sept. 30, 1861, 3 years. Resigned at Camp Wickliffe, Ky., Jan. 22, 1862.

JOHN W. STEELE. Age 24. See Co. H.

1st LIEUTENANTS.

W. J. MORGAN. Age 23. Entered the service Aug. 27, 1861, 3 years. Promoted to Captain Co. H Jan. 9, 1862. Resigned at Readyville, Tenn., March 24, 1863. Battles engaged in: Shiloh, Tenn., April 7, 1862; Stone River, Tenn.

R. B. HARDY. Age 22. See Co. C.

HARRY W. JONES. Age 23. Entered the service Sept. 19, 1861, 3 years. Promoted to 1st Lieut Co. K from 2d Lieut. Feb. 8, 1862. Transferred from Co. K Aug. 6, 1862. Was at the siege of Corinth, Miss.

TRUMAN C. CUTLER. Age 24. See Co. A.

FERDINAND D. COBB. Age 22. See Co. F.

2d LIEUTENANTS.

ELIAS A. FORD. Age 21. See Co. B.

WALTER BLYTHE. Age 30. See Field and Staff.

FREDERICK A. McKAY. Age 19. Entered the service Sept. 30, 1861, 3 years. Promoted from Sergeant Nov. 24, 1862. Was in all battles of the regiment to the fall of Atlanta, Ga., except Mission Ridge, Tenn. Wounded at the battle of Orchard Knob, Tenn., Nov. 23, 1863. Resigned Nov. 20, 1864.

1st SERGEANTS.

ALBERT E. VIRGLE. Age 27. Entered the service Sept. 12, 1861, 3 years. Died at St. Louis, Mo., ——, of wounds received April 7, 1862, in battle of Shiloh, Tenn.

BENJAMIN WOOD. Age 21. Entered the service Sept. 27, 1861, 3 years. Appointed Sergt. from Private Jan. 20, 1864; 1st Sergt. June 8, 1864. Was in all the battles of the regiment. Mustered out with company Nov. 27, 1865. VETERAN. Slightly wounded at Shiloh, April 7, 1862, also at Mission Ridge, Tenn., Nov. 25, 1863.

SERGEANTS.

WILLIAM H. DRUM. Age 19. Entered the service Sept. 13, 1861, 3 years. Appointed from Corporal Jan. 20, 1864. Was in all the battles of the regiment. Mustered out with company Nov. 27, 1865. VETERAN.

JACOB R. CRESSINGER. Age 18. Entered the service Aug. 27, 1861, 3 years. Appointed from Musician April 1, 1865. Was in all the battles of the regiment. Mustered out with company Nov. 27, 1865. VETERAN.

HENRY SIMONS. Age 21. Entered the service Aug. 27, 1861, 3 years. Killed December 31, 1862, in battle of Stone River, Tenn. Was in all previous battles.

WILLIAM LYNCH. Age 29. Entered the service Aug. 27, 1861, 3 years. Discharged at Nashville, Tenn., on surgeon's certificate of disability, June 1, 1862.

JAMES MURRAY. Age 33. Entered the service Oct. 2, 1861, 3 years. Appointed from Private Feb. 28, 1863. Mustered out at Pulaski, Tenn., on expiration of term of service, Nov. 2, 1864. Detailed to build monument on battle field of Stone River, July —, 1863. Returned to company July, 1864. Battles engaged in: Shiloh, Siege of Corinth, Stone River and Siege of Atlanta, Ga.

WILLIAM PATRIDGE. Age 19. Entered the service Oct. 2, 1861, 3 years. Appointed from Private Feb. 28, 1863. Mustered out at Columbus, Ohio, on expiration of term of service, Nov. 2, 1864. Wounded severely in the battle of Orchard Knob, Tenn., Nov. 23, 1863.

CORPORALS.

JOHN CULLEN. Age 35. Entered the service Sept. 12, 1861, 3 years. Killed April 7, 1862, in battle of Shiloh, Tenn.

CHARLES RANDLES. Age 25. Entered the service Oct. 2, 1861, 3 years.

WILLIAM EDWARDS. Age 23. Entered the service Sept. 12, 1861, 3 years. Discharged at Cincinnati, Ohio, by order of War Department, Feb. 21, 1863.

THOMAS POWERS. Age 18. Entered the service Aug. 27, 1861, 3 years. Discharged Sept. 16, 1862, on account of wounds received in battle of Shiloh, April 7, 1862.

MUSICIANS.

SYLVESTER WINCHESTER. Age 52. Entered the service Oct. 4, 1861, 3 years. Killed Dec. 31, 1862, in battle of Stone River, Tenn. Was in all battles prior to his death.

WARRAN K. SCOTT. Age 29. Entered the service Aug. 27, 1861, 3 years. Mustered out at Columbus, Ohio, April 5, 1865.

PRIVATES.

ANNIS, LEMON. Age 18. Entered the service Aug. 27, 1861, 3 years. Discharged at Camp Dennison, Ohio.

ARNOTT, JAMES. Age 18. Entered the service Aug. 27, 1861, 3 years. Transferred to 154th Co., 2d Battalion, Veteran Reserve Corps, Feb. 2, 1864. Was in all battles of the regiment previous to his transfer.

BARBER, JAMES. Age 25. Entered the service Sept. 2, 1861, 3 years. Discharged at Louisville, Ky., May 12, 1862.

BARBER, CASWELL. Age 28. Entered the service Aug. 27, 1861, 3 years. Discharged at Louisville, Ky., May 12, 1862.

BEARD, ALEXANDER. Age 35. Entered the service Aug. 27, 1861, 3 years. Discharged at Glasgow, Ky., Nov. 8, 1862. Was in battle of Shiloh and Siege of Corinth, Miss.

CHAPMAN, MATHEW B. Age 20. Entered the service Feb. 29, 1864, 3 years. Mustered out with company Nov. 27, 1865.

CORBITT, DENNIS. Age 19. Entered the service Sept. 4, 1861, 3 years. Was in all battles of the regiment up to the date of his discharge. Mustered out at Pulaski, Tenn., on expiration of term of service, Nov. 2, 1864. Wounded at Lost Mountain, Ga.

CORBITT, TIMOTHY. Age 31. Entered the service Aug. 27, 1861, 3 years. Killed Dec. 31, 1862, in battle of Stone River, Tenn. Was in the battle of Shiloh, Tenn., and Siege of Corinth, Miss.

CHALK, MICHAEL. Age 31. Entered the service Oct. 6, 1861, 3 years. Died June 18, 1862, at St. Louis, Mo., of wounds received April 7, 1862, in battle of Shiloh, Tenn.

COLBY, SAMUEL. Age 27. Entered the service Aug. 27, 1861, 3 years. Mustered out at Pulaski, Tenn., on expiration of term of service, Nov. 2, 1864. Wounded at Shiloh, Tenn., April 7, 1862, which disabled him from field service. Was on detailed duty at Nashville, Tenn., until mustered out.

CONWAY THOMAS. Age 18. Entered the service Aug. 27, 1861, 3 years. Mustered out at Pulaski, Tenn., on expiration of term of service, Nov. 2, 1864. Was in all battles of regiment up to date of discharge. Wounded at Stone River, Tenn., Dec. 31, 1862.

CONWAY, HENRY. Age 19. Entered the service Aug. 27, 1861, 3 years. Discharged at Louisville, Ky., Aug. 12, 1863, on surgeon's certificate of disability, caused by wounds received at Stone River, Tenn., Dec. 31, 1862.

CALDWELL, JOHN. Age 18. Entered the service Sept. 12, 1861, 3 years. Discharged at Louisville, Ky., July 22, 1863, on surgeon's certificate of disability, caused by wounds received Dec. 31, 1862, in battle of Stone River.

CANFIELD, JOHN. Age 20. Entered the service Dec. 10, 1861, 3 years. Discharged at Huntsville, Ala., June 14, 1865, on surgeon's certificate of disability. Was in all the battles of the regiment. Wounded severely Dec. 31, 1862, in battle of Stone River, Tenn.

COCHRAN, DAVID. Age 22. Entered the service Sept. 14, 1861, 3 years. Mustered out at Pulaski, Tenn., on expiration of term of service, Nov. 2, 1864. Detailed to build monument on battle field of Stone River, Tenn. Rejoined his company at Atlanta, Ga. Wounded Dec. 31, 1862, in battle of Stone River, Tenn. Battles engaged in: Shiloh, Siege of Corinth, Stone River, Atlanta and Lovejoy Station, Ga.

COYKENDALL, HENRY S. Age 21. Entered the service Aug. 27, 1861, 3 years. Mustered out at Pulaski, Tenn., on expiration of term of service, Nov. 2, 1864.

CHESLEY, CHARLES. Age 21. Entered the service Aug. 27, 1862, 3 years. Killed Nov. 23, 1863, in battle of Orchard Knob, Tenn. Was in all battles of regiment from Stone River to Orchard Knob.

DONNELLY, JAMES. Age 29. Entered the service Feb. 29, 1864, 3 years.

DAVIDSON, ROBERT. Age 29. Entered the service Sept. 30, 1861, 3 years. Mustered out at Pulaski, Tenn., on expiration of term of service, Nov. 2, 1864. Was in all battles of the regiment up to his discharge.

EVANS, JAMES. Age 26. Entered the service Sept. 8, 1861, 3 years. Mustered out at Columbus, Ohio, on expiration of term of service, Jan. 30, 1865. Wounded and taken prisoner at battle of Chickamauga, Ga.

ECKHART, ARTHUR. Age 23. Entered the service Aug. 27, 1861, 3 years. Mustered out on expiration of term of service, Nov. 2, 1864. Was in all battles of regiment up to date of discharge.

FLANNIGAN, PATRICK. Age 18. Entered the service Sept. 14, 1861, 3 years. Mustered out with company Nov. 27, 1865. VETERAN. Was in all battles of the regiment.

FLUETT, GEORGE Age 20. Entered the service Aug. 22, 1861, 3 years. Mustered out with company Nov. 27, 1865. VETERAN. Was in all battles of regiment from Stone River, Dec. 31, 1862, to Nashville, Dec. 15, 1864.

FAUST, ERNEST. Age 22. Entered the service Sept. 10, 1861, 3 years.

FLYN, MICHAEL. Age 20. Entered the service Feb. 29, 1864, 3 years.

FARRELL, PATRICK. Age 18. Entered the service Sept. 6, 1861, 3 years. Mustered out at Columbus, O., on expiration of term of service, Feb. 18, 1865. Was taken prisoner Sept. 19, 1863, in battle of Chickamauga, Ga. Was in all battles of regiment up to date of capture.

FULWELLER, ENSIGN. Age 18. Entered the service Aug. 27, 1861, 3 years. Discharged Nov. 16, 1862, for wounds received April 7, 1862, in battle of Shiloh, Tenn.

FITZPATRICK, EDWARD. Age 19. Entered the service Sept. 12, 1861, 3 years. Discharged Aug. 22, 1862, for wounds received April 7, 1862, in battle of Shiloh, Tenn.

FERRELL, WILLIAM. Age 22. Entered the service Aug. 22, 1862, 3 years. Transferred to Veteran Reserve Corps April 1, 1865. Discharged at Knoxville, Tenn., by order of War Department, July 12, 1865.

GODMAN, WILLIAM. Age 22. Entered the service Aug. 31, 1862, 3 years. In battles of Stone River, Woodbury, Chickamauga, Brown's Ferry and around Chattanooga.

GORDON, JOHN. Age 19. Entered the service Sept. 12, 1861, 3 years. Discharged at Columbus, Ohio, June 13, 1862, for wounds received April 7, 1862, in battle of Shiloh, Tenn.

GRIFFIN, MICHAEL. Age 33. Entered the service Oct. 3, 1861, 3 years. Mustered out at Columbus, Ohio, on expiration of term of service, Feb. 21, 1865. Taken prisoner Sept. 20, 1863, in battle of Chickamauga, Ga. Was in all battles of the regiment up to date of capture.

HERLING, CHARLES. Age 18. Entered the service Oct. 9, 1861, 3 years. Killed May 27, 1864, in battle of Pickett's Mills, Ga. Was in all battles of the regiment to date of death. VETERAN.

HAYES, JOHN. Age 18. Entered the service Sept. 12, 1861, 3 years. Died June 15, 1862, at Cincinnati, O., of wounds received April 7, 1862, in battle of Shiloh, Tenn.

HIGHLAND, WILLIAM. Age 19. Entered the service Aug. 27, 1861, 3 years. Died Dec. 26, 1863, in hospital at Chattanooga, Tenn., of wounds received Nov. 25, 1863, in battle of Mission Ridge, Tenn. Was in all battles of regiment up to date of death.

HOGAN, DANIEL. Age 18. Entered the service Aug. 27, 1861, 3 years. Discharged at Cleveland, Ohio, Aug. 5, 1862.

HELPIN, JOHN. Age 19. Entered the service Sept. 1, 1861, 3 years. Discharged at Camp Dennison, O. Was in battle of Shiloh, Tenn, April 7, 1862.

HODGE, FREDERICK. Age 18. Entered the service Aug. 27, 1861, 3 years. Discharged at Cleveland, Ohio, Nov. 6, 1862.

HARVEY, URSON. Age 18. Entered the service Oct. 9, 1861, 3 years. Discharged ——, at Camp Dennison, Ohio.

HOBERT, OLIVER. Age 18. Entered the service Aug. 27, 1861, 3 years. Discharged at Columbus, Ohio, March 31, 1863.

HOWARD, MICHAEL. Age 22. Entered the service Aug. 23, 1862, 3 years. Transferred to 42d Co., 2d Battalion, Veteran Reserve Corps, Oct. 29, 1863. Discharged June 29, 1865, by order of War Department.

HUBBELL, AUGUSTUS. Age 34. Entered the service Aug. 27, 1861, 3 years. Discharged Feb. 10, 1862, at Camp Wickliffe, Ky., on surgeon's certificate of disability, caused by a kick from a horse on Jenkins' farm, W. Va.

JOHNSON, EDWARD. Age 19. Entered the service Aug. 27, 1861, 3 years. Mustered out at Columbus, Ohio, on expiration of term of service, Nov. 12, 1864. Wounded and taken prisoner in battle of Chickamauga, Ga., Sept. 20, 1863. Was in all battles of the regiment up to date of capture.

KEPLER, JOHN. Age 42. Entered the service Sept. 10, 1861, 3 years. Died at Nashville, Tenn., Jan. 18, 1863. Was in battles of Shiloh, Corinth and Stone River.

KANE, MICHAEL. Age 40. Entered the service Aug. 26, 1862, 3 years. Mustered out at Nashville, Tenn., by order of War Department, June 13, 1865. Battles engaged in: Stone River; Woodbury; Chickamauga, Ga., and at Chattanooga, Tenn.

LANGELL, WILLIAM. Age 18. Entered the service Aug. 27, 1861, 3 years. Mustered out with company Nov. 27, 1865. VETERAN. Was in all battles of the regiment.

LOBDELL, JOHN. Age 18. Entered the service Aug. 27, 1861, 3 years. Mustered out with company Nov. 27, 1865. VETERAN.

LAMBIER, JAMES. Age 22. Entered the service Sept. 1, 1861, 3 years. Killed April 7, 1862, in battle of Shiloh, Tenn.

LAMB, ROBERT. Age 33. Entered the service Sept. 1, 1861, 3 years. Discharged at Camp Dennison, Ohio, Jan. 22, 1863. Battles engaged in: Shiloh, and Siege of Corinth, Miss.

MONTREAL, ANTHONY. Age 19. Entered the service Sept. 4, 1861, 3 years. Killed April 7, 1862, in battle of Shiloh, Tenn.

MILLER, JAMES. Age —. Entered the service Feb. 29, 1864, 3 years.

MILLER, MITCHELL. Age 19. Entered the service Dec. 10, 1861, 3 years. Discharged at Huntsville, Ala., on expiration of term of service, Jan. 14, 1865. Wounded April 7, 1862, in battle of Shiloh, Tenn. Was in all battles of the regiment.

MARTIN, JAMES. Age —. Entered the service Feb. 29, 1864, 3 years.

MOSES, JOSEPH. Age 29. Entered the service Sept. 5, 1861, 3 years. Discharged at Cincinnati, Ohio, May 18, 1862.

MATTISON, ANDREW. Age 22. Entered the service Sept. 12, 1861, 3 years. Discharged on surgeon's certificate of disability, Jan. 15, 1862.

MARONEY, JAMES. Age 22. Entered the service Sept. 2, 1862, 3 years. Discharged at Camp Dennison, Ohio, Aug. 3, 1864. Wounded at Stone River, and Chickamauga, Ga.

NALLY, WILLIAM. Age 31. Entered the service Sept. 12, 1861, 3 years. Mustered out with company Nov. 27, 1865. VETERAN. Was in all battles of the regiment.

NAY, THOMAS. Age 43. Entered the service Aug. 25, 1862, 3 years. Mustered out with company Nov. 27, 1865.

NEVILLE, RICHARD. Age 18. Entered the service Oct. 2, 1861, 3 years. Discharged at Pulaski, Tenn., on expiration of term of service, Nov. 2, 1864. Was in all battles of regiment up to date of discharge. Wounded Dec. 31, 1862, in battle of Stone River, Tenn.

NEVILLE, JOHN. Age 19. Entered the service Aug. 27, 1861, 3 years. Mustered out at Pulaski, Tenn., on expiration of term of service, Nov. 2, 1864. Was in all battles of regiment up to date of discharge.

OVIATT, WILLIAM. Age 39. Entered the service Oct. 8, 1861, 3 years. Discharged at Camp Chase, Ohio.

O'RILEY, RICHARD. Age 34. Entered the service Aug. 27, 1861, 3 years. Discharged at Columbus, Ohio, Jan. 20, 1863. Was in battles of Shiloh, Siege of Corinth, Miss., and Stone River, Tenn.

PARTRIDGE GEORGE. Age 18. Entered the service Aug. 27, 1861, 3 years. Absent sick; Mustered out to date, Nov. 27, 1865, by order of War Department. Was in all battles of the regiment up to and including July 5, 1864.

PHILLIPS, JOHN. Age 25. Entered the service Aug. 18, 1862, 3 years.

PHILLIPS, DAVID. Age 30. Entered the service Aug. 27, 1861, 3 years. Discharged at Louisville, Ky., Jan. 2, 1863. Wounded at Shiloh, April 7, 1862.

PALMER, JOHN. Age 18. Entered the service Sept. 8, 1861, 3 years. Mustered out at Nashville, Tenn., by order of War Department, June 13, 1865. Wounded in battle of Chickamauga, Ga.

PRICE, JOHN. Age 48. Entered the service Sept. 27, 1861, 3 years. Mustered out at Pulaski, Tenn., on expiration of term of service, Nov. 10, 1864. Was in battles of Shiloh and Stone River.

QUICK, JESSE. Age 35. Entered the service Aug. 27, 1861, 3 years. Killed Dec. 31, 1862, in battle of Stone River, Tenn. Was in all battles of regiment up to date of death.

RAWLINGS, JOHN. Age 26. Entered the service Aug. 27, 1861, 3 years. On detached duty. Mustered out with company Nov. 27, 1865. VETERAN.

RITTICKER, HENRY. Age 43. Entered the service Aug. 18, 1862, 3 years. Discharged at Nashville, Tenn., July 21, 1863.

RYAN, JOHN. Age 24. Entered the service Sept. 12, 1861, 3 years. Transferred to 125th Co., 2d Battalion, Veteran Reserve Corps, Dec. 18, 1863. Wounded Dec. 31, 1862, in battle of Stone River, Tenn.

ROSSITER, RICHARD. Age 20. Entered the service Nov. 7, 1861, 3 years. Discharged on account of wounds, Dec. 19, 1864. Was in all battles of regiment up to Mission Ridge. Transferred to Co. E, 19th Regt. Veteran Reserve Corps, April 28, 1864. Wounded in right hip Nov. 25, 1863, in battle of Mission Ridge, Tenn.

STROCK, ABRAM. Age 19. Entered the service Aug. 27, 1861, 3 years. Died June 10, 1864, at Chattanooga, Tenn., of wounds received in battle of Resaca, Ga., May 15, 1864. Was in all battles of regiment up to date of death.

SINGLETARY, CYRUS. Age 27. Entered the service Sept. 1, 1861, 3 years. Died July 17, 1864, in hospital at Louisville, Ky. Was in all battles of the regiment up to and including the advance on Chattanooga, Tenn.

SMITH, ALVA. Age 19. Entered the service Oct. 9, 1861, 3 years. Died March 3, 1862, in hospital at Nelson's Furnace, Ky.

SCHMIDT, FREDERICK. Age 36. Entered the service Oct. 1, 1861, 3 years.

SPONSELLER, SAMUEL. Age 20. Entered the service Aug. 27, 1861, 3 years. Discharged Oct. 5, 1867, at Columbus, Ohio, to date July 2, 1865. VETERAN.

SWEENEY, JOHN. Age 18. Entered the service Sept. 28, 1861, 3 years.

SUCH, WILLIAM. Age 18. Entered the service Oct. 9, 1861, 3 years. Discharged June 27, 1864, for wounds received Nov. 25, 1863, in battle of Mission Ridge, Tenn. Was in all battles of the regiment up to date of being wounded.

STEBBINS, NELSON. Age 24. Entered the service Sept. 1, 1861, 3 years. Mustered out at Pulaski, Tenn., on expiration of term of service, Nov. 2, 1864. Was in all battles of regiment up to date of discharge.

STRIKER, CORNELIUS. Age 42. Entered the service Sept. 12, 1861, 3 years. Discharged March 31, 1864, at Chattanooga, Tenn., on surgeon's certificate of disability.

SULLIVAN, DANIEL. Age 37. Entered the service Aug. 27, 1862, 3 years. Transferred to Co. D, 20th Regt., Veteran Reserve Corps, April 18, 1864. Discharged by order of War Department, June 30, 1865.

TREAT, DELOS. Age 17. Entered the service Feb. 29, 1864, 3 years. Mustered out with company Nov. 27, 1865. Was in the Atlanta campaign.

TREAT, LEMON. Age 18. Entered the service Aug. 27, 1861, 3 years. Killed July 5, 1864, in skirmish near Chattahoochee River, Ga. VETERAN. Was in all battles of the regiment up to date of his death.

TOMPKINS, JAMES. Age 18. Entered the service Aug. 27, 1861, 3 years. Absent, sick at Cincinnati, O. No further record found.

VANTASSELL, GEORGE. Age 18. Entered the service Feb. 29, 1864, 3 years. Mustered out at Nashville, Tenn., May 20, 1865, by order of War Department.

WILLIAMS, CYRUS. Age 18. Entered the service Aug. 27, 1861, 3 years. Mustered out with company Nov. 27, 1865. VETERAN. Was in all battles of the regiment.

WAUSSEN, CLYDE. Age 18. Entered the service Sept. 16, 1862, 3 years. Mustered out with company Nov. 27, 1865.

WRIGHT, EDWARD. Age 29. Entered the service Sept. 12, 1861, 3 years.

COMPANY F.

During May and June, 1861, Ephraim S. Holloway enlisted about half a company of men in Mahoning county. They were not taken into camp until October 9, when Holloway reported, with his men, at Camp Wood. There a union was effected with a company partly filled, enlisted under D. S. Leslie, in Lorain and Ottawa counties. Leslie was made Captain; Holloway, First Lieutenant, and John D. Kirkendall, Second Lieutenant. The union of the two bodies of men made a full company.

This was one of the strong companies of the regiment. Not only was it strong in numbers, but the men were rugged and hardy, with capacity for great endurance. It was admirably fitted for its position of second company in the line, having many men above the average stature—a solid, heavy company, a safe reliance in time of emergency. The death roll shows something of the service performed by this company, but not the whole. From first to last it was one of the stronger companies.

CAPTAINS.

DANIEL S. LESLIE. Age 36. Entered the service Sept. 2, 1861, 3 years. Wounded April 7, 1862, in battle of Shiloh, Tenn. Resigned Sept. 9, 1862.

EPHRAIM S. HOLLOWAY. Age 30. Entered the service Oct. 10, 1861, 3 years. Promoted from 1st Lieut. Sept. 8, 1862; to Major Nov. 26, 1864; Lieut. Colonel March 18, 1865; Colonel May 31, 1865, but not mustered; Brevet Brigadier General at expiration of service, Nov. 27, 1865. Wounded slightly Dec. 31, 1862, in battle of Stone River; also June 21, 1864, at or near Kenesaw Mountain, Ga., slightly.

THOMAS H. SOMERS. Age 26. See Co. H.

1st LIEUTENANTS.

JOHN D. KIRKENDALL. Age 30. Entered the service Sept. 2, 1861, 3 years. Promoted from 2d Lieut. Jan. 9, 1862. Transferred to Co. B Jan. 27, 1862; to Captain, Co. I Jan. 1, 1863. Discharged Nov. 10, 1864.

JAMES N. CLARK. Age 19. See Co. C.

PHILO A. BEARDSLEY. Age 20. Entered the service Oct. 10, 1861, 3 years. Appointed Sergt. from Private Jan. 20, 1864; 1st Sergt. Dec. 9, 1864. Promoted to 1st Lieut. March 18, 1865. Mustered out with company Nov. 27, 1865. VETERAN.

2d LIEUTENANTS.

CHARLES J. JAMES. Age —. Entered the service Jan. 9, 1862, 3 years. Commissioned, but not mustered. Resigned March 16, 1862.

FERDINAND D. COBB. Age 22. Entered the service Sept. 2, 1861, 3 years. Promoted from 1st Sergt. March 17, 1862; to 1st Lieut. Co. E May 21, 1862. Mustered out with Co. E Nov. 27, 1865. Wounded Dec. 16, 1864, in battle of Nashville, Tenn.

WILLIAM E. BOOTHE. Age 26. See Field and Staff.

LESTER F. MILLER. Age 22. Entered the service Sept. 26, 1862, 3 years. Appointed Sergt. from Private July 8, 1864. Promoted Q. M. Sergt. May 1, 1865; 2d Lieut. May 11, 1865. Mustered out with company Nov. 27, 1865. Was with the regiment in every battle or skirmish from Stone River to the close of the war.

1st SERGEANTS.

HENRY G. DELKER. Age 25. Entered the service Sept. 2, 1861, 3 years. Appointed from Sergt. Jan. 20, 1864. Promoted to 1st Lieut. Co. H Nov. 26, 1864. Mustered out with Co. H Nov. 27, 1865. VETERAN. Wounded Dec. 16, 1864, in battle of Nashville, Tenn.

JOHN C. CHAPIN. Age 18. Entered the service Oct. 15, 1861, 3 years. Appointed Corporal Jan. 20, 1864; Sergt. Dec. 12, 1864; 1st Sergt. March 28, 1865. Mustered out with company Nov. 27, 1865. VETERAN.

SERGEANTS.

JOB BURNHAM. Age 22. Entered the service Oct. 1, 1861, 3 years. Appointed from Private Jan. 20, 1864. Mustered out with company Nov. 27, 1865. VETERAN.

WARRAN L. RIPLEY. Age 19. Entered the service Oct. 10, 1861, 3 years. Appointed from Private Jan. 20, 1864. Mustered out with company Nov. 27, 1865. VETERAN.

JOHN PENNELL. Age 20. Entered the service Oct. 10, 1861, 3 years. Appointed Corporal Jan. 20, 1864; Sergt. Dec. 12, 1864. Mustered out with company Nov. 27, 1865. VETERAN.

ORESTES T. ENGLE. Age 21. Entered the service Sept. 2, 1861, 3 years. Appointed Corporal July 20, 1864; Sergt. July 1, 1865. Mustered out with company Nov. 27, 1865. VETERAN.

IRAM KILGORE. Age 28. Entered the service Oct. 29, 1861, 3 years. Appointed from Private Sept. 1, 1862. Died in Rebel prison. Wounded Sept. 19, 1863, in battle of Chickamauga, Ga.

JACOB RENNER. Age 22. Entered the service Sept. 2, 1861, 3 years. Wounded Sept. 19, 1863, in battle of Chickamauga, Ga., and died on the battle field. Interred in National Cemetery at Chattanooga, Tenn.

ANDREW GAULT. Age 19. Entered the service Oct. 10, 1861, 3 years. Appointed from Private Jan. 20, 1864. Died Aug. 8, 1864, at Nashville, Tenn., of wounds received May 27, 1864, in battle of Pickett's Mills, Ga. VETERAN.

ORLANDO P. KILMER. Age 33. Entered the service Sept. 2, 1861, 3 years. Appointed from Corporal ——. Died April 22, 1862, at Cincinnati, O., of wounds received April 7, 1862, in battle of Shiloh, Tenn.

ROBERT A. GAULT. Age 22. Entered the service Oct. 10, 1861, 3 years. Appointed from Corporal March 17, 1862. Promoted Sergt. Major May 1, 1863; to 1st Lieut. Co. G Nov. 26, 1864; Captain March 18, 1865. Mustered out with Co. G Nov. 27, 1865. VETERAN. Wounded Dec. 31, 1862, in battle of Stone River, Tenn. Was in all the battles of the regiment.

CHARLES COOPER. Age 26. Entered the service Sept. 2, 1861, 3 years. Discharged on surgeon's certificate of disability, March 25, 1863.

ALFRED MILLER. Age 23. Entered the service Aug. 29, 1862, 3 years. Appointed Corporal Nov. —, 1862; Sergeant March 28, 1865. Mustered out by order of War Department, June 13, 1865.

WALTER SMITH, JR. Age 24. Entered the service Oct. 10, 1861, 3 years. Died Feb. 26, 1862, at New Haven, Ky.

CORPORALS.

AGUSTUS NEIDING. Age 22. Entered the service Sept. 2, 1861, 3 years. Appointed Corporal July 9, 1864. Mustered out with company Nov. 27, 1865. VETERAN.

CHARLES EDNEY. Age 19. Entered the service Oct. 10, 1861, 3 years. Appointed Corporal July 9, 1864. Was in all the battles of the regiment. Mustered out with company Nov. 27, 1865. VETERAN. Wounded Dec. 31, 1862, in left knee, in battle of Stone River, Tenn.

HENRY OLDER. Age 20. Entered the service Oct. 10, 1861, 3 years. Appointed Corporal Dec. 12, 1864. Was in all battles of the regiment. Mustered out with company Nov. 27, 1865. VETERAN. Wounded Dec. 31, 1862, in battle of Stone River, Tenn. Was struck by a shell and left for dead, but recovered.

GEORGE A. WEBB. Age 20. Entered the service Oct. 21, 1861, 3 years. Appointed Corporal Dec. 12, 1864. Mustered out with company Nov. 27, 1865. VETERAN.

WILLIAM T. HAZEL. Age 25. Entered the service March 5, 1864, 3 years. Appointed Corporal April 1, 1865. Mustered out with company Nov. 27, 1865.

ALEXANDER GAULT. Age 24. Entered the service Nov. 4, 1862, 3 years. Appointed Corporal April 1, 1865. Mustered out with company Nov. 27, 1865. Was in all battles of the regiment from Chickamauga, Ga., to the end of the war.

CHARLES SHOEMAKER. Age 33. Entered the service Sept. 2, 1861, 3 years. Killed Nov. 25, 1863, in battle of Mission Ridge, Tenn.

REUBEN H. AYLSWORTH. Age 33. Entered the service Sept. 2, 1861, 3 years. Appointed Corporal Aug. 1, 1862. Died of wounds received Sept. 19, 1863, in battle of Chickamauga, Ga.

FRANK MASER. Age 32. Entered the service Oct. 10, 1861, 3 years. Died March 23, 1862, at Nashville, Tenn.

ISAAC FLANKER. Age 26. Entered the service Oct. 10, 1861, 3 years. Died Feb. 13, 1862, at Nelson's Barracks, Ky.

HENRY A. BRANSTETTER. Age 24. Entered the service Oct. 10, 1861, 3 years. Discharged at Columbus, O., on surgeon's certificate of disability, Nov. 19, 1862.

ALEXANDER BUSHONG. Age 21. Entered the service Oct. 10, 1861, 3 years. Discharged at Nashville, Tenn., on surgeon's certificate of disability, Nov. 4, 1862.

WILLIAM M. GUTHRIE. Age 24. Entered the service Oct. 10, 1861, 3 years. Appointed Corporal March 17, 1862. Discharged at Camp Dennison, O., on surgeon's certificate of disability, Dec. 18, 1862.

JAMES W. PERKINS. Age 25. Entered the service Oct. 10, 1861, 3 years. Appointed Corporal March 17, 1862. Discharged at Columbus, O., on surgeon's certificate of disability, Aug. 29, 1862.

JOHN ROOF. Age 30. Entered the service Aug. 29, 1862, 3 years. Appointed Corporal May 26, 1863. Mustered out by order of War Department, June 13, 1865.

BENJAMIN F. WILBER. Musician. Age 18. Entered the service Sept. 2, 1861, 3 years. Discharged at Louisville, Ky., on surgeon's certificate of disability, May 21, 1862.

ROBERT FULLERTON. Wagoner. Age 29. Entered the service Oct. 10, 1861, 3 years.

PRIVATES.

ATKINSON, EDGAR. Age 18. Entered the service Feb. 26, 1864, 3 years. Wounded May 27, 1864, in battle of Pickett's Mills, Ga. Absent. Mustered out by order of War Department, Nov. 27, 1865.

ANDERSON, HENRY. Age 38. Entered the service Sept. 23, 1864, 1 year. Drafted. Discharged at Columbus, O., to date July 20, 1865.

ALLEN, MARVIN W. Age 42. Entered the service Oct. 10, 1861, 3 years.

AKINS, DAVID. Age 22. Entered the service Aug. 29, 1862, 3 years. Mustered out by order of War Department, June 13, 1865.

APEL, HENRY. Age 18. Entered the service Aug. 26, 1864, 1 year. Discharged by order of War Department, June 23, 1865.

BRIDGE, GEORGE. Age 18. Entered the service Sept. 2, 1861, 3 years. Mustered out with company Nov. 27, 1865. VETERAN.

BRUCKER, FREDERICK. Age 34. Entered the service Sept. 2, 1861, 3 years. Mustered out with company Nov. 27, 1865. VETERAN.

BELLARD, THOMAS H. Age 22. Entered the service Oct. 10, 1861, 3 years. Discharged at Louisville, Ky., on surgeon's certificate of disability, Dec. 20, 1862.

BELLARD, ROBERT P. Age 21. Entered the service Aug. 23, 1862, 3 years. Mustered out by order of War Department, June 13, 1865.

BOWMAN, JACOB. Age 20. Entered the service Feb. 24, 1864, 3 years. Mustered out with company Nov. 27, 1865.

BOWMAN, WILLIAM. Age —. Entered the service Feb. 29, 1864, 3 years. Discharged Sept. 17, 1864, at Dennison U. S. A. general hospital for wounds received May 25, 1864, in battle of Dallas, Ga.

BAKER, THOMAS P. Age 37. Entered the service Sept. 2, 1861, 3 years. Killed Sept. 19, 1863, in battle of Chickamauga, Ga.

BAKER, SIMEON. Age 27. Entered the service Sept. 21, 1864, 1 year. Drafted. Mustered out by order of War Department, June 13, 1865.

BOVIA, JOSEPH. Age 18. Entered the service Sept. 2, 1861, 3 years. Killed Nov. 25, 1863, in battle of Mission Ridge, Tenn.

BLANDEN, JOHN M. Age —. Entered the service Feb. 29, 1864, 3 years. Killed May 27, 1864, in battle of Pickett's Mills, Ga.

BILLINGS, LYMAN C. Age 38. Entered the service Sept. 2, 1861, 3 years. Discharged at Camp Dennison, O., on surgeon's certificate of disability, Dec. 3, 1862.

BURTRAM, AUGUSTUS. Age 40. Entered the service Aug. 1, 1864, 1 year. Substitute. Mustered out by order of War Department, June 13, 1865.

BEHME, ALBERT. Age 25. Entered the service Sept. 23, 1864, 1 year. Drafted. Mustered out by order of War Department, June 13, 1865.

BIGHAM, WILLIAM. Age 19. Entered the service Oct. 1, 1864, 1 year. Substitute. Mustered out on expiration of term of service, Oct. 16, 1865.

BOAN, DANIEL. Age 20. Entered the service Oct. 1, 1864, 1 year. Substitute. Mustered out on expiration of term of service, Oct. 16, 1865.

BOWDRE, GEORGE W. Age 21. Entered the service Oct. 7, 1864, 1 year. Substitute. Mustered out on expiration of term of service, Oct. 16, 1865.

BROWN, HENRY A. Age 18. Entered the service June 18, 1861, 3 years. Transferred from Co. E, 6th Regt., O. V. I., June 26, 1864. Killed Aug. 6, 1864, in action near Atlanta, Ga.

BROWN JOHN W. Age 22. Entered the service Sept. 30, 1864, 1 year. Substitute. Mustered out by order of War Department, June 13, 1865.

BARR, JOSEPH. Age 18. Entered the service Oct. 7, 1864, 1 year. Substitute. Mustered out at Camp Dennison, O., by order of War Department, May 30, 1865.

CLARY, JAMES K. Age 18. Entered the service Sept. 2, 1861, 3 years. Perished by explosion of Steamer Sultana, on Mississippi river, April 27, 1865. VETERAN.

CHRISTMAN, PETER. Age 35. Entered the service Sept. 20, 1864, 1 year. Drafted. Mustered out at Camp Dennison, O., by order of War Department, May 30, 1865.

CROWLEY, MARTIN. Age 35. Entered the service Oct. 4, 1864, 1 year. Substitute. Mustered out at Camp Dennison, O., by order of War Department, May 30, 1865.

CLARK, JOHN. Age 40. Entered the service Sept. 2, 1861, 3 years. Transferred to Co. I Oct. 1, 1861.

DARBY, BENJAMIN. Age 19. Entered the service Sept. 2, 1861, 3 years. Mustered out with company Nov. 27, 1865. VETERAN.

DUER, DILLION P. Age 19. Entered the service Oct. 10, 1861, 3 years. Mustered out with company Nov. 27, 1865. VETERAN. Was in all the battles of the regiment. Wounded in head April 7, 1862, in battle of Shiloh, Tenn.; also in hand May 27, 1864, in battle of Pickett's Mills, Ga.

DUER, THOMAS. Age 31. Entered the service Oct. 10, 1861, 3 years. Died May 4, 1862, at Cincinnati, O.

DAVIS, JAMES. Age 18. Entered the service Sept. 2, 1861, 3 years. Killed Dec. 31, 1862, in battle of Stone River, Tenn.

DELKER, MICHAEL J. Age 18. Entered the service Feb. 26, 1864, 3 years. Killed May 27, 1864, in battle of Pickett's Mills, Ga. Interred in National Cemetery at Marietta, Ga.

DELANTA, JOHN. Age 40. Entered the service June 14, 1864, 3 years. Drafted. Mustered out at Camp Dennison, O., by order of War Department, July 5, 1865.

DEVON, LOUIS. Age 18. Entered the service Sept. 2, 1861, 3 years. Transferred to Co. I Oct. 1, 1861, as Louis Duvoo.

EDNEY, ANDREW. Age 18. Entered the service Oct. 10, 1861, 3 years. Killed Nov. 25, 1863, in battle of Mission Ridge, Tenn.

ECKENROAD, JOHN. Age 42. Entered the service Oct. 22, 1861, 3 years. Discharged at Chattanooga, Tenn., on surgeon's certificate of disability, Jan. 18, 1864.

ECKENROAD, DANIEL. Age 43. Entered the service Oct. 22, 1861, 3 years. Discharged at Nashville, Tenn., on surgeon's certificate of disability, Nov. 25, 1862.

EWING, SAMUEL J. Age 18. Entered the service Aug. 29, 1862, 3 years. Died April 20, 1863, at Jackson, ——, of wounds received Dec. 31, 1862, in battle of Stone River, Tenn.

FABER, ALBERT. Age 21. Entered the service Sept. 1, 1861, 3 years. Discharged Sept. 3, 1862, for wounds received April 7, 1862, in battle of Shiloh, Tenn.

FLORENCE, WILLIAM. Age 44. Entered the service Aug. 29, 1862, 3 years. Discharged at Louisville, Ky., on surgeon's certificate of disability, Sept. 7, 1863.

FREDERICK, PETER. Age 24. Entered the service Sept. 2, 1861, 3 years. Mustered out at Pine Mountain, Ga., on expiration of term of service, Oct. 17, 1864.

FREDERICK, MATHIAS. Age 21. Entered the service Sept. 2, 1861, 3 years. Transferred to Co. G, 12th Regt., Veteran Reserve Corps, May 17, 1864.

GREENE, WILLIAM D.

GREEN, CHARLES. Age 18. Entered the service Sept. 2, 1861, 8 years. Discharged ——, at Nelson's Barracks, Ky., on surgeon's certificate of disability.

GOFF, JULIUS L. Age 21. Entered the service Sept. 2, 1861, 3 years. Mustered out with company Nov. 27, 1865. VETERAN.

GORNIA, FRANK. Age 26. Entered the service Sept. 2, 1861, 3 years. Killed May 27, 1864, in battle of Pickett's Mills, Ga.

GIBSON, JAMES B. Age 18. Entered the service Feb. 29, 1864, 3 years. Mustered out by order of War Department, June 21, 1865.

HAGERMAN, MATHIAS. Age 22. Entered the service Sept. 2, 1861, 3 years. Died May 12, 1862, at St. Louis, Mo., of wounds received April 7, 1862, in battle of Shiloh, Tenn.

HARMON, ANDREW. Age 22. Entered the service Oct. 7, 1864, 1 year. Substitute.

HOBBS, JOHN. Age 26. Entered the service Oct. 4, 1864, 1 year. Substitute. Discharged by order of War Department, June 19, 1865.

HUNT, JACKSON. Age 21. Entered the service Oct. 10, 1861, 3 years. Wounded Dec. 31, 1862, in battle of Stone River, Tenn.

HAZEL, HENRY. Age 22. Entered the service Sept. 2, 1861, 3 years. Discharged at Camp Wickliffe, Ky., on surgeon's certificate of disability, Jan. 18, 1862.

HARRIFF, HENRY. Age 22. Entered the service Oct. 10, 1861, 3 years. Discharged at Columbus, O., on surgeon's certificate of disability, July 24, 1862.

HOFFMAN, BENJAMIN M. Age 22. Entered the service Aug. 21, 1862, 3 years. Mustered out by order of War Department, June 13, 1865.

HUGHES, JAMES Age 18. Entered the service Feb. 29, 1864, 3 years. Mustered out at Camp Dennison, O., by order of War Department, June 7, 1865.

IRY, WILLIAM. Age 27. Entered the service Oct. 10, 1861, 3 years. Discharged at Cincinnati, O., March 30, 1863, for wounds received Dec. 31, 1862, in battle of Stone River, Tenn.

JOHNSON, JOHN. Age 33. Entered the service Oct. 10, 1864, 1 year. Substitute. Mustered out at New Orleans, La., by order of War Department, June 29, 1865.

JOHNSTON, DAVID E. Age 20. Entered the service Aug. 18, 1862, 3 years. Mustered out by order of War Department, June 13, 1865.

JACKSON, WILLIAM. Age 40. Entered the service Oct. 5, 1864, 1 year. Substitute.

KECK, WILLIAM. Age 20. Entered the service Oct. 10, 1861, 3 years. Mustered out with company Nov. 27, 1865. VETERAN.

KIDWELL, LOVY. Age 22. Entered the service Sept. 23, 1861, 3 years. Killed Dec. 31, 1862, in battle of Stone River, Tenn.

KRECKLE, ANTHONY. Age 42. Entered the service Sept. 2, 1861, 3 years. Mustered out at Pine Mountain, Ga., on expiration of term of service, Oct. 17, 1864.

KIRKPATRICK, JAMES M. Age 21. Entered the service Oct. 10, 1861, 3 years. Promoted Com. Sergt. April 1, 1863; 1st Lieut. Co. B Nov. 26, 1864. Appointed Regt. Quartermaster March 1, 1865. Mustered out with regiment Nov. 27, 1865. VETERAN.

LEE, JOSEPH. Age 30. Entered the service March 22, 1865, 1 year. Mustered out with company Nov. 27, 1865.

LA FOUNTAIN, MARSHALL. Age 21. Entered the service Sept. 2, 1861, 3 years. Died Jan. 27, 1863, at Nashville, Tenn.

LEHMAN, ALEXANDER. Age 18. Entered the service Oct. 10, 1861, 3 years. Died ——, of wounds received April 7, 1862, in battle of Shiloh, Tenn.

LEACH, JOHN. Age 43. Entered the service Oct. 10, 1861, 3 years.

LAWRENCE, PETER. Age 18. Entered the service Aug. 28, 1862, 3 years. Mustered out by order of War Department, June 13, 1865.

LOWRY, ROBERT. Age 24. Entered the service Sept. 22, 1862, 3 years. Mustered out by order of War Department, June 13, 1865. Wounded at Stone River, Dec. 31, 1862. Was in all the battles of the regiment after Stone River.

LUDWICK, LEWIS. Age 21. Entered the service Aug. 25, 1862, 3 years. Mustered out by order of War Department, June 13, 1865.

LEONARD, ORANGE D. Age 24. Entered the service Sept. 23, 1864, 1 year. Drafted. Mustered out by order of War Department, June 13, 1865.

LITTEN, SILAS M. Age 18. Entered the service Oct. 8, 1864, 1 year. Substitute. Mustered out at San Antonio, Tex., on expiration of term of service, Oct. 16, 1865.

McCOY, JOHN. Age 40. Entered the service Oct. 8, 1862, 9 months. Drafted. Mustered out at Manchester, Tenn., on expiration of term of service, July 11, 1863.

McILVAIN, ROBERT. Age 44. Entered the service Sept. 23, 1864, 1 year. Drafted. Mustered out by order of War Department, June 13, 1865.

MILLER, ADAM. Age 21. Entered the service Sept. 2, 1861, 3 years. Discharged at Cincinnati, O., on surgeon's certificate of disability, July 22, 1862.

MESSERMAN, DAVID. Age 24. Entered the service Aug. 23, 1862, 3 years. Mustered out by order of War Department, June 13, 1865.

MANSHART, JACOB. Age 41. Entered the service Oct. 5, 1864, 1 year. Substitute. Mustered out at San Antonio, Tex., on expiration of term of service, Oct. 16, 1865.

MENKER, HENRY. Age 23. Entered the service Oct. 8, 1864, 1 year. Substitute. Discharged at Nashville, Tenn., on surgeon's certificate of disability, July 22, 1865.

MURDOCK, JOHN. Age 40. Entered the service Oct. 5, 1864, 1 year. Substitute. Mustered out at Victoria, Tex., on expiration of term of service, Oct. 4, 1865.

MEIHLIG, SEBASTIAN. Age 37. Entered the service Sept. 21, 1864, 1 year. Drafted. Discharged at Cincinnati, O., on surgeon's certificate of disability, May 30, 1865.

MERRIS, GEORGE W. Age 37. Entered the service Sept. 29, 1864, 1 year. Drafted. Mustered out by order of War Department, June 13, 1865.

NEWBURY, CHARLES. Age 18. Entered the service Feb. 24, 1864, 3 years. Died June 19, 1864, of wounds received May 27, 1864, in battle of Pickett's Mills, Ga.

NOSS, HENRY. Age 27. Entered the service Sept. 23, 1864, 1 year. Drafted. Mustered out by order of War Department, June 13, 1865.

NEWTON, CHARLES. Age 43. Entered the service Oct. 10, 1861, 3 years. Discharged Aug. 5, 1862, for wounds received April 7, 1862, in battle of Shiloh, Tenn.

OHL, HENRY. Age 34. Entered the service Feb. 29, 1864, 3 years. Mustered out with company Nov. 27, 1865.

ORR, RODNEY. Age 38. Entered the service Aug. 31, 1862, 3 years. Mustered out by order of War Department, June 13, 1865.

PARISH, JOSEPH. Age 25. Entered the service Oct. 10, 1861, 3 years. Killed Dec. 31, 1862, in battle of Stone River, Tenn.

PETEE, JOHN. Age 19. Entered the service Sept. 2, 1861, 3 years. Discharged at Louisville, Ky., on surgeon's certificate of disability, May 29, 1862.

RIPLEY, WARD. Age 18. Entered the service Oct. 10, 1861, 3 years. Mustered out with company Nov. 27, 1865. VETERAN.

RYAN, WILLIAM. Age 18. Entered the service Sept. 2, 1861, 3 years. Mustered out with company Nov. 27, 1865. VETERAN.

ROLLAND, DAVID. Age 28. Entered the service Feb. 24, 1864, 3 years. Mustered out with company Nov. 27, 1865.

RICE, ABRAHAM J. Age 21. Entered the service Sept. 18, 1861, 3 years. Killed April 7, 1862, in battle of Shiloh, Tenn.

REMLEY, JOSEPH R. Age 19. Entered the service Oct. 21, 1861, 3 years. Discharged on surgeon's certificate of disability, Oct. 17, 1862.

ROCHESTER, SAMUEL. Age 18. Entered the service Sept. 2, 1861, 3 years. Transferred to Co. I Dec. 31, 1863.

SHIRLEY, JACOB. Age 18. Entered the service Sept. 2, 1861, 3 years. Mustered out with company Nov. 27, 1865. VETERAN.

SHIRLEY, FRANK B. Age 19. Entered the service Sept. 2, 1861, 3 years. Died April 24, 1862, of wounds received April 7, 1862, in battle of Shiloh, Tenn.

SWANK, HENRY O. Age 20. Entered the service Jan. 26, 1865, 1 year. Mustered out with company Nov. 27, 1865.

SWANK, CHARLES W. Age 34. Entered the service Oct. 10, 1861, 3 years. Promoted Hospital Steward May 1, 1865. Mustered out with the regiment Nov. 27, 1865. VETERAN.

STACY, MAHLON. Age 19. Entered the service Sept. 9, 1862, 3 years. Killed Sept. 19, 1863, in battle of Chickamauga, Ga.

SISCO, JOHN A. Age —. Entered the service Feb. 24, 1864, 3 years. Killed May 27, 1864, in battle of Pickett's Mills, Ga.

SANTURE, ALEXANDER. Age 33. Entered the service Sept. 2, 1861, 3 years. Died Jan. 15, 1862, in hospital at St. Louis, Mo.

SHISLER, ELI. Age 28. Entered the service Oct. 10, 1861, 3 years. Lost on board Steamer Echo No. 2, June 9, 1865. VETERAN.

SHISLER, SAMUEL. Age 18. Entered the service Aug. 29, 1862, 3 years. Discharged May 31, 1863, for wounds received in action near Readyville, Tenn.

SMITH, CHARLES. Age 20. Entered the service Oct. 21, 1861, 3 years. Died May 10, 1862, at Covington, Ky.

SNYDER, BENJAMIN M. Age 20. Entered the service Sept. 18, 1861, 3 years. Died March —, 1862, at Nelson's Barracks, Ky.

SPAULDING, HOMER. Age 18. Entered the service Oct. 10, 1861, 3 years. Died Dec. 2, 1862, at Ellsworth, O., of wounds received April 7, 1862, in battle of Shiloh, Tenn.

STEWART, PLIMPTON. Age 38. Entered the service Oct. 10, 1861, 3 years. Died June 21, 1862, in field hospital near Corinth, Miss.

SANDERSON, HENRY. Age 18. Entered the service Sept. 2, 1861, 3 years. Discharged at Nelson's Barracks, Ky., June 3, 1862.

STANDEN, JOHN A. Age 18. Entered the service Sept. 2, 1861, 3 years. Discharged at Columbus, O., Sept. 18, 1862, for wounds received April 7, 1862, in battle of Shiloh, Tenn.

SULLIVAN, DENNIS. Age 27. Entered the service Sept. 29, 1864, 1 year. Drafted. Mustered out by order of War Department June 13, 1865.

SHOEMAKER, REUBEN. Age 22. Entered the service Aug. —, 1862, 3 years. Transferred to Co. A, 1st U. S. V. V. Engineers, July 18, 1864.

SCOTT, CHARLES A. Age 18. Entered the service Sept. 10, 1864, 1 year. Substitute. Discharged at U S. general hospital, Quincy, Ill., May 11, 1865.

SHAFFER, DAVID. Age 17. Entered the service Oct. 6, 1861, 3 years. Discharged by civil authority Oct. 26, 1861, (minor).

SHARKEY, JAMES. Age 18. Entered the service Sept. 2, 1861, 3 years. Transferred to 126th Co., 2d Battalion, Veteran Reserve Corps, Dec. 28, 1863.

THOMPSON, EBENEZER J. Age 41. Entered the service Sept. 2, 1861, 3 years. Discharged Dec. 2, 1865, by S. O. No. 55, Headquarters District of Ohio.

UTMAN, SIMEON D. Age 22. Entered the service Oct. 4, 1864, 1 year. Substitute.

UNDERWOOD, JOSEPH. Age 23. Entered the service Sept. 21, 1864, 1 year. Drafted. Discha ged at Columbus, O., May 11, 1865, for wounds received Dec. 16, 1864, in battle of Nashville, Tenn.

WIGGINS, ZENAS H. Age 22. Entered the service Oct. 7, 1864, 1 year. Substitute.

WAITE, JOHN T. Age 18. Entered the service Oct. 1, 1861, 3 years. Discharged at Camp Dennison, O., Aug. 5, 1862, on surgeon's certificate of disability.

WORDEN, JOSEPH. Age 18. Entered the service Sept. 2, 1861, 3 years. Discharged at Camp Dennison, O., by order of War Department, June 21, 1865. VETERAN.

WAITE, JOHN. Age 30. Entered the service Sept. 23, 1864, 1 year. Drafted. Mustered out by order of War Department, June 13, 1865.

WILSON, JOHN A. Age 28. Entered the service Sept. 30, 1864, 1 year. Substitute. Mustered out by order of War Department, June 13, 1865.

WYANT, JOHN. Age 27. Entered the service Sept. 21, 1864, 1 year. Substitute. Was in the battles of Franklin, Tenn., Sept. 30, 1864, and Nashville, Tenn., Dec. 15 and 16, 1864. Discharged by order of War Department, June 13, 1865.

WRIGHT, JOSEPH H. Age 44. Entered the service Sept. 26, 1864, 1 year. Drafted. Mustered out by order of War Department, June 13, 1865.

WINFIELD, WILLIAM C. Age 18. Entered the service Oct. 8, 1862, 9 months. Drafted. Mustered out at Manchester, Tenn., on expiration of term of service, July 11, 1863.

WEBBER, PHILIP D. Age 25. Entered the service Oct. 1, 1864, 1 year. Substitute. Mustered out at San Antonio, Tex., on expiration of term of service, Oct. 16, 1865.

WHITE, LEWIS. Age 19. Entered the service Oct. 2, 1864, 1 year. Substitute. Mustered out at San Antonio, Tex., on expiration of term of service, Oct. 16, 1865.

WEITZELL, WILLIAM. Age 26. Entered the service Sept. 2, 1861, 3 years. Died May 10, 1862, at Cincinnati, O., of wounds received April 7, 1862, in battle of Shiloh, Tenn.

YANELL, JAMES D. Age 18. Entered the service Oct. 7, 1864, 1 year. Substitute. Died March 11, 1865, in hospital at Jeffersonville, Ind.

ZAUVERS, WILLIAM. Age 27. Entered the service Sept. 2, 1861, 3 years.

COMPANY G.

G company, as well as B, was enlisted in Geauga county—G mostly from the townships of Hampden, Huntsburg, Claridon and Munson. Hampden contributed more than thirty men to the company. There were fourteen pairs of brothers in the company. There were no cities or large towns in the county, and most of the men were from the farms, and somewhat larger in stature than the average in the regiment. The company was recruited mainly by Martin H. Hamblin, who served in the Mexican war, and was also in the three months service of the 19th Ohio. While recruiting, the company was known as the Geauga Zouaves, and at first it was expected to go to the 20th Ohio, Col. Lewis P. Buckley, who was Major of the 19th Ohio. B company of the Forty first—known locally as the Hitchcock Guards—had just been enlisted in the county, and many men had gone to other regiments; but in about twenty days there were eighty men for G company. The company was gathered in Chardon, and about Sept. 10th it left for Camp Wood, escorted by the Claridon Martial Band. At the Cleveland railroad station the company was met by the Hitchcock Guards (B company) and escorted to camp. At this time the company had only about eighty men, but it was soon filled to the maximum. Martin H. Hamblin was chosen Captain; Zelotus Sisson, First Lieutenant, and Horatio P. Kile, Second Lieutenant.

The company lost, during its service, thirteen killed in action, five died of wounds and eighteen died of disease. Four of the killed were at Pickett's Mills, seven at Chickamauga and two at Stone River. Fifteen of the dead of the company are buried in the National Cemetery at Chattanooga, and one lies in the cemetery at Indianola, Tex.

CAPTAINS.

MARTIN H. HAMBLIN. Age 33. Entered the service Sept. 10, 1861, 3 years. Resigned Jan. 5, 1862.

WILLIAM W. MUNN. Age 32. See Co. B.

EDWIN B. ATWOOD. Age 23. See Field and Staff.

ROBERT A. GAULT. Age 20. See Co. F.

1st LIEUTENANTS.

ZELOTUS C. SISSON. Age 38. Entered the service Sept. 10, 1861, 3 years. Resigned Jan. 5, 1862.

HORATIO P. KILE. Age 22. Entered the service Sept. 10, 1861, 3 years. Promoted from 2d Lieut. to 1st Lieut. Jan. 1, 1862; to Captain Co. H March 24, 1863. Mustered out at Pulaski, Tenn., on expiration of term of service, Nov. 10, 1864. Was in all battles of the regiment to date of muster out, except Shiloh. Wounded at battle of Mission Ridge, Nov. 25, 1863.

HENRY S. DIRLAM. Age 27. See Co. H.

CHARLES HAMMOND. Age 23. See Co. D.

PETER HERRIFF. Age 19. See Co. D.

2d LIEUTENANTS.

TIMOTHY D. BROWN. Age —. Entered the service Sept. 5, 1862, 3 years. Resigned Dec. 21, 1862.

LLOYD FISHER. Age 20. See Co. D.

1st SERGEANTS.

EUGENE R. EGGLESTON. Age 23. Entered the service Sept. 10, 1861, 3 years. Promoted Sergeant Major Nov. 1, 1862; to 2d Lieut. Co. C March 24, 1863. Resigned Sept. 30, 1864. Was in all battles of regiment from Stone River to date of resignation. Was commissioned 1st Lieut., but not mustered.

SILO P. WARRINER. Age 22. Entered the service Sept. 10, 1861, 3 years. Appointed from Sergt. Nov. 1, 1862. Promoted 1st Lieut. Co K March 18, 1865. Mustered out with Co. K Nov. 27, 1865. VETERAN. In all battles of the regiment except Nashville. Wounded in battle of Chickamauga, Sept. 20, 1863, also in battle of Orchard Knob, Nov. 23, 1863.

HENRY S. YOUNG. Age 21. Entered the service Sept. 10, 1861, 3 years. Appointed Sergt. from Private July 20, 1864; 1st Sergt. April 1, 1865. Mustered out with company Nov. 27, 1865. VETERAN. Wounded in battle of Chickamauga, Sept. 19, 1863.

SERGEANTS.

GEORGE W. STOCKING. Age 27. Entered the service Sept. 10, 1861, 3 years. Appointed from Private Jan. 20, 1864. Mustered out with company Nov. 27, 1865. VETERAN.

GEORGE W. HODGES. Age 34. Entered the service Sept. 10, 1861, 3 years. Appointed Corporal Jan. 20, 1864; Sergt. April 1, 1865. Mustered out with company Nov. 27, 1865. VETERAN. Was in all battles of the regiment except Shiloh; his company was back guarding regimental wagon train.

WILLIAM GARRETT. Age 19. Entered the service Sept. 10, 1861, 3 years. Appointed from Corporal Jan. 20, 1864. Mustered out with company Nov. 27, 1865. VETERAN.

ELIJAH BAKER. Age 20. Entered the service Oct. 17, 1861, 3 years. Appointed Corporal Jan. 20, 1864; Sergt. May 1, 1865. Mustered out with company Nov. 27, 1865. VETERAN.

CHARLES LILLEY. Age 21. Entered the service Sept. 10, 1861, 3 years. Appointed from Corporal ——. Died March 31, 1863, at Readyville, Tenn.

BERNEY D. MILLARD. Age 22. Entered the service Sept. 10, 1861, 3 years. Discharged at Louisville, Ky., Jan. 22, 1863.

GEORGE WATTS. Age 22. Entered the service Sept. 10, 1861, 3 years. Discharged at Louisville, Ky, May 18, 1862, on surgeon's certificate of disability.

LESTER F. MILLER Age 22. Entered the service Sept. 26, 1862, 3 years. Appointed from Private July 8, 1864. Promoted to Q. M. Sergt. May 1, 1865; 2d Lieut. Co. F May 11, 1865. Mustered out with Co. F Nov. 27, 1865. Was in all the battles of the regiment from Stone River to close of the war.

WILLIAM HANSARD. Age 19. Entered the service Sept. 10, 1861, 3 years. Promoted to 2d Lieut. Co. D Sept. 8, 1862; to 1st Lieut. Co. H March 24, 1863; to Captain Co. K Oct. 12, 1864. Died Jan. 9, 1865, in hospital at Nashville, Tenn., of wounds received Dec. 15, 1864, in battle of Nashville, Tenn.

CORPORALS.

HENRY J. WARNER. Age 22. Entered the service Sept. 10, 1861, 3 years. Appointed Corporal July 8, 1864. Mustered out with company Nov. 27, 1865. VETERAN.

GARDNER PICKET. Age 19. Entered the service Sept. 10, 1861, 3 years. Appointed Corporal Feb. 20, 1865. Mustered out with company Nov. 27, 1865. VETERAN.

CHARLES SNETHEN. Age 18. Entered the service Oct. 26, 1861, 3 years. Appointed Corporal April 1, 1865. Mustered out with company Nov. 27, 1865. VETERAN. Was in all battles of the regiment except Shiloh, Tenn. Wounded in the battle of Mission Ridge, Tenn.

ORVILLE CRIPPEN. Age 32. Entered the service Sept. 30, 1862, 3 years. Appointed Corporal July 8, 1864. Mustered out with company Nov. 27, 1865.

MORRIS HARPER. Age 20. Entered the service Sept. 10, 1861, 3 years. Died March 2, 1862, at Nelson's Furnace, Ky.

WEBSTER HATHAWAY. Age 22. Entered the service March 23, 1864, 3 years. Appointed Corporal Feb. 20, 1865. Mustered out with company Nov. 27, 1865.

PHILO SEARL. Age 28. Entered the service Sept. 10, 1861, 3 years. Appointed Corporal July 27, 1863. Killed Sept. 19, 1863, in battle of Chickamauga, Ga.

CLARK D. CALKINS. Age 19. Entered the service Sept. 26, 1862, 3 years. Died Dec. 8, 1863, at Chattanooga, Tenn., of wounds received in action.

BURTON ARMSTRONG. Age —. Entered the service Nov. 2, 1861, 3 years. Discharged at Columbus, Ohio, July 11, 1862, on surgeon's certificate of disability.

JOHN BRIDGEMAN. Age 20. Entered the service Sept. 10, 1861, 3 years. Appointed Corporal Feb. 1, 1862. Discharged Nov. 21, 1863.

HENRY COON. Age 34. Entered the service Oct. 7, 1861, 3 years. Promoted to 2d Lieut. Co. K Feb. 3, 1862. Resigned April 7, 1862.

LYMAN NEWTON. Age 18. Entered the service Sept. 10, 1861, 3 years. Appointed Corporal Feb. 1, 1862. Discharged April 3, 1863.

JOHN QUIGGLE. Age 44. Entered the service Sept. 10, 1861, 3 years. Discharged at Louisville, Ky., on surgeon's certificate of disability, May 3, 1862.

OTIS A. SHATTOCK. Age 28. Entered the service Aug. 30, 1862, 3 years. Appointed Corporal Nov. 1, 1862. Mustered out at Nashville, Tenn., by order of War Department, June 13, 1865.

GEORGE D. SANGER. Age 26. Entered the service Sept 10, 1861, 3 years. Discharged on surgeon's certificate of disability, May 3, 1862.

DARIUS W. YOUNG. Age 22. Entered the service Oct. 24, 1861, 3 years. Appointed Corporal Dec. 10, 1862. Mustered out at Pulaski, Tenn., on expiration of term of service, Nov. 14, 1864.

MUSICIANS.

ROSWELL H. BEACH. Age 25. Entered the service Sept. 10, 1861, 3 years. Discharged at Nashville, Tenn., May 3, 1862.

EDWARD A. FERRIS. Age 38. Entered the service Sept. 10, 1861, 3 years. Discharged at Columbus, O., July 21, 1862.

EDWARD LAMPMAN. Wagoner. Age 47. Entered the service Oct, 9, 1861, 3 years. Discharged at Cincinnati, O., on surgeon's certificate of disability, March 27, 1863.

PRIVATES.

ALEXANDER, WILLIAM. Age 20. Entered the service Oct. 1, 1863, 3 years. Killed May 27, 1864, in battle of Pickett's Mills, Ga.

ADAMS, FRANK. Age 25. Entered the service Oct. 7, 1864, 3 years. Substitute. Discharged June 15, 1865.

ADAMS, E. T. Age 22. Entered the service Aug. 30, 1862, 3 years. Discharged at Nashville, Tenn., Jan. 21, 1863.

BARKER, FRANK. Age 28. Entered the service Sept. 26, 1862, 3 years. Killed Sept. 19, 1863, in battle of Chickamauga, Ga.

BROWN, ROBERT M. Age 18. Entered the service Sept. 10, 1861, 3 years. Died Sept. 15, 1865, at Indianola, Tex. VETERAN.

BROWN, AMENZO. Age 19. Entered the service Oct. 17, 1861, 3 years. Mustered out at Pulaski, Tenn., on expiration of term of service, Nov. 2, 1864.

BROWN, HOSEA T. Age 31. Entered the service Oct. 18, 1862, 9 months. Drafted. Mustered out at Manchester, Tenn., on expiration of term of service, July 17, 1863.

BEATTY, ALEXANDER. Age 24. Entered the service Sept. 20, 1864, 1 year. Substitute. Mustered out at Nashville, Tenn., by order of War Department, June 13, 1865.

BUELL, HENRY M. Age 20. Entered the service Oct. 17, 1861, 3 years. Discharged at Columbus, Ohio, July 25, 1862.

BOWMAN, BAYLES S. Age 18. Entered the service Oct. 8, 1864, 1 year. Substitute. Mustered out at San Antonio, Tex., on expiration of term of service, Oct. 16, 1865.

BOOTH, ORSEMUS. Age 26. Entered the service Sept. 10, 1861, 3 years. Transferred to U. S. Engineers. VETERAN.

COLBY, GEORGE D. Age 28. Entered the service Sept. 10, 1861, 3 years. Mustered out with company Nov. 27, 1865. VETERAN.

COLBY, ALONZO T. Age 20. Entered the service Sept. 10, 1861, 3 years. Mustered out at Pulaski, Tenn., on expiration of term of service, Nov. 2, 1864.

CALKINS, PERRIN H. Age 17. Entered the service Oct. 9, 1861, 3 years. Mustered out with company Nov. 27, 1865. VETERAN.

CORNISH, ROSWELL. Age 25. Entered the service Sept. 10, 1861, 3 years. Killed September 19, 1863, in battle of Chickamauga, Ga.

COOK, AUSTIN. Age 19. Entered the service Oct. 22, 1861, 3 years. Died June 12, 1862, at Louisville, Ky.

COON, CLARK. Age —. Entered the service Sept. 26, 1862, 3 years. Discharged Dec. 31, 1862, on surgeon's certificate of disability.

CAREY, JOHN. Age 24. Entered the service Oct. 5, 1864, 1 year. Substitute. Discharged at Camp Dennison, Ohio, Aug. 24, 1865.

DAVIS, FRANCIS W. Age 18. Entered the service Oct. 5, 1861, 3 years. Died April 7, 1862, at Nashville, Tenn.

DICKENS, SHERMAN. Age 19. Entered the service Sept. 10, 1861, 3 years. Died March 8, 1862, at Louisville, Ky.

DICKENS, FAYETTE. Age 21. Entered the service Sept. 10, 1861, 3 years. Discharged April 1, 1863.

DINES, JOSEPH. Age —. Entered the service Oct. 3, 1861, 3 years. Discharged on surgeon's certificate of disability, Dec. 8, 1862.

EVANS, BLAIR K. Age 19. Entered the service Oct. 12, 1864, 1 year. Substitute. Battles engaged in: Franklin and Nashville, Tenn. Mustered out at San Antonio, Tex., Oct. 16, 1865.

FOWLER, LUCIUS. Age 23. Entered the service Sept. 26, 1862, 3 years. Discharged at Nashville, Tenn., March 3, 1863, on surgeon's certificate of disability.

FOOT, ALVIN. Age 18. Entered the service Oct. 5, 1861, 3 years. Mustered out at Pulaski, Tenn., on expiration of term of service, Nov. 14, 1864.

GRISWOLD, BRADFORD H. Age 18. Entered the service Sept. 10, 1861, 3 years. Mustered out at Pulaski, Tenn., on expiration of term of service, Nov. 2, 1864. Wounded in battle of Pickett's Mills, Ga., May 27, 1864. Was in all the battles of the regiment except Shiloh, Tenn., up to date of discharge.

GROCE, SAMUEL N. Age 18. Entered the service Sept. 30, 1864, 3 years. Substitute. Mustered out at Nashville, Tenn., by order of War Department, June 13, 1865.

GREY, BENJAMIN. Age 44. Entered the service Sept. 10, 1861, 3 years. Discharged at Nashville, Tenn., on surgeon's certificate of disability, April 21, 1862.

GREY, JAMES. Age 24. Entered the service Aug. 30, 1862, 3 years. Discharged at Louisville, Ky., on surgeon's certificate of disability, March 14, 1863.

GREY, JEFFERSON T. Age 28. Entered the service Aug. 30, 1862, 3 years. Mustered out at Nashville, Tenn., by order of War Department, June 13, 1865.

GRIFFIN, HORACE. Age 21. Entered the service Sept. 10, 1861, 3 years. Discharged on surgeon's certificate of disability, April 1, 1863.

GAEBELIN, JOHN. Age 18. Entered the service Sept. 27, 1864, 1 year. Substitute. Mustered out at Nashville, Tenn., June 13, 1865, by order of War Department. Was in battle of Nashville, Tenn., Dec. 15 and 16, 1864.

GREEN, JONATHAN. Age 29. Entered the service Feb. 27, 1864, 3 years. Wounded at Resaca, Ga. Battle engaged in: Resaca, Ga. Discharged at Columbus, O., Dec. —, 1865. Transferred to Co. D, 22d Regt., Veteran Reserve Corps, April 21, 1865.

HAZEN, ANDREW. Age 18. Entered the service Sept. 10, 1861, 3 years. Mustered out with company Nov. 27, 1865. VETERAN. In all battles of the regiment except Shiloh. Slightly wounded twice.

HOARD, JOHN R. Age 21. Entered the service Feb. 12, 1864, 3 years. Mustered out with company Nov. 27, 1865.

HOLLOWAY, ADOLPHUS. Age 18. Entered the service Sept. 10, 1861, 3 years. Mustered out with company Nov. 27, 1865. VETERAN.

HOLLOWAY, BERT. Age 18. Entered the service Sept. 10, 1861, 3 years. Discharged at Louisville, Ky., on surgeon's certificate of disability, June 3, 1862.

HUGHES, IRA. Age 24. Entered the service Sept. 10, 1861, 3 years. Killed May 27, 1864, in battle of Pickett's Mills, Ga.

HUGHES, HARRISON T. Age 24. Entered the service Nov. 4, 1861, 3 years. Killed Dec. 31, 1862, in battle of Stone River, Tenn.

HUGHES, HOWARD M. Age —. Entered the service Nov. 4, 1861, 3 years. Discharged at Nashville, Tenn., June 14, 1863.

HAINES, ORIN. Age 19. Entered the service Nov. 2, 1861, 3 years. Died June 25, 1862, at Corinth, Miss.

HAINES, ELIAS. Age 33. Entered the service Sept. 10, 1861, 3 years. Mustered out at Pulaski, Tenn., on expiration of term of service, Nov. 2, 1864.

HALL, WILLIAM. Age 24. Entered the service Oct. 5, 1861, 3 years. Died Feb. 8, 1862, at Louisville, Ky.

HALL, SIDNEY, JR. Age 17. Entered the service Oct. 7, 1861, 3 years. Discharged on surgeon's certificate of disability at Cincinnati, O., Nov. 29, 1862.

HOFFMAN, REUBEN. Age 19. Entered the service Sept. 10, 1861, 3 years. Died Jan. 18, 1863, at Nashville, Tenn.

HUNT, HARVEY B. Age 25. Entered the service Sept. 10, 1861, 3 years. Transferred to Veteran Reserve Corps, ——. Discharged Oct. 7, 1865. VETERAN.

HOUCK, ALEXANDER. Age 35. Entered the service Oct. 3, 1864, 1 year. Substitute. Died Dec. 16, 1864, at Nashville,Tenn.

HATHAWAY, JAMES E. Age 24. Entered the service Sept. 10, 1861, 3 years. Discharged at Columbus, O., on surgeon's certificate of disability, July 20, 1862.

HATHAWAY, WEBSTER. Age 20. Entered the service Sept. 10, 1861, 3 years. Discharged at Cincinnati, O., on surgeon's certificate of disability, Nov. 10, 1862.

HENKEY, LEWIS. Age 25. Entered the service Sept. 30, 1864, 1 year. Substitute. Mustered out at Nashville, Tenn., by order of War Department, June 13, 1865.

HUNTOON, HENRY. Age 23. Entered the service Sept. 10, 1861, 3 years. Discharged on surgeon's certificate of disability, April 1, 1863.

HILL, GEORGE. Age 32. Entered the service Aug. 25, 1862, 3 years. Mustered out at Nashville, Tenn., by order of War Department, June 13, 1865.

HARPER, CHARLES (CARLOS). Age 19. Entered the service Sept. 10, 1861, 3 years. Discharged at Columbus, O., on surgeon's certificate of disability, July 12, 1862.

HARPER, CARLOS. Age 19. Entered the service Sept. 26, 1862, 3 years. Mustered out at San Antonio, Tex., on expiration of term of service, Oct. 16, 1865.

HOUSWORTH, LEWIS A. Age 36. Entered the service Aug. 25, 1862, 3 years. Mustered out at Nashville, Tenn., by order of War Department, June 13, 1865.

HOUSWORTH, LEVI W. Age 34. Entered the service Aug. 25, 1862, 3 years. Mustered out at Nashville, Tenn., by order of War Department, June 13, 1865.

HANSARD, CHARLES. Age 44. Entered the service Sept. 10, 1861, 3 years. Discharged on surgeon's certificate of disability, May 9, 1863.

HOSFORD, ISAAC. Age 24. Entered the service Sept. 26, 1862, 3 years. Discharged on surgeon's certificate of disability, Dec. 29, 1862.

HENDERSON, WILLIAM H. Age 25. Entered the service Sept. 20, 1861, 3 years. Eye injured at Camp Wickliffe, Ky. Discharged at Columbus, O., on surgeon's certificate of disability, July 1, 1862.

JACKSON, THOMAS W. Age 18. Entered the service Sept. 10, 1861, 3 years. Mustered out at Pulaski, Tenn., on expiration of term of service, Nov. 2, 1864. Wounded at Chickamauga, Ga. Battles engaged in: Stone River, Tenn., and Chickamauga, Ga.

JOHNSON, JULIUS. Age 25. Entered the service Sept. 10, 1861, 3 years. Mustered out at Pulaski, Tenn., on expiration of term of service, Nov. 14, 1864.

JAMES, GEORGE B. Age 21. Entered the service Oct. 4, 1864, 1 year. Substitute. Mustered out at San Antonio, Tex., on expiration of term of service, Oct. 16, 1865.

KOENIGER, LEWIS. Age 25. Entered the service Oct. 7, 1864, 1 year. Substitute. Died June 6, 1865, at Louisville, Ky.

KICKLAND, MARTIN. Age 23. Entered the service Oct. 12, 1861, 3 years. Transferred to Co. E, 19th Regt., Veteran Reserve Corps, April 7, 1864.

KABLE, CHRISTIAN. Age 22. Entered the service Sept. 23, 1864, 8 years. Drafted. Mustered out at Nashville, Tenn., by order of War Department, June 13, 1865.

LANNUM, ELIAS. Age 27. Entered the service Sept. 10, 1861, 3 years. Mustered out with company Nov. 27, 1865. VETERAN.

LITTLE, WALLACE. Age 18. Entered the service Sept. 26, 1862, 3 years. Died Oct. 31, 1862, at Bardstown, Ky.

LEWIS, PHILO. Age 44. Entered the service Sept. 10, 1861, 3 years. Discharged at Nashville, Tenn., on surgeon's certificate of disability, April 1, 1862.

LEWIS, JOHN. Age 19. Entered the service Oct. 5, 1864, 1 year. Substitute.

LEHMAN, ABRAM. Age 24. Entered the service Sept. 26, 1864, 1 year. Drafted. Mustered out at Nashville, Tenn., by order of War Department, June 13, 1865.

LYONDS, MATTHEW. Age 33. Entered the service Oct. 5, 1864, 1 year.

MILLER, ALBERT W. Age 18. Entered the service March 1, 1864, 3 years. Mustered out with company Nov. 27, 1865.

MAXWELL, DAYTON. Age 18. Entered the service Sept. 10, 1861, 3 years. Killed May 27, 1864, in battle of Pickett's Mills, Ga. VETERAN.

MORSE, LORENZO. Age 20. Entered the service Sept. 10, 1861, 3 years. Died January 14, 1862, at Camp Wickliffe, Ky.

MAYNARD, THOMAS. Age 36. Entered the service Sept. 10, 1861, 3 years. Mustered out at Pulaski, Tenn., on expiration of term of service, Nov. 2, 1864.

MANNING, GEORGE. Age 18. Entered the service Sept. 10, 1861, 3 years. Discharged April 1, 1863.

MOSS, CHARLES N. Age 19. Entered the service Sept. 10, 1861, 3 years. Mustered out at Pulaski, Tenn., on expiration of term of service, Nov. 2, 1864.

McCREA, HIRAM. Age 18. Entered the service Oct. 5, 1864, 1 year. Substitute. Mustered out on expiration of term of service, Oct. 16, 1865, at Pulaski, Tenn.

MOSS, GEORGE W. Age 19. Entered the service Oct. 4, 1864, 1 year. Substitute.

NYE, EBENEZER. Age 40. Entered the service Oct. 12, 1861, 3 years. Discharged April 1, 1863.

PARSONS, EDWIN. Age 19. Entered the service Sept. 10, 1861, 3 years. Died Jan. 30, 1862, at Camp Wickliffe, Ky.

PIERSTOCK, JOHN. Age 24. Entered the service Sept. 21, 1864, 1 year. Drafted. Discharged at Nashville, Tenn., by order of War Department, June 13, 1865.

RODGERS, WILLIAM. Age 44. Entered the service Aug. 25, 1862, 3 years. Died Feb. 14, 1863, at Nashville, Tenn.

RODGERS, JOSHUA. Age 18. Entered the service Oct. 26, 1861, 3 years. Killed Sept. 19, 1863, in battle of Chickamauga, Ga.

RICHARDS, JOHN L. Age 18. Entered the service Feb. 12, 1864, 3 years. Discharged on surgeon's certificate of disability, Oct. 26, 1864.

REED, SHERBIN. Age 19. Entered the service Sept. 10, 1861, 3 years. Discharged at Readyville, Tenn., on surgeon's certificate of disability, April 20, 1863.

REEDER, SENECA. Age 19. Entered the service Oct. 8, 1864, 1 year. Substitute. Mustered out at St. Louis, Mo., by order of War Department, Sept. 18, 1865.

STANSELL, CHARLES. Age 22. Entered the service Sept. 10, 1861, 3 years. Died April 1, 1863, at Readyville, Tenn.

SEARL, MARTIN. Age 20. Entered the service Aug. 30, 1862, 3 years. Died Jan. 28, 1863, at Readyville, Tenn.

SNETHEN, BENJAMIN. Age 18. Entered the service March 1, 1864, 3 years. Died July 25, 1864, of wounds received in action.

SNETHEN, JOHN. Age 24. Entered the service Feb. 12, 1864, 3 years. Mustered out with company Nov. 27, 1865.

STEPHENSON, ONEY. Age 21. Entered the service Sept. 10, 1861, 3 years. Mustered out on expiration of term of service, Jan. 14, 1865.

STEPHENSON, HENRY. Age 41. Entered the service Aug. 30, 1862, 3 years. Killed Sept. 19, 1863, in battle of Chickamauga, Ga.

STARKS, LORENZO. Age 19. Entered the service Sept. 10, 1861, 3 years. Discharged on surgeon's certificate of disability, at Columbus, Ohio, Sept. 24, 1864.

SICKER, WILLIAM. Age 30. Entered the service Oct. 12, 1864, 1 year. Substitute. Mustered out at San Antonio, Tex., on expiration of term of service. Oct. 16, 1865.

STILES, ANDREW. Age 33. Entered the service Sept. 10, 1861, 3 years. Mustered out at Nashville, Tenn., by order of War Department, June 13, 1865.

SAYER, DANIEL B. Age 20. Entered the service Oct. 5, 1864, 1 year. Substitute.

SMITH, HORTON. Age 18. Entered the service Sept. 10, 1861, 3 years. Killed May 27, 1864, in battle of Pickett's Mills, Ga.

STRONG, JOEL. Age 21. Entered the service Sept. 10, 1861, 3 years. Killed Dec. 31, 1862, in battle of Stone River, Tenn.

THAYER, PETER. Age 19. Entered the service Sept. 10, 1861, 3 years. Captured May 27, 1864, at battle of Pickett's Mills, Ga. Discharged at Camp Chase, O., June 26, 1865. VETERAN.

TRAVER, HENRY B. Age 18. Entered the service Oct. 5, 1861, 3 years. Killed Sept. 19, 1863, in battle of Chickamauga, Ga.

TUCKER, WILLIAM. Age 18. Entered the service Sept. 21, 1864, 1 year. Substitute. Mustered out at Nashville, Tenn., by order of War Department, June 13, 1865.

TAYLOR, DAVID. Age 18. Entered the service Sept. 30, 1864, 1 year. Substitute. Mustered out at Nashville, Tenn., by order of War Department, June 13, 1865.

TAYLOR, JOSHUA V. Age 21. Entered the service Sept. 23, 1864, 1 year. Drafted. Mustered out at Nashville, Tenn., by order of War Department, June 13, 1865.

VARNEY, ALLISON. Age 18. Entered the service Oct. 13, 1863, 3 years. Mustered out by order of War Department, May 16, 1865.

WATTS, CHESTER. Age 18. Entered the service Sept. 10, 1861, 3 years. Mustered out with company Nov. 27, 1865. VETERAN.

WATTS, MORTIMER F. Age 25. Entered the service Sept. 10, 1861, 3 years. Killed Sept. 19, 1863, in battle of Chickamauga, Ga.

WHITNEY, ORIN. Age 22. Entered the service Sept. 10, 1861, 3 years. Died March 27, 1862.

WORTHINGTON, DANIEL H. Age 28. Entered the service Sept. 10, 1861, 3 years. Died Feb. 8, 1863, of wounds received in action. Died at Nashville, Tenn.

WEAVER, WILLIAM O. Age 44. Entered the service Sept. 30, 1862, 3 years. Discharged at Camp Dennison, O., July 10, 1865.

WARRINER, HENRY. Age 22. Entered the service Sept. 10, 1861, 3 years. Discharged at Columbus, Ohio, Sept. 26, 1862.

WEIGAND, JOHN. Age 37. Entered the service Sept. 30, 1864, 1 year. Substitute. Mustered out at Nashville, Tenn., June 13, 1865.

WEIGLE, WILLIAM. Age 18. Entered the service Oct. 7, 1864, 1 year. Substitute. Mustered out Sept. 29, 1865.

WARD, JOHN. Age 30. Entered the service Oct. 7, 1864, 1 year. Substitute.

YEARGAN, JAMES. Age 18. Entered the service Oct. 6, 1864, 1 year. Substitute. Mustered out at San Antonio, Tex., on expiration of term of service, Oct. 16, 1865.

COMPANY H.

The enlistment of Company "H," 41st Regt., O. V. I., was begun at Oberlin, Lorain county, about the middle of August, 1861. Capt. Alonzo H. Pease, a resident of that place, had organized and commanded a company of Ohio militia and acquired a little knowledge of military affairs in that service. About the first of August, 1861, he determined to enter the service, and suggested to John W. Steele that he join in raising a company. At this time a regiment was being formed at Jefferson, Ashtabula county, Ohio, called after the Hon. Joshua R. Giddings "The Giddings Regiment." It was finally agreed between us that we should try to raise a company in Lorain county for this regiment, to be called the "Lorain Guards." Enlistment rolls were procured and without further authority the enlistment of the company was undertaken. Several men from Oberlin and Pittsfield signed these rolls, but learning that such enlistment was illegal, or at least informal, the work was suspended until, on proper application, authority was granted September 4th, 1861, to Capt. Pease, to form a company for the 41st Regt., O. V. I. The men who had already enlisted signed the new rolls and the effort to fill the company was pushed in Lorain and adjoining counties. Meetings were held in Pittsfield, Huntington and Camden, of Lorain county, and in Wakeman, Huron county. The Hon. James Monroe and Prof. Henry E. Peck, of Oberlin College, addressed these meetings and rendered valuable assistance in the matter of recruiting. Ebenezer Kingsburry and Albert McRoberts, of Pittsfield, Capt. Alonzo Pease and John W. Steele, of Oberlin, Lorain county, and William H. Pierce, of Wakeman, Huron county, were among the most active in securing enlistments. Within ten days from the receipt of authority to enlist, fifty-two men had joined the company and were ordered to rendezvous at Oberlin, Monday, Sept. 16, 1861, prepared to join the regiment at Camp Wood, Cleveland, Ohio. In pursuance to this order, the company (fifty-two in all) reported at Oberlin during the forenoon of the 16th. The people of the town gave them a hearty reception. Dinner was given at the Palmer House; patriotic addresses were made by the leading citizens, and at one o'clock p. m. the company formed and marched to the Lake Shore depot, boarded the train, and amid cheers and other demonstrations of good will, accompanied by several friends, they started for Camp Wood, where they arrived at 4 o'clock p. m.

The regiment, then numbering about 500 men, Col. W. B. Hazen commanding, was drawn up to receive them. They were mustered in, and marched to their quarters under escort of Company "A." Their tents were already pitched and, after being assigned to quarters and baggage disposed of, supper was prepared and the company with its guests joined in their first meal as soldiers. Soon after Capt. Pease formed the company, three cheers were given for the departing friends and then the company retired for their first night in military service. On the morning of the 17th of September the company by unanimous vote elected Alonzo H. Pease, Captain, who soon after appointed non-commissioned officers and the company entered on their duties as soldiers.

About the 10th of October the enrollment exceeded eighty men. The company then elected John W. Steele, 1st Lieut. and Albert McRoberts, 2d Lieut. On the 29th of October the company (three commissioned officers and eighty-three enlisted men) was mustered into the U. S. service by James P. W. Neill, 1st. Lieut., 18th U. S. Infantry. Five new recruits were received in October, 1862, and eleven in the month of February, 1864, making a total of ninety-nine enlisted men who served with Company H during the war.

Probably not far from 75 per cent. of the enlisted men were farmers; fifteen per cent. mechanics, and the remainder were of various other pursuits. They were mostly descendants from New England stock who settled the Western Reserve. They were fairly well educated, industrious, honest and thrifty. Most of them enlisted from a patriotic sense of duty. Many of them were connected with protestant denominational churches and were zealous in their religious beliefs. Soon after their enlistment they organized weekly religious services and kept this organization up throughout their term of enlistment. As a characteristic of the company: Soon after entering Camp Wood the majority of its members drew up a written remonstrance against profanity among the officers of the regiment. This remonstrance was written in moderate language and rather in the tone of a petition than of a complaint. A committee was appointed, who presented the remonstrance to the Colonel. They were told that such action was subversive of military discipline and were not a little surprised at the spirit in which the petition was received; they, however, ventured the remark that profanity was not only in violaton of the commandment, but also a violation of the United States regulations for the army. The company was known as the praying company, and many new recruits received after going to Camp Wood, attracted by these sterling qualities, enlisted in this company. The average age of the men was about twenty-seven years.

From a letter just received from Capt. Horatio P. Kile, who commanded the company twenty months, I clip the following: "The men of Company H were as a whole, as grand, noble and brave a lot of men as could be mustered in a company organization in any community, therefore to its survivors, descendants and friends is due a recognition of their worth and work."

The following resume of the roster of enlisted men of Company H will give its condition up to the time of discharge from the service.

Commissioned and promoted to other companies...................... 4
Killed, ... 15
Died in the service... 13
Died at Andersonville... 1
Discharged wounded 3
Discharged on surgeon's certificate and mustered out.................. 26
Transferred to Veteran Reserve Corps............................... 7
Transferred to Co. K.. 3
Mustered out at expiration of service............................... 9
Mustered out with company.. 15
Absent sick, ... 1
Transferred to Signal Corps... 1
Appointed Quarter Master's Sergeant................................. 1
                                                                  ———
                                                                   99

Veteranized, 11; prisoners of war, 3.

CAPTAINS.

ALONZO H. PEASE. Age 40. Entered the service Oct. 8, 1861, 3 years. Resigned at Camp Wickliffe, Ky., Jan. 9, 1862.

WILLIAM J. MORGAN. Age 23. See Co. E.

HORATIO P. KILE. Age 22. See Co. G.

EZRA DUNHAM. Age 23. See Co. C.

JOHN P. PATTERSON. Age 18. See Co. C.

WILLIAM M. BEEBE. Age 21. See Co. I.

JAMES M. McCLEERY. Age 20. See Co. A.

1st LIEUTENANTS.

CHARLES D. GAYLORD. Age 22. See Co. K.

JAMES B. CLEVELAND. Age 27. See Co. B.

WILLIAM HANSARD. Age 19. See Co. G.

HENRY G. DELKER. Age 25. See Co. F.

ALBERT WHITTLESEY. Age 18. Entered the service Oct. 10, 1861, 3 years. Appointed Sergt. from Private. Promoted 2d Lieut. from Sergt. Nov. 7, 1862; 1st Lieut. to date April 13, 1864. Was detailed at Readyville, Tenn., May, 1863, while 2d Lieut. to the Pioneer Corps. Returned to Regt. in 1864. Resigned at the expiration of his 3 years service, Nov. 20, 1864.

JOHN W. STEELE. Age 24. Entered the service Sept. 16, 1861, 3 years. Promoted to Captain Co. E Feb. 3, 1862; to Major and A. D. C. Nov. 7, 1864.

2d LIEUTENANTS.

ALBERT McROBERTS. Age 30. Entered the service Oct. 8, 1861, 3 years. Resigned May 27, 1862.

WILLIAM H. PIERCE. Age 21. Entered the service Sept. 16, 1861, 3 years. Appointed Sergt. from Corporal ——. Promoted to 2d Lieut. May 24, 1862. Transferred to Co. B Feb. 1, 1863; to 1st Lieut. June 27, 1863, but not mustered. Mustered out at expiration of his three years service, Jan. 27, 1865.

1st SERGEANTS.

JAMES McMAHON. Age 25. Entered the service Sept. 16, 1861, 3 years. Appointed Sergt. from Private Sept. —, 1861; 1st Sergt. Oct. —, 1861. Promoted to 2d Lieut. Co. I Dec. 21, 1862; 1st Lieut. Co. A April 13, 1864; Captain Nov. 26, 1864. Wounded severely Dec. 16, 1864, in battle of Nashville, Tenn. Discharged Feb. 24, 1865, from hospital at Cincinnati, O., by special order of Sec. of War, for wounds. Was in all battles of regiment.

HENRY S. DIRLAM. Age 27. Entered the service Sept. 16, 1861, 3 years. Appointed Sergt. from Private ——; 1st Sergt. April —, 1863. Promoted 1st Lieut. Co. G March 24, 1863. Was in all battles to date of death. Died Dec. 18, 1863, of wounds received Nov. 25, 1863, in battle of Mission Ridge, Tenn. Was also wounded Dec. 31, 1862, in battle of Stone River, Tenn.

DANIEL H. SMITH. Age 30. Entered the service Oct. 8, 1861, 3 years. Appointed Sergt. from Corporal —; 1st Sergt. May —, 1863. Wounded at battles of Stone River, Tenn., Chickamauga, Ga., and Orchard Knob, Tenn. Discharged at Cleveland, O., from hospital, June 3, 1865. VETERAN. Battles engaged in: All battles of regiment up to and including Kenesaw Mountain, June 27, 1864.

JOSEPH CROSS. Age 25. Entered the service Sept. 26, 1861, 3 years. Appointed from Private July 1, 1865. Was in all the battles of the regiment except Pickett's Mills, Ga., May 27, 1864. Was wounded Dec. 31, 1862, in battle of Stone River, Tenn. Mustered out with company Nov. 27, 1865. VETERAN.

SERGEANTS.

NATHAN WHITNEY. Age 34. Entered the service Sept. 16, 1861, 3 years. Died Feb. 3, 1862, at Louisville, Ky.

HARVEY H. GREEN. Age 33. Entered the service Sept. 16, 1861, 3 years. Discharged at Camp Wickliffe, Ky., Feb. 13, 1862, on surgeon's certificate of disability.

JOHN O. STRONG. Age 26. Entered the service Sept. 16, 1861, 3 years Discharged at Columbus, Ohio, Jan. 23, 1863.

THOMAS H. SOMERS. Age 26. Entered the service Sept. 16, 1861, 3 years. Appointed from Corporal Dec. 27, 1861. Promoted to Q. M. Sergt. June 20, 1862; to 2d Lieut. Co. F May 29, 1863; 1st Lieut. Co. K Oct. 12, 1864; Captain Co. F Nov. 26, 1864. Was with the regiment in all its battles. Mustered out with Co. F Nov. 27, 1865.

WILLIAM H. ROSSITER. Age 23. Entered the service Sept. 16, 1861, 3 years. Appointed from Corporal July 8, 1864. Mustered out with company Nov. 27, 1865. VETERAN.

JOSIAH STAPLES. Age 20. Entered the service Oct. 8, 1861, 3 years. Appointed from Corporal ——. Killed May 27, 1864, in battle of Pickett's Mills, Ga. VETERAN.

JOHN G. MILLS. Age 25. Entered the service Oct. 8, 1861, 3 years. Appointed Sergt. from Private ——. Killed May 27, 1864, in battle of Pickett's Mills, Ga. VETERAN.

GEORGE M. ROGERS. Age 18. Entered the service Sept. 16, 1861, 3 years. Appointed from Private April 1, 1865. Was in all the battles of the regiment. Wounded in battle of Chickamauga, Ga., Sept. 19, 1863. Mustered out with company Nov. 27, 1865. VETERAN.

CORPORALS.

GEORGE W. CLARK. Age 18. Entered the service Oct. 16, 1861, 3 years. Appointed Corporal July 8, 1864. Wounded in battle of Mission Ridge, Tenn., Nov. 25, 1863. Mustered out with company Nov. 27, 1865. VETERAN. Was in all battles of the regiment.

WILLIAM A. MILLS. Age 19. Entered the service Sept. 16, 1861, 3 years. Killed Nov. 23, 1863, in battle of Orchard Knob, near Chattanooga, Tenn.

CHESTER J. CASE. Age 35. Entered the service Oct. 10, 1861, 3 years. Appointed Corporal Oct. —, 1862. Records do not show him to be a sergeant. Discharged at Cleveland, O., Sept. 2, 1863. Wounded Dec. 31, 1862, in battle of Stone River, Tenn. Was in battle of Shiloh.

EDWARD R. LOVELAND. Age 24. Entered the service Oct. 10, 1861, 3 years. Appointed Corporal soon after his enlistment. Wounded severely April 7, 1862, in battle of Shiloh, Tenn. Discharged Oct. 31, 1862, at St. Louis, Mo.

JAMES H. GRANT. Age 19. Entered the service Sept. 16, 1861, 3 years. Appointed Corporal——. Killed Nov. 23, 1863, in battle of Orchard Knob, near Chattanooga, Tenn.

SYLVESTER B. CHAPMAN. Age 30. Entered the service Oct. 10, 1861, 3 years. Appointed Corporal soon after his enlistment. Discharged at Nashville, Tenn., 1862.

ROBERT L. SIMMONDS. Age 22. Entered the service Sept. 16, 1861, 3 years. Discharged at Louisville, Ky., on surgeon's certificate of disability, Sept. 16, 1863.

RAYMOND A. WILDER. Age 22. Entered the service Sept. 24, 1861, 3 years. Discharged at Cincinnati, O., Oct. 2, 1862, on surgeon's certificate of disability from wound received before Corinth, Miss., May 21, 1862.

EDWARD P. HASKELL. Age 18. Entered the service Oct. 8, 1861, 3 years. Appointed Corporal ——. Transferred to Signal Corps Oct. 22, 1863.

MUSICIANS.

HORACE WILCOX. Age 15. Entered the service Oct. 14, 1861, 3 years. Discharged at Camp Chase, O., Nov. 1, 1862, on surgeon's certificate of disability.

ALONZO HOSFORD. Age 29. Entered the service Oct. 8, 1861, 3 years. Mustered out at Pulaski, Tenn., on expiration of term of service, Nov. 9, 1864.

PRIVATES.

ALLEN, THOMAS. Age 43. Entered the service Feb. 22, 1864, 3 years. Wounded at Altoona Mountain, Ga. Mustered out with company Nov. 27, 1865. Was with the company in the Atlanta campaign, and back to Nashville, Tenn., and in the battles of the regiment during said time.

BRICE, EDWIN. Age 19. Entered the service Sept. 16, 1861, 3 years. Mustered out with company Nov. 27, 1865. VETERAN. Was in all battles of regiment.

BRUMBY, JOHN H. Age 19. Entered the service Feb. 24, 1864, 3 years. Mustered out with company Nov. 27, 1865.

BLACKWELL, JAMES W. Age 23. Entered the service Oct. 8, 1861, 3 years. Killed Nov. 23, 1863, in battle of Orchard Knob, near Chattanooga, Tenn.

BEAM, EPHRAIM T. Age 29. Entered the service Sept. 16, 1861, 3 years. Mustered out at Pulaski, Tenn., Nov. 9, 1864, on expiration of term of service.

BIGELOW, MARLIN M. Age 28. Entered the service Sept. 16, 1861, 3 years. Transferred to 42d Co., 2d Battalion, Veteran Reserve Corps, Oct. 10, 1863. Mustered out at Washington, D. C., on expiration of term of service.

BUTSON, GEORGE. Age 18. Entered the service Feb. 27, 1864, 3 years. Killed May 27, 1864, in battle of Pickett's Mills, Ga.

BROWN, HYMAN A. Age 23. Entered the service Sept. 16, 1861, 3 years. Died May 30, 1862, near Corinth, Miss.

CAMP, SENECA. Age 24. Entered the service Sept. 16, 1861, 3 years. Killed April 7, 1862, in battle of Shiloh, Tenn.

CAMP, RANSOM H. Age 23. Entered the service Oct. 14, 1861, 3 years. Discharged at Columbus, O., July 1, 1862, on surgeon's certificate of disability.

CLARK, JOHN. Age —. Entered the service Feb. —, 1864, 3 years. Killed May 27, 1864, in battle of Pickett's Mills, Ga.

CLARK, ALBERT J. Age 19. Entered the service Sept. 16, 1861, 3 years. Died May 14, 1862, near Corinth, Miss.

CLARK, GEORGE C. Age 22. Entered the service Oct. 8, 1861, 3 years. Died Jan. 23, 1862, at Camp Wickliffe, Ky.

CHAMBERLAIN, MATTHEW. Age 29. Entered the service Oct. 2, 1861, 3 years. Killed April 7, 1862, in battle of Shiloh, Tenn.

CHAMBERLAIN, ANDREW. Age 21. Entered the service Oct 2, 1861, 3 years. Discharged at Louisville, Ky., June 18, 1862, on surgeon's certificate of disability.

CROSS, JOHN. Age 25. Entered the service Sept. 26, 1861, 3 years. Discharged at Louisville, Ky., June 3, 1862.

DOTY, ELLIS E. Age 29. Entered the service Oct. 10, 1861, 3 years. Died Aug. 10, 1864, in Rebel prison at Andersonville, Ga. Wounded and taken prisoner in battle of Chickamauga, Ga., Sept. 19, 1863.

DIRLAM, VEROZANO. Age 22. Entered the service Sept. 16, 1861, 3 years. Mustered out at Pulaski, Tenn., Nov. 9, 1864, on expiration of term of service.

DANFORTH, CHARLES. Transferred to Co. K.

ELDRED, ZENAS. Age 28. Entered the service Oct. 10, 1861, 3 years.

FISHELL, SAMUEL. Age 40. Entered the service Oct. 10, 1861, 3 years. Transferred to 126th Co., 2d Battalion, Veteran Reserve Corps, Dec. 28, 1863. Wounded Dec. 31, 1862, in battle of Stone River, Tenn.

GOODELL, SYDNEY S. Age 42. Entered the service Sept. 16, 1861, 3 years.

GUNSAUL, CHARLES. Age 19. Entered the service Oct. 10, 1861, 3 years. Killed Nov. 23, 1863, in battle of Orchard Knob, near Chattanooga, Tenn. Interred in National Cemetery at Chattanooga, Tenn.

GETNER, FREDERICK. Age 36. Entered the service Oct. 8, 1862, 9 months. Drafted. Mustered out at Manchester, Tenn., on expiration of term of service, July 17, 1863.

GILLETT, GEORGE J. Age 37. Entered the service Oct. 8, 1862, 9 months. Drafted. Mustered out at Manchester, Tenn., on expiration of term of service, July 17, 1863.

HOOVER, JACOB. Age 42. Entered the service Sept. 16, 1861, 3 years. Mustered out with company Nov. 27, 1865. VETERAN.

HASBROOK, EDWIN. Age 21. Entered the service Sept. 16, 1861, 3 years. Mustered out with company Nov. 27, 1865. VETERAN. Wounded in battle of Chickamauga, Ga., Sept. 19, 1863.

HOLCOMB, WILLIAM J. Age 23. Entered the service Feb. 1, 1864, 3 years. Mustered out with company Nov. 27, 1865.

HATCH, JOHN M.. Age 26. Entered the service Oct. 10, 1861, 3 years. Discharged at Louisville, Ky., July 31, 1862, on surgeon's certificate of disability.

HARRISON, ALFRED. Age 28. Entered the service Oct. 8, 1862, 9 months. Drafted. Mustered out at Manchester, Tenn., on expiration of term of service, July 17, 1863.

HUDSON, RICHARD. Age 27. Entered the service Oct. 14, 1861, 3 years. Discharged at Louisville, Ky., Oct. 1, 1862, on surgeon's certificate of disability.

KINGSBERRY, EBENEZER. Age 41. Entered the service Sept. 16, 1861, 3 years. Killed Nov. 23, 1863, in battle of Orchard Knob, near Chattanooga, Tenn.

KELLOGG, ALBERT M. Age 17. Entered the service Sept. 16, 1861, 3 years. Died March 18, 1862, at Louisville, Ky.

KELLOGG, HUGH H. Age 46. Entered the service Sept. 16, 1861, 3 years. Discharged at Gallatin, Tenn., Feb. 27, 1863, on surgeon's certificate of disability.

KELLOGG, MARTIN H. Age 23. Entered the service Sept. 16, 1861, 3 years. Transferred to Veteran Reserve Corps April 6, 1864.

LAUGHREY, HOMER J. Age 18. Entered the service Feb. 24, 1864, 3 years. Mustered out at Columbus, O., July 3, 1865, by order of War Department.

LENHART, JOHN C. Age 25. Entered the service Sept. 16, 1861, 3 years. Killed Dec. 31, 1862, in battle of Stone River, Tenn.

LAWRENCE, DANIEL. Age 44. Entered the service Sept. 16, 1861, 3 years. Died June 4, 1862, in hospital at Bardstown, Ky.

LINCOLN, JOSEPH H. Age 43. Entered the service Sept. 16, 1861, 3 years. Died March 20, 1862, at his home, Pittsfield, O.

LYNDES, ANSON. Age 19. Entered the service Sept. 16, 1861, 3 years. Captured Sept. 12, 1863, near Gorden's Mills, Ga., and served several months in Libby prison, Richmond, Va. Mustered out at Pulaski, Tenn., Nov. 2, 1864, on expiration of term of service.

LUMER, LEVI. Age 39. Entered the service Feb. 6, 1864, 3 years. Mustered out with company Nov. 27, 1865.

MAINES, AQUILLA. Age 17. Entered the service Oct. 8, 1861, 3 years. Mustered out with company Nov. 27, 1865. VETERAN.

MOORE, HARRISON. Age 21. Entered the service Sept. 16, 1861, 3 years. Transferred to 125th Co., 3d Battalion, Veteran Reserve Corps, Dec. 18, 1863, on account of wounds received in battle of Stone River, Tenn.

MURRAY, CHARLES F. Age 18. Entered the service Sept. 16, 1861, 3 years. Mustered out at Pulaski, Tenn., Nov. 14, 1864, on expiration of term of service.

MILLER, GEORGE W. Age 19. Entered the service Sept. 16, 1861, 3 years. Discharged June 3, 1862, on surgeon's certificate of disability, at Louisville, Ky.

MORTON, LEANDER L. Age 42. Entered the service Sept. 16, 1861, 3 years. Discharged Oct. 20, 1862, at Nashville, Tenn., on surgeon's certificate of disability.

MARCEY, ADELBERT. Age 17. Entered the service Oct. 8, 1861, 3 years. Discharged at Louisville, Ky., May 12, 1862, on surgeon's certificate of disability.

MESLER, WILLIAM. Age 40. Entered the service Oct. 8, 1862, 9 months. Drafted. Mustered out at Manchester, Tenn., July 17, 1863, on expiration of term of service.

MARKS, LESTER E. Age 23. Entered the service Feb. 28, 1864, 3 years, Mustered out with company Nov. 27, 1865.

MARKS, LESTER E. Age 19. Entered the service Sept. 16, 1861, 3 years. Discharged at Camp Chase, O., June 18, 1862, on account of wounds received April 7, 1862, in battle of Shiloh, Tenn.

NORTON, SAMUEL H. Age 28. Entered the service Oct. 8, 1861, 3 years. Discharged at Nashville, Tenn., Oct. 6, 1862, on surgeon's certificate of disability.

PORTER, WILLIAM H. Age 18. Entered the service Sept. 16, 1861, 3 years. Killed April 7, 1862, in battle of Shiloh, Tenn.

PORTER, JOHN. Age 40. Entered the service Sept. 16, 1861, 3 years. Discharged at Camp Wickliffe, Ky., Feb. 10, 1862 on surgeon's certificate of disability.

POMEROY, FRANKLIN. Age 18. Entered the service Sept. 16, 1861, 3 years. Died Jan. 19, 1862, near Camp Wickliffe, Ky.

PRINCE, WILLIAM H. Age 35. Entered the service Sept. 16, 1861, 3 years. Discharged at Camp Dennison, O., March 16, 1863, on surgeon's certificate of disability from wound received in battle of Stone River, Dec. 31, 1862. Battles engaged in: Shiloh and Stone River.

ROSSITER, EMER A. Age 20. Entered the service Sept. 16, 1861, 3 years. Killed Dec. 31, 1862, in battle of Stone River, Tenn.

ROSSITER, FLOYD. Age 18. Entered the service Oct. 3, 1861, 3 years. Discharged near Corinth, Miss., June 1, 1862, on surgeon's certificate of disability.

ROLLINSON, WILLIAM. Age 24. Entered the service Sept. 16, 1861, 3 years.

ROSER, JOHN C. M. Age 28. Entered the service Sept. 16, 1861, 3 years. Transferred to Co. I, 19th Regt., Veteran Reserve Corps, March 25, 1864. Discharged at Elmira, N. Y., Oct. 30, 1864. Wounded in battle of Shiloh, Tenn., also wounded in battle of Mission Ridge, Nov. 25, 1863. Battles engaged in: Shiloh, Stone River, Chickamauga, Mission Ridge.

SANDERS, DANIEL. Age 42. Entered the service Feb. 5, 1864, 3 years. Discharged at Tripler's hospital, Columbus, O., May 16, 1865.

SIMONDS, GEORGE D. Age 18. Entered the service Oct. 16, 1861, 3 years. Transferred to Co. H, 12th Regt., Veteran Reserve Corps, May 20, 1864.

SMITH, JOHN E. Age 18. Entered the service Oct. 27, 1861, 3 years. Discharged at Nashville, Tenn., Oct. 6, 1862, on surgeon's certificate of disability.

SMITH, OLIVER M. Age 26. Entered the service Sept. 24, 1861, 3 years. Died June 13, 1862, at Spencer O.

SANDERSON, HARVEY. Age 24. Entered the service Sept. 24, 1861, 3 years. Died June 22, 1862, near Corinth, Miss.

SPANGLER, PHILIP. Age —. 3 years. Died June 5, 1863, at Readyville, Tenn., of disease. Interred in Summit county, O.

TAYLOR, ZACHARIAH. Transferred to Co. K.

TOOZE, WILLIAM. Age 34. Entered the service Feb. 27, 1864, 3 years. Absent, sick at Cleveland, Tenn., May 2, 1864. No further record found.

TOOZE, JAMES. Age 33. Entered the service Sept. 16, 1861, 3 years. Was taken prisoner at Chickamauga, Ga., Sept. 20, 1863. Seventeen months in Rebel prison. Discharged at Columbus, Ohio, April 5, 1865. Battles engaged in: Shiloh; Stone River; Chickamauga, Ga.

TODD, CHARLES M. Age 21. Entered the service Sept. 16, 1861, 3 years. Died April 7, 1862, at Columbia, Tenn.

TURNER, LEVI. Age 30. Entered the service Feb. 6, 1864, 3 years. Mustered out with company Nov. 27, 1865

TIFT, GEORGE G. Age 18. Entered the service Sept. 16, 1861, 3 years. Transferred to Co. I, 5th Regt., Veteran Reserve Corps, Dec. 15, 1863, on account of wounds received Dec. 31, 1862, in battle of Stone River, Tenn.

TALCOTT, PHILANDER. Age 19. Entered the service Oct. 14, 1861, 3 years. Discharged at Louisville, Ky., June 20, 1862, on surgeon's certificate of disability.

WORCESTER, NORTON T. Age 18. Entered the service Feb. 24, 1864, 3 years. Mustered out with company Nov. 27, 1865. Wounded in battle of Pickett's Mills, Ga., May 27, 1864.

WEST, HENRY. Age 22. Entered the service Sept. 16, 1861, 3 years. Killed April 7, 1862, in battle of Shiloh, Tenn.

WEST, BENONI B. Age 37. Entered the service Sept. 16, 1861, 3 years. Died Nov. 2, 1864, at Oberlin, Ohio, of disease.

WHITTLESEY, FREDERICK. Age 21. Entered the service Aug. 15, 1862, 3 years. Transferred to Co. K.

WHITNEY, GEORGE F. Age 27. Entered the service Sept. 16, 1861, 3 years. Wounded in battle of Shiloh, Tenn., April 7, 1862. Discharged at Columbus, O., July 21, 1862, on surgeon's certificate of disability.

COMPANY I.

When the first call for volunteers was made in April, 1861, a full company of 100 men was formed in Port Clinton, Ottawa county, but so many companies were being offered to the government at the time that the Port Clinton company could not find a place in any regiment, and it was finally disbanded. But a few men, who afterwards formed the nucleus of Company "I," kept together, and about the 1st of September, 1861, organized a new company which became Company "I" of the 41st Ohio. John Mitchell was elected Captain; John H. Williston, 1st Lieutenant, and Wm. Rymers, 2d Lieutenant. When the company arrived in Cleveland Col. Hazen refused to recommend Mitchell for a commission as Captain and made Williston Captain; Rymers, 1st Lieutenant, and W. M. Beebe, (not of the company) 2d Lieutenant. Mitchell served in the ranks as private until March 1, 1862, when he was commissioned 2d. Lieutenant.

The rejection of John Mitchell was as great a mistake as Hazen made in the whole work of organization. Mitchell's record in all grades up to captain abundantly vindicated him. There was no more reliable, sturdy and faithful soldier in the regiment.

The company lost thirteen killed in action, four died of wounds. and eighteen died of disease. Four of the killed in action were at Shiloh, and three at Pickett's Mills.

CAPTAINS.

JOHN H. WILLISTON. Age 28. Entered the service Sept. 16, 1861, 3 years. Promoted to Major Jan. 1, 1864. Wounded July 5, 1864, in action at Chattahoochee River, Ga. Discharged on surgeon's certificate of disability, Oct. 22, 1864.

JOHN D. KIRKENDALL. Age 31. See Co. F.

JAMES McMAHON. Age 25. See Co. H.

WILSON S. MILLER. Age 22. Entered the service Sept. 16, 1861, 3 years. Appointed 1st Sergt. from Sergt. April 18, 1863. Promoted 1st Lieut. Nov. 26, 1864; Captain March 18, 1865. Mustered out with company Nov. 27, 1865. VETERAN.

1st LIEUTENANTS.

WILLIAM RYMERS. Age 33. Entered the service Sept. 16, 1861, 3 years. Promoted to Captain Co. C March 1, 1862. Resigned Sept. 9, 1862.

CHARLES D. GAYLORD. Age 22. See Co. K.

LESTER T. PATCHIN. Age 26. See Co. B.

JOHN MITCHELL. Age 28. Entered the service Sept. 16, 1861, 3 years. Promoted 2d Lieut. from Private to date March 1, 1862; 1st Lieut. to date Nov. 20, 1862. Resigned Oct. 10, 1864.

JOHN CRONKHITE. Age 19. Entered the service Oct. 5, 1861, 3 years. Appointed Corporal Feb. 4, 1862; Sergt. Nov. 23, 1863; 1st Sergt. Dec. 6, 1864. Promoted Sergt. Major Feb. 1, 1865; 1st Lieut. April 20, 1865. Mustered out with company Nov. 27, 1865. VETERAN.

2d LIEUTENANTS.

WILLIAM M. BEEBE. Age 21. Entered the service Oct. 29, 1861, 3 years. Resigned April 16, 1862. Recommissioned 1st Lieut. June 1, 1862. Promoted Captain Co. C April 13, 1864. Transferred to Co. H March 28, 1865; Brevet Major March 13, 1865; Lieut. Colonel 128th Regt., U. S. Col. Troops, April 28, 1865.

PETER HERRIFF. Age 19. See Co. D.

RUSH JAMESON. Age 19. See Co. C.

1st SERGEANTS.

WILLIAM W. WATSON. Age 23. Entered the service Sept. 16, 1861, 3 years. Promoted to 2d Lieut. Co. K May 24, 1863. Killed Nov. 25, 1863, in battle of Mission Ridge, Tenn. Interred in National cemetery at Chattanooga, Tenn.

GEORGE O. BAILEY. Age 19. Entered the service Sept. 16, 1861, 3 years. Appointed Corporal Aug. 1, 1862; Sergt. Dec. 6, 1864; 1st Sergt. Feb. 1, 1865. Mustered out with company Nov. 27, 1865. VETERAN.

SERGEANTS.

CHARLES F. CLOSE. Age 26. Entered the service Sept. 16, 1861, 3 years. Appointed Corporal March 1, 1862; Sergt. March 26, 1864. Mustered out with company Nov. 27, 1865. VETERAN. Was in all the battles of the regiment. Wounded at Shiloh, April 7, 1862.

GUSTAVIUS A. KRAEMER. Age 21. Entered the service Sept. 16, 1861, 3 years. Appointed Corporal April 18, 1863; Sergt. March 26, 1864. Mustered out with company Nov. 27, 1865. VETERAN. Was in all the battles of the regiment. In the charge on Orchard Knob, Tenn., Nov. 23, 1863, he captured the flag of the 28th Alabama Regt., C. S. A., from the Color Sergt. and handed it to Capt. McMahon who handed it over to Col. Wiley on the works.

WILLIAM McCLANATHAN. Age 22. Entered the service Sept. 16, 1861, 3 years. Discharged at Nashville, Tenn., May 27, 1865. VETERAN.

CALVIN BROWN. Age 19. Entered the service Oct. 5, 1861, 3 years. Appointed Corporal March 26, 1864; Sergt. Feb. 20, 1865. Mustered out with company Nov. 27, 1865. VETERAN.

WILLIAM A. FETTERLY. Age 24. Entered the service Sept. 16, 1861, 3 years. Appointed from Private July 1, 1865. Mustered out with company Nov. 27, 1865. VETERAN.

CHARLES A. KIRK. Age 24. Entered the service Sept. 16, 1861, 3 years. Appointed from Private Aug. 18, 1862. Killed Nov. 23, 1863, in battle of Orchard Knob, near Chattanooga, Tenn.

THOMAS J. WONNELL. Age 25. Entered the service Sept. 16, 1861, 3 years. Appointed from Corporal Feb. 4, 1862. Discharged at Columbus, O., Aug 18, 1862, on surgeon's certificate of disability.

JOHN HOUSEMAN. Age 34. Entered the service Sept. 16, 1861, 3 years. Appointed from Corporal April 18, 1863. Transferred to Veteran Reserve Corps Sept. 1, 1863.

CORPORALS

WILLIAM H. SILVERWOOD. Age 19. Entered the service Sept. 16, 1861, 3 years. Appointed Corporal Sept. 17, 1862. Mustered out with company Nov. 27, 1865. VETERAN.

GEORGE W. CARROLL. Age 23. Entered the service Sept. 16, 1861, 3 years. Appointed Corporal March 26, 1864. Mustered out with company Nov. 27, 1865. VETERAN.

WALLACE W. JOHNSON. Age 33. Entered the service Feb. 29, 1864, 3 years. Appointed Corporal July 9, 1864. Mustered out with company Nov. 27, 1865.

HENRY TUTTLE. Age 36. Entered the service Oct. 5, 1861, 3 years. Appointed Corporal July 9, 1864. Mustered out with company Nov. 27, 1865. VETERAN.

JOSEPH EBY. Age 18. Entered the service Oct. 2, 1861, 3 years. Appointed Corporal Dec. 6, 1864. Mustered out with company Nov. 27, 1865. VETERAN.

JAMES FITZGERALD. Age 18. Entered the service Aug. 27, 1861, 3 years. Appointed Corporal Feb. 20, 1865. Mustered out with company Nov. 27, 1865. VETERAN.

ELMER N. WILKINSON. Age 18. Entered the service Oct. 5, 1861, 3 years. Appointed Corporal April 1, 1865. Mustered out with company Nov. 27, 1865. VETERAN.

GEORGE D. PARKER. Age 17. Entered the service Oct. 2, 1861, 3 years. Died Dec. 26, 1861, at Louisville, Ky.

DANIEL MOORE. Age 17. Entered the service Sept. 16, 1861, 3 years. Appointed Corporal May 1, 1865. Mustered out with company Nov. 27, 1865. VETERAN.

JEREMIAH K. SNYDER. Age 31. Entered the service Sept. 16, 1861, 3 years. Appointed Corporal Aug. 1, 1862. Killed Dec. 31, 1862, in battle of Stone River, Tenn.

WILLIAM F. GRAM. Age —. Entered the service Sept. 16, 1861, 3 years. Appointed Corporal March 26, 1864. Killed May 27, 1864, in battle of Pickett's Mills, Ga. VETERAN.

WILLIAM D. GILL. Age 21. Entered the service Sept. 16, 1861, 3 years. Died April 23, 1862, at Evansville, Ind., of wounds received April 7, 1862, in battle of Shiloh, Tenn.

DISBRO JUSTICE. Age 31. Entered the service Sept. 16, 1861, 3 years. Died July 5, 1862, at Athens, Ala. Buried at Athens, Ala.

GEORGE E. SANGER. Age —. Entered the service Nov. 1, 1861, 3 years. Appointed Corporal Feb. 4, 1862. Discharged at Columbus, Ohio, July 3, 1863.

WILLIAM U. BAKER Age 24. Entered the service Sept. 16, 1861, 3 years. Discharged at Columbus, O., Sept. 16, 1862, on surgeon's certificate of disability.

HENRY J. ENGELBECK. Age 21. Entered the service Sept. 16, 1861, 3 years. Appointed Corporal April 18, 1863. Promoted to Sergeant Major May 1, 1865. Mustered out with regiment Nov. 27, 1865. VETERAN. Wounded at Kenesaw Mountain, Ga., June 24, 1864.

MUSICIANS.

CHARLES H. COWELL. Age 35. Entered the service Sept. 16, 1861, 3 years. Mustered out with company Nov. 27, 1865. VETERAN.

SHEPHERD SCOTT. Age 18. Entered the service Oct. 2, 1861, 3 years. Missing Sept. 20, 1863, at battle of Chickamauga, Ga. Died Aug. 9, 1864, in Rebel prison at Andersonville, Ga. Grave No. 5133.

PRIVATES.

ALGO, CYRENUS. Age 23. Entered the service Feb. 29, 1864, 3 years. Mustered out with company Nov. 27, 1865.

ARNOLD, TIMOTHY. Age 15. Entered the service Sept. 26, 1861, 3 years. VETERAN.

APPLEGATE, CHARLES. Age 24. Entered the service Sept. 16, 1861, 3 years. Wounded Sept. 19, 1863, in battle of Chickamauga, Ga. Mustered in as John Applegate. Discharged at Columbus, O., Nov. 1, 1864, on expiration of term of service.

ACKLEY, JOSEPHUS. Age 18. Entered the service Aug. 27, 1861, 3 years. Discharged at Jeffersonville, Ind., March 29, 1865. VET-ERAN.

ATWATER, SAMUEL. Age —. Entered the service Feb. 24, 1864, 3 years. Discharged at Nashville, Tenn., March 15, 1865, on surgeon's certificate of disability.

ALSPAUGH, BENJAMIN. Age 21. Entered the service Oct. 10, 1863, 3 years. Transferred to Co. A, 17th Regt., Veteran Reserve Corps, Jan. 16, 1865.

BERRY, LEWIS. Age 19. Entered the service Feb. 24, 1864, 3 years. Mustered out with company Nov. 27, 1865.

BICE, JOHN. Age 18. Entered the service Feb. 24, 1864, 3 years. Mustered out with company Nov. 27, 1865.

BODIE, DAVID. Age 39. Entered the service Feb. 8, 1865, 1 year. Mustered out with company Nov. 27, 1865.

BATTIN, CHRISTOPHER. Age 18. Entered the service Feb. 29, 1864, 3 years. Killed May 27, 1864, in battle of Pickett's Mills, Ga.

BROWER, GEORGE W. Age —. Entered the service Sept. 29, 1864, 1 year. Substitute. Killed Dec. 16, 1864, in battle of Nashville, Tenn.

BELL, JOSEPH M. Age 19. Entered the service Sept. 16, 1861, 3 years. Died Sept. 20, 1862, at Nashville, Tenn.

BALDWIN, ISAAC P. Age 24. Entered the service Sept. 16, 1861, 3 years. Discharged at Columbus, Ohio, Sept. 16, 1862, on surgeon's certificate of disability.

BARTLEBAUGH, GEORGE J. Age —. Entered the service Sept. 4, 1864, 1 year. Substitute. Discharged at Nashville, Tenn., June 13, 1865, by order of War Department.

BRITT, THOMAS. Age —. Entered the service Oct. 8, 1864, 1 year. Substitute. Mustered out at San Antonio, Tex., Oct. 16, 1865, on expiration of term of service.

CARROLL, WALTER. Age 21. Entered the service Feb. 29, 1864, 3 years. Mustered out with company Nov. 27, 1865.

COUCHAIN, FELIX H. Age 18. Entered the service Feb. 29, 1864, 3 years. Mustered out with company Nov. 27, 1865.

COUCHAIN, ANDREW J. Age 18. Entered the service Sept. 16, 1861, 3 years. Wounded Dec. 31, 1862, in battle of Stone River, Tenn. Was in all battles of regiment up to date of being wounded. Discharged at Louisville, Ky., March 23, 1863, on surgeon's certificate of disability.

CHAPMAN, WILLIAM. Age 18. Entered the service Feb. 29, 1864, 3 years. Mustered out with company Nov. 27, 1865.

CHAPMAN, JAMES E. Age 18. Entered the service Feb. 29, 1864, 3 years. Mustered out with company Nov. 27, 1865.

CLUCKY, EDWARD. Age 19. Entered the service Feb. 24, 1864, 3 years. Mustered out with company Nov. 27, 1865.

CLUCKY, LEWIS. Age 29. Entered the service Feb. 8, 1865, 1 year. Died Oct. 4, 1865, at Victoria, Tex.

CLUCKY, PETER. Age 31, Entered the service Feb. 24, 1864, 3 years. Wounded in battle of Resaca, Ga. Battles engaged in: Resaca; Dallas; Kenesaw Mountain; Siege of Atlanta; Franklin, Tenn. Mustered out at Nashville, Tenn., May 16, 1865, by order of War Department.

COOCHER, SAMUEL. Age 36. Entered the service Feb. 8, 1865, 1 year. Mustered out with company Nov. 27, 1865.

COOCHER, DAVID. Age 25. Entered the service Feb. 8, 1865, 1 year. Mustered out with company Nov. 27, 1865.

COOPER, GEORGE A. Age 22. Entered the service Feb. 24, 1864, 3 years. Died June 3, 1865, at Nashville, Tenn.

CLARK, JOHN. Age 40. Entered the service Sept. 2, 1861, 3 years. Wounded Nov. 25, 1863, in battle of Mission Ridge. Lost a leg above the knee. Transferred from Co. F Oct. 1, 1861. Discharged at Nashville, Tenn., July 25, 1864, on surgeon's certificate of disability.

CULLUMBER, HENRY P. Age 24. Entered the service Sept. 23, 1864, 1 year. Drafted. Prisoner of war since Dec. 1, 1864. No further record found.

DAWSON, SYLVESTER M. Age 18. Entered the service Oct. 3, 1861, 3 years. Mustered out with company Nov. 27, 1865. VETERAN.

DEAL, JACOB. Age 20. Entered the service Oct. 10, 1863, 3 years. Mustered out with company Nov. 27, 1865.

DAVENPORT, HOLLIS. Age 26. Entered the service Feb. 29, 1864, 3 years. Mustered out with company Nov. 27, 1865.

DUBSEY, GABRIEL. Age 18. Entered the service Feb. 26, 1864, 3 years. Mustered out with company Nov. 27, 1865.

DAVIS, ALBERT C. Age 24. Entered the service Feb. 24, 1864, 3 years. Killed May 27, 1864, in battle of Pickett's Mills, Ga.

DOUGHERTY, CHARLES. Age 33. Entered the service Sept. 16, 1861, 3 years. Discharged at Knoxville, Tenn., March 31, 1864, on surgeon's certificate of disability.

DEWITT, ANDREW J. Age 24. Entered the service Sept. 16, 1861, 3 years. Discharged at Camp Wickliffe, Ky., Feb. 15, 1862.

DEPEW, GEORGE H. Age 21. Entered the service Sept. 16, 1861, 3 years. Discharged at Louisville, Ky., Jan. 29, 1863, on surgeon's certificate of disability.

DUVOO, LEWIS. Age 18. Entered the service Sept. 2, 1861, 3 years. Transferred from Co. F Oct. 1, 1861, as Lewis Devon. Mustered out at Pulaski, Tenn., Nov. 14, 1864, on expiration of term of service.

EBY, JOHN. Age 18. Entered the service Feb. 29, 1864, 3 years. Mustered out with company Nov. 27, 1865.

ELLSWORTH, CHARLES. Age 19. Entered the service Sept. 14, 1861, 3 years. Mustered out at Pulaski, Tenn., Nov. 14, 1864, on expiration of term of service.

ELLWILL, GEORGE. Age 18. Entered the service Oct. 8, 1861, 3 years. Discharged at Columbus, O., Feb. 19, 1863, on surgeon's certificate of disability.

FARRON, EDWARD. Age 41. Entered the service Feb. 8, 1865, 1 year. Mustered out with company Nov. 27, 1865.

FETTERLY, CHARLES. Age 18. Entered the service Feb. 8, 1865, 1 year. Mustered out with company Nov. 27, 1865.

FELTER, MARTIN. Age —. Entered the service Feb. 29, 1864, 3 years. Died May 20, 1864, of wounds received May 15th, 1864, in battle of Resaca.

FOSTER, THOMAS. Age —. Entered the service Sept. 29, 1864, 1 year. Substitute. Mustered out at Nashville, Tenn., June 13, 1865, by order of War Department.

FIELDS, GEORGE W. Age 18. Entered the service Oct. 25, 1861, 3 years. Killed April 7, 1862, in battle of Shiloh, Tenn.

GODDARD, WILLIAM. Age 39. Entered the service Oct. 16, 1861, 3 years. Died Feb. 1, 1862, at Louisville, Ky.

GOUCH, FREDERICK. Age 18. Entered the service Oct. 2, 1861, 3 years. Died April 21, 1863, at Readyville, Tenn.

GREINER, CYRUS. Age 19. Entered the service Sept. 19, 1861, 3 years. Died July 9, 1863, at Tullahoma, Tenn.

GRAM, CASPER. Age 20. Entered the service Sept. 16, 1861, 3 years. Wounded May 27, 1864, in battle of Pickett's Mills, Ga. Battles engaged in: All of the Atlanta campaign up to date of being wounded. Mustered out at Camp Dennison, O., Sept. 29, 1864, on expiration of term of service.

GRANT, JAMES. Age —. Entered the service Oct. 5, 1864, 1 year. Substitute. Discharged Oct. 18, 1865, by order of War Department.

GREEN, WILLIAM. Age 20. Entered the service Feb. 24, 1864, 3 years. Mustered out at Jeffersonville, Ind., June 7, 1865, by order of War Department.

GLEASON, JOHN. Age 21. Entered the service Jan. 4, 1864, 3 years. Mustered out at Camp Dennison, O., July 1, 1865.

GRAFF, H. A. W. Age —. Entered the service Sept. 26, 1864, 1 year. Drafted. Mustered out at Nashville, Tenn., June 13, 1865, by order of War Department.

HERRING, ANDREW. Age 27. Entered the service Oct. 10, 1863, 3 years. Mustered out with company Nov. 27, 1865.

HERRING, JOSIAH. Age 26. Entered the service Oct. 10, 1863, 3 years. Mustered out with company Nov. 27, 1865.

HERRING, ZACHARIAH. Age 21. Entered the service Oct. 10, 1863, 3 years. Mustered out with company Nov. 27, 1865.

HESS, WILLIAM J. Age 28. Entered the service Feb. 29, 1864, 3 years. Mustered out with company Nov. 27, 1865.

HARTMAN, FREDERICK. Age 18. Entered the service Oct. 5, 1861, 3 years. Killed April 7, 1862, in battle of Shiloh, Tenn.

HALL, JOHN W. Age 19. Entered the service Oct. 2, 1861, 3 years. Died Sept. 12, 1863, at Poe's Tavern, Tenn.

HOLMES, HENRY. Age 20. Entered the service Oct. 2, 1861, 3 years. Was in all battles of regiment to date of discharge. Mustered out at Columbus, O., Nov. 1, 1864, on expiration of term of service.

HADLOCK, URIAH. Age 45. Entered the service Sept 22, 1861, 3 years. Discharged at Louisville, Ky., Jan. 31, 1862, on surgeon's certificate of disability.

HASKELL, SHERM R. Age 22. Entered the service Sept. 24, 1864, 3 years. Discharged at Columbus, O., Jan. 9, 1865, on surgeon's certificate of disability.

JOHNSON, JOHN O. Age 22. Entered the service Feb. 24, 1864, 3 years. Mustered out with company Nov. 27, 1865.

JERAMAY, ISAAC. Age 27. Entered the service Dec. 6, 1864, 1 year. Mustered out with company Nov. 27, 1865.

JONES, WILLIAM H. Age 28. Entered the service Oct. 20, 1861, 3 years.

JOHNSON, JOHN. Age 22. Entered the service Oct. 7, 1864, 1 year. Substitute. Mustered out at San Antonio, Tex., Oct. 16, 1865, on expiration of term of service.

KARL, AUGUSTINE. Age 37. Entered the service Feb. 29, 1864, 3 years. Mustered out with company Nov. 27, 1865.

KLEINHAUS, GEORGE H. Age 18. Entered the service Nov. 14, 1863, 3 years. Captured Dec. 16, 1864, at battle of Nashville, Tenn. No further record found.

KAEFER, GEORGE W. Age 17. Entered the service Oct. 16, 1861, 3 years. Died Jan. 24, 1862, at Louisville, Ky.

KAEFER, ABRAHAM. Age 20. Entered the service Sept. 16, 1861, 3 years. Mustered out at Nashville, Tenn., June 13, 1865, by order of War Department.

KENNEDY, JOHN. Age 35. Entered the service Sept. 8, 1861, 3 years. Discharged at Louisville, Ky., Dec. 11, 1862, on surgeon's certificate of disability.

KOCHE, EDWARD. Age 20. Entered the service Oct. 10, 1863, 3 years. Mustered out at Chattanooga, Tenn., May 18, 1865.

KLENNINGER, FRANCIS. Age 31. Entered the service Jan. 1, 1864, 3 years. Discharged at Camp Dennison, O., June 21, 1865, on surgeon's certificate of disability.

KING, GEORGE W. Age —. Entered the service Sept. 30, 1864, 1 year. Substitute. Mustered out at Nashville, Tenn., June 13, 1865, by order of War Department.

LEGGETT, ALBERT M. Age 18. Entered the service Feb. 24, 1864, 3 years. Mustered out with company Nov. 27, 1865.

LEEDERS, CHARLES. Age —. Entered the service Feb. 24, 1864, 3 years. Died April 12, 1864, at Nashville, Tenn.

LOCKWOOD, ALFRED R. Age 18. Entered the service Feb. 29, 1864, 3 years. Died April 1, 1864, at Louisville, Ky.

LADOW, JOHN. Age 17. Entered the service Aug. 27, 1861, 3 years.

LYMBURNER, JOHN. Age 20. Entered the service Sept. 16, 1861, 3 years. VETERAN. Left sick at Port Clinton, O., while on Veteran furlough.

LOVEJOY, GEORGE W. Age —. Entered the service Oct. 4, 1864, 1 year. Substitute. Mustered out at San Antonio, Tex., Oct. 16, 1865, on expiration of term of service.

MINIER, DANIEL. Age 35. Entered the service Feb. 23, 1865, 1 year. Mustered out with company Nov. 27, 1865.

MINIER, CHRISTOPHER. Age 21. Entered the service Sept. 16, 1861, 3 years. Discharged at Cleveland, O., Feb. 2, 1865, on surgeon's certificate of disability.

MINIER, BENJAMIN. Age 19. Entered the service Feb. 23, 1865, 1 year. Mustered out with company Nov. 27, 1865.

MINIER, JOSEPH. Age 25. Entered the service Sept. 16, 1861, 3 years. Died June 7, 1862, at Corinth, Miss.

MYER, JOHN. Age 26. Entered the service Sept. 16, 1861, 3 years. Died Aug. 25, 1864, at Nashville, Tenn. VETERAN.

MILLER, SAMUEL M. Age —. Entered the service Sept. 22, 1864, 1 year. Drafted. Died Jan. 10, 1865, at Jeffersonville, Ind.

MILLER, ABRAHAM. Age —. Entered the service Sept. 9, 1864, 3 years. Substitute.

MANTKIN, WILLIAM. Age —. Entered the service Oct. 12, 1864, 1 year. Substitute.

MOORE, BUCYRUS. Age 30. Entered the service Sept. 16, 1861, 3 years. Discharged at Columbus, O., Aug. 8, 1862, on surgeon's certificate of disability.

METTY, MOSES. Age 19. Entered the service Feb. 24, 1864, 3 years. Mustered out at Nashville, Tenn, May 18, 1865.

NAPIER, ORRIS P. Age 20. Entered the service Feb. 24, 1864, 3 years. Mustered out with company Nov. 27, 1865.

NAGLE, JOHN. Age —. Entered the service Oct. 12, 1864, 1 year. Substitute. Mustered out at San Antonio, Tex., Oct. 16, 1865, on expiration of term of service.

PARTLOW, WILLIAM. Age 22. Entered the service Sept. 16, 1861, 3 years. Died Dec. 26, 1861, at Louisville, Ky.

PARK, ISAAC. Age 18. Entered the service Oct. 6, 1861, 3 years. Died Feb. 1, 1862, at Camp Wickliffe, Ky.

POWERS, MIFFLIN. Age 18. Entered the service Sept. 16, 1861, 3 years. Died April 23, 1862, at Cincinnati, Ohio.

PHILLIPS, WILLIAM. Age —. Entered the service Oct. 29, 1861, 3 years.

PATTERSON, WILLIAM S. Age —. Entered the service Sept. 22, 1864, 1 year. Substitute. Discharged at Camp Dennison, O., May 30, 1865, on surgeon's certificate of disability.

PETERS, MARTIN. Age —. Entered the service Oct. 5, 1864, 1 year. Substitute. Mustered out at San Antonio, Tex., Oct. 16, 1865, on expiration of term of service.

PROVONSHA, JOSEPH. Age 22. Entered the service Sept. 16, 1861, 3 years. Mustered out with company Nov. 27, 1865. VETERAN.

PETEE, EDGAR A. Age 23. Entered the service Feb. 26, 1864, 3 years. Mustered out with company Nov. 27, 1865.

ROCHESTER, SAMUEL. Age 18. Entered the service Sept. 2, 1861, 3 years. Transferred from Co. F Dec. 31, 1863. Mustered out with company Nov. 27, 1865. VETERAN.

REED, SAMUEL. Age 34. Entered the service March 9, 1865, 1 year. Mustered out with company Nov. 27, 1865.

REED, HENRY Age 19. Entered the service Sept. 16, 1861, 3 years. Killed April 7, 1862, in battle of Shiloh, Tenn.

REED, WILLIAM. Age 21. Entered the service Sept. 16, 1861, 3 years. Mustered out at Nashville, Tenn., Oct. 28, 1864, on expiration of term of service.

ROHLOFF, JOHN F. H. Age 22. Entered the service Oct. 5, 1861, 3 years. Killed Nov. 23, 1863, in battle of Orchard Knob, near Chattanooga, Tenn.

RING, DENNIS. Age —. Entered the service Oct. 29, 1864, 1 year. Substitute.

RATHBURN, WILLIAM. Age 25. Entered the service Feb. 24, 1864, 3 years. Discharged at Louisville, Ky., March 29, 1865.

ROBINSON, CHARLES. Age 21. Entered the service Sept. 16, 1861, 3 years. Died May 20, 1864, of wounds received May 17, 1864, in battle of Adairsville, Ga.

SWOPE, GEORGE. Age 22. Entered the service Feb. 8, 1865, 1 year. Mustered out with company Nov. 27, 1865.

SUCH, JOHN. Age 17. Entered the service Sept. 20, 1861, 3 years. VETERAN.

SMITH, JOHN D. Age —. Entered the service Oct. 12, 1864. 1 year. Substitute.

STORMS, GEORGE M. Age 43. Entered the service Oct. 12, 1861, 3 years. Discharged at Louisville, Ky., May 3, 1862, on surgeon's certificate of disability.

SOLO, GLODE. Age 29. Entered the service Feb. 24, 1864, 3 years. Mustered out at Louisville, Ky., June 9, 1865.

SNYDER, WILLIAM P. Age 24. Entered the service Sept. 16, 1861, 3 years. Discharged at Camp Dennison, O., Jan. 9, 1863, on surgeon's certificate of disability.

SILVERWOOD, JACKSON. Age 20. Entered the service Jan. 4, 1864, 3 years. Discharged at Columbus, O., March 30, 1864, on surgeon's certificate of disability.

SESLER, MARTIN. Age —. Entered the service Sept. 27, 1864, 1 year. Drafted. Mustered out at Nashville, Tenn., June 13, 1865, by order of War Department.

SAHL, JACOB. Age —. Entered the service Oct. 4, 1864, 1 year. Substitute. Mustered out at San Antonio, Tex., Oct. 16, 1865, on expiration of term of service.

STREETMAKER, CHARLES. Age —. Entered the service Sept. 22, 1864, 1 year. Drafted. Mustered out at Nashville, Tenn., June 13, 1865, by order of War Department.

TILLOTSON, SAMUEL H. Age 23. Entered the service Sept. 16, 1861, 3 years. Killed April 7, 1862, in battle of Shiloh, Tenn.

TROUTMAN, EBENEZER C. Age 18. Entered the service Sept. 16, 1861, 3 years. Killed Dec. 31, 1862, in battle of Stone River, Tenn.

TALCOTT, HENRY. Age 44. Entered the service Oct. 5, 1861, 3 years. Killed Nov. 23, 1863, in battle of Orchard Knob, near Chattanooga, Tenn.

TANNER, DAVID B. Age —. Entered the service Oct. 4, 1864, 1 year. Substitute. Mustered out at Nashville, Tenn., June 13, 1865, by order of War Department.

VALLAD, PETER. Age 28. Entered the service Dec. 6, 1864, 1 year. Mustered out with company Nov. 27, 1865.

VALEQUETTE, ELI. Age 38. Entered the service Feb. 10, 1865, 1 year. Mustered out with company Nov. 27, 1865.

VANGORDER, DAVID. Age —. Entered the service Oct. 4, 1864, 1 year. Substitute. Mustered out at San Antonio, Tex., Oct. 16, 1865, on expiration of term of service.

WORMWOOD, FRANCIS P. Age 19. Entered the service Sept. 16, 1861, 3 years. Mustered out with company Nov. 27, 1865. VETERAN. He reports being in ten battles, but don't name them.

WITMER, HENRY. Age 18. Entered the service Sept. 19, 1861, 3 years. Mustered out with company Nov. 27, 1865. VETERAN.

WELSH, AMBY W. Age 24. Entered the service Sept. 24, 1865, 1 year. Mustered out with company Nov. 27, 1865.

WELSH, ROBERT, A. Age 21. Entered the service Feb. 24, 1865, 1 year. Mustered out with company Nov. 27, 1865.

WARREN, GEORGE. Age 17. Entered the service Oct. 22, 1861, 3 years. Wounded May 27, 1864, in battle of Pickett's Mills, Ga. Was in all battles of the regiment up to and including Pickett's Mills, Ga. Discharged at Cleveland, O., Jan. 21, 1865, on surgeon's certificate of disability. VETERAN.

WELLS, CHARLES. Age 18. Entered the service Sept. 14, 1861, 3 years. Wounded slightly April 7, 1862, in battle of Shiloh, Tenn. Was in all battles of the regiment except Franklin and Nashville, Tenn. Mustered out at Columbus, O., June 17, 1865. VETERAN. Taken prisoner Nov. 29, 1864, at Spring Hill, Tenn. In Andersonville prison 5 months, and in other prisons.

WALKER, WILLIAM. Age 27. Entered the service Sept. 16, 1861, 3 years. Mustered out at Pulaski, Tenn., Nov. 4, 1864, on expiration of term of service.

WALKER, ETHAN A. Age —. Entered the service Sept. 24, 1864, 1 year. Drafted. Was in battles of Franklin and Nashville, Tenn. Mustered out at Nashville, Tenn., June 13, 1865, by order of War Department.

WILLIAMS, JAMES M. Age 19. Entered the service Sept. 16, 1861, 3 years. Mustered out at Pulaski, Tenn., Nov. 4, 1864, on expiration of term of service.

WILLIS, GEORGE. Age —. Entered the service Oct. 12, 1864, 1 year. Substitute. Mustered out at San Antonio, Tex., Oct. 16, 1865, on expiration of term of service.

WHITEHEAD, AMOS. Age —. Entered the service Sept. 27, 1864, 1 year. Drafted. Mustered out at Nashville, Tenn., June 13, 1865, by order of War Department.

YOUNG, JOHN A. Age 18. Entered the service Jan. 10, 1865, 1 year. Mustered out with company Nov. 27, 1865.

ZEALEY, ADAM. Age 19. Entered the service Oct. 5, 1861, 3 years. Died Feb. 20, 1862, at Belmont Furnace, Ky.

COMPANY K.

The tenth company, "K," was organized in Camp Wood, in October, 1861. James Horner, who had served in the regular army, enlisted in "A" company at Camp Wood, Aug. 26, and was soon detailed by Col. Hazen as a drillmaster, and served as such until the beginning of October. Then he was given a furlough of several days, and went to Vienna, Trumbull county, where he enlisted ten men. With these he returned to Camp Wood. This was the beginning of the tenth company. C. D. Gaylord, of Cleveland, brought several men to Horner, and engaged in recruiting for the company. The recruits were sent out, and brought other men, until about sixty had been secured. About the end of October, Wm. Goodsell came in with sixteen men, and these with a few transfers from the stronger companies, made the minimum of eighty-four for the company, and on the 29th of October it was mustered. Wm. Goodsell was Captain; James Horner, First Lieutenant; Charles D. Gaylord, Second Lieutenant.

During its term of service the company lost three men killed in action, six who died of wounds, and fifteen who died of disease. Two of the killed in action were at the battle of Pickett's Mills, where the company went in with eleven men, and all but two were killed or wounded.

CAPTAINS.

WILLIAM GOODSELL. Age 23. Entered the service Oct. 29, 1861, 3 years. Resigned Feb. 1, 1862.

JAMES HORNER. Age 34. Entered the service Oct. 29, 1861, 3 years. Promoted from 1st Lieut. Feb. 8, 1862. Resigned March 30, 1864.

WILLIAM HANSARD. Age 19. See Co. G.

EDWIN B. ATWOOD. Age 23. See Field and Staff.

1st LIEUTENANTS.

H. W. JONES. Age 23. See Co. E.

CHARLES D. GAYLORD. Age 22. Entered the service Oct. 1, 1861, 3 years. Promoted 1st Lieut. Co. H from 2d Lieut. Feb. 3, 1862. Transferred to Co. I May 24, 1862; transferred to Co. K Aug. 31, 1862. Resigned Nov. 24, 1862.

WILLIAM M. BEEBE. Age 21. See Co. I.

THOMAS H. SOMERS. Age 26. See Co. H.

SILO P. WARRINER. Age 22. See Co. G.

2d LIEUTENANTS.

HENRY COON. Age 34. See Co. G.

ELIAS A. FORD. Age 21. See Co. B.

HARLAN P. WALCOTT. Age 23. Entered the service Oct. 15, 1861, 3 years. Wounded in left arm April 7, 1862, in battle of Shiloh. Lost left leg Dec. 31, 1862, in battle of Stone River, Tenn. Promoted from 1st Sergt. Oct. 1, 1862 to Major and Paymaster May 27, 1863.

WILLIAM W. WATSON. Age 23. Killed Nov. 25, 1863, in battle of Mission Ridge, Tenn. See Co. I.

1st SERGEANTS.

JOHN ORR. Age 24. Entered the service Oct. 3, 1861, 3 years. Mustered as Corporal. Appointed 1st Sergt. ———. Died Jan. 3, 1863, of wounds received Dec. 31, 1862, in battle of Stone River, Tenn.

JOHN W. WAMPLER. Age 18. Entered the service Jan. 11, 1864, 3 years. Promoted from Private July 1, 1865. Transferred from Co. I, 93d Regt., O. V. I., June 5, 1865. Mustered out with company Nov. 27, 1865.

SERGEANTS.

JOHNSON P. BUTTON. Age 20. Entered the service Aug. 23, 1861, 3 years. Appointed from Private Feb. 28, 1865. Mustered out with company Nov. 27, 1865. VETERAN.

PETER KERON. Age 18. Entered the service Feb. 9, 1864, 3 years. Appointed from Private July 1, 1865. Transferred from Co. B, 93d O. V. I., June 6, 1865, as Peter Krun. Mustered out with company Nov. 27, 1865.

MATTHEW E. TAWPLIN. Age 18. Entered the service Jan. 4, 1864, 3 years. Appointed from Private July 1, 1865. Transferred from Co. I, 93d O. V. I., June 6, 1865. Mustered out with company Nov. 27, 1865.

STEPHEN O. EARL. Age 18. Entered the service Oct. 19, 1861, 3 years. Appointed Corporal July 9, 1864; Sergt. July 1, 1865. Mustered out with company Nov. 27, 1865. VETERAN.

LEANDER LOVELACE. Age 35. Entered the service Oct. 18, 1861, 3 years. Died April 24, 1862, at Cincinnati, O., of wounds received in action.

G. S. DWIGHT. Age —. Entered the service Nov. 27, 1861, 3 years. Appointed Sergt. from Private ———. Died July 14, 1862, in hospital at Louisville, Ky.

CHARLES GRIFFIN. Age 20. Entered the service Oct. 16, 1861, 3 years. Appointed from Private ——. Died June 18, 1864, at Marietta, Ga. VETERAN.

JAMES O'BRIAN. Age 27. Entered the service Oct. 3, 1861, 3 years. Appointed from Corporal ——.

JOHN THOMPSON. Age 28. Entered the service Oct. 8, 1861, 3 years. Wounded at Stone River and Chickamauga. Appointed from Private. Battles engaged in: Shiloh, Stone River, Chickamauga, Mission Ridge. VETERAN.

WILLIAM R. LITTLE. Age 43. Entered the service Oct. 16, 1861, 3 years. Discharged at Columbus, Ohio, May 10, 1862, on surgeon's certificate of disability.

ALBERT L. BLISS. Age 24. Entered the service Oct. 16, 1861, 3 years. Discharged at Columbus, Ohio, Dec. 29, 1862, on surgeon's certificate of disability.

FRANK H. SNOW. Age 31. Entered the service Oct. 11, 1861, 3 years. Discharged at Columbus, Ohio, Oct. 18, 1862, on surgeon's certificate of disability.

LINNEAS O. SMITH. Age 29. Entered the service Oct. 16, 1861, 3 years. Appointed from Private ——. Discharged at Louisville, Ky., Aug. 22, 1863, on surgeon's certificate of disability.

CORPORALS.

HENRY H. BELDEN. Age 23. Entered the service Feb. 2, 1864, 3 years. Appointed Corporal July 1, 1865. Transferred from Co. B, 93d Regt., O. V. I., June 6, 1865. Mustered out with company Nov. 27, 1865.

SANFORD BARNES. Age 18. Entered the service Oct. 14, 1861, 3 years. Appointed Corporal July 1, 1865. Mustered out with company Nov. 27, 1865. VETERAN. Battles engaged in: Shiloh, Chickamauga and the Atlanta campaign.

DAVID H. JOHNSON. Age 22. Entered the service Feb. 2, 1864, 3 years. Appointed Corporal July 1, 1865. Transferred from Co. E, 93d Regt., O. V. I., June 6, 1865. Mustered out with company Nov. 27, 1865.

MICHAEL RHIAN. Age 18. Entered the service Feb. 1, 1864, 3 years. Appointed Corporal July 1, 1865. Transferred from Co. C, 93d Regt., O. V. I., June 6, 1865. Mustered out with company Nov. 27, 1865.

SAMUEL VANSLYKE. Age 18. Entered the service Feb. 25, 1864, 3 years. Appointed Corporal July 1, 1865. Transferred from Co. F, 93d Regt., O. V. I., June 6, 1865. Mustered out with company Nov. 27, 1865.

EDWARD DALTON. Age 37. Entered the service Oct. 7, 1861, 3 years. Appointed Corporal ——.

JOSEPH BEARD. Age 40. Entered the service Oct. 18, 1861, 3 years. Appointed Corporal ——. Died May 8, 1862, at Cincinnati, O., of wounds received in action.

WILLIAM PRICE. Age 35. Entered the service Oct. 21, 1861, 3 years. Appointed Corporal ——. Died ——, at Chattanooga, Tenn., of wounds received in action.

BRUCE H. LAKE. Age 19. Entered the service Oct. 15, 1861, 3 years. Discharged at Columbus, O., Dec. 4, 1862, on surgeon's certificate of disability.

MYRON CLARK. Age 21. Entered the service Oct. 21, 1861, 3 years. Discharged at Columbus, Ky., Oct. 31, 1862, on surgeon's certificate of disability.

EDWARD DANFORTH. Age 30. Entered the service Sept. 25, 1861, 3 years. Discharged at Columbus, O., July 24, 1862, on surgeon's certificate of disability. Battle engaged in: Shiloh.

SAMUEL A. UDALL. Age 18. Entered the service Oct. 18, 1861, 3 years. Discharged at Camp Wickliffe, Ky., Feb. 10, 1862, on surgeon's certificate of disability.

SHELDON F. HIGLEY. Age 28. Entered the service Oct. 16, 1861, 3 years. (See Co. I, 171st Regt., O. V. I.)

JAMES MILLER. Wagoner. Age 45. Entered the service Oct. 24, 1861, 3 years. Discharged at Nashville, Tenn., Dec. 19, 1862, on surgeon's certificate of disability.

PRIVATES.

ASHALD, JOHN. Age 29. Entered the service Oct. 21, 1861, 3 years. Mustered out with company Nov. 27, 1865. VETERAN.

ASHALD, ABEL. Age 44. Entered the service Oct. 24, 1861, 3 years. Discharged Jan. 21, 1862, on surgeon's certificate of disability.

ALCOE, HAMILTON. Age —. Entered the service Jan. 25, 1862, 3 years.

AKEL, JOHN. Age 26. Entered the service Jan. 19, 1864, 3 years. Transferred from Co. K, 93d Regt., O. V. I., June 6, 1865.

ARNOLD, HENRY. Age 19. Entered the service Oct. 14, 1861, 3 years. Wounded Sept. 19, 1863, in battle of Chickamauga, Ga. Transferred to Co. H, 19th Regt., Veteran Reserve Corps, March 23, 1864.

APLAIN, JAMES. Age 21. Entered the service Oct. 25, 1861, 3 years. Mustered out on expiration of term of service, Nov. 2, 1864.

BOUGUE, ALONZO.   Age 39.   Entered the service Oct. 17, 1861, 3
years. In battles of Shiloh, Stone River, Chickamauga, Mission
Ridge, Pickett's Mills, and all others of the regiment. Mustered
out with company Nov. 27 1865. VETERAN.

BABCOCK, WILLIAM.   Age 37.   Entered the service Oct. 8, 1861, 3
years. Wounded in battle of Chickamauga, Ga. Mustered out with
company Nov. 27, 1865. VETERAN. Battles engaged in: Shiloh,
Stone River, Chickamauga, Mission Ridge.

BRUMSON, WILLIAM A.   Age 18.   Entered the service Jan. 5, 1865, 3
years. Transferred from Co. E, 93d Regt., O. V. I., June 6, 1865.
Mustered out with company Nov. 27, 1865. See Roll of Honor.

BRITTON, LEWIS.   Age 18.   Entered the service Dec. 22, 1863, 3 years
Transferred from Co. I, 93d Regt., O. V. I., June 6, 1865. Absent
in hospital. No further record found.

BRASHER, GEORGE.   Age 22.   Entered the service Jan. 22, 1864, 3
years. Mustered out with company Nov. 27, 1865.

BOYLE, CORNELIUS.   Age 21.   Entered the service Oct. 21, 1861, 3
years.

BRENNER, JESSE.   Age 18.   Entered the service Feb. 18, 1865, 1 year.
Transferred from Co. B, 93d Regt., O. V. I., June 6, 1865.

BRENNER, JACOB J.   Age 21.   Entered the service Feb. 18, 1865, 1 year.
Transferred from Co. B, 93d Regt., O. V. I., June 6, 1865. Discharged
March 3, 1867, to date June 19, 1865.

BRICE, JOHN M.   Age 35.   Entered the service Feb. 15, 1865, 1 year.
Transferred from Co. B, 93d Regt., O. V. I., June 6, 1865. Discharged
March 3, 1867, to date June 19, 1865.

BATTLES, NEWTON.   Age 33.   Entered the service Aug. 24, 1861, 3
years. Died Dec. 20, 1861, at Camp Wickliffe, Ky.

BURR, HARVEY.   Age 18.   Entered the service Aug. 20, 1861, 3 years.
Died Oct. 9, 1862, in hospital at Bowling Green, Ky.

BARNES, FRANK E.   Age —.   Entered the service Feb. 15, 1864, 3 years.
Discharged at Columbus, Ohio, July 3, 1865, on surgeon's certificate
of disability.

BARNES, DANFORTH.   Age 18.   Entered the service Oct. 14, 1861, 3
years. Mustered out with company Nov. 27, 1865. This man must be
a VETERAN from date of enlistment and muster out. (Committee.)

BRADLEY, RAWSON A.   Age 18.   Entered the service Oct. 14, 1861, 3
years. VETERAN. Discharged at St. Louis, Mo., March 9, 1865, on
surgeon's certificate of disability.

BROWN, LAFAYETTE. Age 18. Entered the service Oct. 4, 1861, 3 years. Discharged at Camp Wickliffe, Ky., Jan. 21, 1862, on surgeon's certificate of disability.

BANCROFT, THEODORE E. Age 17. Entered the service Aug. 17, 1861, 3 years. Mustered out on expiration of term of service, Nov. 2, 1864.

BAIN, ALONZO. Age 17. Entered the service Oct. 14, 1861, 3 years. Mustered out on expiration of term of service, Jan. 27, 1865.

CANFER, PETER. Age 18. Entered the service Jan. 20, 1865, 1 year. Transferred from Co. E, 93d Regt., O. V. I., June 6, 1865, as Peter Coafer. Mustered out with company Nov. 27, 1865.

COOK, WILLIAM. Age 18. Entered the service Jan. 11, 1864, 3 years. Transferred from Co. I, 93d Regt., O. V. I., June 6, 1865. Mustered out with company Nov. 27, 1865.

COBLENTZ, DANIEL. Age 18. Entered the service Jan. 7, 1865, 1 year. Transferred from Co. B, 93d Regt., O. V. I., June 6, 1865.

COWDRY, EDWARD M. Age 19. Entered the service Oct. 15, 1861, 3 years. Discharged at Columbus, Ohio, Sept. 13, 1862, for wounds received in action.

DITTMAN, JACOB. Age 42. Entered the service Jan. 6, 1865, 1 year. Transferred from Co. G, 93d Regt., O. V. I., June 6, 1865. Mustered out with company Nov. 27, 1865.

DEAN, EDWARD. Age 24. Entered the service Dec. 16, 1864, 3 years. Transferred from Co. H, 93d Regt., O. V. I., June 6, 1865.

DECKER, JOHN. Age 20. Entered the service Aug. 20, 1861, 3 years. Killed May 27, 1864, in battle of Pickett's Mills, Ga. VETERAN.

DOLAN, JOHN. Age 23. Entered the service Nov. 17, 1863, 3 years. Transferred from Co. I, 93d Regt., O. V. I., June 6, 1865.

DONALDSON, JOHN. Age 36. Entered the service Oct. 10, 1861, 3 years. Mustered out on expiration of term of service, Nov. 2, 1864.

DICKERSON, WILLIAM. Age 40. Entered the service Aug. 23, 1861, 3 years.

DICKERSON, WALTER. Age 17. Entered the service Aug. 22, 1861, 3 years. Discharged at Nashville, Tenn., June 19, 1862, on surgeon's certificate of disability.

DUNBAR, GEORGE W. Age 25. Entered the service Oct. 16, 1861, 3 years. Mustered out on expiration of term of service, Nov. 15, 1864.

DANFORTH, CHARLES. Age —. Transferred from Co. H. Transferred to Co. I, 5th Regt., Veteran Reserve Corps, Dec. 15, 1863.

ELSNER, JOHN. Age 18. Entered the service Feb. 11, 1864, 3 years. Transferred from Co. B, 93d Regt., O. V. I., June 6, 1865. Mustered out with company Nov. 27, 1865.

EARL, BEEMAN W. Age 31. Entered the service Oct. 26, 1861, 3 years. Wounded in battle of Shiloh, Tenn. Discharged at Columbus, O., Dec. 3, 1862, on surgeon's certificate of disability.

FULTZ, LUTHER M. Age 18. Entered the service Feb. 18, 1864, 3 years. Transferred from Co. G, 93d Regt., O. V. I., June 6, 1865. Mustered out with company Nov. 27, 1865.

FOX, BENJAMIN. Age 20. Entered the service Jan. 22, 1864, 3 years. Transferred from Co. D, 93d Regt., O. V. I., June 6, 1865. Mustered out with company Nov. 27, 1865.

FOX, GEORGE. Age 22. Entered the service Jan. 22, 1864, 3 years. Transferred from Co. D, 93d Regt., O. V. I., June 6, 1865. Absent in hospital at New Orleans July 7, 1865. Died at Jefferson Barracks, Mo., Oct. 2, 1865.

FOOT, LEVI. Age 19. Entered the service Aug. 23, 1861, 3 years. Died Jan. 3, 1862, in hospital at Louisville, Ky.

GOOD, JOHN. Age 18. Entered the service March 8, 1864, 3 years. Transferred from Co. B, 93d Regt., O. V. I., June 6, 1865. Mustered out with company Nov. 27, 1865.

GLEASON, MATTHEW. Age 31. Entered the service Jan. 5, 1864, 3 years. Transferred from Co. I, 93d Regt., O. V. I., June 6, 1865. Mustered out with company Nov. 27, 1865.

GOLDNER, WILLIAM. Age 28. Entered the service Aug. 24, 1861, 3 years. Discharged at Camp Wickliffe, Ky., Jan. 21, 1862, on surgeon's certificate of disability.

HURD, EMI W. Age 17. Entered the service Oct. 10, 1861, 3 years. Mustered out with company Nov. 27, 1865. VETERAN.

HOFFMAN, WILLIAM C. Age 19. Entered the service Feb. 18, 1864, 3 years. Transferred from Co. K, 93d Regt., O. V. I., June 6, 1865. Mustered out with company Nov. 27, 1865.

HELLRIGLE, HENRY H. Age 34. Entered the service Feb. 29, 1864, 3 years. Transferred from Co. D, 93d Regt., O. V. I., June 6, 1865. Mustered out with company Nov. 27, 1865.

HENRY, DARWIN. Age 44. Entered the service Oct. 6, 1861, 3 years. Discharged at Murfreesboro, Tenn., Aug. 8, 1862, on surgeon's certificate of disability.

HOSKINS, WILLIAM H. Age 20. Entered the service Oct. 10, 1861, 3 years. Killed May 27, 1864, in battle of Pickett's Mills, Ga.

HEWITT, HENRY. Age 18. Entered the service Feb. 12, 1864, 3 years. Transferred from Co. E, 93d Regt., O. V. I., June 6, 1865, as Henry Huiet. Discharged by order of War Department, June 28, 1865.

HUTCHIN, JOHN L. Age 22. Entered the service Aug. 10, 1861, 3 years. Discharged at Camp Wickliffe, Ky., Jan. 20, 1862, on surgeon's certificate of disability.

HITCHCOCK, CHARLES. Age 18. Entered the service Aug. 15, 1861, 3 years. Discharged at Camp Wickliffe, Ky., March 31, 1862, on surgeon's certificate of disability.

JAMES, JOSEPH C. Age 19. Entered the service Jan. 5, 1864, 3 years. Transferred from Co. I, 93d Regt., O. V. I., June 6, 1865, while absent sick. Mustered out at Camp Dennison, O., May 16, 1865, as of Co. I, 93d Regt., O. V. I.

KINELLE, JOHN A. Age 28. Entered the service Aug. 11, 1862, 3 years. Transferred from Co. G, 93d Regt., O. V. I., June 6, 1865. Mustered out with company Nov. 27, 1865.

KICK, CHRISTOPHER. Age 18. Entered the service Feb. 29, 1864, 3 years. Transferred from Co. D, 93d Regt., O. V. I., June 6, 1865. Mustered out with company Nov. 27, 1865.

KIRBY, TIMOTHY. Age 18. Entered the service Feb. 1, 1864, 3 years. Transferred from Co. C, 93d Regt., O. V. I., June 6, 1865. Mustered out with company Nov. 27, 1865.

KELLEY, JOHN T. Age 36. Entered the service Oct. 11, 1861, 3 years. Mustered out at Pulaski, Tenn., Nov. 2, 1864, on expiration of term of service.

LAPE, JOHN. Age 38. Entered the service Feb. 24, 1864, 3 years. Transferred from Co. E, 93d Regt., O. V. I., June 6, 1865. Mustered out with company Nov. 27, 1865.

LEMON, FRANKLIN. Age 19. Entered the service Aug. 2, 1862, 3 years. Transferred from Co. B, 93d Regt., O. V. I., June 6, 1865. Mustered out at Columbus, O., Aug. 10, 1865, on expiration of term of service.

McREYNOLDS, CHARLES. Age 18. Entered the service March 17, 1864, 3 years. Transferred from Co. B, 93d Regt., O. V. I., June 6, 1865. Mustered out with company Nov. 27, 1865.

McCROSSEN, JOHN. Age 24. Entered the service Jan. 6, 1865, 1 year. Transferred from Co. F, 93d Regt., O. V. I., June 6, 1865. Mustered out by order of War Department, June 19, 1865.

McWILLIAMS, EDWARD. Age 22. Entered the service Dec. 30, 1863, 3 years. Transferred from Co. I, 93d Regt., O. V. I., June 6, 1865. Wounded May 14, 1864. Absent in hospital at Indianapolis, Ind. No further record found.

McEACHARN, WILLIAM. Age 39. Entered the service Oct. 14, 1861, 3 years. Wounded Dec. 31, 1862, in battle of Stone River. Transferred to 125th Co., 2d Battalion, Veteran Reserve Corps, Dec. 18, 1863.

McKEAN, JOHN. Age 44. Entered the service Dec. 30, 1863, 3 years. Transferred from Co. C, 93d Regt., O. V. I., June 6, 1865. Mustered out at Camp Dennison, O., May 16, 1865, by order of War Department.

MOYER, PERRY. Age 20. Entered the service Feb. 25, 1864, 3 years. Transferred from Co. E, 93d Regt., O. V. I., June 6, 1865. Wounded May 27, 1864, in battle of Pickett's Mills, Ga. Absent. No further record found.

MITCHELL, JOHN. Age 23. Entered the service Dec. 24, 1863, 3 years. Transferred from Co. G, 93d Regt., O. V. I., June 6, 1865. Absent, sick in hospital. Mustered out at Camp Chase, O., June 28, 1865, as of Co. G, 93d Regt., O. V. I.

MERCER, ROBERT M. Age 21. Entered the service Jan. 2, 1864, 3 years. Transferred from Co. I, 93d Regt., O. V. I., June 6, 1865, while absent sick. Mustered out at Camp Chase, O., June 8, 1865, as of Co. I, 93d Regt., O. V. I.

MEREDITH, CONRAD. Age 18. Entered the service March 7, 1864, 3 years. Transferred from Co. B, 93d Regt., O. V. I., June 6, 1865. Mustered out with company Nov. 27, 1865.

MIZENER, ROBERT. Age 22. Entered the service Aug. 22, 1861, 3 years. Died Feb. 13, 1862, in hospital at Louisville, Ky.

MILLER, CHARLES. Age 20. Entered the service Oct. 16, 1861, 3 years. Died Feb. 9, 1863, in hospital at Readyville, Tenn.

MILLER, MILTON. Age 17. Entered the service Oct. 16, 1861, 3 years.

MANNY, NAPOLEON B. Age 18. Entered the service Oct. 17, 1861, 3 years. Mustered in as Napoleon Bonapart. Mustered out with company Nov. 27, 1865.

O'CONNER, PATRICK. Age 18. Entered the service Jan. 12, 1864, 3 years. Transferred from Co. D, 93d Regt., O. V. I., June 6, 1865. Mustered out with company Nov. 27, 1865.

PENDLETON, JOHN. Age 18. Entered the service Sept. 1, 1861, 3 years. Discharged at Columbus, O., Sept. 2, 1862, on surgeon's certificate of disability.

POTTER, SAMUEL. Age 33. Entered the service Aug. 15, 1861, 3 years. Mustered out at expiration of term of service, Nov. 2, 1864.

QUINN, ALFRED. Age 18. Entered the service Sept. 14, 1861, 3 years. Mustered out with company Nov. 27, 1865. VETERAN.

RINEL, JOSEPH. Age 26. Entered the service Oct. 23, 1863, 3 years. Transferred from Co. G, 93d Regt., O. V. I., June 6, 1865. Mustered out with company Nov. 27, 1865.

QUINN, ARTHUR. Age 43. Entered the service Aug. 27, 1861, 3 years. Discharged at Camp Wickliffe, Ky., Jan. 18, 1862, on surgeon's certificate of disability.

QUILLING, ALBERT. Age 18. Entered the service July 31, 1862, 3 years. Transferred from Co. H, 93d Regt., O. V. I., June 6, 1865.

REEL, JAMES B. Age 23. Entered the service Feb. 18, 1865, 1 year. Transferred from Co. B, 93d Regt., O. V. I., June 6, 1865.

RUSHER, JACOB. Age 27. Entered the service Oct. 21, 1861, 3 years. Killed April 7, 1862, in battle of Shiloh, Tenn.

RODECK, WILLIAM P. Age 18. Entered the service Oct. 9, 1861, 3 years. Prisoner of war. Mustered out on expiration of term of service, March 20, 1865.

RAND, BENJAMIN. Age 41. Entered the service Sept. 14, 1861, 3 years. Discharged at Murfreesboro, Tenn., Aug. 14, 1862, on surgeon's certificate of disability.

REEVES, WILLIAM. Age 27. Entered the service Oct. 17, 1861, 3 years. Discharged at Camp Wickliffe, Ky., Jan. 21, 1862, on surgeon's certificate of disability.

REGAN, DANIEL. Age 25. Entered the service Oct. 7, 1861, 3 years. Transferred to Veteran Reserve Corps, Sept. 26, 1863.

STOVER, DAVID A. Age 35. Entered the service March 31, 1864, 3 years. Transferred from Co. D, 93d Regt., O. V. I., June 6, 1865. Mustered out with company Nov. 27, 1865.

SMITH, JEFFERSON. Age 19. Entered the service Aug. 20, 1861, 3 years. Mustered out with company Nov. 27, 1865. VETERAN.

SMITH, JAMES W. C. Age 33. Entered the service Dec. 29, 1863, 3 years. Transferred from Co. C, 93d Regt., O. V. I., June 6, 1865.

SMITH, WILLIAM K. Age —. Entered the service Feb. 21, 1864, 3 years. Died May 3, 1865, in hospital at Nashville, Tenn.

SCHLOSSER, SAMUEL. Age 20. Entered the service Dec. 24, 1863, 3 years. Transferred from Co. I, 93d Regt., O. V. I., June 6, 1865; to 80th Co., 2d Battalion, Veteran Reserve Corps, May 4, 1865.

SHAFFER, JOHN B. Age 44. Entered the service Dec. 30, 1863, 3 years. Transferred from Co. C, 93d Regt., O. V. I., June 6, 1865. Discharged Feb. 22, 1868, to date June 19, 1865.

SHORT, SIMON. Age 17. Entered the service Oct. 24, 1861, 3 years.

SCHOCK, CONRAD. Age 24. Entered the service Oct. 16, 1861, 3 years.

SHERMAN, GILBERT. Age 19. Entered the service Aug. 27, 1861, 3 years. Died Feb. 27, 1862, in hospital at Belmont, Ky.

STEWART, JOHN. Age 39. Entered the service Oct. 16, 1861, 3 years. Died Oct. 14, 1863, in hospital at Chattanooga, Tenn.

SYNOD, MARCUS. Age 47. Entered the service Oct. 15, 1861, 3 years. Mustered out on expiration of term of service, Jan. 10, 1865.

SEXTON, DENNIS. Age 42. Entered the service Aug. 27, 1861, 3 years. Died April 29, 1802, at Mound City, Ill., of wounds received April 7, 1862, in battle of Shiloh, Tenn

TINGLE, WILLIAM E. Age 19. Entered the service Feb. 18, 1864, 3 years. Transferred from Co. G, 93d Regt., O. V. I., June 6, 1865, while absent in hospital. Mustered out at Cincinnati, O., May 24, 1865; Co. G, 93d Regt., O. V. I.

TAFT, SETH. Age 21. Entered the service Oct. 15, 1861, 3 years. Discharged at Louisville, Ky., Jan. 23, 1862, on surgeon's certificate of disability.

TAFT, REUBEN. Age 18. Entered the service Oct. 15, 1861, 3 years. Discharged at Louisville, Ky., Jan. 23, 1862, on surgeon's certificate of disability.

TOMPKINS, JAMES. Age 46. Entered the service Oct. 15, 1861, 3 years. Mustered out Feb. 26, 1863, at Gallatin, Tenn., on expiration of term of service.

TRYAN, JAMES. Age 28. Entered the service Aug. 22, 1861, 3 years. Discharged at Louisville, Ky., Jan. 1, 1863, on surgeon's certificate of disability.

TAYLOR, ZACHARIAH. Age —. Transferred from Co. H. No further record found.

TAYLOR, SAXTON. Age 19. Entered the service Oct. 14, 1861, 3 years. Wounded April 7, 1862, in battle of Shiloh, Tenn. Re-enlisted in Co. F, 81st Regt., New York Volunteers. Discharged from 41st Regt., O. V. I., May 13, 1862, by order of War Department.

THAYER, ASAHEL. Age 40. Entered the service Sept. 14, 1861, 3 years. Died Oct. 13, 1862, in hospital at Bowling Green, Ky.

VANDIVER, HENRY F. Age 19. Entered the service Oct. 29, 1863, 3 years. Transferred from Co. E, 93d Regt., O. V. I., June 6, 1865, as Henry F. Vanerveer. Mustered out with company Nov. 27 1865.

WITTERS, WILLIAM H. Age 19. Entered the service Aug. 9, 1862, 3 years. Transferred from Co. K, 93d Regt., O. V. I., June 6, 1865. Mustered out with company Nov. 27, 1865.

WILLIAMS, JOHN. Age 24. Entered the service Jan. 4, 1865, 3 years. ɪransterred from Co. D, 93d Regt., O. V. I., June 6, 1865. Mustered out with company Nov. 27, 1865.

WYRICK, SAMUEL. Age 39. Entered the service Feb. 25, 1864, 3 years. Transferred from Co. G, 93d Regt., O. V. I., June 6, 1865. Mustered out with company Nov. 27, 1865.

WOLFE, SAMUEL. Age 38. Entered the service Dec. 25, 1863, 3 years. Transferred from Co. I, 93d Regt., O. V. I., June 6, 1865. Mustered out with company Nov. 27, 1865.

WALLACE, WILLIAM B. Age 22. Entered the service Aug 6, 1862, 3 years. Transferred from Co. C, 93d Regt., O. V. I., June 6, 1865, as William R. Wallace. Mustered out with company Nov. 27, 1865.

WHITNEY, CHARLES. Age 45. Entered the service Oct. 15, 1861, 3 years.

WHITE, ELIPHAZ W. Age 23. Entered the service Oct. 18, 1861, 3 years. Died Dec. 25, 1861, at Camp Wickliffe, Ky.

WHITE, MATTHEW. Age 35. Entered the service Oct. 12, 1861, 3 years. Discharged at Nashville, Tenn., March 16, 1862, on surgeon's certificate of disability.

WALKER, JOSEPH. Age 31. Entered the service Aug. 21, 1861, 3 years.

WAGONER, NICHOLAS. Age 42. Entered the service Oct. 8, 1861, 3 years. Died July 16, 1862, at Athens, Ala.

WAGNER, HENRY. Age 18. Entered the service Oct. 9, 1861. Transferred to 25th Co., 2d Battalion, Veteran Reserve Corps, Nov. —, 1863. Discharged on expiration of term of service at Indianapolis, Ind., Nov. 2, 1864. Re-enlisted Feb. 20, 1865, Co. I, 193d Regt., O. V. I., 1 year. Mustered out at Winchester, Va., Aug. 4, 1865, by order of War Department.

WHEELOCK, EMERY L. Age 23. Entered the service Oct. 19, 1861, 3 years. Transferred to 87th Co., 2d Battalion, Veteran Reserve Corps, Nov. 3, 1863.

WINTERS, ANDREW. Age 17. Entered the service Aug. 22, 1861, 3 years. Transferred to 67th Co., 2d Battalion, Veteran Reserve Corps, Oct. 2, 1863.

WHITTLESEY, FREDERICK. Age 21. Entered the service Aug. 15, 1862, 3 years. Transferred from Co. H, ——. Discharged July 5, 1864, to accept promotion.

YOUNG, JACOB. Age 21. Entered the service April 11, 1864, 3 years. Transferred from Co. C, 93d Regt., O. V. I., June 6, 1865. Mustered out with company Nov. 27, 1865.

ZIMMERMAN, JOHN. Age 22. Entered the service Oct. 19, 1861, 3 years. Discharged at Camp Wickliffe, Ky., June 30, 1862, on surgeon's certificate of disability.

TOM ——. Age 33. Entered the service May 27, 1863, 3 years. Transferred from Co. B, 93d Regt., O. V. I., June 6, 1865. Colored cook. Mustered out with company Nov. 27, 1865.

RECAPITULATION.

Field and Staff, number enrolled,			42	Transferred,	26
Company A,	"	"	151	"	3
" B,	"	"	145	"	4
" C,	"	"	173	"	5
" D,	"	"	142	"	3
" E,	"	"	113	"	6
" F,	"	"	172	"	3
" G,	"	"	157	"	7
" H,	"	"	115	"	10
" I,	"	"	178	"	6
" K,	"	"	166	"	9

Total, ... 1554   82

Less Transfers, . . 82

Total number in Regiment, . 1472

Total number in Regiment, ... 1472
Less drafted, 1 year men, ... 73
" " 9 months men, ... 30
" Substitutes and other one year men, . . 138
" " that were assigned but never
reported, ... 9

Tota!, ... 250
Less Transfers from 93d Ohio, 1865, . . . 59
                                        —— 309

Total men in Regiment who did about all the
duty and fighting, ... 1163

Of the above 309, one was killed in battle, two died of wounds and seven died of disease. Total, 10. Which is only 3 per cent.; so that of the 1163 three years men, as shown above, the total deaths were 312, which is nearly 27 out of every 100.

ROLL OF HONOR.

COMPANY A.

KILLED IN ACTION.

AMES, HORACE B. Corp. Killed April 7, 1862, in battle of Shiloh. Interred in Shiloh cemetery.

BARNES, GEORGE. Private. Killed May 27, 1864, in battle of Pickett's Mills, Ga. Interred in National cemetery, Chattanooga.

BENNETT, SAMUEL. Private. Killed April 7, 1862, in battle of Shiloh, Tenn. Interred in National cemetery, Shiloh, Tenn.

BRADEN, WALLACE W. Corp. Killed Sept. 19, 1863, in battle of Chickamauga, Ga. Interred in National cemetery, Chattanooga.

HART, CALVIN C. 1st Lieut. Killed Dec. 31, 1862, in battle of Stone River. Interred at Hartford, Trumbull county, O.

McFARLAND, ALBERT. Private. Killed Dec. 31, 1862, in battle of Stone River, Tenn. Interred in Stone River cemetery, section 10, grave 28.

RITCHIE, MILO. Private. Killed Nov. 25, 1863, in battle of Mission Ridge, Tenn. Interred in National cemetery, section C, grave 1118, Chattanooga.

SADDLER, THOMAS. Private. Killed Oct. 27, 1863, in battle of Brown's Ferry, Tenn. Interred in National cemetery, section C, grave 1115, Chattanooga.

SMITH, CHARLES R. Corp. Killed May 27, 1864, in battle of Pickett's Mills, Ga. Interred in National cemetery, Chattanooga, Tenn.

WAGONER, JOHN. Private. Killed Dec. 31, 1862, in battle of Stone River, Tenn. Interred in Stone River cemetery, Hazen's Brigade lot.

WARD, JOHN. Private. Killed April 7, 1862, in battle of Shiloh, Tenn. Interred in National cemetery, Shiloh, Tenn.

DIED OF WOUNDS.

BACON, CLINTON. Private. Died Sept. 26, 1863, of wounds received Sept. 19, 1863, in battle of Chickamauga, Ga. Interred in National cemetery, Nashville, Tenn., section B, grave 440.

BENNETT, AVERY. Private. Died Jan. 17, 1863, of wounds received Dec. 31, 1862, in battle of Stone River, Tenn. Interred in National cemetery, Nashville, Tenn.

BENNETT, CHARLES H. Sergt. Died Dec. 9, 1863, in hospital at Nashville, Tenn., of wounds received Oct. 27, 1863, in battle of Brown's Ferry, Tenn. Interred in National cemetery, Nashville, Tenn.

HOLCOMB, JUDSON, B. Private. Died Feb. 3, 1864, of wounds received Sept. 19, 1863, in battle of Chickamauga, Ga. Interred in National cemetery at Nashville, Tenn.

HOLCOMB, MARQUIS D. Private. Died June 9, 1864, of wounds received May 27, 1864, in battle of Pickett's Mills, Ga. Interred in National cemetery at Chattanooga, Tenn., section E, grave 11351.

HEWETT, ASBURY. Private. Wounded and captured in battle of Pickett's Mills, Ga., May 27, 1864. Died in Rebel prison. No further account of him.

PHILLIPS, IRA N. Private. Died Dec. 11, 1864, of wounds received in action Dec. 7, 1864, in front of Nashville, Tenn. Interred in National cemetery at Nashville, Tenn.

RALPH, RANSOM. Private. Died Sept. 26, 1863, of wounds received Sept. 19, 1863, in battle of Chickamauga, Ga. Interred in National cemetery, section A, grave 308.

RICHMOND, WILFORD J. Private. Died April 13, 1862, at Mound City, Ill., of wounds received April 7, 1862, in battle of Shiloh, Tenn. Interred in National cemetery, Mound City, Ill., section B, grave 1427.

SHIREY, WILLIAM. Private. Died Sept. 25, 1863, of wounds received Sept. 19, 1863, in battle of Chickamauga, Ga. Interred in National cemetery at Chattanooga, Tenn., section C, grave 1236.

DIED OF DISEASE.

BEECH, CURTLIN. Private. Died Nov. 17, 1862, at Silver Springs, Tenn., of disease. Interred in Stone River cemetery, Murfreesboro, Tenn.

BROCKWAY, DANIEL W. Private. Died March 27, 1864, of disease. Interred at Cleveland, O.

BROWN, HENRY H. Corp. Died Sept. 13, 1864, in Rebel prison at Andersonville, Ga. Interred in National cemetery at Andersonville, Ga., grave 8676.

CURTIS, FRANK. Private. Died Jan. 22, 1862, of disease. Interred in Cave Hill cemetery, Louisville, Ky., section A, range 7, grave 170.

HOLCOMB, VIRGIL. Private. Died June 25, 1863, at Readyville, Tenn., of disease. Interred in Stone River cemetery, Murfreesboro, Tenn.

MURRAY, LOFTUS L. Private. Died Jan. 26, 1863, of disease. Interred in National cemetery, Nashville, Tenn., section B, grave 339.

NORTON, GEORGE. Private. Died March 11, 1862, of disease. Interred in Cave Hill cemetery, Louisville, Ky.

PARKER, ALBERT L. Private. Died Sept. 17, 1865, at Victoria, Tex., of disease. Interred in National cemetery, Brownsville, Tex., grave 950.

PELTON, JAMES. Private. Died Feb. 16, 1862, of disease. Interred in Cave Hill cemetery, Louisville, Ky., section A, range 8, grave 209.

RATLIFF, WILLIAM Private. Died Dec. 24, 1861, of disease, at Camp Wickliffe, Ky. Interred at London, Ky.

SETTLE, JOHN. Private. Died March 17, 1863, of disease, at Parole Camp, near Annapolis, Md. Interred in section 11, grave 1826.

SPENCER, OWEN. Private. Died Aug. 17, 1863, of disease, at Readyville, Tenn. Interred in Stone River cemetery, Murfreesboro, Tenn.

SNACKHAMER, ISAAC. Private. Died May 31, 1865, of disease. Interred at New Albany, Ind., section B, grave 702.

WADSWORTH, JAMES. Private. Died Nov. 17, 1862, of disease. Interred at Nashville, Tenn.

COMPANY B.

KILLED IN ACTION.

BARTLETT, GEORGE S. Private. Killed April 7, 1862, in battle of Shiloh, Tenn. Interred in National cemetery, at Shiloh, Tenn.

BUCK, WILLIAM H. Private. Killed Dec. 31, 1862, in battle of Stone River, Tenn. Interred in Stone River cemetery, Hazen's Brigade lot, Murfreesboro, Tenn.

DINES, JAMES A. Private. Killed July 5, 1864, in action at Chattahoochee River, Ga. Interred in National cemetery, Marietta, Ga., section I, grave 9646.

GILBERT, HARRISON W. Private. Killed Sept. 19, 1863, in battle of Chickamauga, Ga. Interred in National cemetery, Chattanooga, Tenn.

HANSARD, JOHN. Sergt. Killed April 7, 1862, in battle of Shiloh, Tenn. Interred in National cemetery, at Shiloh, Tenn.

ROSE, NELSON E. Private. Killed Sept. 19, 1863, in battle of Chickamauga, Ga. Interred in National cemetery, Chattanooga, Tenn.

SPRINGER, CHARLES H. Private. Killed May 27, 1864, in battle of Pickett's Mills, Ga. Interred in National cemetery, Marietta, Ga., section G, grave 7364.

TALCOTT, CHANCY H. 2d Lieut. Killed April 7, 1862, in battle of Shiloh, Tenn. Interred in National cemetery, at Shiloh, Tenn.

TURRELL, GEORGE E. 1st Sergt. Killed April 7, 1862, in battle of Shiloh, Tenn. Interred in National cemetery, at Shiloh, Tenn.

WILLIAMS, CHARLES H. 1st Sergt. Killed Nov. 25, 1863, in battle of Mission Ridge, Tenn. Interred in National cemetery at Chattanooga, Tenn.

DIED OF WOUNDS.

BELDEN, HARVEY. Corp. Died Nov. 30, 1863, of wounds received in battle of Mission Ridge, Tenn., Nov. 25, 1863. Interred in National cemetery, section D, grave 12036, Chattanooga, Tenn.

CARLTON, EDWARD A. Corp. Died Dec. 25, 1863, of wounds received in battle of Chickamauga, Ga., Sept. 19, 1863. Interred in National cemetery, section H, grave 10794, Chattanooga, Tenn.

MOORE, JOSEPH. Sergt. Died Nov. 25, 1863, of wounds received in battle of Mission Ridge, Tenn. Interred in National cemetery, Chattanooga, Tenn.

MUNN, WILLIAM W. Capt. Died Dec. 2, 1863, at Chattanooga, Tenn., of wounds received Nov. 25, 1863, in battle of Mission Ridge. Interred at Chattanooga, Tenn.

PATCHIN, LESTER T. 1st Lieut. Died Jan. 18, 1863, at Nashville, Tenn., of wounds received Dec. 31, 1862, in battle of Stone River, Tenn. Interred at Nashville, Tenn.

WILDER, GEORGE. Private. Died Feb. 19, 1863, at Murfreesboro, Tenn., of wounds received in battle of Stone River, Tenn. Interred in Stone River cemetery.

DIED OF DISEASE.

ANDREWS, HOMER. Private. Died Jan. 23, 1862, of disease.

BALLARD, LUTHER M. Private. Died Nov. 30, 1863, of disease, at Chattanooga, Tenn. Interred in National cemetery, section D, grave 12048.

BENTON, ORLANDO. Private. Died May 7, 1862, in hospital of 4th Division, near Shiloh, Tenn. Interred in National cemetery, Shiloh, Tenn.

BOSLEY, WILLIAM H. Private. Died June 16, 1862, of disease. Interred at Shiloh, Tenn.

BURNETT, ROBERT P. Private. Died May 7, 1862, of disease, in hospital near Shiloh, Tenn. Interred in National cemetery, Shiloh, Tenn., section D, grave 198.

CARLOSS, DANIEL. Corp. Died Sept. 15, 1862, of disease, at Bowling Green, Ky. Interred in National cemetery, Nashville, Tenn., in section V, grave 185.

GRAY, ERASTUS. Private. Died May 17, 1863, of disease, in hospital at Nashville, Tenn. Interred in National cemetery, in section E, grave 1165.

HARRINGTON, SUMAN. Private. Died Nov. 27, 1862, of disease, at Nashville, Tenn. Interred in National cemetery.

MORTON, DAVID C. Private. Died Dec. 30, 1861, of disease, at Louisville, Ky. Interred in Cave Hill cemetery. No record.

PEBLES, LYMAN W. Private. Died March 24, 1862, of disease, at Louisville, Ky. Interred in Cave Hill cemetery, section D, division 7, grave 3858.

ROOT, RILEY. Private. Died July 17, 1863, of disease, at Manchester, Tenn. Interred in Stone River cemetery, section J, grave 288.

SAVAGE, EDWARD. Private. Died Jan. 26, 1862, of disease, at Louisville, Ky. Interred in Cave Hill cemetery, section A, grave 279.

SEELY, ANDREW J. Private. Died June 12, 1864, of disease, near Atlanta, Ga. Interred in National cemetery, Marietta, Ga.

SLITAR, ENOCH. Private. Died March 20, 1862, of disease, at Louisville, Ky. Interred in Cave Hill cemetery.

SMITH, JAY C. Private. Died Jan. 29, 1862, of disease, at Louisville, Ky. Interred in Cave Hill cemetery.

TAYLOR, MARTIN. Private. Died May 2, 1863, of disease.

WHITE, JAMES. Private. Died Feb. 14, 1865, of disease, at Louisville, Ky. Interred in Cave Hill cemetery, section C, grave 3138.

WHITE, WILLIAM. Private. Died Dec. 20, 1862, of disease.

WILSON, BUELL. Private. Died April 9, 1862, of disease, at Louisville, Ky. Interred in Cave Hill cemetery.

DROWNED.

PELTON, HENRY C. Private. Drowned March 26, 1862, in the Ohio river.

COMPANY C.

KILLED IN ACTION.

ANDERSON, WILLIAM S. Corp. Killed Nov. 25, 1863, in battle of Mission Ridge, Tenn. Interred in National cemetery, Chattanooga, Tenn., section C, grave 1218.

BONHAM, THOMAS. Private. Killed Sept. 19, 1863, in battle of Chick amauga, Ga. Interred at Chattanooga, Tenn.

CAMP, ANTHONY. Private. Killed Nov. 25, 1863, in battle of Mission Ridge, Tenn. Interred at Chattanooga, Tenn.

HARLEY, WILLIAM F. Private. Killed May 27, 1864, in battle of Pickett's Mills, Ga. Interred at Chattanooga, Tenn.

JACKSON, JACOB. Private. Killed May 27, 1864, in battle of Pickett's Mills, Ga. Interred at Chattanooga, Tenn.

LININGER, EDWARD. Corp. Killed May 27, 1864, in battle of Pickett's Mills, Ga. Interred at Chattanooga, Tenn.

MILLER, SOLOMON. Corp. Killed May 31, 1864, in battle of Dallas, Ga. Interred at Marietta, Ga., section C, grave 1873.

SHELLEY, JOHN. Corp. Killed Nov. 25, 1863, in battle of Mission Ridge, Tenn. Interred at Chattanooga, Tenn.

SWEENEY, JOSEPH. Private. Killed April 7, 1862, in battle of Shiloh, Tenn. Interred in National cemetery, Shiloh, Tenn.

WAGONER, SIMON. Private. Killed April 7, 1862, in battle of Shiloh, Tenn. Interred at Shiloh, Tenn.

WEAVER, JOHN. Private. Killed April 7, 1862, in battle of Shiloh, Tenn. Interred at Shiloh, Tenn.

DIED OF WOUNDS.

AXE, JOHN. Private. Died July 20, 1864, at Jeffersonville, Ind., of wounds received May 27, 1864, in battle of Pickett's Mills, Ga. Interred in section B, grave 876, New Albany, Ind.

CARLIN, JOSEPH. Private. Died Dec. 9, 1863, of wounds received Nov. 23, 1863, in battle of Orchard Knob, Tenn. Interred in National cemetery, Chattanooga, Tenn.

COCKLIN, DAVID. Private. Died May 10, 1862, of wounds received April 7, 1862, in battle of Shiloh, Tenn. Interred in Spring Grove cemetery, Cincinnati, O.

DUNN, JOHN. Sergt. Died April 13, 1862, of wounds received April 7, 1862, in battle of Shiloh, Tenn. Interred in section B, grave 1057, New Albany, Ind.

ECKERMAN, FRANKLIN W. Private. Died July 4, 1864, of wounds received May 27, 1864, in battle of Pickett's Mills, Ga. Interred in section E, grave 11587, Chattanooga, Tenn.

GRAYBILL, SAMUEL H. Corp. Died June 15, 1864, of wounds received May 27, 1864, in battle of Pickett's Mills, Ga. Interred in section J, grave 446, Nashville, Tenn.

LAUTZENHEISER, SAMUEL. Private. Died June 20, 1864, of wounds received May 27, 1864, in battle of Pickett's Mills, Ga. Interred in section B, grave 942, Chattanooga, Tenn.

MARKWALDER, JOHN. Private. Died Dec. 25, 1863, of wounds received Nov. 25, 1863, in battle of Mission Ridge, Tenn. Interred in National cemetery, Chattanooga, Tenn.

McGONIGAL, THOMAS. Private. Died Jan. 1, 1863, of wounds received Dec. 31, 1862, in battle of Stone River, Tenn. Interred in Stone River cemetery, grave 2227.

PANCOAST, FRANKLIN E. 1st Lieut. Died May 16, 1862, of wounds received April 7, 1862, in battle of Shiloh, Tenn. Interred at Wooster, Ohio.

ROSSITER, JOSEPH. Corp. Died April 10, 1862, of wounds received April 7, 1862, in battle of Shiloh, Tenn. Interred at Shiloh, Tenn.

REED, LOUIS. Sergt. Died May 11, 1862, of wounds received April 7, 1862, in battle of Shiloh, Tenn. Interred in City cemetery, Massillon, Ohio.

SHANKLIN, JACOB. Private. Died Nov. 27, 1863, of wounds received Nov. 25, 1863, in battle of Mission Ridge, Tenn. Interred at Chattanooga, Tenn.

DIED OF DISEASE.

BERRY, SAMUEL. Sergt. Died Feb. 22, 1862, of disease, at Wooster, Ohio.

BOND, ISAAC. Private. Died Jan. 10, 1865, of disease, at Huntsville, Ala. Interred at Chattanooga, Tenn.

CAMP, MATHIAS. Private. Died Feb. 10, 1862, of disease. Interred in Cave Hill cemetery, Louisville, Ky.

CASWELL, H. S. Private. Died Dec. 1, 1862, of disease. Interred in section B, grave 1074, Nashville, Tenn.

FLICKINGER, JOHN. Private. Died April 11, 1862, of disease. Interred in section A, grave 671, Nashville, Tenn.

GALLOWAY, DAVID W. Private. Died April 8, 1862, of disease. Interred in Stone River cemetery, grave 1679.

GEORGE, WILLIAM. Private. Died Feb. 24, 1862, of disease. Interred in Cave Hill cemetery, secton A, division 11, grave 20.

HARMON, HIRAM. Private. Died Feb. 3, 1864, of disease, in Rebel prison, at Salisbury, N. C. Interred at Danville, Va., in section 1, grave 454.

JACKSON, JAMES. Private. Died June 24, 1862, of disease, at Iuka, Miss. Interred at Corinth, Miss.

KLINE, JOSIAH. Private. Died May 10, 1862, of disease, at Evansville, Ind. Interred at New Albany, Ind.

MAXWELL, ALEXANDER. Private. Died March 25, 1863, of disease, at Readyville, Tenn. Interred in Stone River cemetery, H. B. lot, grave 46.

PERKINS, LEONIDAS. Private. Died March 8, 1865, of disease. Interred in Nashville, Tenn., cemetery.

RAYAL, ALONZO B. Corp. Died March 3, 1862, of disease. Interred in Cave Hill cemetery, Louisville, Ky.

SERGEON, JOSEPH. Private. Died Aug 9, 1863, of disease. Interred in Cave Hill cemetery, Louisville, Ky.

SNYDER, PETER. Private. Died March 23, 1863, of disease, at Readyville, Tenn. Interred in Stone River cemetery, grave 52, H. B. lot.

STRINE, HARRISON. Private. Died March 3, 1862, of disease, at his home in Wooster, Wayne county, Ohio.

SCOTT, LEVI. Private. Died Feb. 17, 1863.

WELLS, THOMAS. Corp. Died Dec. 29, 1862, of disease. Interred in Cave Hill cemetery, Louisville, Ky.

ASDELL, SAMUEL B. 1st Lieut. Died Nov. 17, 1863, of disease.

COMPANY D.

KILLED IN ACTION.

ATHERTON, ALLEN. Private. Killed May 15, 1864, in battle of Resaca, Ga. Interred in National cemetery, Marietta, Ga.

DUNHAM, ROYAL. Private. Killed May 27, 1864, in battle of Pickett's Mills, Ga. Interred in National cemetery, Chattanooga, Tenn.

GARDNER, JOHN. Private. Killed Nov. 25, 1863, in battle of Mission Ridge, Tenn. Interred in National cemetery, Chattanooga, Tenn., section B, grave 351.

RATTLE, WILLIAM. Private. Killed May 27, 1864, in battle of Pickett's Mills, Ga. Interred in National cemetery, Chattanooga, Tenn.

RICHARDSON, LUTHER. Private. Killed May 27, 1864, in battle of Pickett's Mills, Ga. Interred in National cemetery, Chattanooga, Tenn.

TRUMP, ANDREW. Private. Killed May 27, 1864, in battle of Pickett's Mills, Ga. Interred in National cemetery, Chattanooga, Tenn.

DIED OF WOUNDS.

BUTLER, THOMAS. Sergt. Died in Rebel prison, of wounds received May 27, 1864, in battle of Pickett's Mills, Ga.

DUNKEE, WILLIAM. Corp. Died Nov. 25, 1863, of wounds received Nov. 25, 1863, in battle of Mission Ridge, Tenn. Interred in National cemetery, Chattanooga, Tenn.

FITZPATRICK, THOMAS. Private. Died Dec. 8, 1863, of wounds received Nov. 23, 1863, in battle of Orchard Knob, Tenn. Interred in section D, grave 12170, Chattanooga, Tenn.

HECKELMYER, THOMAS. Private. Died Jan. 15, 1865, of wounds received Dec. 16, 1864, in battle of Nashville, Tenn. Interred in Nashville, Tenn.

HIST, JOSEPH. Private. Died Jan. 28, 1863, of wounds received Dec. 31, 1862, in battle of Stone River, Tenn. Interred at Nashville, Tenn.

KELLEY, EDWARD W. Private. Died Aug 12, 1864, in Rebel prison, at Andersonville, of starvation. Wounded in battle of Chickamauga, Sept. 19, 1863. Interred at Andersonville, Ga., grave 15381.

SMELLIE, EMERSON W. Corp. Died Nov. 26, 1863, of wounds received Nov. 25, 1863, in battle of Mission Ridge, Tenn. Interred in Erie street cemetery, Cleveland, Ohio.

SMITH, HENRY W. Private. Died June 22, 1864, of wounds received May 27, 1864, in battle of Pickett's Mills, Ga. Interred at Chattanooga, Tenn., section E, grave 11266.

TOMPKINS, MOSES. Private. Died June 21, 1864, of wounds received May 27, 1864, in battle of Pickett's Mills, Ga. Interred at Chattanooga, Tenn., section E, grave 11295.

TROWBRIDGE, DANIEL. Corp. Died May 9, 1862, of wounds received April 7, 1862, in battle of Shiloh, Tenn. Interred at Shiloh, Tenn.

DIED OF DISEASE.

CORKAL, EDWARD. Private. Died May 18, 1862, at Iuka, Miss., of disease. Interred in National cemetery, Corinth, Miss.

DAVIDSON, JESSE. Private. Died April 22, 1862, of disease, at Louisville, Ky. Interred in Cave Hill cemetery.

GREY, SAMUEL H. Private. Died Dec. 25, 1864, of disease, at Nashville, Tenn. Interred in National cemetery, section G, grave 51.

HARRIS, FRANCIS. Private. Died March 25, 1862, of disease. Interred in Cave Hill cemetery, Louisville, Ky., section A, division 15, grave 389.

IVES, ERASTUS P. Private. Died Feb. 20, 1862, of disease. Interred in Cave Hill cemetery, Louisville, Ky.

JONES, DAVID M. Private. Died Feb. 6, 1863, of disease, at his home in Bedford, Cuyahoga county, Ohio.

MEAD, LEVI. Private. Died April 7, 1862, of disease, at Louisville, Ky. Interred in Cave Hill cemetery.

SAMPSON, SAMUEL. Private. Died Dec. 5, 1865, of disease, at Cairo, Ill.

STUDOR, THOMAS. Private. Died Feb. 16, 1862, of disease, at Louisville, Ky. Interred in Cave Hill cemetery.

UNDERHILL, DANIEL R. Private. Died Jan 15, 1862, of disease, at Camp Wickliffe, Ky. Interred at London, Ky.

COMPANY E.

KILLED IN ACTION.

CHESLEY, CHARLES. Private. Killed Nov. 25, 1863, in battle of Mission Ridge, Tenn. Interred in National cemetery, Chattanooga, Tenn.

CULLEN, JOHN. Corp. Killed April 7, 1862, in battle of Shiloh, Tenn. Interred in National cemetery, Shiloh, Tenn.

HERLING, CHARLES. Private. Killed May 27, 1864, in battle of Pickett's Mills, Ga. Interred in National cemetery, Chattanooga, Tenn.

LAMBIER, JAMES. Private. Killed April 7, 1862, in battle of Shiloh, Tenn. Interred in National cemetery, Shiloh, Tenn.

MONTREAL, ANTHONY. Private. Killed April 7, 1862, in battle of Shiloh, Tenn. Interred in National cemetery, Shiloh, Tenn.

QUICK, JESSE. Private. Killed Dec. 31, 1862, in battle of Stone River, Tenn. Interred in National cemetery, Hazen's Brigade lot.

SIMONS, HENRY. Sergt. Killed Dec. 31, 1862, in battle of Stone River, Tenn. Interred in National cemetery, Hazen's Brigade lot, grave 51.

TREAT, LEMON. Private. Killed July 5, 1864, in action, at Chattahoochee River, Ga. Interred in National cemetery, Marietta, Ga.

WINCHESTER, SYLVESTER. Musician. Killed Dec. 31, 1862, in battle of Stone River, Tenn. Interred in National cemetery, Hazen's Brigade lot, grave 55.

DIED OF WOUNDS.

CHALK, MICHAEL. Private. Died June 18, 1862, of wounds received April 7, 1862, in battle of Shiloh, Tenn. Interred in Jefferson Barracks cemetery, section 64, grave 10890, St. Louis, Mo.

CORBITT, TIMOTHY. Private. Died ——, 1863, of wounds received Dec. 31, 1862, in battle of Stone River, Tenn. Interred in Stone River National cemetery, Murfreesboro, Tenn.

HAYES, JOHN. Private. Died June 15, 1862, of wounds received April 7, 1862, in battle of Shiloh, Tenn. Interred in Spring Grove cemetery, Cincinnati, Ohio.

HIGHLAND, WILLIAM. Private. Died Dec. 26, 1863, of wounds received Nov. 25, 1863, in battle of Mission Ridge, Tenn. Interred in National cemetery, section D, grave 12726, Chattanooga, Tenn.

STROCK, ABRAM. Private. Died June 10, 1864, of wounds received May 14, 1864, in battle of Resaca, Ga. Interred in National cemetery, section B, grave 939, Chattanooga, Tenn.

VIRGIL, ALBERT E. 1st Sergt. Died of wounds received Apr. 7, 1862, in battle of Shiloh, Tenn. Interred in Jefferson Barracks cemetery, St. Louis, Mo. Name does not appear on cemetery record.

DIED OF DISEASE.

KEPLER, JOHN. Private. Died Jan. 18, 1863, of disease, at Nashville, Tenn. Interred in National cemetery, Nashville, Tenn., section B, grave 132.

SINGLETARY, CYRUS. Private. Died July 17, 1864, of disease, in hospital at Louisville, Ky. Interred in Cave Hill cemetery.

SMITH, ALVA. Private. Died March 8, 1862, of disease, at Nelson's Furnace, Ky. Interred at New Albany, Ind., section D, grave 2592.

COMPANY F.

KILLED IN ACTION.

AYLESWORTH, REUBEN H. Corp. Killed Sept. 19, 1863, in battle of Chickamauga, Ga. Interred in National cemetery, Chattanooga, Tenn.

BAKER, THOMAS P. Private. Killed Sept. 19, 1863, in battle of Chickamauga, Ga. Interred in National cemetery, Chattanooga, Tenn.

BLANDEN, JOHN M. Private. Killed May 27, 1864, in battle of Pickett's Mills, Ga. Interred in National cemetery, Chattanooga, Tenn., section B, grave 817.

BOUVIA, JOSEPH. Private. Killed Nov. 25, 1863, in battle of Mission Ridge, Tenn. Interred in National cemetery, Chattanooga, Tenn., section B, grave 795.

BROWN, HENRY M. Private. Killed Aug. 6, 1864, in action near Atlanta, Ga. Interred at Marietta, Ga., section K, grave 4256.

DAVIS, JAMES. Private. Killed Dec. 31, 1862, in battle of Stone River, Tenn. Interred in Stone River cemetery, Murfreesboro, Tenn.

DELKER, MICHAEL, J. Private. Killed May 27, 1864, in battle of Pickett's Mills, Ga. Interred in National cemetery, Chattanooga, Tenn.

EDNEY, ANDREW. Private. Killed Nov. 25, 1863, in battle of Mission Ridge, Tenn. Interred in National cemetery, Chattanooga, Tenn., section B, grave 793.

GARNIA, FRANK. Private. Killed May 27, 1864, in battle of Pickett's Mills, Ga. Interred in National cemetery, Chattanooga, Tenn.

KIDWELL, LOVY B. Private. Killed Dec. 31, 1862, in battle of Stone River, Tenn. Interred in Stone River cemetery, Hazen's Brigade lot, grave 43.

LEHMAN, ALEXANDER. Private. Killed April 7, 1862, in battle of Shiloh, Tenn. Interred in National cemetery, Shiloh, Tenn.

PARISH, JOSEPH. Private. Killed Dec. 31, 1862, in battle of Stone River, Tenn. Interred in Stone River cemetery, Hazen's Brigade lot, grave 48.

RENNER, JACOB. Sergt. Killed Sept. 19, 1863, in battle of Chickamauga, Ga. Interred in National cemetery, Chattanooga, Tenn.

RICE, ABRAM. Private. Killed April 7, 1862, in battle of Shiloh, Tenn. Interred in National cemetery, Shiloh, Tenn.

SHOEMAKER, CHARLES. Corp. Killed Nov. 25, 1863, in battle of Mission Ridge, Tenn. Interred in National cemetery, Chattanooga, Tenn., section C, grave 1339.

STACY, MAHLON. Private. Killed Sept. 19, 1863, in battle of Chickamauga, Ga. Interred in National cemetery, Chattanooga, Tenn.

SISCO, JOHN A. Private. Killed May 27, 1864, in battle of Pickett's Mills, Ga. Interred in National cemetery, Chattanooga, Tenn.

DIED OF WOUNDS.

EWING, SAMUEL J. Private. Died April 20, 1863, in Jackson township, Mahoning county, Ohio, of wounds received April 7, 1862, in battle of Stone River, Tenn. Interred at North Jackson, Ohio.

GAULT, ANDREW. Sergt. Died Aug. 8, 1864, at his home near North Jackson, Ohio, of wounds received May 27, 1864, in battle of Pickett's Mills, Ga. Interred at North Jackson, Ohio.

HAGEMAN, MATHIAS. Private. Died May 12, 1862, of wounds received April 7, 1862, in battle of Shiloh, Tenn. Interred in Jefferson Barracks cemetery, St. Louis, Mo., in section 64, grave 10919.

HUNT, JACKSON. Private. Died March 3, 1863, of wounds received in battle of Stone River, Tenn., Dec. 31, 1862. Interred in Linden Grove cemetery, Covington, Ky., section B, grave 46.

KILGORE, IRAM. Sergt. Died Aug 16, 1864, in Andersonville prison, Ga., of wounds received Sept. 19, 1863, in battle of Chickamauga, Ga. Interred in grave 5813. Name does not appear on cemetery register.

KILMER, ORLANDO P. Sergt. Died April 22, 1862, of wounds received April 7, 1862, in battle of Shiloh Tenn. Interred in Spring Grove cemetery, section A, grave 145, Cincinnati, Ohio.

NEWBURY, CHARLES. Private. Died June 24, 1864, of wounds received May 27, 1864, in battle of Pickett's Mills, Ga. Interred in National cemetery, section A, grave 122, Marietta, O.

SAUTUER, ALEXANDER. Private. Died June 15, 1862, of wounds received, April 7, 1862, in battle of Shiloh, Tenn. Interred in Jefferson Barracks cemetery, St. Louis, Mo., section 65, grave 10315.

SHIRLEY, FRANK B. Private. Died April 24, 1862, of wounds received April 7, 1862, in battle of Shiloh, Tenn. Interred in Spring Grove cemetery, Cincinnati, O.

SPAULDING, HENRY. Private. Died Dec. 2, 1862, of wounds received April 7, 1862, in battle of Shiloh, Tenn. Interred at Ellsworth, O.

WETZEL, WILLIAM. Private. Died May 10, 1862, of wounds received April 7, 1862, in battle of Shiloh, Tenn. Interred in Spring Grove cemetery, Cincinnati, O.

DIED OF DISEASE.

DUER, THOMAS. Private. Died May 2, 1862, of disease. Interred in Spring Grove cemetery, section A, grave 194, Cincinnati, O.

FLAUGHER, ISAAC. Corporal. Died Feb. 13, 1862, of disease. Interred in Cave Hill cemetery, Louisville, Ky. Died at Nelson's Barracks hospital, Ky.

LA FOUNTAIN, MARSHALL. Private. Died Jan. 27, 1863, of disease. Interred in National cemetery, section B, grave 200, Nashville, Tenn.

MASER, FRANK. Corporal. Died March 23, 1862, of disease. Interred in National cemetery, section A, grave 607.

SMITH, CHARLES. Private. Died May 10, 1862, of disease. Interred in Linden Grove cemetery, Covington, Ky.

SMITH, WALTER. Sergeant. Died Feb. 26, 1862, of disease, at New Haven, Ky. Interred at Ellsworth, O.

SNYDER, BENJAMIN M. Private. Died March 8, 1862, of disease, at Nelson's Furnace, Ky. Interred in Cave Hill cemetery, Louisville, Ky.

STEWART, PLIMPTON. Private. Died June 21, 1862, of disease. Interred in National cemetery, Corinth, Miss.

YARNELL, ISAAC. Private. Died March 11, 1865. of disease, at Jeffersonville, Ind. Interred in National cemetery, New Albany, Ind.

KILLED BY ACCIDENT.

CLARY, JAMES K. Private. Perished April 27, 1865, by the blowing up of the steamboat "Sultana" on the Mississippi river, near Memphis. Tenn.

SHISLER, ELI. Private. Lost June 19, 1865, by the sinking of the steamboat "Echo," No. 2, near Cairo, Ill.

COMPANY G.

KILLED IN ACTION.

ALEXANDER, WILLIAM. Private. Killed May 27, 1864, in battle of Pickett's Mills, Ga. Interred in National cemetery, Chattanooga, Tenn.

BARKER, FRANK. Private. Killed Sept. 19, 1863, in battle of Chickamauga, Ga. Interred in National cemetery, Chattanooga, Tenn.

CORNISH, ROSWELL. Private. Killed Sept. 19, 1863, in battle of Chickamauga, Ga. Interred in National cemetery, Chattanooga, Tenn.

HUGHES, IRA. Private. Killed May 27, 1864, in battle of Pickett's Mills, Ga. Interred in National cemetery, Chattanooga, Tenn.

HUGHES, HARRISON T. Private. Killed Dec. 31, 1863, in battle of Stone River, Tenn. Interred in Hazen's Brigade lot, section B, grave 42, Stone River cemetery.

MAXWELL, DAYTON. Private. Killed May 27, 1864, in battle of Pickett's Mills, Ga. Interred in National cemetery, Chattanooga, Tenn.

RODGERS, JOSHUA. Private. Killed Sept. 19, 1863, in battle of Chickamauga, Ga. Interred in National cemetery, Chattanooga, Tenn., section B, grave 821.

SEARL, PHILO. Corporal. Killed Sept. 19, 1863, in battle of Chickamauga, Ga. Interred in National cemetery, Chattanooga, Tenn.

SMITH, HORTON. Private. Killed May 27, 1864, in battle of Pickett's Mills, Ga. Interred in National cemetery, Chattanooga, Tenn.

STEPHENSON, HENRY. Private. Killed Sept. 19, 1863, in battle of Chickamauga, Ga. Interred in National cemetery, Chattanooga, Tenn.

STRONG, JOEL. Private. Killed Dec. 31, 1862, in battle of Stone River, Tenn. Interred in Stone River cemetery, Hazen's Brigade lot, grave 50.

TRAVER, HENRY B. Private. Killed Sept. 19, 1863, in battle of Chickamauga, Ga. Interred in National cemetery, Chattanooga, Tenn.

WATTS, MORTIMER F. Private. Killed Sept. 19, 1863, in battle of Chickamauga, Ga. Interred in National cemetery, Chattanooga, Tenn.

DIED OF WOUNDS.

CALKINS, CLARK D. Corporal. Died Dec. 8, 1863, of wounds received Nov. 25, 1863, in battle of Mission Ridge, Tenn. Interred in National cemetery, Chattanooga, Tenn.

DIRLAM, HENRY S. 1st Lieutenant. Died Dec. 18, 1863, of wounds received Nov. 25, 1863, in battle of Mission Ridge, Tenn. Interred in National cemetery, Chattanooga, Tenn.

SNETHAN, BENJAMIN. Private. Died July 25, 1864, of wounds received in battle of Pickett's Mills, Ga. Interred in National cemetery, section J, grave 171, Nashville, Tenn.

WORTHINGTON, DANIEL H. Private. Died Feb. 8, 1863, of wounds received Dec. 31, 1862, in battle of Stone River, Tenn. Interred in National cemetery, section B, grave 760, Nashville, Tenn.

DIED OF DISEASE.

BROWN, ROBERT M. Private. Died Sept. 15, 1865, of disease. Interred in National cemetery, Brownsville, Texas, grave 852.

COOK, AUSTIN. Private. Died June 12, 1862, of disease. Interred in Cave Hill cemetery, Louisville, Ky.

DAVIS, FRANCIS M. Private. Died April 7, 1862, of disease. Interred in section A, grave 593, National cemetery, Nashville, Tenn.

DICKINS, SHERMAN. Private. Died March 8, 1862, of disease. Interred in Cave Hill cemetery, Louisville, Ky., section A, division 14, grave 376.

HAINES, ORIN. Private. Died June 25, 1862, of disease. Interred at Corinth, Miss.

HALL, WILLIAM. Private. Died Feb. 8, 1862, of disease. Interred in Cave Hill cemetery, Louisville, Ky.

HARPER, MORRIS. Corporal. Died March 2, 1862, of disease, at Nelson's Furnace, Ky. Interred in Cave Hill cemetery, Louisville, Ky.

HOFFMAN, REUBEN. Private. Died Jan. 8, 1863, of disease. Interred in section B, grave 391, National cemetery, Nashville, Tenn.

HOUCK, ALEXANDER. Private. Died Dec. 16, 1864, of disease. Interred at Chattanooga, Tenn.

KOENIGER, LEWIS. Private. Died June 6, 1865, of disease. Interred in Cave Hill cemetery, Louisville, Ky., section C, division 3, grave 2698.

LILLY, CHARLES. Sergeant. Died March 31, 1863, of disease at Readyville, Tenn. Interred in Hazen's Brigade lot, section 1, grave 45, Stone River cemetery.

LITTLE, WALLACE. Private. Died Oct. 31, 1862, of disease, at Bardstown, Ky. Interred at Lebanon, Ky.

MORSE, LORENZO. Private. Died Jan. 14, 1862, of disease, at Camp Wickliffe, Ky. Interred at London, Ky.

PARSONS, EDWIN. Private. Died Jan. 30, 1862, of disease, at Camp Wickliffe, Ky. Interred at London, Ky.

RODGERS, WILLIAM. Private. Died Feb. 14, 1863, of disease. Interred in National cemetery, section E, grave 586, Nashville, Tenn.

SEARL, MARTIN. Private. Died Jan. 28, 1863, at Readyville, Tenn. Interred in Stone River cemetery. No record.

STANSELL, CHARLES. Private. Died April 1, 1863, at Readyville. Tenn. Interred in Stone River cemetery, Hazen's Brigade lot, grave 53.

WHITNEY, ORIN. Private. Died March 27, 1863, of disease. Interred in Cave Hill cemetery, Louisville, Ky.

COMPANY H.

KILLED IN ACTION AND MORTALLY WOUNDED.

BLACKWELL, JAMES W. Private. Killed Nov. 23, 1863, in battle of Orchard Knob, Tenn. Interred at Chattanooga, Tenn.

BUTSON, GEORGE. Private. Killed May 27, 1864, in battle of Pickett's Mills, Ga. Interred at Chattanooga, Tenn.

CAMP, SENECA. Private. Killed April 7, 1862, in battle of Shiloh, Tenn. Interred at Shiloh, Tenn.

CHAMBERLAIN, MATTHEW. Private. Killed April 7, 1862, in battle of Shiloh, Tenn. Interred at Shiloh, Tenn.

CLARK, JOHN. Private. Killed May 27, 1864, in battle of Pickett's Mills, Ga. Interred at Chattanooga, Tenn.

GRANT, JAMES H. Corporal. Killed Nov. 23, 1863, in battle of Orchard Knob, Tenn. Interred at Chattanooga, Tenn.

GUNSAUL, CHARLES. Private. Killed Nov. 23, 1863, in battle of Orchard Knob, Tenn. Interred at Chattanooga, Tenn., in section D, grave 11910.

KINGSBURY, EBENEZER. Sergeant. Killed Nov. 23, 1863, in battle of Orchard Knob, Tenn. Interred at Chattanooga, Tenn.

LENHART, JOHN C. Private. Killed Dec. 31, 1862, in battle of Stone River, Tenn. Interred in Hazen's Brigade lot, grave 44.

MILLS, JOHN G. Sergeant. Killed May 27, 1864, in battle of Pickett's Mills, Ga. Interred at Chattanooga, Tenn.

MILLS, WILLIAM A. Corporal. Killed Nov. 23, 1863, in battle of Orchard Knob, Tenn. Interred at Chattanooga, Tenn., section B, grave 788.

PORTER, WILLIAM H. Private. Killed April 7, 1862, in battle of Shiloh, Tenn. Interred at Shiloh, Tenn.

ROSSITER, EMER A. Private. Killed Dec. 31, 1862, in battle of Stone River, Tenn. Interred in Hazen's Brigade lot.

STAPLES, JOSIAH. Sergeant. Killed May 27, 1864, in battle of Pickett's Mills, Ga. Interred at Chattanooga, Tenn.

WEST, HENRY. Private. Killed April 7, 1862, in battle of Shiloh, Tenn. Interred at Shiloh, Tenn.

DIED OF DISEASE.

BROWN, HYMEN A. Private. Died May 20, 1862, of disease. Interred in grave 2397, Corinth, Miss.

CLARK, ALBERT J. Private. Died May 14, 1862, of disease. Interred at Corinth, Miss.

CLARK, GEORGE C. Private. Died Jan. 23, 1862, at Camp Wickliffe, Ky., of disease. Interred at London, Ky.

DOTY, ELLIS E. Private. Died August, 1864, in Rebel prison. Interred in grave 5299, Andersonville, Ga.

KELLOGG, ALBERT M. Private. Died March 18, 1862, of disease. Interred in Cave Hill cemetery, Louisville, Ky.

LAWRENCE, DANIEL. Private. Died June 4, 1862, of disease, at Bardstown, Ky. Interred in section B, Lebanon, Ky.

LINCOLN, JOSEPH H. Private. Died March 20, 1862, of disease, in Lorain county, Ohio. Interred at Pittsfield, O.

POMEROY, FRANKLIN. Private. Died Jan. 19, 1862, of disease, at Camp Wickliffe, Ky. Interred at London, Ky.

SANDERSON, HARVEY. Private. Died June 22, 1862, of disease, near Corinth, Miss. Interred at Corinth, Miss.

SMITH, OLIVER M. Private. Died June 13, 1862, of disease, at Spencer, Ohio. Interred at Spencer, O.

SPANGLER, PHILIP. Private. Died June 5, 1863, of disease, at Readyville, Tenn. Interred in Stone River cemetery, grave 5004.

TODD, CHARLES M. Private. Died April 7, 1862, of disease, at Columbia, Tenn. Interred in Stone River cemetery. No record.

WEST, BENONI B. Private. Died Nov. 2, 1864, of disease. Interred at Oberlin, O.

WHITNEY, NATHAN H. Sergeant. Died Feb. 3, 1862, of disease. Interred at Cave Hill cemetery, Louisville, Ky.

COMPANY I.

KILLED IN ACTION.

BATTIN, CHRISTOPHER. Private. Killed May 27, 1864, in battle of Pickett's Mills, Ga. Interred in National cemetery, Chattanooga, Tenn.

BROWER, GEORGE W. Private. Killed Dec. 16. 1864, in battle of Nashville, Tenn. Interred in National cemetery, Nashville, Tenn.

DAVIS, ALBERT C. Private. Killed May 27, 1864. in battle of Pickett's Mills, Ga. Interred at Chattanooga, Tenn.

FIELDS, GEORGE W. Private. Killed April 7, 1862, in battle of Shiloh, Tenn. Interred at Shiloh, Tenn.

GRAM, WILLIAM F. Corporal. Killed May 27, 1864. in battle of Pickett's Mills, Ga. Interred at Chattanooga, Tenn.

HARTMAN, FREDERICK. Private. Killed April 7, 1862. in battle of Shiloh, Tenn. Interred at Shiloh, Tenn.

KIRK, CHARLES A. Sergeant. Killed Nov. 23, 1863, in battle of Orchard Knob, Tenn. Interred at Chattanooga, Tenn.

REED, HENRY. Private. Killed April 7, 1862, in battle of Shiloh, Tenn. Interred at Shiloh, Tenn.

ROHLOFF, JOHN F. H. Private. Killed Nov. 23, 1863, in battle of Orchard Knob, Tenn. Interred in section B, grave 796, Chattanooga, Tenn.

SNYDER, JEREMIAH K. Corporal. Killed Dec. 31, 1862, in battle of Stone River, Tenn. Interred in Hazen's Brigade lot, grave 49.

TALCOTT, HENRY. Private. Killed Nov. 23, 1863, in battle of Orchard Knob, Tenn. Interred at Chattanooga, Tenn.

TILLOTSON, SAMUEL H. Private. Killed April 7, 1862, in battle of Shiloh, Tenn. Interred at Shiloh, Tenn.

TROUTMAN, EBENEZER C. Private. Killed Dec. 31, 1862, in battle of Stone River. Tenn. Interred in Hazen's Brigade lot, grave 54.

DIED OF WOUNDS.

GILL, WILLIAM D. Corporal. Died April 23, 1862, at Evansville, Ind., of wounds received April 7, 1862, in battle of Shiloh, Tenn. Interred at New Albany, Ind.

ROBINSON, CHARLES. Private. Died May 20, 1864, of wounds received May 17, 1864, in battle of Adairsville, Ga. Interred at Marietta, Ga.

FELTER, MARTIN. Private. Died May 20, 1864, of wounds received May 15, 1864, in battle of Resaca, Ga.

DIED OF DISEASE.

BELL, JOSEPH M. Private. Died Sept. 29, 1862, of disease. Interred in section A, grave 535, Nashville, Tenn.

CLUCKEY, LEWIS. Private. Died Oct. 4, 1865, of disease. Interred in National cemetery, at Brownsville, Texas, grave 458.

COOPER, GEORGE A. Private. Died June 3, 1865, of disease. Interred in section G, grave 686, Nashville, Tenn.

DISDRO, JUSTICE. Corporal. Died July 5, 1862, of disease. Interred at Athens, Ala.

GODDARD, WILLIAM. Private. Died Feb. 1, 1862, of disease. Interred in Cave Hill cemetery, Louisville, Ky., section A, grave 175.

GOUCH, FREDERICK. Private. Died April 21, 1863, of disease, at Readyville, Tenn. Interred in Stone River cemetery. No record.

GREINER, CYRUS. Private. Died July 9, 1863, of disease, at Tullahoma, Tenn. Interred in Stone River cemetery, section G, grave 1116.

HALL, JOHN W. Private. Died Sept. 12, 1863, of disease, at Poe's Tavern, Tenn. Interred at Chattanooga, Tenn.

KAEFER, GEORGE W. Private. Died Jan. 24, 1862, of disease. Interred in Cave Hill cemetery, Louisville, Ky., section A, division 11, grave 276.

LEEDERS, CHARLES. Private. Died April 12, 1864, of disease. Interred in section C, grave 646, Nashville, Tenn.

LOCKWOOD, ALFRED R. Private. Died April 1, 1864, of disease. Interred in Cave Hill cemetery, Louisville, Ky., section B, range 13, grave 2033.

MILLER, SAMUEL M. Private. Died Jan. 10, 1865, of disease, at Jeffersonville, Ind. Interred at New Albany, Ind.

MINIER, JOSEPH. Private. Died June 7, 1862, of disease. Interred at Corinth, Miss.

MYER, JOHN. Private. Died Aug. 25, 1864, of disease. Interred in section E, grave 2799, Nashville, Tenn.

PARK, ISAAC. Private. Died Feb. 1, 1862, of disease, at Camp Wickliffe, Ky. Interred at London, Ky.

PARKER, GEORGE D. Corporal. Died Dec. 26, 1861, of disease. Interred in Cave Hill cemetery, Louisville, Ky., section A, division 5, grave 121.

PARTLOW, WILLIAM. Private. Died Dec. 26, 1861, of disease. Interred in Cave Hill cemetery, Louisville, Ky.

POWERS, MIFFLIN. Private. Died April 23, 1862, of disease. Interred in Spring Grove cemetery, Cincinnati, O.

SCOTT, SHEPHERD. Musician. Died Aug. 9, 1864, of starvation in Rebel prison, at Andersonville, Ga. Interred in grave 5133.

ZEALEY, ADAM. Private. Died Feb. 20, 1862, of disease, at Belmont Furnace, Ky. Interred in Cave Hill cemetery, Louisville, Ky.

COMPANY K.

KILLED IN ACTION.

DECKER, JOHN. Private. Killed May 27, 1864, in battle of Pickett's Mills, Ga. Interred at Chattanooga, Tenn.

HOSKINS, WILLIAM H. Private. Killed May 27, 1864, in battle of Pickett's Mills, Ga. Interred at Chattanooga, Tenn.

RUSHER, JACOB. Private. Killed April 7, 1862, in battle of Shiloh, Tenn. Interred at Shiloh, Tenn.

WATSON, WILLIAM W. 2d Lieutenant. Killed Nov. 25, 1863, in battle of Mission Ridge. Interred in National cemetery, Chattanooga, Tenn.

DIED OF WOUNDS.

BEARD, JOSEPH. Corporal. Died May 8, 1862, of wounds received April 7, 1862, in battle of Shiloh, Tenn. Interred in Jefferson Barracks cemetery, section 64, grave 10916, St. Louis, Mo.

HANSARD, WILLIAM. Captain. Died Jan. 9, 1865, of wounds received Dec. 15, 1864, in battle of Nashville, Tenn. Interred at Nashville, Tenn.

LOVLACE, LEANDER. Sergeant. Died April 24, 1862, of wounds received April 7, 1862, in battle of Shiloh, Tenn. Interred in Spring Grove cemetery, Cincinnati, O.

ORR, JOHN. 1st Sergeant. Died Jan. 3, 1863, of wounds received Dec. 31, 1862, in battle of Stone River, Tenn. Interred in Stone River cemetery, section 1, grave 165.

PRICE, WILLIAM. Corporal. Died of wounds received in battle of ——. Interred at Chattanooga, Tenn.

SEXTON, DENNIS. Private. Died April 29, 1862, of wounds received April 7, 1862, in battle of Shiloh, Tenn. Interred at Cairo, Ill.

DIED OF DISEASE.

BRUNSON, WILLIAM A. Private. Mustered out Nov. 27, 1865. Died Nov. 28, 1865, of disease. Interred in Green Lawn cemetery, Columbus, O.

BURR, HARVEY. Private. Died Oct. 9, 1862, in hospital at Bowling Green, Ky., of disease. Interred in section M, grave 512, National cemetery, Nashville, Tenn.

BATTLES, NEWTON. Private. Died Dec. 20, 1861, of disease, at Camp Wickliffe, Ky. Interred at London, Ky.

DWIGHT, G. S. Sergeant. Died July 14, 1862, of disease. Interred in Cave Hill cemetery, section A, division 28, grave 10, Louisville, Ky.

FOX, GEORGE. Private. Died Oct. 2, 1865, of disease. Interred in section 45, grave 1589, Jefferson Barracks cemetery, St. Louis, Mo.

FOOT, LEVI. Private. Died Jan. 3, 1862, of disease. Interred in Cave Hill cemetery, Louisville, Ky.

GRIFFIN, CHARLES. Sergeant. Died June 18, 1864, of disease. Interred in section J, grave 9956, Marietta, Ga.

MILLER, CHARLES. Private. Died Feb. 9, 1863, of disease, at Readyville, Tenn. Interred in Stone River cemetery.

MIZENER, ROBERT. Private. Died Feb. 13, 1862, of disease. Interred in Cave Hill cemetery, Louisville, Ky.

SHERMAN, GILBERT. Private. Died Feb. 27, 1862, of disease. Interred in Cave Hill cemetery, Louisville, Ky.

SMITH, WILLIAM R. Private. Died May 3, 1865, of disease. Interred in section H, grave 304, National cemetery, Nashville, Tenn.

STEWARD, JOHN. Private. Died Oct. 14, 1863, of disease. Interred in National cemetery, Chattanooga, Tenn.

THAYER, ASAHEL. Private. Died Oct. 13, 1862, of disease, at Bowling Green, Ky. Interred in National cemetery, Nashville, Tenn.

WAGONER, NICHOLAS. Private. Died July 16, 1862, of disease, at Athens, Ala. Interred in Stone River cemetery, grave 926.

WHITE, ELIPHUS W. Private. Died Dec. 25, 1861, of disease, at Camp Wickliffe, Ky. Interred at London, Ky.

TABLE OF ROLL OF HONOR.

	Killed in Battle.	Died of Wounds.	Died of Disease.	Killed by Accident.
Company A, ...	11	10	14	
" B, ...	10	6	19	1
" C, ...	11	13	19	
" D, ...	6	10	10	
" E, ...	9	6	3	
" F, ...	17	11	9	2
" G, ...	13	4	18	
" H, ...	15	...	14	
" I, ...	13	3	20	
" K, ...	4	6	15	
Total, . . .	109	69	141	3

Total deaths, 322.

The Regimental Roster as shown on pages 137 to 264, is taken from the "Official Roster of the Soldiers of the State of Ohio, in the War of the Rebellion, 1861 to 1865," Volume 4, published 1887.

A number of names omitted there have been added, and many errors have been corrected by individuals and by company reports made while this history was in preparation.

The *Roll of Honor* on pages 265 to 291, was prepared by Col. E. S. Holloway. Here again corrections and additions, not a few, have been made. Every effort has been made to render the Roster and Roll of Honor as complete as possible, and if any errors are found, they are due to the fact that 33 years after the close of the war, and the loss of company and regimental records in the collision on the river at Cairo, Ills., in June, 1865, it is not possible to get the history of every one of our 1472 men, and that the official records are not always accurate.

The company histories preceding each company in the Roster were furnished by the following persons, who were original members of the company : Company A, S. S. Palmer ; Company B, E. A. Ford ; Company C, Aquila Wiley ; Company D, R. L. Kimberly ; Company E, W. J. Morgan ; Company F, R. A. Gault ; Company G, Silo P. Warriner ; Company H, J. W. Steele ; Company I, W. S. Miller ; Company K, James Horner. Any discrepancies between their statements and the roster of the companies as given, is probably due to the fact that they were neeessarily made without having access to the official records.

On a general summing up we find this Regiment traveled during the service 14,500 miles : 5,200 by water, 3,800 by rail and 5,500 on foot. Was engaged in 20 battles, besides a great many skirmishes. Lost, 109 killed in battle, 69 died of wounds, 141 died of disease, and 3 killed by accidents ; total, 322 deaths. There were 616 wounded that are known, and a great many more were slightly wounded, of which there is no record.

                                    COMMITTEE ON HISTORY.

CONTENTS.

CONTENTS. — Continued.

INDEX.

Boldface page numbers indicate photographs.

Other Civil War Books Available from Blue Acorn Press

Dan McCook's Regiment
52nd Ohio Volunteer Infantry 1862-1865
Nixon B. Stewart

Loyal West Virginia 1861-1865
Theodore F. Lang

Two Wars
Samuel G. French

Kennesaw Mountain June 1864
Richard A. Baumgartner & Larry M. Strayer

Echoes of Battle
The Struggle for Chattanooga
Richard A. Baumgartner & Larry M. Strayer

Blue Lightning
Wilder's Brigade in the Battle of Chickamauga
Richard A. Baumgartner

Blood & Sacrifice
The Civil War Journal of a Confederate Soldier
William Pitt Chambers

How Soldiers Were Made
Benjamin F. Scribner

Visit our website on the Internet
www.blueacornpress.com

BLUE ACORN PRESS
P.O. Box 2684 • Huntington, WV 25726 • (304) 733-3917